Developments in British Politics 3

=

D0995767

Also available from Macmillan

Peter Hall, Jack Hayward and Howard Machin (eds)
DEVELOPMENTS IN FRENCH POLITICS

Gordon Smith, William E. Paterson and Peter H. Merkl (eds)
DEVELOPMENTS IN WEST GERMAN POLITICS

Stephen White, Alex Pravda and Zvi Gitelman (eds)
DEVELOPMENTS IN SOVIET POLITICS

Forthcoming

Patrick Dunleavy
ANALYSING BRITISH POLITICS
Gillian Peele, Christopher Bailey and Bruce Cain (eds)
DEVELOPMENTS IN AMERICAN POLITICS

Developments in British Politics 3

Edited by
Patrick Dunleavy
Andrew Gamble
Gillian Peele

MACMILLAN

Publishers' note
This book is designed as a direct replacement
for Developments in British Politics 2 (*see next page*)

First edition 1990
Reprinted 1991, 1992

This book replaces Developments in British Politics (first published 1983, reprinted
1983, revised edition 1984, reprinted with corrections 1985) and Developments in
British Politics 2 (first published 1986, reprinted 1987, reprinted with corrections
1987, revised edition 1988, reprinted 1989).

Published by
THE MACMILLAN PRESS LTD
Houndmills, Basingstoke, Hampshire RG21 2XS
and London
Companies and representatives
throughout the world

Printed in Hong Kong

A catalogue record for this book is available
from the British Library

ISBN 0–333–51367–3 (hardcover)
ISBN 0–333–51368–1 (paperback)

Contents

viii   *Contents*

List of Contributors

Norman Barry is Professor of Politics at the University of Buckingham. Recent publications include *Hayek's Social and Economic Philosophy; The New Right*; and *Welfare*.

Ted Benton is Senior Lecturer in Sociology at the University of Essex, and is researching on social theory and environmental issues.

Colin Crouch is Fellow and Tutor in Politics at Trinity College, Oxford. Recent publications include *The Politics of Industrial Relations*; and *Trade Unions: The Logic of Collective Action*.

Patrick Dunleavy is Professor of Government at the London School of Economics and Political Science. Recent publications include *Theories of the State: The Politics of Liberal Democracy* (co-author); and *Democracy, Bureaucracy and Public Choice*.

Andrew Gamble is Professor of Politics at the University of Sheffield. Recent publications include *Britain in Decline* (third edition); *The Free Economy and the Strong State*; and *Thatcher's Law* (co-editor).

William L. Miller is Professor of Politics at the University of Glasgow. Recent publications include *Irrelevant Elections? The Quality of Local Democracy in Britain*; and *How Voters Change: The 1987 Election Campaign in Perspective* (co-author).

Brendan O'Leary is Lecturer in Public Administration at the London School of Economics and Political Science. Recent publications include *The Asiatic Mode of Production; Theories of the State: The Politics of Liberal Democracy* (co-author); and *The Future of Northern Ireland* (co-editor).

Gillian Peele is Fellow and Tutor in Politics at Lady Margaret Hall, Oxford. Recent publications include *British Party Politics: Competing for Power in the 1990s; The Government of the United Kingdom: Political Authority in a*

Changing Society (second edition) (co-author); and *Developments in American Politics* (co-editor).

David Samways is a graduate student in the Department of Government at the University of Essex, and is researching on the politics of the ozone layer.

Steve Smith is Senior Lecturer in International Relations and Director of the Centre for Public Choice Studies, University of East Anglia. Recent publications include *British Foreign Policy* (co-editor); and *Explaining and Understanding International Relations* (co-author).

Gerry Stoker is Lecturer in Government at the University of Essex. Recent publications include *The Politics of Local Government*; and *The Future of Local Government* (co-editor).

Cento Veljanovski is Research and Editorial Director at the Institute of Economic Affairs. Recent publications include *Selling the State*; and *Law and Economics*.

Helen Wallace is Director of the West European Programme at the Royal Institute of International Affairs, Chatham House. Recent publications include *Europe: The Challenge of Diversity*; and *Policy-Making in the European Community* (co-editor).

Hugh Ward is Lecturer in Government at the University of Essex. Recent publications include 'Environmental Groups' in D. Marsh (ed.), *Pressure Politics*; and 'Neutrality of Sciences and Technology', in A. Reeve and B. Goodin (eds), *Liberal Neutrality*.

Albert Weale is Professor of Politics at the University of East Anglia. Recent publications include *Political Theory and Social Policy* and a number of papers relating political ideas to public policy.

Paul Whiteley is the Pamela V. Harriman Professor of Government and Public Policy at the College of William and Mary, Virginia. Recent publications include *The Labour Party in Crisis*; and *Political Control of the Macroeconomy*.

Geoff Whitty is Goldsmiths' Professor of Policy and Management in Education in the University of London. Recent publications include *Sociology and School Knowledge*; and *The State and Private Education* (co-author).

Preface

This is the third *Developments in British Politics* volume. Like its predecessors, it aims to provide a rigorous analysis of contemporary events and recent changes in the British political scene. As with previous volumes, all the chapters included here are wholly new and, with the exception of the editors, a completely different set of authors has been recruited for this project. These authors represent a range of viewpoints and, while all have been asked to combine sensitivity to theoretical issues with their discussion of empirical issues, there has been no attempt to impose uniformity on the treatment of individual themes.

Readers familiar with the format of *Developments in British Politics* will notice that we have made a number of substantial changes in this volume. Firstly, the interpretative overview written by Patrick Dunleavy with which previous volumes concluded has now been removed and extended into a separate book, *Analysing British Politics* (Dunleavy, forthcoming). Because analytic themes and debates change more slowly than political processes themselves, there seemed little justification for reprinting essentially similar material in each new volume of *Developments in British Politics* especially given the frequency with which we revise and update our material. Instead, we have included in this edition a short introduction which considers some of the major avenues for change in the British political scene open in the 1990s and a concluding chapter which looks at some overarching themes raised by the detailed topic chapters. We hope that this rearrangement of the book, which brings it into line with the companion volumes on German, French, Soviet and American politics which have grown out of our original conception, will make it more accessible and useful for students and teachers.

Secondly, we have given more prominence to the European dimension of British politics. A new Part One chapter focuses on Britain's relations with the European Community. But in addition we asked all our contributors to consider the ways in which British involvement in the European Community has affected their subject area. In most cases substantial new sections of individual chapters have resulted and in all chapters this previously somewhat hidden topic is now explicitly considered. Our focus is still firmly on British politics, but the politics of a Britain increasingly integrated with its European neighbours rather than the freestanding polity beloved of many traditional textbooks.

Thirdly, we have been able to expand our coverage of empirical changes into new areas. Most notably we have responded to the rapid growth of environmental issues and politics by including a new Part Two policy chapter to complement those on social, economic and foreign policy which have appeared in previous editions. In our judgement, increased environmental awareness and the politicisation of 'green' issues is likely to be a permanent feature of the British political scene in the 1990s.

Fourthly, our selection of current issues for coverage in Part Three includes chapters on education (where the government's reforms have been particularly extensive) and the nexus of issues surrounding privatisation and deregulation.

Any contributed volume depends to a large extent for its success on the cooperation of individual authors and their willingness to submit to deadlines and requests for last-minute revisions and changes. We have been fortunate once again in our team. Despite heavy teaching and writing commitments and in some cases the complications of extensive travel, all our authors kept their part of the collective academic bargain.

A special acknowledgement is due to Henry Drucker who left the editorial team after his appointment as Director of Development at the University of Oxford. Henry conceived the idea of *Developments in British Politics*, and was general editor for the first two volumes. We greatly missed his editorial skills this time, and for our part and on behalf of the publishers would like to record our thanks for all he has contributed. We should also like to thank Bruno Bargery, John Barnes, Brendan O'Leary, and Seamus Tucker, all of whom gave special assistance with the production of the book.

As in previous volumes we owe a heavy debt to our publisher Steven Kennedy without whose intellectual input and practical advice the project would be much the poorer.

Finally we thank the many students, teachers, academics, and general readers who have pointed out neglected issues or topics not explored in *Developments in British Politics 2*. We are keen to have as much feedback as possible, and welcome comments on this edition, and suggestions for the future.

Patrick Dunleavy, Dept. of Government, LSE, Houghton St., London WC2A 2AE
Andrew Gamble, Dept. of Politics, University of Sheffield, Sheffield S10 2TN
Gillian Peele, Lady Margaret Hall, Oxford OX2 6QA

1

Introduction: Prospects for British Politics in the 1990s

PATRICK DUNLEAVY

In all aspects of social life the onset of a new decade triggers something of an effort to summarise and characterise the preceding ten years, and to look forward to changes – the onset of a new age. Political life is no exception to this pattern, and scarcely had Margaret Thatcher celebrated ten years continuously in power as Prime Minister in May 1989 than her government entered into a prolonged period of crises and setbacks which culminated in the first challenge to her leadership of the Conservative Party that December.

The 1980s had seen crises of confidence before, notably in late 1981 as the great recession of the Thatcher government's first term reached its height, and in January 1986 as the PM twisted and turned during the Westland affair. But combined with the prolonged Labour lead in the opinion polls during the last part of 1989, plus the return of a deep-seated British economic malaise, the government's problems at the turn of the decade seemed more fundamental than for many years previously.

None of this is to deny that the Conservatives may well pull out of the political doldrums, stabilise the main economic indicators, and win another majority in 1991–2. But even if they do, it seems unlikely that either the Conservatives or Thatcher will recover the dominant, indeed apparently

unchallengeable, position they occupied for most of the previous decade. British politics in the 1990s will hence be
different from the 1980s.

The key problem then is to anticipate in what ways and for
what reasons a qualitative shift in the pattern of British
politics is likely. Four explanations of the origins and direction
of change are briefly reviewed: the ageing of the government;
party pendulum effects; the narrowing down of the New Right
project; and the growth of a new public agenda.

The Ageing of the Government

When a party is newly arrived in power, it can blame its
predecessors in government for many economic problems,
compare its record in funding popular services with the
previous regime, and remind the public in periods of unpopularity about how much worse off or more disgruntled they felt
when the current opposition themselves held power. All these
tactics worked very effectively for the Conservatives in the
early 1980s. Tory election broadcasts in 1983, and even still in
1987, dwelt on the alleged horrors of the 1978–9 'winter of
discontent' in order to convince wavering supporters not to
risk bringing about the return of a Labour government. However, the longer that a government remains continuously in
power the less and less relevant earlier periods may come to
seem. The problems and crises of the past recede into history,
while those of the current administration loom larger in
people's concerns. Previous governments' policy decisions no
longer provide plausible excuses for present failures.

Perhaps as significant, a long-term government has the
chance both to implement its favoured policies and to experience their results. According to neo-conservative critics themselves, politicians have an inherent bias towards making
initiatives rather than following through their implementation
(Minogue, 1978). Launching new policy programmes is a
popular activity for ministers, but reviewing their success or
failure less so – especially when results are negative or
disappointing. Some areas of policy under the Thatcher
government seem to fit this model of 'hyperactivism' well. In

employment training policy, for example, new schemes have been introduced every other year throughout the 1980s, while opposition parties still cite the UK's poor performance in this area as a key reason for lagging economic growth.

On larger and more dramatic issues continuity in office also tends to throw up instances of policy initiatives which back-fire. A constant source of problems is the interaction between one policy problem and adjacent issues, which requires sensitive management to satisfy partially conflicting objectives at the same time – a balance which can be disturbed by strong political interventions. For example, in 1984 Thatcher responded to a press outcry against football hooliganism by launching a crusade to clean up crowd behaviour at soccer matches. An area previously the responsibility of an obscure junior minister in the Department of Environment was suddenly promoted to the level of a Cabinet committee chaired by the PM. One of the key policy changes to follow from this heavyweight intervention included fencing-in soccer grounds. In 1989 after 95 people were crushed to death in a caged stadium at Hillsborough this policy went into sudden reverse, with 'crowd safety now given priority over crowd control.

Government policies also fail because they stimulate countervailing responses by citizens seeking to evade new efforts to control them. For example, throughout the 1980s the government progressively tightened up the restrictions on trade unions' rights and abilities to organise strikes. Unions were compelled to hold ballots before strikes, and forced to run a gamut of legal actions taken by employers. By the summer of 1989 militant union members in London and elsewhere began responding to the decreased ability of official unions to organise effective industrial action by organising unofficial actions, controlled by a secret group of activists whom employers could not even identify to negotiate with (see Chapter 15). The government responded to the emergence of this problem by promising new legislation in 1990 to combat unofficial, wildcat strikes.

Finally government policies (especially in foreign affairs or defence) may fail or become endangered because of unanticipated external developments. In 1984 Britain and China negotiated an agreement about the handover of Hong Kong to

China in 1997, which guaranteed a slow and regulated transition for the colony to full-scale integration into the mainland Chinese system. For the most part Hong Kong people passively accepted this deal, while the UK government position was that the matter was essentially closed. But in the spring of 1989 Hong Kong opinion changed markedly because of the Chinese government's brutal suppression of demonstrations in Tianenmen Square in Beijing. The heightened anxiety naturally caused by these events called in question the UK strategy of moving very slowly to democratise Hong Kong's government (so as not to offend the Chinese), and its reluctance to accord rights of abode in Britain to Hong Kong's ethnic Chinese population (see Chapters 4 and 11).

Party Pendulum Effects

The quickest way in which the 1990s could differ from the previous decade is for there to be a change of governing party. During the 1980s, previous expectations of a regular left/right swing of general election votes between the major parties proved almost completely inapplicable. The 1983 and 1987 election results, for example, were very similar in terms of parties' share of the vote. Yet throughout this period, there were substantial fluctuations of opinion polls showing government mid-term reverses and recovery in the run-up to the election. Labour and the Liberal/SDP alliance won council seats from the Conservatives in most years during the decade, and the Alliance won some stunning by-election victories as well. But neither apparently could make any headway in general elections.

The roots of this situation are well known. From the founding of the Social Democrat Party in 1981 to the botched merger of the SDP and Liberals in the autumn of 1987, the Conservatives occupied the privileged position of a governing party with long-established loyal bases of electoral support facing a divided opposition. The British electoral system – plurality rule – allocates seats to the largest party in each constituency, without any concern with proportionality between a party's seats and votes nationally. In 1983 and 1987 more than one in five Commons seats was allocated to a party which did not win enough votes on a proportionality basis to justify them, with the Conservatives benefiting far more than Labour, both gaining at the expense of the Liberals and SDP.

One analysis of these years argues that the British polity has remained balanced unsteadily between a number of fundamentally different routes of development (Dunleavy and Husbands, 1985) – separated from each other by narrow margins of opinion poll or electoral support (Figure 1.1). The pattern of party fortunes in Thatcher's third term fits this analysis well. At the 1987 general election the parties were in the central rosette of the diagram. When the Liberal/SDP alliance collapsed in the acrimony over attempted merger in the autumn, the Conservatives at first assumed a commanding opinion poll lead, sustained throughout the first part of 1988 by the government's tax cuts. Hence at this period the party system seemed to be moving towards the bottom-right-hand rosette, the scenario in which the Tories become the dominant party. But with worsening economic difficulties and rapidly rising interest rates in early 1989, and the eclipse of the Liberal Democrats by the Greens at that year's Euro-elections, it was the Labour Party which moved ahead, reaching levels of 50 per cent support briefly in the autumn. This shift seemed to push the party system back into the two-party scenario in which fluctuations of Tory and Labour support are decisive and centre parties are marginalised (see Chapter 3).

Yet even if the return to a two-party system proves more permanent than previous mid-term fluctuations, there is no guarantee that a 'party pendulum' effect or feeling that it is 'time for a change' will be enough to produce a Labour government. Long-term analyses suggest that historically the two-party system never operated even-handedly between the Conservatives and Labour, even in its heyday (Dunleavy, 1989a). The Conservatives have controlled government with secure Commons majorities four times as often as Labour since 1918, when Labour first competed nationwide. Recent trends in electoral geography – such as the falling number of marginal seats and the increased incumbency advantage enjoyed by sitting MPs – make it difficult to envisage an overall

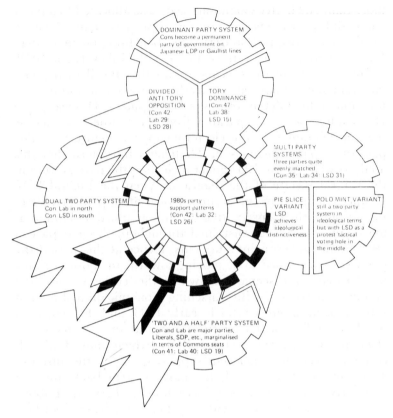

FIGURE 1.1   *Alternative futures for the British party system*
Source: *New Statesman and Society*, 16 September 1988, p. 13.

Labour majority in the 1991–2 general election. And the
government retains the ability to tailor its economic policy
and legislative programmes so as to seek increased popularity
in time for this test.

Development of the New Right Project

When Margaret Thatcher first became premier, she brought
into office an unusually consistent ideology worked out during
her period as Leader of the Opposition. But as numerous

studies have demonstrated her government also made such an immediate and extensive impact upon public policies partly because it drew upon a whole stream of intellectual effort in the USA and Britain over at least two previous decades. 'New Right' concepts and doctrines spanned across macroeconomic policy, social policy, foreign affairs, cultural politics, public management and administration, and political reforms (Green, 1987; King, 1987; Hoover and Plant, 1988; Barry, 1987). Government ministers made it clear that what they wanted to achieve was a reversal of the ways in which British society had been developing from 1945 up to the late 1970s (see Chapter 2).

There were two crucial areas where the first-term Thatcher government sought fundamental changes. The first was macro-economic management where monetarist doctrine urged governments to withdraw from any attempt to fine-tune the economy or boost unemployment levels, in favour of achieving a restrictive financial regime designed to squeeze inflation out of the economy. The second key achievement was to be a renaissance of an 'enterprise culture', of 'the family', and of 'Victorian values', pushing back the 'dependency culture' bred by the post-war welfare state and the 'Wenceslas myth' of unrestricted governmental resources to permit redistribution according to need. At first Thatcher opposed almost all proposals for reorganising public administration systems. These schemes, it was suggested, reflected the inward-looking concerns of the old-style civil service or the misguided energies of the Heath government – which in the early 1970s completely reformed the local government system, created a new structure of NHS authorities, restructured and modernised many public corporations, and reorganised the water industry. Thatcher and her team at that time interpreted this preoccupation with governmental concerns in the midst of a wider economic and cultural decline as akin to reorganising the deckchairs on the *Titanic*. Apart from drastically tightening financial controls in the public sector, and abolishing a single supernumerary tier of health authorities, the Conservatives' first term accordingly avoided institutional reorganisations.

This stance changed during the mid-1980s for three main

reasons. First, monetarist policies were tacitly downgraded in significance in 1982–3, and by 1985 were more or less completely abandoned in favour of pragmatic macroeconomic management (see Chapter 8). Only the twin commitments to reducing the public sector share of GDP and cutting income tax levels survived intact from the government's initial economic programme. Second, the idea of privatising public corporations, which started as a minor sideline, mushroomed into a key government policy, vital for maintaining the momentum of 'rolling back the state'. Third, the government became involved in an escalating battle with Labour local governments which led it into abolishing metropolitan councils, and cumulating layers of ineffective financial regulation. At this period prominent New Right intellectuals began to argue that large-scale changes could not be pushed through by a frontal assault upon welfare state institutions to which public opinion apparently remained committed. Instead, reform would be a 'micro-political' process of tackling individual vested interests one after the other (Pirie, 1988).

The third term of the Thatcher government has turned out to be dominated by a programme of large-scale institutional reforms curiously reminiscent of the Heath government. One centrepiece has been a task shirked by all other post-war governments – the creation of a wholly new local government finance system, replacing traditional property rates with a new poll tax and a unified business rate (see Chapter 6). Almost as fundamental is another complete reorganisation of the National Health Service supposed to usher in an 'internal market' for health care in which the efficiency of hospitals and doctors is increased by forcing them to compete with each other for patients and funds (see Chapter 9). At the same time the privatisation programme has entered a new, more complex phase as the government tries both to avoid simply privatising monopolies (as it did in the middle 1980s with gas and telecommunications) and attempts to cope with public demands for increased public interest regulation (see Chapter 13). Alongside these shifts has been a reconsideration of attitudes among originally hostile public administrators and opposition parties. Many originally rather distinctive and controversial New Right organisational strategies – such as contracting out, performance indicators and incentives, and bureaucratic competition – have been toned down and put into a form which attracts much wider agreement. Hood (1990) terms this consensus 'the new public management' and predicts the widespread adoption of its techniques in the 1990s.

What then has become of the original agenda of fundamental economic, social and cultural change on which Thatcher launched her premiership? The economic euphoria of the middle 1980s has largely disappeared with the return of 'stop–go' cycles induced by a huge balance-of-payments deficit and the revival of 'stagflation' as the dominant economic theme of 1989–90 (see Chapter 8). The government's once proudly proclaimed attachment to 'zero inflation' seems to have foundered on the return of large-scale economic 'overheating' – with wage pressure especially high in the south-east. Here many government policies have increased labour shortages and consequent wage inflation – notably the abandonment of positive regional policies, support for home ownership boosting house prices, and the provision of only modest training programmes. Even the trade-union movement, apparently so decisively crushed by mass unemployment at the start of the decade, has been flexing its muscles, with widespread industrial militancy reviving for the first time since 1979 (see Chapter 15). As for the cultural agenda, change has simply petered out. An ethos of individualistic materialistic advance has undoubtedly become more marked in contemporary Britain, but it is hard to see any signs of the revival of 'the family' as an institution relieving the burden upon the welfare state or law and order services. Nor does opinion poll evidence show any noticeable change in British attitudes. Majority opinion is still supportive of welfare state institutions, stress-ing the need for government to ensure greater equality than would result from unrestricted market operations.

The degeneration of the original New Right 'project' into a long march of institutional reform through one welfare state area after another has been aided by the growth of issues on which the New Right at first had little or nothing to say. The locus of decision-making in some key areas of economic and social development seemed to have shifted away from

Westminster towards Brussels in the run-up to the Single European Market in 1992 (see Chapter 7). Just as previous left-wing governments have found the project of 'socialism in one country' hard to sustain in the face of adverse movements in the international economy, so New Right policies risk being diluted to the extent that the British government loses control of policy areas to the joint decision-making machinery of the European Community. Thatcher's initially successful stance of narrowly defending UK national interests has become more controversial as the momentum towards greater European integration has mounted, leaving Britain protesting unavailingly in its wake, and dividing the Conservative Party more fundamentally than previous conflicts.

There have been previous low points in the ideological drive behind Conservative government policies, notably in early 1986 when the petering-out of the New Right was proclaimed by some observers, only for the government's momentum to revive with radical new policies for the 1987 election manifesto. And there is considerable evidence that both the Prime Minister's and the Conservative Party's fortunes have thrived on the dialectic of mid-term slumps in popularity followed by triumphant re-election. But throughout all these political peaks and troughs, the scope and ambitions of the New Right project seem consistently to have become more political and governmental, and less social and economic in their scope (see Chapter 16).

A New Public Agenda?

The final dimension of change relevant to the future of British politics concerns a deeper-lying shift of attitudes which some observers detect. Hirschman (1985) argues that periods in which public opinion strongly embraces private individual material wellbeing are regularly followed by a shift in people's predominant concerns back towards more publicly orientated issues. People move out of the privatised phase of this cycle because they become disappointed with the material possessions gained through self-advancement, disillusioned with the by-products or side-effects of economic growth, and correspondingly attracted by the promise of new collective issues. In the contemporary UK, such a shift towards public concerns might take place in one of four ways.

First, perhaps the most obvious (because most traditionally left-wing) scenario for a new public agenda would focus on the renewal of the public consensus and political drive behind the welfare state issues. Galbraith's (1965) American complaint about 'private affluence amidst public squalor' finds considerable echo in contemporary Britain. The growth of homeless people and beggars in London; and the declining standards of public services measured by cracked pavements, shabby schools, closed hospital wards, overcrowded commuter trains, and congested roads – these have been the most visible signs of decline lamented by government critics. Less obvious phenomena in the same mould include the lagging prospects of inner-city areas, the creation of an apparently permanent 'underclass' excluded from rising prosperity, and the worsening of social inequality attacked by the churches, concerned professionals, and altruistic pressure groups on behalf of the disadvantaged. For government critics these disparate pieces of evidence are the cumulative outcomes of the Conservative's unreasoning anti-statist orientation. However, expectations of a public reaction against the full range of government policies have been high before without being fulfilled. The issues here seem complex and too diffuse to be easily linked up, except by those with a well-developed non-Conservative ideological orientation. Individual problems can be easily explained away or apparently tackled by modest injections of new funding in the election run-up. Hence it seems unlikely they can act as a viable focus for a new public agenda. Hirschman's theory also stresses that the key actors triggering the shift back to public issues are the newly affluent sections of society – among whom social welfare concerns seem to have least resonance.

Second, environment issues provide an alternative focus for a new public agenda, and one which the Thatcher government appears to take much more seriously. The 1989 Euro-elections were comprehensively won by Labour after 15 per cent of the electorate voted Green, disproportionately in the well-off Conservative heartland areas of the south-east. Green politics is genuinely new in Britain, and provides an alternative ideological framework outside the previous left/right conflicts, within which many of the discontents with social developments in the 1980s can be voiced (see Chapter 10). Environmental concern has become a broad social movement reflected powerfully in company advertising, consumer behaviour, and mass media attitudes – and spanning across national, Euro-wide and global concerns. Even among the New Right there is a grudging recognition that developments such as global warming or the depletion of the Earth's ozone layer could jeopardise ultimate 'collective goods' – which it is a legitimate duty of government to protect against the uncontrolled consequences of free market activities. Little wonder then that the Conservative and Labour parties havè both moved rapidly to try and out-green each other (and to squeeze out the Green party itself) by tapping into these new public attitudes.

Third, a potent area of new public concerns opening up rapidly in the early 1990s concerns the development of Europe. For business decision-makers the transition to a single European market in 1992 has become a major project in itself, which partly explains the adverse elite reactions to Thatcher's perceived isolationist position on Europe during 1988 and 1989 (see Chapter 7). Wider public attitudes remain more suspicious of aspects of the EC (such as farm price subsidies or loss of economic sovereignty) but keen on EC pressure for higher environmental standards and the Social Charter. The collapse of Communist hegemony in Eastern Europe opens up new dimensions for European development – such as the prospect of German reunification – which seems likely to strengthen public interest in integration. If the Russian leader Gorbachev's theme of a 'common European home' also takes off, then the salience of defence (especially nuclear defence) issues is likely to decline in the 1990s (see Chapter 11).

Fourth, the persistence of Conservative political predominance by the late 1980s created a still-nascent public agenda focusing essentially on constitutional issues – such as a bill of rights, electoral reform, and the creation of new checks and balances to curb the unrestrained power of a government with a secure Commons majority. Expressed by groups such as

Charter 88 these concerns can seem just the traditional Liberal party preoccupations, marginalised in British politics for over fifty years by Conservative and Labour agreement to defend the constitutional status quo. Yet what is new here is the extent of Labour (and indeed left Labour) support for change in these areas. The 1989 Labour Policy Review, for example, pledged a reformed House of Lords and new regional assemblies, plus strengthened support for citizen rights. A majority of Labour constituency parties voted against the leadership line at the 1989 party conference to investigate alternative electoral systems as well, a proposal defeated by trade-union bloc votes. If Labour fails to win a Commons majority at the 1991–2 general election (a very hard task starting from the 1987 results), or even fails to achieve a hung Parliament, then Labour support for electoral reform will grow sharply. Paradoxically if Thatcher indeed goes 'on and on' the scale of eventual political system changes will almost certainly increase.

Conclusion

For all the government's appearance of forcing through change in the British state during the 1980s, the pressures for continuity have remained strong. The public sector share of gross domestic product has fallen back from the peaks it reached by 1982–3, but (after allowing for privatisation receipts) still stands within touching distance of its 1978 level. Public employment has declined because of public corporation sell-offs, but governmental expenditure and employment proper remain much as they were at the start of the 'Thatcher decade'. And the proportion of people dependent upon the public sector for their income has almost certainly marginally increased.

Similarly in political life, the prospect of dramatic change in the number or composition of major parties has receded. The Conservative Party remains as strongly based as ever, while Labour has pulled back from the apparently terminal decline of 1981–3. The Alliance challenge, crippled by the plurality rule electoral system, has subsided back, now competing with the emergent Greens. And nationalism in Scotland and Wales continues much as it ever was in the 1970s. Many of the background social changes which provided the seedbed for Thatcherism continue to operate – including the growth of non-manual occupations and loss of manual jobs; the decline or cross-cutting of occupational class as a political influence; and the fall in unionisation and cutbacks of public sector jobs (Dunleavy, 1989b).

These considerations, and the often reiterated textbook stress on gradualism in British political development, all militate against expectations of dramatic change in British politics in the 1990s. With or without party alternations in power or new party leaders, reforms of welfare state institutions on 'new public management' lines are likely to continue, while at the same time public policy shifts to embrace one or more strands of the new public agenda. Yet two motors for more radical change also exist. The first is the changing configuration of Western and Eastern Europe, and its impacts upon British public opinion about European integration and national defence. The second is that the various possibilities for change sketched above may not be alternatives but complementary forces triggered together. The stability of the 1980s may be deceptive, disguising the subterranean cumulation of pressures for change. In which case a change of Prime Minister or of the party in power could go along with the public ditching of much of the New Right project and the substitution of a new public agenda in guiding public debate.

PART ONE
The Political System

2

Ideology

NORMAN BARRY

During the last ten years political debate in Britain has experienced a remarkable transformation. The change is not simply the emergence of new issues – indeed, many of these (the economy, the welfare system, taxation, Europe and so on) are familiar enough and have altered only in detail – but is much more to do with the *language and style* of political argument. The crucial point is that the divisions between political parties have become more ideological since the late 1970s so that political argument involves the use of concepts and values that explicitly refer to competing ways of life and seemingly incommensurable moral and political ideals. Thus the language of British politics is no longer primarily 'adjectival', in which words like 'moderate' and 'extreme' simply refer to different points along a common ideological spectrum, but contains nouns, especially 'market' and 'state', 'individual' and 'community', which denote radically conflicting suggestions, and, indeed, injunctions, for the organisation of a modern democratic state.

It is possible that this uncharacteristically confrontational style of British political life may only be a momentary aberration from the normal course of political development and that a kind of dialectical process will generate a new synthesis, 'consensus', out of the current apparently contradictory value positions. For the time being, however, any observer of the contemporary British political scene has to

17

account for some un-Anglican, discordant voices and to explain radically divergent purported solutions to rather familiar economic, political and social problems.

It is an exaggeration to assert that the current disharmony is entirely a consequence of the so-called Thatcherite Revolution of the past decade. It is true that the policies of her government have been consciously and, more important, *systematically*, at odds with the pre-1979 consensus but their theoretical and conceptual sources pre-date her first election victory. Although it is not inaccurate to describe the post-war period up to the mid-1970s as one of a consensus among political thinkers around a small number of key themes in public morality and political economy, with debate more or less confined to the problems within that consensus rather than focusing on its intellectual foundations, there was always a strong undercurrent of dissent, both from the left and right of the political spectrum. The objections to the consensus that emanated from what is conventionally known as the Right are the most important if only because they, in political terms at least, were simply successful. The individualistic, pro-market and anti-statist political philosophies not only penetrated the leadership of the Conservative Party, but their partial implementation since 1979 has left an indelible mark on other parties' political programmes as well as on political thought in general. Thus despite the hostility that much of Margaret Thatcher's programme and political philosophy has aroused, she has in a very real sense set the agenda of current political argument; and the rethinking of socialism that is now going on is partly, if not mainly, a response to the economic and political theory that she espouses. But it should be stressed that there is nothing particularly original in these ideas: innovative though the Thatcherite revolution may be in direct policy terms its social theory represents a recrudescence of ideas that had been obscured but not obliterated by the post-war consensus (see Green, 1987; Barry, 1987; King, 1987).

Although much of contemporary political thought from both the left and right sides of the political divide centres around the alleged failures of the post-war ideological consensus it should not be assumed that that system has no defenders. The common policy ends of government-inspired full employment with low inflation, a limited welfare state and a mixed economy produced not only an ideological truce between the extremes of socialism and capitalism but also coincided with reasonable prosperity and a more stable social and political order than Britain had experienced in the inter-war years. It is true that individualist and collectivist political theorists had predicted its demise, and attempted to restructure doctrines independently of its main features, but there are still powerful ideological forces that argue both that its disintegration was not inevitable and that a reconstituted social and economic philosophy based on Keynesian economic principles and more 'rational' interventionist policies in the fields of welfare and redistribution is essential. Although commentators often write of the 'collapse' of the consensus it is not true to say that it is in ruins, for some of the harshest critics of the Thatcher decade desire a return to those halcyon days in which the extremes of Left and Right were tempered and moderated by a belief in an overriding public good.

Consensus: An Ancien Régime?

The consensus that dominated British political thought from the early 1950s until the 1970s covered economic, social and constitutional matters and in essence presupposed an agreement about the broad aims of public policy. However, this concord tolerated disagreement, sometimes quite fierce, about the detailed application of these aims and also their implications.

The ruling consensus covered four major areas of political thought: an expansive role for government in the use of macroeconomic powers for the securing of full employment; an agreement about the appropriate 'mix' of private and public ownership of resources; a guaranteed provision of welfare based upon objective needs; and a continued acceptance of the traditional features of the constitution (the electoral system, the sovereignty of parliament and collective and individual responsibility of ministers under the Cabinet system). There were subsidiary items in this comprehensive agenda. The most important was perhaps the recognition of the necessity for the incorporation of pressure groups into the political process, especially trade unions; they were to become heavily involved in negotiating the items of the new agenda (mainly as a result of successive governments' commitment to full employment). It was this involvement, however, that put a particular strain on the constitutional consensus since the influence of trade unions on public policy through their direct dealing with government undermined the whole system of parliamentarianism (see Chapter 16).

The consensus did represent a significant departure from the main course of ideological development in Britain. For conservative thinkers the most important issue was the re-definition of the role of the state. The question of the state is an exceedingly complex one for conservative political theorists, for in this area tradition does not speak with one authoritative voice but is systematically ambiguous.

It is not the ultimate power of the state that is contested in conservative thought but the *extent* of its legitimate authority. The division here is between those conservatives who restrict the state to the role of enforcing universal rules over individuals playing a social and economic 'game' which has no necessary outcome (in this view it is not the business of political authority to promote economic growth or provide extensive social welfare), and those who impose on the state further *social* obligations, notably the political implementation of a common hierarchy of values embracing cultural, moral and economic ends. In this latter concept the state becomes an active participant in the social game, working with particular groups rather than merely containing them.

Sources of Disharmony

Astute political observers pointed to the tensions within the political consensus and the social science paradigm that underlay it. The main problem was the very possibility of a 'middle way', an exquisite *modus vivendi* between, on the one hand, the potentially awesome power of a fully-fledged socialist state and, on the other, a possibly socially destructive capitalism, driven entirely by self-interest and indifferent to social welfare in its quest for the immediate gratification of consumers. The series of crises that afflicted the history of the consensus can be traced to the fact that its social ends (desirable or otherwise) were imposed on a community whose basic institutions, and the motivations of its inhabitants, were still individualistic. The attempt, for example, to secure full employment without runaway inflation required self-restraint on the part of a trade-union movement whose rationale was precisely to secure the highest wages for its members within a still nominal market system. Again, in a parliament with absolute powers, there could be no guarantee that politicians driven by the need to maximise votes would engage in redistributive activities for the general welfare rather than press for the sectional interests of their client groups. These weaknesses in the theoretical structure of consensus thought were almost bound to lead to a reassertion of the old Left–Right divide.

Theoretical Origins of Thatcherism

The theoretical rejuvenation of conservative political thought, which began in the mid-1970s, incorporates a curious mixture of classical liberal individualist principles and traditional conservative values of authority and legitimacy. It is important to note that a crucial objection to the consensus which conservatives made was the undermining of the traditional authority of the state that was thought to be occurring throughout the 1970s. Although the classical liberal economists were primarily concerned with the onset of inflation and the enervating effect that even modest interventions in the private enterprise economy had on efficiency, conservatives pointed to the irony that an over-expanded state, burdened with a plethora of welfare and economic functions, had degenerated into a weak state unable to control insubordinate groups, especially trade unions. Lord Hailsham (1978) pointed to the phenomenon of 'elective dictatorship', a sovereign parliament elected by a minority of the voters, and was an early advocate of constitutional reform. However, in practice the authority of the supposedly 'strong' state was constantly flouted.

The new conservative social philosophy was from the outset concerned with both traditional Tory questions of authority and legitimacy *and* economic matters. What was unusual was its 'intellectualisation' of the problems that faced Britain in the mid-1970s. In a series of speeches and pamphlets Sir Keith Joseph (see especially, Joseph, 1976) incorporated ideas imported from a variety of 'foreign' sources, notably American public choice theory and neo-classical economics. Although the followers of Sir Keith Joseph and Margaret Thatcher were originally a small minority in the Conservative Party, they effected a revolution in conservative thought, dispensing with that caution, adjustment to circumstances and outright pessimism about the possibility of reversing the tide of collectivism, that had been such a feature of previous conservative speculation on politics. Unlike orthodox conservative thinkers, they made use of contemporary developments in the social sciences: they founded their normative politics on a rational understanding of social affairs and a more critical view of tradition. The intellectual progenitors of this are the economists Milton Friedman (1962, 1979) and F. A. von Hayek (1960) (who is also very much the *philosopher* of liberal-conservatism), and the public choice economists James Buchanan (1975), Buchanan and Tullock (1962), and Mancur Olson (1965). In fact, many of their ideas were distilled and made palatable by the financial journalist and political economist, Samuel Brittan (1973, 1983, 1988). In the writings of all those theorists there is a subtle blending of economic and political analysis.

'Marketing' the Market

The first and most important intellectual innovation was the rehabilitation of the market system as an important engine of prosperity and liberty. Although Keynesian macroeconomics itself did not dispense with the market as an efficient allocator of resources at the micro level, theorists of the consensus were sceptical both of its morality of self-interest and its efficiency. The reason for the former claim was that intellectual opinion had identified the noun 'public' with unselfish action directed towards the well-being of the community, and 'private' with selfish behaviour which brought personal gratification to the cost of society at large: this dichotomy neglected the obvious possibility that the actions of public officials could be self-regarding and that self-interested action could, unintentionally, generate the public interest. Although this insight was by no means new (it was the lynchpin of Adam Smith's political economy), it is the key to the thinking of the 'radical Right', undercutting the claims of both traditionalist conservatives and state socialists. What was new was the careful analysis of how the pursuit of self-interest by members of groups smaller than the state was ultimately destructive of the well-being of those group members themselves; the behaviour of trade unions is the obvious example of this process (see Barry, 1987, ch. 5).

The market was venerated for reasons of both efficiency and personal liberty. As a signalling device it indicates relative scarcities: the price system simply draws the factors of production into those activities where they are most usefully employed. The phrase 'usefully employed' means satisfying the desires of atomised individuals. The reason why the market is claimed to be superior to the state in an efficiency sense is that since economic knowledge, i.e. information about consumer tastes, production costs and so on, is widely dispersed in a complex society it cannot be centralised in one mind or institution. Since constant change is a feature of such complex societies the comparison between the market and the state turns largely upon the speed of response to such changes; and the liberal economists argued that prices act quicker than cumbersome political decision-making.

However, the major dissent from the Keynesian macro-economics concerns unemployment and monetary policy. Since the liberal economists assumed that the market is a self-correcting mechanism, the unemployment of any factor of production, including labour, must be caused by some impediment to that process of automatic adjustment: if willing workers are unemployed it is a consequence of monopoly unions fixing the price of labour above its market clearing price, or some other politically induced obstacle to the free movement of workers. Stimulating demand by inflation could only have a temporary effect in raising employment and, like the taking of drugs (an analogy often used by liberal economists), it requires larger and larger doses for smaller and smaller beneficial effects (Hayek, 1975). Indeed, inflation involves the breach of the obligation of government to maintain the value of its currency, a traditional Tory doctrine. It was, of course, breached by Conservative governments during the period of consensus. Indeed, Margaret Thatcher has not been entirely successful in taming the inflationary 'tiger' (see Chapter 8).

Markets and Conservative Morality

The more overtly moral justification for the market turned upon the questions of liberty and autonomy. The new conservatism adopted a largely 'negative' view of liberty: a person is free to the extent that his actions are not impeded by the (alterable) actions of another, normally in the form of laws and prohibitions by coercive government. In this conception a person's freedom is not limited by adverse economic conditions, such as poverty or unemployment. They may limit his *ability* or power to do things but not his liberty. Although it looks as if the periods of unemployment that undoubtedly occur during the course of even unimpeded capitalist development reduce liberty, at least in the sense of opportunity, the fact that they are not the product of intention and are more or less unalterable means that, for the new conservative, they are simply facts of life, unavoidable phenomena, like the weather. It is true that the commitment to liberty opens up embarrassing tensions within conservative thought. When market freedom is limited only by general laws of the protection type it does sanction the exercise of liberty, especially in matters of personal conduct, which do not gel with traditional conservative moral standards. This points up the contrast between the liberal-conservative who regards morality as a matter of personal choice, with rules functioning as artifices to prevent conflict, and the traditionalist who claims that there are more or less objective moral standards that are embedded in traditional practices; and those ought not to be cast lightly aside at the behest of an abstract and rationalist conception of liberty (Scruton, 1981). In British conservative thought economic liberty is almost always ranked higher than personal liberty; in socialist libertarianism the converse is the case.

The Attack on Social Justice

There is greater unity among conservative thinkers in their forthright rejection of the goal of social justice or substantive equality. Redistribution, although occupying a dominant position in socialist thought, never held a secure place in the consensus. This was because post-war conservatives, although they favoured an activist state in certain economic spheres, did not sanction a particularly redistributive role with regard to property and income: what they lacked was a coherent ethical and economic defence of that anti-egalitarianism. To the more radical spokesman for the consensus the traditional Tory defence of inequality, and its somewhat mystical argument for the necessity of a social hierarchy, looked uncomfortably like a rationalisation of privilege.

The impact of individualistic classical liberalism on the new conservatism's conception of justice was decisive, for it gave a sophisticated argument for inequality that was claimed to be consistent with both economics and ethics (see Joseph and Sumption, 1979).

The case for inequality rested upon a crucial distinction between procedural justice and social justice. The former refers to those rules (of contract, property, tort and crime) that are essential for the operation of a market system; moral 'blame', as well as legal sanctions, is appropriate for the breach of them. The distribution of income, as determined by the free exchange system, has nothing to do with justice, it is merely the unintended outcome of the interactions of many individuals. Social justice, however, presupposes that the spread of incomes that results from a market can be evaluated by reference to principles external to the market and which are independent of the rules of procedural (or commutative) justice that service it: these principles are normally need, desert and merit, and sometimes equality for its own sake (or for its contribution to fraternity or social solidarity). It was this view of justice that influenced Labour governments during the consensus and underlay much of welfare provision and redistributive taxation.

However, the new conservatives argued that the pursuit of social justice was both economically inefficient and destructive of a proper morality. It rested upon an unsustainable distinction between the 'laws' of production and the 'laws' of distribution of an exchange economy. In liberal theory, the 'earnings' of the factors of production are simply those inducements required to allocate them to their most efficient uses, and to interfere, for example, with wage determination by heavily progressive taxation is to distort this allocative process to the detriment of society as a whole. This is no more than the argument for the necessity of incentives for the efficient exploitation of natural resources. However, it depended also on the claim that in a free society there can be no *agreement* on the values of desert and need which are supposed to function as extra-market criteria of redistribution. In the absence of such a hierarchy of values, the *political* determination of income leads to an unseemly scramble for distributive shares by strategically placed groups (see Brittan, 1975).

Questioning the Welfare State

However, throughout much of the post-war period, equality was pursued by high public spending, especially on the familiar welfare services, as recommended by C. A. R. Crosland (1956). Ironically, many critics of this type of intervention have exploited the work of socialist political economists who pointed out that this 'strategy of equality' had alarmingly *inegalitarian* effects: Julian Le Grand (1982) showed that public spending on education (especially higher education), health, housing and so on was systematically to the benefit of the middle classes and that it probably produced more inequality than if the market had been left alone in these areas. The crucial point here is that Le Grand based his arguments on an alternative social science paradigm, the individualistic model of man found in classical liberal economics: he used simple economic reasoning to show how the middle classes could exploit, for example, higher education at low to zero cost, and subsidies to private housing and press politically for their retention. This is not an argument about the values of the consensus but a critique of the paradigm of social science that underlay it, i.e. the assumption that the self-interested features of human action would diminish in the context of a semi-collectivised society.

The attack on social justice is inextricably bound up with the question of welfare: for a large part of the new conservative assault on the consensus derived from the perceived economic and moral effects of state-supplied pensions, health, education and so on. Few conservatives of the New Right objected to the welfare state as such, and even fewer would recommend the abrogation of those entitlements that had accumulated in the welfare status quo, yet they were exercised by its foundations, which, they claimed, led inevitably to its expansion. This was said to be so because of a flaw in the social science of the consensus: the theorists of welfare neglected a basic principle of human nature, that if a good or service is supplied at zero price, as much of welfare is, then demand will rise, leaving tremendous allocation problems for government. The democratic process itself will encourage spending on welfare since voters are not the immediate bearers of its cost. Conservative critics argued that the welfare state is a vast complex of vested interests, inefficiencies and opportunities for the exercise of discretionary power over the private lives of individuals. The main problem was that since many of its services are supplied universally rather than selectively, its benefits had no necessary tendency to be delivered to those in need, its original rationale. But a further conservative argument was that the welfare state encouraged dependency rather than autonomy; this was compounded by the fact that welfare entitlements were treated as rights flowing from citizenship. To both traditional Tories and New Right classical liberals this had the effect of undermining the obligations which welfare recipients had to the society that provided them (see Chapter 9).

Traditionalism, Modernism, and Thatcherism

The incorporation of classical liberal ideas into conservative thought and practice since the mid-1970s caused a certain ideological disarray. For many traditionalists, notably Sir Ian Gilmour (1983), lamented the decline of 'One Nation' Toryism, and its partial replacement by a market-powered materialism and individualism, as a betrayal of the obligation to govern in the interests of all. They argued that a society organised according to market principles, in which the profitability of an enterprise is the only indicator of its social value, and which is prepared to tolerate heavy unemployment as a necessary cost in the pursuit of adjustment to changing economic circumstances, is as potentially unstable and divisive as one divided into antagonistic classes. In fact, the spokesmen for this point of view are not so much theorists of traditional conservatism but rather spokesmen for the return of the kind of Keynesian economic management and collective welfare state that characterised the Macmillan era. The philosophical objection to the new conservatism is that a communal social order, held together by unquantifiable bonds of affection, has been replaced by an *anonymous* society of traders, held together by an unstable cash nexus.

It could just as plausibly be maintained, however, that the 'Thatcherite revolution' is more consonant with traditional Tory values, and that the Macmillan–Heath era was the aberrant phase. The long-term effect of consensus policies was the undermining of political authority and the 'capture' of state machinery by interest groups. The authority of the state was restored in 1979 by rigorous enforcement of the traditional constitutional machinery, primarily the sovereignty of Parliament. This process has continued, producing a curious hybrid of a free market economy overlaid by a heavily *dirigiste* political system. Lord Hailsham's potentially more radical constitutional proposals of the 1970s were never entertained; precisely because they would have entailed a diminution of centralised political power.

Yet in a curious way, Margaret Thatcher has revived, if not entirely successfully, two principles of the 'tacit' constitution, despite her well-publicised opposition to any formalised constitutional change. These are the obligations of a government to balance its budget and to maintain the value of the national currency: they had fallen into desuetude since the 1930s. This illustrates the curious combination of traditionalism and radicalism that is such a feature of contemporary conservative ideology. There has been a break with the past, but only the *immediate* past.

A Retreat from Theory?

Despite the political and economic success of the New Right it would be misleading to say that it has a coherent programme for the future, or that there is a unity of purpose within its ranks. Active conservative politicians have expressed disquiet at the pace of the privatisation programme; some of which appears to many as a gratuitous exercise in pure ideology. Furthermore, the attempts to introduce elements of consumer choice into such sacrosanct areas as the law and the National Health Service have met with stiff opposition from the *professions*, which had hitherto been protected from Thatcherite individualism. Again, any tampering with the welfare system is likely to meet with opposition from the general public, most of whom simply do not want freedom in this area.

Further extensions of the choice mechanism to traditional British social and economic institutions will reopen the old debate between pragmatic conservatism and radical individualism. The pragmatists claim that while there is a public opinion favourable to anti-inflationary monetary policies, to legal controls over trade unions and to the rehabilitation and extension of private property and the profit motive, this does not extend to, for example, a rapid withdrawal of the state in the areas of welfare and health. To this extent, the battle of ideas between individualism and collectivism that raged throughout the 1970s and 1980s may now be over: not because either side has 'won' but because in modern complex societies it is impossible to rely on the intellectual *purity* of a doctrine alone for its successful implementation.

It is likely that the next stage of conservative thinking will be less concerned with high theory and more to do with detailed enquiries into how particular aspects of a programme may be implemented. This strategy has been aptly called 'micropolitics' by Madsen Pirie (1988). He argues that such is the range of the entrenched interests in British society that a wholesale transition to *laissez-faire* (whatever its theoretical virtues) would meet with opposition from minority groups which, for public choice reasons, have a disproportionate influence over public affairs. In an implicit rejection of the 'potency of ideas' school Pirie maintains that to overcome their opposition these groups will have to be offered inducements. In an explicit rejection of the claims of the ideologues, he writes that they:

> constantly criticise government for its failure to create a pure free market situation and regard measures to trade benefits with interest groups as a sign of weakness and lack of commitment. They show no sign of understanding that it is these trade-offs which make the exercise possible in the first place. (Pirie, 1988, p. 181)

Pirie maintains that the reason for the success of the Thatcher administrations, in comparison to the 1970–4 Heath experiment in free market policies, is that her government, in its reform of trade unions, the privatisation programme and the management of the economy in general, proceeded in a step-by-step manner, ensuring that at each stage of the process, potential opposition could be offered something in return for the giving up of a privilege. The method was illustrated in a spectacular fashion with the privatisation programme where potentially disruptive managements and workers in state industries were bought off with private monopoly status and financial inducements. If Pirie is right, and I suspect that the real test will come in a sustained attack on the professions and on the reform of the welfare state, then the future course of conservative thinking will be in detailed policy research rather than exercises in grand theory. The implication of Pirie's analysis is that freedom must be 'bought', like any other commodity.

Socialism in Crisis

If there is some disarray within conservatism as a result of the dramatic changes in the past decade, then the position of socialist thought is surely more confusing. The curious thing is that although socialist thinkers have kept a vociferous opposition to the new conservatism, the re-writing of their ideology has incorporated significant elements of classical liberalism. Although no one book comparable to Crosland's *The Future of Socialism* has emerged, a number of important studies have appeared in the past decade which, in a sense, chart the development of socialist ideas. Of particular interest is the work of the Socialist Philosophy Group (Forbes, 1979) which aims to counter those academic theories of market capitalism which have been so influential on contemporary conservative thought. While much of socialist writing is confined to the *criticism* of existing conservative thought and policy there have been some substantive developments. The most important of these has been the attempt to recapture the market for socialism and to drive a wedge between capitalism and freedom. Nevertheless, it cannot be denied that developments in socialist thought represent a *response* to events and ideas, whereas for a very long time collectivism of some kind had set the agenda of British political and economic debate.

It is doubtful whether any serious socialist thinker believes in the wholesale nationalisation of the means of production, the abolition of the market and its replacement by a centrally planned system. The problems of knowledge and coordination that a completely socialist system entails, as well as the threat to personal liberty that it poses, have been recognised. However, the state will remain a key institution in socialist thought and practice for the reason that markets, however, egalitarian and well-organised they may be, are essentially *random* and, without the guidance of central authority, unlikely to maximise the objective ends of a community. At the heart of all socialist economic philosophy is the belief that there are economic and social ends worthy of pursuit which are not revealed in the subjective choices of individuals. No matter how much socialists might now reject comprehensive economic planning the belief remains that individuals will discount the future at a higher rate than is good for society as a whole. Furthermore, socialists display a preference for political controls over the self-correcting mechanisms of the market.

Again, the socialist, although less likely to believe in the inevitability of class conflict does emphasise the importance of collective organisations within the state. The liberal conception of the atomised individual, abstracted from a pre-existing form of social organisation, is just as much a fiction for the socialist as it is for the traditionalist, anti-individualist conservative. The difference is that the socialist identifies individuals as members of industrial groups rather than of the nation, and this is why trade unions will continue to occupy a prominent place in socialist thought and practice: without collective forms of organisation individuals would be defenceless against capitalist owners. Thus whereas central control has been rejected as an inefficient form of economic organisation it has been, in theory at least, replaced by different forms of collectivism.

At the more general level, Roy Hattersley's book, *Choose Freedom* (1987), represents a sustained attempt to found socialism on libertarian principles. His argument involves a specific rejection of negative liberty, which is associated with unbridled capitalism, and a redefinition of freedom in terms of increased opportunities: the provision of which would require a continuing and substantial role for the state. Whereas previous socialist theorists had proposed some kind of trade-off between equality and liberty, usually in order to preserve the superficially more liberal concept of negative liberty, Hattersley argues that liberty is only possible with a substantially more equal spread of wealth and income than could ever be achieved by the operation of spontaneous forces. The freedom that the market offers is illusory if it is accompanied by the inequalities created by capitalism: inequalities which also invest the few with *power* over the many.

Socialism and the Market

This brings us directly to the question of market socialism. Although this is talked of frequently by contemporary socialist theorists few significant books have appeared in contemporary literature (Miller, 1989; Estrin and Le Grand, 1989). However, its features are clear enough. The main theoretical point is the claim that although the market mechanism is, in principle, a welfare-maximising device, an indicator of value in individualist–subjectivist terms, the capitalist system, because of its inequalities of wealth, power and privilege, is an ineffective expression of this welfare criterion. Market socialists get very close to the odd conclusion that capitalism, at least that operative in existing societies, is incompatible with the market.

However, this acceptance of the market, despite the attempted dissociation of it from capitalism, does mark a radical departure from a whole tradition of socialism. For this did understand the exchange relationship itself as divisive, and a source of alienation, whatever the economic conditions under which it is conducted. By maximising subjective wants, and operating through the motive of self-interest, it undermined those cooperative and altruistic sentiments on which a fraternal socialist order depends. Yet Hattersley (1987, p. 149) writes: 'Most Labour party members understand and accept that, for a large proportion of the economy, markets must determine price and the allocation of resources.' Markets are also conceded, guardedly, to be freedom-enhancing in comparison to some allocative mechanism of the state (p. 151). Is there a *theory* behind this claim for the compatibility of socialism and markets?

Market socialism has only recently been taken up by political theorists but it was a prominent feature of socialist economics in the 1930s. It derives from the work of general equilibrium theory in microeconomics; and was an attempt to show how freedom, efficiency and some equality could be combined (see Lavoie, 1985). In a *perfectly competitive* market that array of goods and services which is produced exactly reflects consumer preferences, and the factors of production that are required are paid just that income which is necessary to keep them efficiently employed. All 'entrepreneurial' profit, i.e. income above marginal productivity, has been whittled away by competition and market 'power' is absent. A perfectly competitive 'outcome' is in theory significantly egalitarian.

What prevented it occurring was the existing structure of capitalist society with its intrinsic privileges and 'irrational' inequalities. The role of the state is to *replicate* the theoretical equilibrium of perfect competition without socially wasteful profit and the private ownership of resources. State managers, responding to market-led consumer demands, would replace entrepreneurs.

Leaving aside the technical problems of this model, it is easy to see why it has attracted some socialists: it eliminates socially unproductive 'profit', the traditional target for the egalitarian, while maintaining freedom of choice in consumption and occupation. Contemporary individualist conservatives argue that it is profit which is required to power the whole system and that it is impossible to eliminate it without eliminating prosperity. It is doubtful, too, whether British market socialists would dispense with profit entirely either, and they would be sceptical of the practicability of the *original* theoretical model. Although contemporary writers talk frequently of market socialism, a coherent account of it has yet to be given. Unlike the original theory, it tends to mean that certain parts of the economy, those concerned with the production of consumer goods, should be left in *private ownership*, subject to supply and demand and powered by the profit motive. This, however, should proceed only in the context of a redistributive and welfare state, with reserve powers of overall planning.

In view of all this one might well ask: what is left of socialism? Furthermore, if socialist ideology has incorporated so much of market philosophy, why does there still appear to be a great difference between the two major parties in comparison to the 1950s and 1960s? I think the answers to these questions revolve around the extent to which the market mechanism should apply to social affairs. The nouns 'market' and 'state' continue to reflect mutually antagonistic positions because there is no consensus about their respective roles, even though everyone accepts the necessity of both.

The new individualist conservatives would like the market to penetrate all aspects of social life, while the market socialist would insist that some areas should be exempt from it. Certain basic welfare needs, including pensions, housing, health, education and so on, should be satisfied before subjective choice and market allocation are allowed to operate freely. In fact, under market socialism that list would still leave a wide area of social life under state control and therefore pressure would continue to be put on public spending. It is for this reason that a new consensus around the market is unlikely to emerge, irrespective of the problem of the role of profit under market socialism.

Welfare and Citizenship

It is the welfare issue that illustrates the point that competing and irreconcilable value differences still occur. Socialist theorists are now developing a concept of citizenship derived originally from T. H. Marshall (1950) which is sharply at odds with that anonymous individualism of the new conservatism. Such a concept grants welfare entitlements, which are of equal weight with the familiar civil and political rights, and they constitute a claim on resources irrespective of the contribution the beneficiaries make to the output of an economy (see Hoover and Plant, 1989). Conservatives do not deny that some state welfare is essential but this is, strictly speaking, an aspect of benevolence; to the market socialist, or any other kind of socialist, it is an obligation of justice. The argument here is that the relentless allocative method of the market produces innocent victims of change, excluded from its benefits through no fault of their own. There is also the danger of an 'under class' being created that is permanently alienated from society and which constitutes a possible threat to its stability.

It is here that socialists join hands with traditionalist, non-individualistic conservatives: both schools of thought understand a society as a complex network of reciprocal obligations which cannot be dissolved into individual transactions under general and impersonal rules. In a consistent application of this philosophy the recipient of a welfare benefit is under an obligation, where possible, to perform certain social duties. 'Workfare' would then be compatible with collectivism (indeed, community work is already a condition of welfare benefit in some socialist countries).

Civil Liberties and the Constitution

A further area in which socialists are beginning to distinguish themselves sharply from conservatives is in constitutional reform. Although the leadership of the Labour Party is as wedded to the constitutional *ancien régime* as is Margaret Thatcher, intellectuals within the broad socialist movement are now demanding a bill of rights enforceable at law, proportional representation, and a diminution of the sovereignty of parliament under a written constitution (see Radice, 1989). Ironically, they are saying much the same thing as Lord Hailsham said in the mid-1970s. No doubt, this is a consequence of the increasing *dirigisme*, in non-economic matters at least, of the Thatcher government, and Britain's rather poor record before the European Court of Human Rights.

In fact, this new interest in civil liberties may mark a decline in the importance of economics in the Labour Party. It may be the case that the party has achieved a 'Bad Godesberg' (it was this conference, in 1959, at which the German Social Democratic Party formally abandoned its Marxist, class-based economics and initiated a highly successful relationship with market capitalism) in a typically British and evolutionary manner. Even on the left of the Labour Party, in the writings of Tony Benn (1980a) the stress is as much on the necessity for the democratisation of political institutions as it is on reconstituting the economic order. Abolition of the House of Lords, election of the Cabinet and removal of the privileges and prerogatives of the Prime Minister seem to be as important as nationalisation or even extensive redistribution of resources.

However, this may not reflect a lessening of the tensions between the major political factions, or a cooling of the ideological debate, but rather a recognition of the fact that it was the peculiarly permissive British constitutional system that allowed the 'Thatcher revolution' to proceed to the extent that it has. *Mutatis mutandis*, was not this the reasoning that motivated conservative constitutional reformers in the heyday of Labour intervention in the economy in the mid-1970s, its granting of extra immunities to the unions, and its threat to individual economic liberties? It is doubtful if political leaders in Britain possess that 'constitutional attitude' which is required if institutional restraints are to achieve any permanence.

The Response of the 'Old' Left

It would not be true to say that the Left's economic ideology has been completely jettisoned from Labour's thinking. The *Labour Policy Review* (1989) incorporates some of the new market philosophy and rejects the 'shopping list' of national- isation proposals that was such a feature of the 1983 General Election campaign but the evolution toward this has provoked resistance from the Bennite Left. Although there have been few, if any, theoretical restatements of *traditional* socialist values (see Benn, 1980b), a movement called the Socialist Conference, which incorporates the Bennite Left Labour MPs as well as fringe groups including the Socialist Workers Party, and some intellectuals, has been formed to propagate a more collectivist brand of socialism. It published its own Socialist Policy Review (1989) which, in addition to the aforemen- tioned scheme to democratise the British Constitution, pro- claimed a belief in traditional nationalisation and state man- agement of the economy, including controls over imports and multinational companies.

There is still then a powerful minority of anti-market socialists within the Labour Party who are likely to resist too great an intrusion of the price system and individual choice into the collectivist strategy; but their appeal is now a limited one. What they lack is a coherent theoretical statement of a socialist system that does not embody the electorally unattrac- tive features of nationalisation and trade-union power. However, their lack of popular support, or indeed intellectual appeal for the 1990s, should not be taken to mean that they will not continue to have a voice in the Labour movement.

Continued Conflict or a New Consensus?

Although it is possible that many of the reforms that have come about in the 1980s will survive a hypothetical future change of government, this does not necessarily mean that a new consensus has emerged, and that the resurgence in ideological differences that occurred in the late 1970s has subsided. It is almost certain that the prevailing constitutional machinery will remain intact (subject to changes necessitated only by Britain's membership of the European Communities) and this does allow for fairly rapid about-turns in policy. The fact that market institutions have now been morally and economically validated does not mean that a new set of overriding common purposes has emerged to which all groups can give an unqualified allegiance.

Therefore, despite the persistence of intellectual support for the old consensus the conditions for a successful rehabilitation of it do not obtain. To a greater extent than other western democracies British society is characterised by interest groups, driven by the 'logic of the situation' to press for sectional advantages at the potential cost of benefits that accrue from cooperative activity (of the kind, that apparently obtains, for example, in Sweden, Austria and West Germany). That voluntary wage restraint, which is required for employment to be raised by demand management policies, is unlikely to be forthcoming given the prevailing organisation of trade unions. Thus economic problems will have to be tackled either by the continuation of the present *laissez-faire* approach in the manner recommended by Pirie or by a greater level of state control (which may well be incompatible with traditional liberties). Again, the recognition that the present welfare system is inefficient, and from which the middle classes benefit substantially, is one thing; correcting it in the context of a competitive party system in which the vote motive compels political entrepreneurs to extend and preserve its inequities, quite another. Interest groups in Britain, as Olson (1982) astutely observed, are not wide, all-encompassing and united by a sense of common purpose, but are medium-sized, numerous, well-organised and identified by the pursuit of narrow ends.

The European elections of 1989, however, produced a phenomenon not analysable in these conventional terms: the emergence of the Green (ecology) Party. Their electoral achievement of 15 per cent of the poll not only displaced the

Liberal Democrats as the third party but introduced a new ideology that will have an effect on all the major political parties. The party's overriding concern for the protection of the environment, and its open commitment to a policy of *reduced* economic growth, runs counter to the main economic themes of the post-war era. It is claimed to be the 'most dynamic social and political movement since the birth of socialism' (Porritt, 1985, p. xiv) (see Chapter 10).

The political thought of the Green Party is not addressed primarily to the problems of Britain but to global issues: the despoliation of the environment, the 'greenhouse effect' and the damaged ozone layer, the possibility of ultimate nuclear disaster and the rapid industrialisation of the past 100 years, all of which produced an alienated proletariat whose vision of the good life is limited to a (manufactured) demand for an endless supply of consumer goods. It is argued that, since the pursuit of industrialism is ultimately self-defeating, the real interests of all would be served by a process of de-industrialisation. Britain then should be part of an international movement to avert what social scientists call the 'tragedy of the commons'.

Since growth has been the aim of Conservative and Labour governments alike one would expect that Green political economy would be even-handed in its condemnation of socialism and capitalism. To some extent this is true: large-scale unionisation, nationalisation, and big government are as objectionable to Greens as are multinational corporations and *laissez-faire* capitalism. However, despite the emphasis on decentralisation their practical policies are statist and regulatory. A Green government would make economic growth impossible; by statutory controls, taxation and redistribution. Small business would be fostered by Regional Enterprise Boards (Porritt, ch. 10). Whether the drop in living standards (at least in terms of the availability of consumer goods), which would occur as a consequence of the adoption of Green policies, could ever be attractive to Labour voters is quite another matter.

Nevertheless, the Greens represent a strand of opinion which is likely to influence the major parties. Margaret Thatcher has expressed a concern for these matters and leading conservative economists (see Pearce *et al.*, 1989) have shown how the problems identified by the Greens are soluble by market pricing methods, e.g. protecting the environment by 'charging' polluters and rigorously enforcing (and possibly redefining) property rights.

Nevertheless, Thatcherite orthodoxy is almost bound to set the agenda for the next decade, even though its programme is likely to be less ideological and more pragmatic. One suspects that the imperative of the next election and the perceived unpopularity of recent policies will deter Conservatives from radical experiments. One significant question is just how much longer Margaret Thatcher will continue to lead the Conservative Party. The post-1985 laxity in monetary policy (see Congdon, 1989) has been damaging and many conservatives will be keen to return to the original rationale of the Thatcher government – the maintenance of political *authority* and the restoration of a sound currency. With regard to the latter ideal, post-Thatcher Conservatives are likely to favour a closer integration with Europe through the EC's monetary mechanism. However, the 'social agenda' of the EC will be resisted because of its implicit threat to much of the 'Thatcherite revolution'; especially in relation to trade unions and social policy.

The ideological task of Labour is awesome by comparison with that of the Conservatives. Having suffered three successive electoral defeats the party has been forced to re-think its theoretical and political strategy. At the intellectual level, its major problem is to integrate successfully the popular elements of the market with traditional socialist values. But the achievement, both in theory and practice, of market freedom without capitalism is extraordinarily difficult. Socialist theorists have often looked to decentralised industrial operations subject to worker's control rather than capitalist ownership. However, experiments in Yugoslavia, and elsewhere, suggest that without a private capital market, the state inevitably determines investment programmes, on political grounds, to the detriment of innovation and enterprise. However, over the next ten years, a comprehensive theory of market socialism for the British context is likely to be produced: it is clearly needed.

At the practical level, Labour politicians will be more concerned to protect areas of social life, especially welfare, from penetration by the market. And for this reason ideological debate with Thatcherism is likely to continue with the same intensity. Practical politics will impel policy reviewers to define and limit the area of the capitalist market rather than attempt to adopt a genuine *socialist* market; even if there is a viable theoretical model. Private control, including wider share-ownership, is presumably too well-entrenched in Britain. For this reason, the theory and practice of socialism are likely to unite over the defence of the welfare state; reinforced by a further elaboration of the philosophy of citizenship.

The current affection for EC institutions may turn out to be a tactical ploy against Thatcherism rather than a genuine commitment to the European ideal. A full integration would involve the kind of constitutional restraint, especially in the monetary field, which Labour leaders have resented as much as conservatives have. There is a similarity here with the Labour leadership's lack of interest in internal constitutional reform proposals of the 'Charter 88' (1988) group; for in practice these measures and strict EC rules necessitate substantive limitations on the sovereignty of parliament – a constitutional device socialists have found so useful in the past. In this area, at least, the old consensus remains intact.

Note

This chapter was completed while the author was Visiting Scholar at the Social Philosophy and Policy Center, Bowling Green State University.

3

Voting and the Electorate

W. L. MILLER

Voting is not just a matter of personal choice. Obviously voters are more likely to vote for a party they like than one they dislike, but their likes and dislikes are influenced and conditioned by a variety of outside forces – in particular, by their social and family background and by the way the parties are presented in the media. And whatever their political opinions, voters cannot vote for a party that does not put forward a candidate in their ward or constituency. Even when their preferred party does contest an election, voters may be reluctant to vote for it if they feel it has no chance of winning. At other times (especially at byelections) voters may vote for a party precisely because they are sure that it cannot win power. So it makes little sense to discuss voting without paying attention to the circumstances that surround the vote, the 'voting context'.

Various models of voting have been proposed to explain why people vote the way they do. Figure 3.1 sets out a general model summarising and synthesising these accounts. It has six elements:

(1) *Social context* includes not only the voter's own class, age, sex, religion, region etc., but also the social characteristics and political attitudes of the voter's family, neighbours, workmates and friends.
(2) *Party identification* has been a key concept in the most

popular models of voting behaviour. It means the voter's sense of attachment to, or 'identification' with a political party. There are two aspects to party identification: first, its direction (which party); second, its strength.

(3) *Attitudes* include how voters feel about issues, performance, personalities, values and ideology. For example: the *issue* of unilateralism; the *performance* of the government in managing the economy; the *personality* of Thatcher; the *values* or *ideology* of egalitarianism or self-help.

(4) *The voting context* includes people's assessment of the point or purpose of the election and the range of credible options available. If voters feel the election is pointless they may ignore it and abstain. If it is a byelection they may feel it is a suitable and safe opportunity for a protest. If it is a local government election they may feel that it is appropriate to express a view on the Poll Tax but not on Defence policy. Their choice of party *must* be limited by the range of candidates available in their constituency; it *may* also be limited by the viability of the parties (i.e. their perceived chances of success) nationally or locally.

(5) *The media context* includes political advertising, reporting and commentaries in newspapers, on radio and especially on television.

(6) *Government and party actions* are almost self-explanatory except that we need to stress the leading role of government. The governing party is far more than 'first among equals'.

Figure 3.1 also shows the causal arrows which link these elements with each other and with voting behaviour. An arrow indicates that one element *influences* another, but does not imply that one element completely *determines* another.

Arrow *A* says that voters' social and family backgrounds influence their sense of party identification. For example, working-class children with working-class, Labour-voting parents, who grow up in a working-class neighbourhood are more likely to identify themselves with the Labour Party than those who came from a different background. Links *B* and *C* suggest that voters' political attitudes are influenced by their background *and* by this pre-existing sense of party identification.

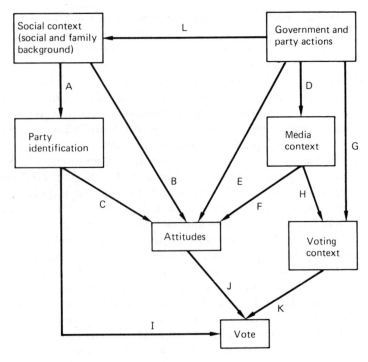

FIGURE 3.1   *A general model of voting*

Link *D* suggests that the content and style of the mass media is influenced by the actions of government and the parties. In one sense that is obvious since the political content of the media largely consists of reports on the activities of the parties. But, in addition, all the parties try to manipulate the news and the government is particularly well-placed to do so. The actions of government and parties influence voters' attitudes *directly* through personal experience (e.g. of inflation, or unemployment) shown by link *E*; and *indirectly* through media reports (e.g. about defence policy) represented by link *F*. Similarly voters' perceptions of party credibility are influenced by direct experience (e.g. the availability of local candidates, whether they have been leafleted or canvassed) shown by link *G*; and by media reports (e.g. opinion poll projections of the parties' chances) represented by link *H*.

The voter's ultimate decision about which way to vote is based upon a mix of influences from party loyalty (link *I*), political attitudes (link *J*) and the voting context (link *K*). Until the 1980s we could have ended the model description there. But a significant new feature of Thatcherism is its explicit attempt to 'bury socialism' by eradicating socialism's social base – not, of course, by eradicating the poor, but by eradicating the council tenant, the public employee, and the 'welfare scrounger'. So we need to add a new link in the model (link *L*) to represent the purposive influence of government upon social background. Obviously nothing can be done to change voters' family backgrounds but it is quite easy to change their own social circumstances by selling them council houses, privatising their employers, and encouraging them to rely on private health care organisations instead of the NHS.

In broad terms the elements on the left-hand side of Figure 3.1 are the voters' social background and party identification – originally conceived as the 'enduring' elements of political motivations. On the right are party activity, media reports, voters' attitudes and voters' perceptions – originally conceived as the 'ephemeral' elements of political motivations. Any change in the balance of influence between the elements on the left and the right of the diagram would affect the stability and continuity of voting behaviour. A system dominated by social background and party loyalty should tend towards stability; a system dominated by yesterday's dramatic government announcement, cabinet scandal or eye-catching headline should tend towards volatility.

On the other hand, slow but cumulative and relatively irreversible changes are more likely to flow from changes in social background or party identification. Conversely, forces towards stability can be found on the right-hand side of the diagram. Issues are not always 'ephemeral'. Sometimes they are so persistent and multifaceted as to merit the description 'values' or 'ideology'. Under a self-consciously ideological government the issues that crop up day after day are *not* independent of one another and the general thrust of policy and debate does *not* change. Moreover, parties are not equal in their power to influence events, news reports and public attitudes. If inequalities in the structure of party power persist then party activity itself may be a force for stability rather than change.

The literature on voting behaviour is littered with the names of voting models which stress particular aspects of the general model set out in Figure 3.1: the Sociological Model, the Party Identification Model, the Rational Choice Model and the Dominant Ideology Model, for example. Differences between these models are not essentially differences of principle, so much as differences of focus and emphasis. Political scientists who see particular value in one of these partial models do not necessarily deny the value of others. The question is not which model is *the correct one*, but which models are *relevant* to our understanding of political behaviour. In current British politics a restricted focus would be difficult to justify. It is clear that the relationship of social structure to voting is still significant; that party identification is still influential; that voters' attitudes do change and do affect voting choice; that party credibility has a major impact; and that there is disturbing if inconclusive evidence of hegemonic forces at work. In short, *nothing* in the general model is
redundant. But there is too much in the general model to discuss all at once; so we can use the partial models as a useful way to focus attention on different parts of the general model in turn.

Sociological Model

The basic claim of the *sociological model* is that social groups will vote for the party that serves their interests. Individuals as completely independent decision-makers do not exist. What voters' claim to be their own carefully thought-out political attitudes may simply reflect the interests of the group to which they belong. To what extent this model fits the facts can be measured by the degree of *social alignment*: the extent to which particular social groups vote for particular parties or the extent to which opposite sides of a social divide vote for different parties. Because different social divisions cross-cut one another, we look at the correlations between social divisions and voting. Amongst the obvious social divisions that relate to group interests and voting behaviour are class, industrial sector, sex, ethnicity, religion and region. Whatever the differences in their group interests, voting differences between men and women are relatively small (Crewe, 1987, p. 3). Ethnic and religious alignments are closely linked: most catholics have an Irish connection, most moslems an Asian, most presbyterians a Scottish connection. Since religion is not central to any of the modern parties, ethnic/religious groups are free to 'negotiate' a home in any (or every) party. As long as they feel a disadvantaged minority, religious/ethnic groups have a natural affinity for Labour but there is nothing permanent or intrinsic about their political allegiance. Anwar (1986) shows that Asians and Afro-Caribbeans are still overwhelmingly Labour voters. Catholics are still roughly 15 per cent more Labour than are Anglicans in the same class (Rose and McAllister, 1986, p. 73). But Alderman (1989) has drawn attention to the way Jews have switched from Labour to Conservative as they have become more prosperous.

Traditionally, Labour has been the party of social and collective approaches to industry, housing and welfare. Those who work in the public sector, or who depend upon the public sector, have an interest in electing Labour governments. We might expect a public/private voting alignment in terms of housing, employment, even share-ownership. Middle-class public-sector workers are slightly less Conservative than the rest of the middle class, and those who own houses or shares are much more Conservative.

But the social alignments that have attracted most attention have been *class* and *region*. Over the last three decades the class alignment has declined sharply while geographical and regional alignments have intensified. Class polarisation has declined to little more than half its post-war peak while regional polarisation has grown rapidly to rival class polarisation in intensity (Figure 3.2). Over the period 1955–87 the swing in the South and Midlands of England was more favourable to the Conservatives than in Britain as a whole; but in the North of England it was more favourable to *Labour*; and in Scotland very much more favourable to Labour (Curtice and Steed, 1988, p. 330). Of course, the most extreme

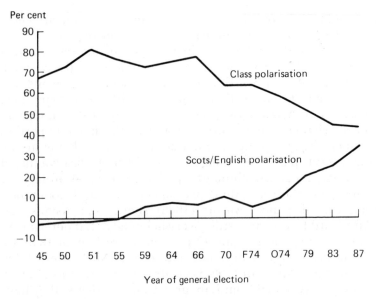

FIGURE 3.2   *Trends in Con/Lab polarisation (1945–87)*

Definitions:
Polarisation between social groups is defined in terms of the Conservative lead over Labour (CON LEAD) as a per cent of a group's total votes.

Class polarisation = CON LEAD in middle class
                    minus CON LEAD in working class.

Scots/English polarisation = CON LEAD in England
                            minus CON LEAD in Scotland.

Scots/English polarisation was slightly negative from 1945 to 1955 since the Scots were more Conservative than the English at that time.

Sources: Class polarisation calculated by the author from data in Heath *et al.* (1985, p. 30) and Butler (1989, p. 62). Scots/English polarisation calculated by the author from data in Craig (1989).

regional polarisation affects only the opposite ends of the kingdom (Scotland and the south of England), and relatively few people live in Scotland; but the existence of separate institutions north of the border adds significance to Scots/ English party polarisation.

Heath, Jowell and Curtice (1985) have argued that the evidence of class dealignment has been overstated if, indeed, any class dealignment has occurred at all. The middle class of the 1980s was much more 'professional' and less 'bourgeois' than the middle class of the 1950s and 1960s – its income and status much more dependent upon education than wealth. Their evidence suggests that *if* we could ignore the growth of Alliance voting and *if* we could ignore the changing class structure then there was not much evidence of class dealignment. But, of course, we cannot ignore those changes. The growth of Alliance voting meant that increasing numbers of voters opted for a party that did not represent class interests. The growth of the professional salariat, coupled with a static bourgeoisie and a declining working class means that the sum total of class groups whose interests are clearly represented by parties is shrinking. So in terms of the *sociological model* class dealignment is real and is in part due to a growing mis-match between the available parties and the classes as social interest groups.

It is not too difficult to argue that both class dealignment and growing north/south alignments reflect the interests of social groups. The 1966–70 and 1974–9 Labour governments both had major confrontations with the unions and could only legitimately claim a mildly more egalitarian record than Conservative governments. Conversely, in the late 1970s and 1980s, there appeared to be an increasingly good fit between regional interests and parties. Between 1979 and 1987 employment grew in every region in southern England – by 5 per cent overall, while it *dropped* in Scotland, Wales and every region of northern England – by 9 per cent overall (Lewis and Townsend, 1989, p. 9).

Overall, despite the decline in the class alignment among individuals, social groups within the British electorate have *not* become more politically homogeneous. Parliamentary constituencies have never been more politically polarised and, in consequence, the number of marginal constituencies held by small majorities has halved since the 1960s (Curtice and Steed, 1988, p. 354).

Party Identification Model

The *party identification model* (sometimes called the 'socialisation' model or the 'expressive' model) stresses the importance of enduring partisan commitment. It emphasises the power of links *A*, *C* and *I* in the general model. Its basic claims are that:

(1) substantial numbers of voters (but not all) self-consciously identify with a party;
(2) their party identification is a relative stable and enduring part of their political outlook – certainly more stable than their attitudes towards issues and personalities;
(3) their party identification influences (but does not completely determine) their attitudes towards issues, personalities and government performance;
(4) in addition, their party identification also directly affects their voting choice: i.e., it partially outweighs their attitudes as well as influencing them.

How far are these claims still true? Just under half the electorate regularly claim to be party 'supporters'. Substantial numbers of voters still do identify with parties even though their strength of commitment appears to have dropped sharply in the 1970s (Figure 3.3). Moreover, the number of 'supporters' appears to rise by about 16 per cent, and the number of 'very strong' identifiers by 8 per cent at election time compared with mid-term surveys (Miller *et al.*, 1990, ch. 1). So self-conscious party commitment remains significant, even at the lower levels found in the 1980s.

The only way to assess the *stability* of party identification is by means of a panel survey, which interviews the same respondents at least twice. In a panel of voters questioned for the British Local Election Study in November 1985 and again in June 1986, 82 per cent identified with the same party in both interviews (Miller, 1988, p. 43). The *direction* of party identification was less stable than choice of morning newspaper but much more stable than any aspect of political knowledge, opinion or attitude. Heath and McDonald (1988) also found, in their 1983–7 British Election Study panel that party identification was more stable than any one issue-attitude though no more stable than general left–right value orientations. Much of the instability was associated with the Alliance option. In the 1985–6 Local Election study, for example, if we restrict attention to voters with a Conservative or Labour

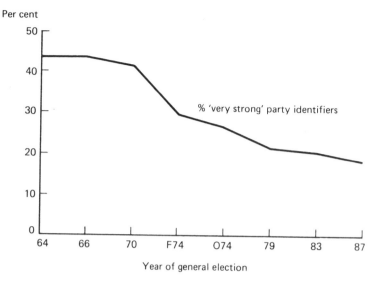

FIGURE 3.3   *Trends in party identification (1964–87)*

Definition: Percentage of electors who describe themselves as 'very strongly' Conservative, Labour, Liberal, etc. It includes all very strong party identifiers, irrespective of party.

Source: Heath and McDonald (1988).

identification, 97 per cent chose the same party in the two interviews. However, while the *direction* of party identification was stable, its strength was more variable.

One explanation for the apparent increase in electoral volatility in the 1970s is simply that the ties of party identification were loosened: a drop in the strength of party commitment meant more votes were 'up for grabs'. Disillusionment with the records of Wilson's 1964–70 Labour governments and Heath's 1970–4 Conservative government almost halved the numbers of strongly committed partisans and allowed Liberals and Nationalists to make spectacular gains in votes in 1974. The argument is persuasive, particularly as an explanation of electoral volatility in the 1970s, if not in the 1980s when other factors were at work. But since we now know that the strength of party identification is so unstable it is also possible that the decline in the strength of partisanship accompanied but did not precede the rise in voter volatility.

Conversely there is nothing immutable about current lower levels of partisan strength.

Correlations between party identification and attitudes predictably reveal a connection but give no hint of whether it is partisanship that influences attitudes or vice versa. We need a process test: does party identification influence emerging changes in voters' opinions? A striking feature of the winter of 1986–7 was the sudden increase in economic optimism. Crewe (1987, p. 7) has attributed the Conservatives' re-election solely to this surge in optimism. There were only 2 per cent more optimists than pessimists in the early summer of 1986 but this figure reached 41 per cent by March 1987 – a large increase. Needless to say, Conservatives were the most optimistic and Labour voters the most pessimistic. What is interesting, however, is the way optimism developed within the different partisan groups. Among those who declared themselves party *supporters* in 1986 (half the electorate), net economic optimism increased during the following year by 40 percentage points among Conservative supporters, by 24 percentage points among Alliance supporters and by only 18 percentage points among Labour supporters (Miller *et al.*, 1990, ch. 4). So party identification had a marked effect upon the development of economic attitudes in at least that half of the electorate who declared themselves to be party supporters.

Finally, party identification does appear to have a direct effect upon voting choice even after taking into account the influence of judgements about economic performance, issue attitudes, personalities and tactical voting (Miller *et al.*, 1990, ch. 7). Rose and McAllister (1986, p. 135) deny this but they use a statistical test that is biased against such a conclusion: it does not treat the range of possible influences equally.

Rational Choice Model

The *rational choice model* focuses attention on only one link in the general model, link *J*. It ignores the question of where voters get their attitudes from, and confines its attention to the fit between voters' attitudes and their voting choice. A variety of more specific names are sometimes used for rational choice models, depending upon the particular attitudes that best predict voting choice. So the model may be called an 'issue voting' model, a 'value' model, a 'prospective' model (if votes fit best with attitudes towards party policies for the future), a 'retrospective' model (if votes fit best with attitudes towards the government's past record in handling the economy, for example), or a 'leader personality' model.

The basic claim of this model is that voters make up their own minds about issues, performance and personalities and then vote for the party that comes closest to delivering the policies and performance that they want. Simple enough in principle the model is extremely difficult to apply in practice because of the open-ended nature of the voters' decision criteria. Any analysis that shows voters do *not* decide their vote on the basis of particular issues is open to the challenge that perhaps there were some other, hidden issues – a secret agenda – that really determined the result.

The rational choice model fails simple tests in spectacular fashion but perhaps that is the fault of the tests rather than the model. The Conservatives won the 1983 election by a margin of 15 per cent, and yet Heath, Jowell and Curtice (1985, p. 97) note that if people had voted *on the issues* Labour would have tied with the Conservatives. If each voter had voted for the party they thought was best, on the issue which they said was most important for themselves, Labour and the Conservatives would each have won 35 per cent. Crewe (1987, p. 7) repeated this analysis for the 1987 election and found that if each voter had voted for the party they preferred, on the issue they themselves regarded as most important, Labour would then have beaten the Conservatives by 2 per cent instead of trailing behind by 12 per cent.

The mystery is deepened by the fact that all the way through the 1980s a large and growing majority of voters have said they want more public services even at the expense of higher taxes – an ideological position directly opposed to Thatcherism. According to Crewe, 'private prosperity' was the 'key to the Conservative victory'. Labour might have been ahead on ideology and ahead on the most important issues but the electorate associated the Conservatives with economic prosperity. By a majority of two-to-one, voters chose the

Conservatives as the party best able to maintain economic prosperity in 1987 – whether for Britain as a whole, or for the voter and his/her family.

But as always a correlation does not prove causation. We know that partisanship influenced voters' economic perceptions. Perhaps they praised the Conservatives' economic competence because they liked the Conservatives for other reasons. Is there any direct evidence that economic perceptions actually swung voters towards the Conservatives? Once again we can turn to the 1986–7 panel of voters from the British Campaign Study.

Over the winter of 1986–7 roughly half the panel became more optimistic, a quarter stayed the same and a quarter became more pessimistic. Party supporters (half the electorate) were not much influenced by their changing economic optimism but the rest of the voters were. The Conservative Party gained 20 per cent among those who (i) did not have a firm sense of party identification and (ii) became more optimistic about the economy. The party gained nothing among those who became more pessimistic about the economy; and only 4 per cent among those who became more optimistic but had a firm sense of identification with one or other of the parties (Miller *et al.*, 1990, ch. 4). (See Figure 3.4.)

These findings are consistent with *both* the party identification *and* the rational choice models. Further analysis shows that over the winter preceding the 1987 election: (i) *among party supporters* (roughly half the electorate) their party preference had more influence over the development of their economic attitudes than vice versa; but (ii) *among the other half of the electorate*, their developing economic attitudes had more influence over their party preference than vice versa. So, at least in terms of economic attitudes, the behaviour of half the electorate (party 'supporters') was governed by a party identification model, while the behaviour of the rest was governed by a rational choice model.

It is, of course, as rational to vote for prosperity as for a better health service or for policies to reduce unemployment. Indeed rational choice theorists would probably regard voting for the party best able to advance your family's economic prosperity as rational voting *par excellence*. However, other

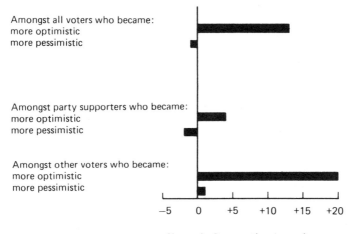

FIGURE 3.4 *The effect of changing optimism on Conservative voting intentions (1986–7)*

Source: Miller *et al.* (1990, ch. 4)

evidence from the 1987 Campaign Study confirms the findings from many earlier studies that voters were primarily motivated by their judgements about the *government's record on managing the economy* rather than by their own economic fortunes (which they quite properly recognise depend a great deal upon their own efforts and good luck). What is not entirely clear is whether rational choice theorists regard this predominant 'sociotropic' (or society-centred) motivation as being 'rational' for individuals.

Dominant Ideology Model

The basic claim of the *dominant ideology* model is that powerful groups in society are able to influence public opinion, through the structure of public institutions and control of the mass media (Dunleavy and Husbands, 1985). The argument can get quite metaphysical. Let us consider it in a concrete form: can the parties or the government control public opinion? They certainly try.

Trade unionists tend to vote Labour. Conservative policies

have succeeded in reducing their numbers, and curbing their influence. But the unions have become rather more popular as they have become smaller and less powerful (ICM poll in the *Guardian*, 18 September 1989, p. 20). In 1984 the government also attacked the financial base of the Labour Party by imposing a system of ballots on the use of union funds for political purposes. But all the ballots voted to retain these funds and the unions were encouraged to spend more, not less, on political campaigning.

Council tenants tend to vote Labour. The Conservative government sold over a million council houses (at massive discounts) to the sitting tenants, turning them into owner-occupiers. Yet some studies argue that there is 'no indication that the sale of council houses produced new recruits for Thatcherism' (Heath *et al.*, 1989, p. 13). Council house purchasers were certainly relatively Conservative council tenants *before* their purchase, but they became no more so *after* their purchase. However, other studies have claimed more indirect benefit to the Conservatives from council house sales, such as a shift from Labour to Alliance voting (Williams *et al.*, 1987; Stubbs, 1988, pp. 154–5).

Workers in nationalised industries tend to vote Labour. Several nationalised industries were privatised. But 'while the privatisations certainly extended popular capitalism perhaps to a further 12 per cent of the electorate, it is not clear that this had any direct effect upon voting behaviour' (Heath *et al.*, 1989, p. 8). Those who purchased shares were relatively Conservative *before* they did so and became no more so *afterwards*. Many sold their newly acquired shares quite quickly. Workers in the newly privatised industries may be encouraged to support the Conservatives and discouraged from voting Labour. But since the nationalised industries were never popular with their customers, the Conservatives may lose some support by switching customer-resentment to the private sector. One clear though limited gain for the Conservatives: several newly privatised industries, including British Airways and Rolls-Royce, made large donations to the Conservative Party's election funds (Pinto-Duschinsky, 1989).

In terms of the media system, all the major London-based papers except for the *Mirror*, the *Guardian* and the *Independent* are biased towards the Conservatives and explicitly endorse the party in election campaigns. Over two-thirds of newspaper readers detect bias in the papers they themselves read; and they describe the bias as pro-Conservative, anti-Labour and especially anti-Alliance. By contrast television and radio are required by law to maintain political balance in their news. During election campaigns this is particularly tightly controlled by an explicit inter-party agreement. Broadly, the ratio of television news time reflects the parties' recent voting strengths. In 1987 the Alliance was granted exact equality with the other two parties. But a detailed study of the content of television news reveals that in the event there was a massive bias towards the government (Miller *et al.*, 1990, ch. 8).

There is a simple reason for this paradox. The parties, as parties, did indeed receive approximately equal coverage. But the incumbent ministers, *as a government*, then received as much again. So in non-controversial news items during the campaign, the Conservative government got twice as much coverage as any other party. Most of these non-controversial items were helpful to its image – items about Thatcher meeting Gorbachev or attending the Venice summit of Western leaders, items about Sir Geoffrey Howe threatening the Iranians with dire consequences unless they released a Britisher held in Tehran (the Iranians released him shortly before election day), and so on.

In more controversial news items television tended either to present the views of all three parties *or* present the controversy as a Conservative/Labour battle (and not, for example, as a Conservative/Alliance or Labour/Alliance battle). As the campaign drew to a close, television focused increasingly on the Conservative/Labour two-party battle which marginalised the Alliance. In terms of issues television was biased towards the Conservative agenda. The issues that voters told the pollsters they thought were most important to them, and the issues they said should be discussed were social issues – unemployment, health, education. But election-news focused as much on security issues (defence, law and order) as on social issues; and non-election news on television during the campaign gave five times as much attention to security as to social affairs. In short, television news stressed the kind of issues that usually benefit right-wing parties.

Bias does not prove domination. To what extent did television succeed in setting the voters' agenda? Its influence seems limited but certainly not negligible. In the first week of the 1987 election campaign only 5 per cent of television's election-news focused on defence; only 3 per cent of voters thought the parties were actually stressing the issue; and only 3 per cent of voters wanted the parties to stress the issue. But by the middle of the campaign 26 per cent of television's election-news focused on defence; 39 per cent of voters now thought it was the Conservative party's main campaign issue; and 11 per cent of voters now thought it should be the main issue to be discussed by the parties. So television easily conveyed the message that the Conservatives wanted to talk about defence but only raised the number of voters seeing defence as a priority from 3 per cent to 11 per cent. It would be an exaggeration to say that television was able to *set* the voters' agenda, but correct to say that television was able to *influence* the voters' agenda (see Figure 3.5).

Particularly disturbing is evidence of the lengths to which government is now prepared to go to increase the inevitable advantages of incumbency by manipulating the news. In the 1980s government used its control of official statistics to alter the formula for calculating unemployment rates about two dozen times – nearly always to *reduce* the official unemployment rate. Cumulatively, these adjustments cut published unemployment figures by about a quarter. When inflation rates became inconveniently high towards the end of the decade, ministers even considered excluding mortgage repayments from the inflation calculation.

Government is now regularly in the list of the top ten spenders on advertising and it has stepped outside previous conventions by running advertising campaigns in support of government policies *before* their passage into law. A television advertising campaign about 'Action for Jobs' policies in the spring of 1987 turned out to be aimed at middle-class opinion-formers who already had jobs, rather than at the jobless. Advertising slots were aimed at the prosperous South rather than the unemployed North, and chosen to coincide

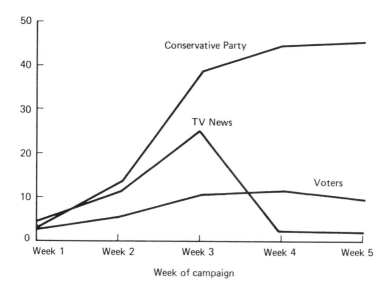

FIGURE 3.5   *Stress on the defence issue in the 1987 campaign*

Definitions:

Conservative Party = Per cent of electors who say the Conservative Party seems to be talking mainly about Defence.

Voters = Per cent of electors who say the main subject the parties *should* be discussing is Defence.

TV News = Per cent of election news items on TV which focus on Defence. TV includes the BBC's *Six O'Clock News*, and *Nine O'Clock News*, plus ITN's *News at 5.40*, and *New at Ten*.

Source: Miller *et al.* (1990, ch. 6).

with ITN's up-market *News at Ten* rather than the soap-operas watched by the unemployed (*Panorama*, 4 September 1989). Perhaps most disturbing of all, ministers apparently attempted to intimidate the BBC by stridently alleging left-wing bias in 1986–7 (despite repeated survey evidence that the public thought the BBC had a *right*-wing bias); by supporting a police raid on the BBC's Scottish Headquarters to seize a complete series of documentaries) and by helping to promote the sacking of the BBC's Director General. All this is only coincidentally an attempt at right-wing domination of the media; it is primarily just an attempt by an incumbent government to secure its position. It is also clear that in some obvious respects it was unsuccessful. For example, the BBC-Scotland series on the *Secret Society* won much more attention by being seized in a police raid than it would have received if it had been broadcast on schedule.

Finally, let us reconsider the evidence on economic optimism. Crewe (1987) argued that this was the 'key to the Conservative victory' in 1987. We have seen that, over the winter preceding the general election, (i) economic optimism increased dramatically and (ii) the Conservative recovery was confined to voters who became more optimistic. From a narrow perspective that seemed an eloquent justification for the *rational choice* model. But *why* did voters become more optimistic at that time? If they did so as a consequence of the government's efforts to manipulate the media and the economy then this is evidence for the *dominant ideology* model. The government not only adjusted the calculation of economic statistics, used public funds for political advertising, and put extreme pressure on the BBC, it also manipulated the real economy. Monetarism was abandoned, the growth of money supply (M3) stepped up, taxes cut, public spending increased, rising inflation tolerated and real (not just statistical), unemployment reduced (see Chapter 8). So voters' optimism in 1987 was stimulated by a real pre-election consumer boom as well as by careful news management.

So do the parties compete on a level playing field? Certainly not. The system is biased towards the Conservative Party and (quite separately) towards the incumbent government. But even large media biases seem to have had small effects; attempts to manipulate the social structure do not seem to have paid the expected political dividends; and only a good old-fashioned pre-election boom had a large effect. Labour's 1989 'Policy Review' was very popular with the voters and Labour increased its lead over the Conservatives 'on the issues' though lingering doubts remain about its ability to manage the economy (NOP poll in the *Independent*, 16 September 1989). In the run-up to the next election the media will be full of good economic news (real, imaginary or manufactured) and that will help the government. Against that the government will have to defend its unpopular policies on the NHS, privatisation and the Poll Tax. Defence may be a less useful distraction now that Labour has reverted to its traditional defence policy and the Soviet Union seems less threatening. The team at the bottom of the hill may still win even though the odds are against it.

Voting Contexts

Academics have paid remarkably little attention to voters' perceptions of the electoral context though they loom large in journalists' accounts of electoral change which discuss 'tactical voting', 'protest voting', 'party credibility' or a 'byelection atmosphere'. If we had to devise a name for explanations of voting that stressed this kind of voter motivation then the most inclusive label would be the *voting context model*.

These accounts emphasise the link K (from voters' perceptions of the electoral context to the vote) and also G and H (the influence of party actions and media reports on voters' perceptions of party credibility). Voters take account not only of their personal preferences but also of the *likely consequences* of their vote. Those consequences depend upon the nature of the election, the available range of electoral options, and the credibility of those options. The model implies that voters' preferences for parties are not so extreme that they absolutely refuse to consider alternatives, but we know from multi-wave panels that almost half the British electorate switched between Conservative, Labour and the Alliance at least once during the 1980s (Miller *et al.*, 1990, ch. 1), and if half the electorate *actually* switched then at least half, and probably more, are *potential* switchers.

There are clear interactions between the type of election and party credibility. Constituency boundaries are crucial under Britain's first-past-the-post electoral system since they define the local credibility of each party. A voter may live in an ultra-safe Conservative *local government ward*, within a marginal Conservative/Democrat *parliamentary constituency*, that is located within a marginal Conservative/Labour *Euro-constituency*. Clearly the tactical voting pressures on that voter depend very much upon which of these boundaries is relevant to the election in question. A Labour partisan in such a situation might well decide to abstain in the local government election, vote tactically for the Democrats in the parliamentary election and vote his/her party identification in the European election – without even considering the different candidates or issues in the three contests. In addition, some issues are peculiar to specific contests, and different types of elections lead to a change of focus within the range of issues. Defence and relations with the superpowers have a higher profile in *parliamentary* elections; environmental protection and relations with Europe have a higher profile in *Euro-elections*; the Poll Tax and central/local relationships have a higher profile in *local government elections*. In a sense all of these are 'national' issues simply because they all involve the UK national government. Yet each of them also involves conflict (or cooperation) between the national government and a different adversary (or partner).

The Local Election Context

The British Local Election Study showed that 84 per cent of local election voters in 1986 voted for the party they said they would prefer at a parliamentary election. Among local election voters who said they were voting on *national* issues the fit between local and national preferences rose to 93 per cent, and among those who said they were voting for the *party* rather than the candidate it touched 91 per cent. But just over half the panel said they voted on *local* issues in local elections and among them only 75 per cent voted their national preference. A third said they voted for the *candidate* rather than the party in local elections (very few said that about national elections) and among them only 55 per cent voted for a candidate of the party they preferred nationally (Miller, 1988, p. 167).

In 1987 there were local elections exactly five weeks before the parliamentary general election. Obviously any difference between local and national choice could reflect a trend in opinion over those five weeks as well as the difference between a national and a local government contest. On the other hand we can compare real votes at both levels and do not have to rely upon hypothetical preferences. In 1987 only 71 per cent of local election voters voted for the same party they chose in the parliamentary election a mere five weeks later. Among those who said they voted for the party rather than the candidate in local elections this figure rose to 78 per cent; but among those who said they voted more for the *candidate* than the party in local elections the fit between national and local election votes sank to 48 per cent. There were substantial shifts from voting Labour in the local elections to voting Alliance in the parliamentary election; and from voting Alliance in the local elections to voting both Labour and Conservative in the parliamentary.

The Byelection Context

The normal electoral cycle of government popularity has usually been reflected in byelections, but as Norris (1990) notes, relatively 'long-term trends in government popularity can rarely explain the short-term changes in voting intentions which can occur during the two or three week period of a by-election campaign', and 'the traditional theory has difficulty explaining the rapid shifts in support from one party in opposition to another – for example the sudden switch from Labour to the Alliance recorded in the polls at Bermondsey (1983) and Greenwich (1987)'. There was a similar dramatic switch from Labour to the SNP in the closing stages of the Govan byelection in 1988.

Norris proposes a *two-stage model* of byelection voting. The first stage is the erosion of government popularity that regularly happens in the mid-term; together with local circumstances that defines the parties' popularity at the start of the byelection campaign. The second stage is a very short-term but frequently very large shift in voting intentions between the start and the end of the byelection campaign. Here third parties – Liberals, SDP, Alliance, Nationalists, Democrats (and perhaps Greens in the future) – are well placed to aggregate the votes of temporarily disaffected government supporters with those of the main opposition party whose overriding objective may be to beat the government candidate or grab the maximum media attention for their grievances.

The third parties' chief asset is that they are less off-putting for government supporters to back, rather than that they are intrinsically attractive.

Using data from 10 BBC *Newsnight* byelection surveys, Norris divides voters into three main types. *Core* voters are those who decide at the start of the campaign and would not consider switching even if their chosen candidate had no chance of victory; only 39 per cent of the total fell in this group. Tactical voters are those who have a clear first preference but would consider switching to a second party to keep out a third that they dislike more than the second; 37 per cent are in this group. *Floating voters* (9 per cent) are simply undecided. Finally there are *abstainers* (15 per cent) with no intention of voting at all.

General Elections

During the run-up to the 1987 general election, voters were asked to give a 'mark out of ten' for how inclined they were to vote Conservative, another for how inclined they were to vote Labour, and a third for how inclined they were to vote Alliance. Typically they gave a mark of 8 to their first choice, 5 to their second and 2 to their third. Very few voters ended up voting for the party they had placed third at the start of the campaign. Their effective choice was between the parties they placed first and second and their likelihood of eventually switching to their second choice depended upon *how much* lower a rating they gave it initially. Around 90 per cent of those who initially put their first choice three or more points ahead of their second ended up voting for their original first choice; but only 80 per cent of those who originally put their first choice only 2 points ahead; and just 73 per cent of those who originally put their first choice only 1 point ahead (Miller *et al.*, 1989). There was clearly a sliding scale of voting indecision with considerable power to influence their final choice. Remember that tossing a coin to decide between first and second choices would lead 50 per cent to vote for their original first choice.

How many voters were located at different points on this scale of voting indecision? Among the majority of the electorate who were considering supporting either one of the two major parties or the Alliance over half (57 per cent) put their initial first preference only 2 or less points ahead of their second; and about a third (30 per cent) put their initial first preference only one point ahead or initially rated both parties equally. So between a third and a half of all voters had such a narrow preference for their first party over their second that they were potential switchers.

Voters in the panel were asked to assess each party's electoral chances, both nationally and local, at different stages in the campaign. It seems that voters' perceptions of party chances, particularly in the *local constituency*, and particularly in the *last few days* of the campaign, had a substantial effect upon their final voting choice. Looking at potential Labour/ Alliance switchers, among those who thought Labour had the best chance of beating the Conservatives locally, Labour's lead over the Alliance rose from 43 per cent at the start of the campaign to 75 per cent at the end; among those who thought the Alliance had the best chance of beating the Conservatives locally, Labour began with a narrow lead of 3 per cent over the Alliance but ended the campaign 12 per cent behind. However, voters were also influenced by perceptions of the parties' national credibility in the longer term. Indeed, perceptions of the parties' chances in local constituencies at the end of the campaign were to some extent the product of earlier assessments of the parties' chances nationally.

The Euro-Election Context

Euro-elections achieved a new status in June 1989, partly reflecting new powers given to the European Parliament between 1984 and 1989, and partly stronger party campaigning. Labour launched its policy review, and Thatcher chose to run on an anti-European platform which provoked her predecessor, Heath, into a vigorous defence of Europe. In Scotland the SNP pushed its new policy of 'Independence in Europe'. All of this raised turnout rates by 3 per cent in Britain as a whole, and by over twice that amount in Scotland.

The Liberal Democrats' standing in national opinion polls

was very low by 1989, but their local credibility in particular areas of local strength with sitting MPs or local councillors helped them win a respectable 20 per cent at the English country elections in May 1989. A month later they faced the Euro-elections with neither national nor local credibility. Because the Euro-constituencies were so large all but five seats in Scotland and Ulster were effectively a straight fight between Conservative and Labour. The Democrats also faced a sudden strong challenge by the Green party. Thatcher herself had legitimised the notion of Green politics with a much publicised meeting with environmentalists during the winter. European institutions had a high profile on matters such as food quality and environmental protection, which made a Euro-election a good time to think about environmental issues. With only 78 mainland constituencies to fight, although the Greens had few members and scant funds they found it much easier to find the candidates and deposits to contest every seat – boosting media coverage and the party's credibility. In the event, Labour beat the Conservatives by 5 per cent – its first nationwide victory since 1974 – and the Greens scored 15 per cent as the Liberal Democrats dropped to 6 per cent.

The Greens had no previous record of success in Britain. In 294 contests at general elections from 1979 to 1987 they had never won as much as 4 per cent in any parliamentary constituency and they had averaged only 1 per cent. At the English local government elections a month earlier they had averaged just under 9 per cent in 209 four-cornered fights, but still nothing like the 15 per cent nationwide which they won at the Euro-elections. Kellner's (1989) analysis suggested that it was 'almost certain that more ... Green voters in fact voted Alliance in 1987 than supported any other party'. Greens also gained substantial votes from those who had voted Conservative in 1987 and a few (one in eight) from former Labour voters. So Green support in 1989 came mainly from those who had voted Alliance in the past plus those who would have switched to them in 1989 if the Alliance had not fallen apart in fratricidal quarrelling after the 1987 elections. The longer-term support for Green policies seems unclear still; it is perhaps only half the party's 1989 vote.

Conclusions

When voters were asked, in 1987, to give the British system of elections 'a mark out of ten' they gave it an average of 7. Conservatives gave it the highest rating and Alliance voters the lowest. Very strong Conservative identifiers gave it one mark *more* than Conservative leaners, while very strong Alliance identifiers gave it one mark *less* than Alliance leaners (see Figure 3.6). By a narrow majority (50 per cent to 45 per cent) voters described the electoral system as 'unfair'. But they swung increasingly against coalition government – by the end of the 1987 campaign they were *marginally* against coalition and by the week after the election (when the Liberals and SDP were quarrelling merrily) they were *massively* against. And despite the fact that the Conservative victors won only 42 per cent, a small majority of voters (50 per cent to 45 per cent) said they were pleased with the result. Naturally enough, 96 per cent of Conservatives were pleased by the result but so were 30 per cent of Alliance voters.

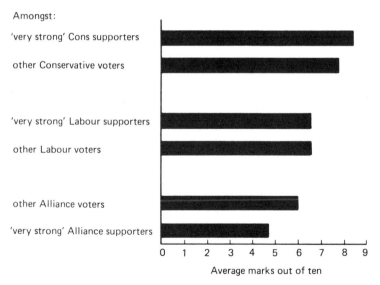

FIGURE 3.6 *Marks out of ten for the electoral system (1987)*
Source: Miller *et al.* (1990, ch. 8).

These data help put into perspective the oft-repeated claim that the Thatcher government depends only on an electoral minority. The government's legitimacy was more broadly accepted by voters after the 1987 election than its 43 per cent support alone might suggest. Nevertheless, one of the more interesting areas of change in voting patterns in the 1990s might follow from the introduction of new more proportional voting systems currently being discussed in the Labour Party and always supported by the Liberal Democrats, SDP and Greens. Whether such ideas get translated into practice – for example, for European elections or for a Scottish Convention – will be important in the 1990s.

4

Parties, Pressure Gro⹂ and Parliament

GILLIAN PEELE

By the end of the 1980s the British system of representation seemed to have undergone a complete cycle of change. From a situation at the beginning of the 1980s where many aspects of the party system seemed to have been transformed by a collapse of Labour support and a resurgence of the centre parties, the political framework of the late 1980s had apparently returned to the familiar structure of two-party competition. For the Conservatives a series of mid-term policy problems, particularly over the poll tax, the economy and the NHS, and controversy over Mrs Thatcher's leadership produced electoral setbacks in the local and the European elections and the loss of a safe seat in the mid-Staffs byelection. For Labour, a wide-ranging policy review, accompanied by byelection, local and European poll successes and in 1990 their highest ever opinion poll rating created a new mood of confidence which was reflected at all levels of party activity.

Beneath the apparent restoration of the structure of two-party politics in Britain, however, there were signs that the fabric of British political life had been permanently changed by the events of the Thatcher decade. The emergence of the Greens in the European elections in 1989 underlined the degree of this change. For not merely did the growth in ral support for the Greens (jumping to 15 per cent of the vote from the 0.5 per cent registered in the European ctions of 1984) signal the continuing volatility of the public d the willingness to switch to a new party; more importantly it ignalled the capacity of single issues to alter electoral behaviour and the extent to which the electorate might be mobilised by short-term factors which had gained publicity rather than long-term factors such as class identity (see Chapter 3). In this chapter, therefore, attention will be focused not merely on the parties which seek to aggregate interests and opinions into a majority capable of supporting a government but on the pressure groups which articulate interests and mobilise public opinion around issues. For often it is at the level of pressure group activity, rather than at the level of formal party activity, that the first signs of political and cultural change are detectable. Finally, the chapter examines some aspects of the way Parliament has worked in the period of Thatcher government in order to ascertain whether the experience of such a sustained period of government by one party has left any legacy.

The Nature of the Party System

Margaret Thatcher's dramatic achievement in winning three general elections in a row – together with Labour's sustained period of demoralisation – caused many observers to wonder whether Britain had become a one-party dominant system (Gamble, 1988; Peele, 1989). At every level in the 1980s – ideological, organisational and electoral – the Conservatives seemed to have the edge over the opposition and factors such as constituency redistribution seemed likely to work in their favour also.

For some on the left, indeed, the strategies of the Conservative Party after 1979 were geared towards the establishment of a political superiority which went far beyond the simple capture of national power for a prolonged period. For them the transformation of the Conservative Party under Margaret Thatcher was part of a much more radical project – an attempt to establish control of the values of society as well as the institutions of government (Hall, 1988). For other observers, especially those who had seen the evolution of Conservative policy and followed the policy debates in detail, no such over-arching strategy could be discerned (Riddell, 1989) (see Chapter 16). The Conservatives had simply combined a shrewd understanding of the public mood with a courageous determination to shake the British economy and society out of its lethargy. Electoral success had been the product of the Conservatives' apparent unity of purpose and the contrasting divisions among the opposition parties.

However, the experience of the European elections in 1989 – causing a loss of thirteen Conservative (or EDG) Euro-seats – prompted a reassessment of the strengths and weaknesses of the Conservative Party. It became apparent that, while the Conservative machine had generally operated effectively in *national* elections, it was not invulnerable. Moreover, it was not always the case that the Conservatives would display a united front in the face of an election. The issues associated with the character of the European Community divided the Conservative Party in Westminster as well as in Strasbourg and the decision to mount a campaign which emphasised the need to protect British interests against Community intervention angered many pro-European Tories. Subsequent debates over the pace of political and economic integration in Europe often found a majority of Conservative MEPs arguing a line quite different from that of the prime minister. Thus in November 1989 a majority of the depleted Conservative representation in the European Parliament signed a letter to *The Times* which was clearly more supportive of closer political integration than the Conservative leadership.

This division within the Conservative Party seems likely to last at least for the duration of Margaret Thatcher's tenure of Number 10 Downing Street. The prime minister herself appeared to recognise the potential danger of the split between herself and the Conservative MEPs when she announced in early January 1990 that she would be calling a meeting with them to resolve differences. However, one MEP, Peter Price, made public the extent of the disagreement and argued that not merely was much of the split the result of the leadership's negativism, but that virtually the whole group of Conservative

MEPs wanted faster integration and was supportive of a European central bank and a common currency, policies which were of course anathema to Mrs Thatcher.

Apart from their relevance to the substance of European policy, the results of the European elections underlined two further points about the party system. Firstly, electoral opinion remained volatile and gave little evidence for any form of realignment. Secondly, it was possible that such a long period of Conservative government might carry with it the seeds of its own demise. The electorate might become weary of having one party in power for so long – to say nothing of having a single leader in Number 10; and it was always likely that other parties would adapt their programmes and organisations to mount an effective challenge to the government.

The Conservatives in Power

The Conservative Party was itself well aware of the dangers inherent in too long a period of power. The need to keep itself fresh in the minds of the electorate was one reason for the emphasis on radical measures in its third term which some Conservatives thought should be a consolidating one. Yet there was evidence that public support for further radicalism of a free market sort had waned. While the support for the early measures of privatisation achieved fairly solid levels of public approval, the determination to extend the principle of privatisation to electricity and to water appeared much less welcome to the public. A poll taken in late June 1989 found that 79 per cent of the public was opposed to the privatisation of the water industry and that professional investors were almost equally opposed to it. Ironically, much of the opposition had been generated by a growing environmental awareness, fostered in part by the government itself (*Observer/ Harris Poll* reprinted in the *Observer*, 2 July 1989). Nevertheless the government did not abandon the policy and when the time came for selling shares in water to the public the offer was over-subscribed.

In addition to the concern about the quality of British water, there was fear that privatisation would lead to higher costs being passed on to the consumer – a fear which was also a factor in the controversy surrounding the electricity industry. The handling of electricity privatisation indeed suffered a major setback when the government was forced to retain Britain's nuclear power stations in public ownership because of the high costs associated with their modernisation.

The progress of privatisation (see Chapter 13) was of great symbolic significance for the government. The reduction of the public sector and the rolling back of the frontiers of the state had been central themes in Conservative philosophy under Margaret Thatcher's leadership (Peele, 1989). Yet, although there was plenty of evidence that the public was impatient with the inefficiencies of the nationalised industries, there was never much substantial evidence of the commitment to the neo-liberal values of Thatcherism. The most that could be said was that the electorate was willing to give a conditional degree of support to measures which were generally deemed unlikely to make matters worse in a policy area where the status quo was also deeply unpopular.

It was not only in relation to the next stages of privatisation that the radical agenda of the government ran into difficulties however. The government had long argued that there was a need to reform the National Health Service. Initially it seemed that reform might involve introducing an insurance principle into medical provision, but it became apparent that the political support for the principles of the existing health care system was such as to preclude such an option. Instead it was decided to try to make the system more responsive to the market by making general practitioners and hospitals more responsible for their own budgets and to give them greater choice in the selection of patient care. Such proposals however met with opposition from the medical profession (see Chapter 9).

The campaign by doctors met with great sympathy from the public and the future of the National Health Service emerged as a major issue for the Labour Party. Less likely to resonate with the public but embarrassing for the government was a concerted campaign by the legal profession to resist proposals by the Lord Chancellor to eliminate restrictive practices in the legal profession. Nevertheless the strength of the opposition was such that concessions had to be made.

The more radical parts of the Conservative legislative programme thus encountered sustained opposition at a time when there was controversy over the handling of the economy and disagreement between the Prime Minister and the Chancellor of the Exchequer about the measures needed to reduce the rate of inflation and about British participation in the European monetary system. The conflict was exacerbated by public statements by the Prime Minister's economic adviser Sir Alan Walters – statements which created uncertainty about who was in charge of the government's economic policy. In October 1989 the Chancellor of the Exchequer, Nigel Lawson, resigned, apparently after having made it plain to the Prime Minister that he could no longer tolerate a situation in which there was doubt about the direction of key issues related to the economy (see Chapter 8).

The Future of the Conservative Leadership

The resignation of the Chancellor threw the Conservative Party into disarray. Nigel Lawson had been regarded as a key figure in maintaining financial confidence and the whole affair appeared symptomatic of the Prime Minister's leadership style. Increasingly she had come to seem isolated from the rest of the cabinet and liable to rely on her own advisers. The charge of authoritarianism which surfaced during the Westland affair was again levelled at the Prime Minister and critics suggested that the very fact that she had allowed so senior a figure to resign was a sign that she was losing her political touch.

There had already been a perception of disunity in government ranks in the summer of 1989 when one of the customary devices for refreshing the image of the government – a reshuffle – had backfired. Although this reorganisation of the government had brought forward a new generation of leaders and provided some much needed strengthening both at the Department of the Environment (where Chris Patten replaced Nicholas Ridley) and at Central Office (where Kenneth Baker replaced Peter Brooke) it left some senior ministers feeling aggrieved. The replacement of Sir Geoffrey Howe by Mr John

Major at the Foreign Office was resented in certain sections of the party, although Sir Geoffrey was able to insist on the title of Deputy Prime Minister in addition to his role as Leader of the House of Commons. The resignation of the Chancellor of the Exchequer forced the Prime Minister to make other changes, bringing John Major back to the Treasury as Chancellor of the Exchequer and promoting Douglas Hurd to the Foreign Office.

In these circumstances of doubt and uncertainty there was increasing discussion about the Prime Minister's own future. Although no senior political figure would challenge her, a backbencher – Sir Anthony Meyer – was nominated in 1989 to contest the leadership and test opinion on the backbenches. The result was interpreted differently by the Prime Minister's supporters and opponents. But the fact that 60 members of the Conservative Party either cast their ballots for Sir Anthony or abstained suggested to many observers that there was a substantial wedge of opposition to the leadership.

The Prime Minister herself reacted in a somewhat confusing manner to the discontent and speculation. An early statement implying that she would retire after the next election was contradicted by a subsequent interview in which she stated that there was no definite date for retiring in her mind and that as long as she had party and electoral support she would contemplate continuing for another election after that.

The first challenge to Margaret Thatcher's leadership could be interpreted in a number of ways. For some it cleared the air and resolved an issue which would otherwise have continued to give rise to speculation. For others it threatened to be the first of a series of challenges. There was some speculation about the wisdom of allowing a challenge to be mounted on the basis of limited open support within the party and in 1990 the 1922 Committee made some minor changes to the rules for election to the leadership. One aspect of the events of late 1989 which did emerge was that the Prime Minister would prefer if posssible her successor as party leader to come not from her own generation of politicians such as Sir Geoffrey Howe but from a younger generation which included John Major and Chris Patten. Yet how far she would be able to dictate the dictate the party's choice of the next leader was increasingly an open question as the party slipped behind in the opinion polls.

Conservative Party Dissent

The government could take comfort from the fact that it had been through such troughs before and that it was still only the mid-term of the Parliament. But, whereas in previous Parliaments it had to face an official Opposition in disarray, by 1989 it was clear that it was the centre that had collapsed while Labour had revived. Disunity within the Conservative Party ranks would therefore be extremely damaging to the overall fortunes of the party. Apart from Europe and the general handling of the economy, one issue which seemed capable of causing such disunity was that of Hong Kong and in particular the extent to which guarantees should be given to any group of the colony's citizens of a right of abode in the United Kingdom. The government wanted to grant a limited right of abode (extending to perhaps 200,000 people) to reassure key elites and prevent them from emigrating. Populist Conservatives such as Norman Tebbit argued that the United Kingdom should not be asked to absorb further immigration of this sort.

Norman Tebbit's opposition to government policy on this issue was a sign of how far the government had moved towards the political centre despite its proclaimed radicalism. Tebbit had started out as one of Margaret Thatcher's most loyal lieutenants and was himself an archetype of the new style of conservatism. Yet by 1989 on many issues it was the Right which had been forced to concede ground. Despite the rhetoric of the Prime Minister and such pressure groups as the Bruges Group, the Thatcherite position on Europe looked increasingly isolated even within the government. The promotion of able left-of-centre ministers such as Chris Patten underlined the extent to which the Conservatives still needed the 'one nation' wing. And the Prime Minister's emphasis on community values and caring in speeches made at the very end of 1989 underlined her appreciation that the public mood was changing as the country entered the 1990s.

Thus, although the supremacy of the Conservative Party was an undoubted feature of the party politics of the 1980s, there was a degree of change in the party which underlined its determination to adapt to a perceived shift in the public mood. For it was not at all clear how solid were the foundations on which that supremacy was built. The Tory optimists might believe that their interpretation of victories built on the rock of realignment was justified. Sceptics could point to the victories being the product of a superior ability to take advantage of fluctuating party fortunes, the ability to manipulate the business cycle and disarray within the opposition ranks.

Whatever the cause of the Tory victories, however, the Conservatives' ability to win three general elections and to enact a large part of an ambitious and radical programme forced the other parties to respond.

Rebuilding the Labour Party

The period from the general election of 1979 until the acceptance of the loss of the 1987 general election was one of the darkest in Labour's history. Admittedly, the structure of the Labour Party and its coalitional nature had always made it more difficult to lead than the Conservative Party. But for almost a decade the splits within Labour's ranks had deepened and had been so visible as to make the party unelectable.

The most public split had occurred in 1981 when the Social Democratic Party had been formed by a group of senior Labour politicians disillusioned with Labour policy shifts on defence and Europe and hostile to the changes in party structure advocated by the Campaign for Labour Party Democracy – all of which were designed to give the party greater control over policy. These changes – in the method of leadership election, in the candidate selection process and in the way the manifesto was made – were also calculated to shift party policy towards the left.

The Labour Party usually moves to the left in opposition but the degree of the ideological shift in 1979 had made it virtually impossible for many on the right of the party – and especially the pro-Europeanists – to remain within the Labour fold. James Callaghan's replacement as leader – Michael Foot – was clearly not a long-term appointment. It was not until Neil Kinnock replaced Foot that the scene was set for a series of changes designed to make the party more responsive to the mood of the electorate.

Labour's Image

The changes which Kinnock backed were of three kinds. First, there was the need for Labour to change its image to accord with the more modern style of European socialism in the 1980s. A large part of this change was effected by Peter Mandelson, the Labour Communications Director. Mandelson had been trained in television and was sensitive to the importance of party presentation and of the interaction between television and press. In an election campaign it is essential to provide television with the material it needs and set the agenda for the morning newspapers. By knowing how the media operated the Labour Party could ensure that its campaign was covered as effectively as possible.

The detailed attention given to communications under Mandelson's direction was important because it represented a major change of party style and a first step back from the position of isolation and insulation which had so weakened the Labour Party in the early 1980s. The idea of using up-to-date communications methods was itself fairly radical since the Labour Party was traditionally suspicious of marketing men and reluctant to spend money on selling itself. But as Kinnock and Mandelson realised, Labour was already handicapped in competition with the Conservatives. Any government has formidable publicity resources available to it; but under Thatcher the government had deployed those resources with calculated shrewdness. Moreover the Conservative Party had been studying how best to adapt the modern campaign techniques familiar in America to the British context and their position was greatly helped both by superior access to money and by the anti-Labour bias of the press. Professional handling of publicity and a special concentration on television (where most electors received political information) were therefore essential to Labour.

Transforming Labour's image was controversial. Replacing the red flag by the red rose was a very explicit identification with the democratic socialist parties of Europe and a retreat from Labour fundamentalism. Glossy packaging by yuppies with filofaxes struck many activists as inappropriate to the party's traditions and it was obvious that the modernisation of this aspect of the party's action had a hidden agenda of providing the party with a set of policies which could be sold to the public.

The Policy Review

The second aspect of rebuilding the Labour Party was the comprehensive policy review announced after the 1987 election. It was designed to force Labour to rethink its policy positions in the light of developments under three Conservative administrations but also to convince the party of the need to scrap the most unpopular aspects of Labour policy. In particular Labour's commitment to unilateral nuclear disarmament needed to be reconsidered since it was clear that this policy issue had given the Conservatives a powerful campaign weapon. Equally, it was clear by 1987 that Labour's 1983 commitment to leave the European Community needed reconsideration especially in the light of the changing nature of the Community.

Seven policy reports were issued in May 1989 under the title *Meet the Challenge: Make the Change* and the Labour Party accepted these documents at its annual conference in 1989. The reports dealt with a range of topics in a way designed to modify Labour policies to take account of the changed climate brought about by Thatcherism. On economic policy, for example, the party moved away from the highly progressive tax rates of the pre-1979 period. Instead the party recommended a tax-banding system starting below 20 per cent and rising to a top rate of 50 per cent, which would mean lower tax rates for the very poorest and a slightly higher top rate than the Conservatives had introduced.

On the sensitive question of the status of the various items of trade-union legislation, the policy review suggested keeping the legislation, providing a framework for union democracy but modifying aspects of the legislation to broaden the scope of legal strikes and to protect union funds from sequestration. The party also dropped its commitment to the closed shop once it became clear that this was incompatible with the provisions of the European Social Charter (see Chapters 7 and 15).

On the vexed issue of defence, the report *Britain in the World* instead of proposing that Britain renounce nuclear weapons unilaterally, argued that Britain should join the superpowers in disarmament negotiations and promote policies calculated to reduce the dependence on nuclear weapons. This change had been prefigured in a personal and controversial about-turn on defence policy by the Labour leader and was supported by the TUC in September 1989.

Other aspects of the Labour review presented policies designed to appeal to consumer interests, minorities and women. Labour had placed a special emphasis on issues likely to appeal to women in its 1987 manifesto and had promised that a ministry for women would be established. (In part this coincided with increasing concern for feminism in socialist ranks; in part it was a reflection that women in Britain – as in the USA – found themselves at the hard edge of policies designed to reduce the role of the state.)

Black Sections

Minorities constituted something of a problem for Labour. On the one hand it was clear that the ethnic minority population was an important constituency to which Labour could appeal successfully. The national party had made a series of efforts to appeal to black voters from the late 1970s onwards, although many of these national initiatives were rather tardy responses to local and grass roots activity. Between 1979 and 1987 the number of black parliamentary candidates had risen from 5 to 27 and in 1987 four black Labour MPs were elected to Parliament. A black parliamentary caucus was established as was a black section councillors group. In 1989 one of the black Labour MPs, Paul Boateng, was given front bench status.

On the other hand there was a danger that too overt a solicitation of blacks would alienate white voters, especially the working-class electors whom Labour desperately needed to draw back into its fold. In addition there was the problem that black activists within Labour's ranks also wanted special provision – notably black sections analogous to women's sections. The battle over the demand for black sections (as well as a series of clashes over candidate selection, on one occasion involving the removal of an extreme ethnic candidate and the imposition by the NEC of a more moderate one) created tension in the Labour ranks over ethnic participation. Following the reference back of an amendment in favour of black sections at the conference in 1983 a working party was set up to study and defuse the issue. In 1985 a report was published recommending black sections but this proved unacceptable to the leadership and a series of defeats for the whole idea followed in 1986 and 1987. In July 1989 it seemed a compromise was possible with black members of the Labour Party being allowed to organise in a new affiliated society. Although this society was not a black section, an extra seat was to be created in the affiliated societies section (effectively at present a Cooperative Society seat) and only candidates from the society would be able to contest it. However, the annual conference considered two composite motions in 1989 – one a demand for black sections and the other the more moderate NEC proposal. Conference rejected both proposals thereby ensuring that the debate would rumble on despite the potentially embarrassing effects for Labour.

Constitutional Reform

The policy review also emphasised the need for constitutional reform, although the tone was very different from that adopted by Tony Benn and some previous manifestos. Thus the House of Lords would become an elected chamber designed to represent regional and local interests. This proposal was in stark contrast to earlier demands for its complete abolition. There was no commitment to a bill of rights or proportional representation, although the fact that the issue was gaining support within the party was underlined by a conference debate in 1989. Although conference rejected a proposal to set up a working party on electoral reform by 4,592,000 to 1,443,000, it is probable that another election defeat would bring a somewhat different result. On constitutional themes, the policy review called for a commitment to decentralisation and devolution – themes likely to have special resonance in Scotland.

Party Organisation

The third aspect of rebuilding the Labour Party involved the complex structure of the party itself. Kinnock was determined to change the party into a mass individual membership party based on the principle of one person one vote. Accordingly a membership drive was launched in January 1989 aimed at an ultimate target of one million but a short-term target of 600,000. A broader membership was considered not merely the key to ending damaging conflicts over the reselection of candidates by constituency parties but also an important component in transforming the image of the party. The decline of the Labour Party's individual membership had been dramatic and had allowed unrepresentative cliques to gain influence at constituency level. But, as the figures of individual membership revealed in September 1989 suggested, building a transformation of the Labour Party on an individual membership drive could be a slow process. Individual membership had fallen to 265,000 during 1988–9, a drop of 23,000. At the very least such figures suggested that the goal of 600,000 members by 1990 was unlikely to be reached. Although the membership drive had added some new members the recruits only made up the ground lost after the election of 1987 (*The Independent*, 12 September 1989).

Even without new individual members, the indirect power structure of the party as a whole – with the huge block votes for the unions – was now problematic. For the general public the intricate and arcane processes of Labour Party politics were unappealing. Government legislation had brought greater awareness of the internal decision processes of trade unions and had to some extent reformed them. It therefore seemed anomalous to leave the Labour Party itself in the grip of an undemocratic structure.

Trade unions were indeed the crucial element in any reform of party structure since they exercised 90 per cent of the conference votes. However, they also provided the overwhelming share of the cash which Labour needed to operate effectively. Kinnock wanted union members to join their local party as individuals in their own right rather than simply being affiliated by the union. As individual membership increased, it was hoped that the balance of power at conference would be altered, and the block vote reduced in influence.

Some advocates of reform wanted a much more swift alteration of the balance of power in the party. But in July 1989 the NEC voted to make firm proposals for change in principle to the 1990 conference but to postpone any change in practice until after the next general election. The annual conference accepted a resolution calling for wide consultation about the party's policy-making procedures including the block vote so that a report could be presented to the 1990 conference.

The unions' attitudes towards the revision of Labour policies and structures varied considerably. Ron Todd, the leader of the Transport and General Workers' Union (TGWU) – the largest union – had signalled opposition to many aspects of the revision process in the Tribune Lecture at the 1988 annual conference. On the other hand, many union leaders were aware both of the need for change in the trade-union movement and of the disadvantage of a further period out of power. Thus electoral considerations and industrial realities seemed to point towards a transformation of the relationship between the unions and the party. This even Ron Todd himself seemed to recognise as he accepted the defeat over unilateralism at the 1989 TUC conference with a pledge not to keep the issue simmering.

The clearest indication of Labour's renewed self-confidence and determination to mount an effective challenge to the Conservatives came however in the attitudes towards Mr Kinnock's leadership and the degree of support given to his strategy for party reform. The decisive defeat of Tony Benn's challenge to the leadership in 1988 effectively neutralised the Left and established Mr Kinnock's position in the party. Following the shadow cabinet elections of 1989, Kinnock was able to deploy a new team of front bench spokesmen who included a number of women and Paul Boateng as well as such fluent performers as Gordon Brown, John Smith and Bryan Gould.

The Fragmentation of the Centre

Part of the reason for the Conservatives' ascendancy over Labour in the 1980s had undoubtedly been the split in the Labour Party and the emergence of the Alliance between the Liberal Party and the Social Democratic Party (SDP). However, the strains inherent in the Alliance made the maintenance of a loose union of two parties untenable after 1987. In particular the 1987 election witnessed major organisational and campaigning difficulties for the Alliance with two parties and two leaders. David Steel's preemptive proposal for merger engendered a divisive debate inside both the Liberal Party and the SDP, although in the long run the process of merger was probably much more damaging for the SDP which found itself split between a pro-mergerite majority (representing 65.3 per cent of SDP members) and an anti-mergerite minority of 34.7 per cent. However, the minority opposed to merger contained the SDP's most visible spokesman – David Owen. He had resigned the leadership in August 1987 in order to be able to oppose the proposed merger.

Initially Owen thought that he could keep the SDP alive as a separate party even after the merger vote went against him and he relaunched the SDP in March 1988. But by May 1989 it was clear that the chances of the SDP having the resources to continue a fight on its own were remote and the national committee announced that there would be reduction in the party's activities. Although the party might continue to field some candidates at all levels of the political system, it had recognised that it no longer had the capacity to fight a national campaign.

The fratricide within the erstwhile partnership of the

Alliance had three main consequences. First and most important for the character of the British party system, it underlined the difficulty of changing the political style of British parties. Both the Liberals and the SDP had to some extent advocated a shift from the adversarial pattern of politics towards a more cooperative mode. Yet, as their critics were quick to point out, the arguments between two parties who had everything to gain from working together augured ill for a more radical shift towards a multi-party system.

Second, much of the enthusiasm which had greeted the formation of the SDP and the subsequent move towards an alliance with the Liberals was dissipated. Party membership, funding and electoral support all fell off after 1987. It is not clear whether the difficulties of the Alliance parties after 1987 will create new opportunities for an alternative party such as the Green Party or whether the two major parties will be the principal beneficiaries of the Alliance's collapse.

Third, the new merged party born from the ashes of the Liberal Party and a majority of the SDP lacked identity. The name Social and Liberal Democrats (SLD) caused some confusion and the poor performance of the SLD in the European elections prompted some members to seek a reopening of the debate about the name. In October 1989 the SLD decided, after a postal ballot, to use the short title of Liberal Democrats – a decision which kept the word Liberal firmly to the fore but somewhat diminished the social democratic component of the party.

The lack of identity of the new party, however, was much more deep-rooted than its name. It lacked a clear philosophical or ideological identity (see Chapter 2). 'Different Visions' offered an amalgam of philosophies but little with the capacity to inspire either activists or voters. It is true that some individuals such as David Marquand had set out a well-argued statement of political values and that the SLD itself had tried to emphasise citizenship and community as an alternative to the polar forces of the market and state socialism (Marquand, 1988). But much of it failed to get across to the general public. The searing merger debate had meant that many of the major figures associated with the Liberal Party and the SDP were no longer available to lead the new party. Paddy Ashdown, the new leader of the SLD, lacked political experience and exhibited a different style from that of David Steel. Although the 1989 conference saw some victories for the SLD leadership in terms of defence policy and the manner of party decision-making, there was a range of problems in the background. The Social Democratic faction of the party showed signs of feeling aggrieved about its input into the new party; and the issue of alliances with other parties remained a difficult one. Above all, the opinion poll ratings, as well as questions of funding and membership, confirmed the extent to which the feuding of the years 1987–9 had damaged the former parties of the Alliance.

In these circumstances it was hardly surprising if support for other parties grew. The advances made by the Greens were in areas where the old Alliance parties would have expected to do well prior to the merger debate – a factor which was important in the SLD leader's decision to attack the Green Party at the 1989 SLD conference. Yet as the Green Party's 1989 conference at Wolverhampton revealed, the party was itself organisationally unprepared for a major political role. Its ideology precluded the designation of a single leader, although Sara Parkin (one of the co-chairs of the party) emerged as a major national figure whose own views on the major policy issues were for a time given much prominence by the media (Parkin, 1989). Its policies were still in a process of revision, and on some, such as the commitment to a specific cut in population, it was forced to make a rather humiliating reversal of its stance. And it feared infiltration from other groups anxious to capitalise on the Green's advances at the polls.

Scotland and the National Question

In Scotland the Scottish National Party experienced a resurgence of support. The loss of the devolution referendum in 1979 had taken the edge off SNP support for a period but the experience of Conservative government encouraged a revival of nationalism, albeit in slightly different form than prior to 1979. There were two main reasons for the emergence of a distinctively Scottish reaction to government policies. The first was that, although the government had a United Kingdom majority, it was a minority party in Scotland. This was so in 1979 and became increasingly so as a result of the 1983 and 1987 general elections when the Conservatives were reduced to ten MPs out of seventy-one.

The second factor which proved conducive to Scottish nationalism was the ideological character of government policies. The free market thrust of Conservative economic policy, the centralising trend of welfare policy and the reduced autonomy accorded to local government all took on an added dimension of insensitivity in a Scottish context.

All the opposition parties in Scotland sought to capitalise on the unpopularity of the Conservative Party. Leading figures in the Alliance parties such as David Steel and Robert McLennan had Scottish constituencies and their emphasis on constitutional reform fitted well with Scottish demands for greater autonomy. But the real contest was between the Scottish Labour Party and the Scottish National Party.

Labour had become more sympathetic to the idea of devolution after 1979 but it had to be careful not to support any proposals which might deprive it of the seats needed for governing the United Kingdom as a whole. The SNP for its part had identified a theme which it felt might make the idea of Scottish independence less cataclysmic for voters – the idea of an independent Scotland within the European Community. However, some of the SNP policies which restricted land ownership to Scottish residents seemed difficult to reconcile with an increasingly international European Community.

In some ways the SNP had acquired a new generation of leaders and a new agenda. Apart from the leader – Gordon Wilson – there were several prominent figures, notably Jim Sillars, Margaret Ewing and Alex Salmond. The party programme emphasised investment and planning and an industrial strategy calculated to restore the infrastructure of Scotland.

The salience of the question of a separate Scottish Parliament was underlined when a Scottish Constitutional Convention representing all political parties in Scotland except the SNP and the Conservatives met in March 1989 to draw up a

Claim of Right demanding a Scottish Assembly. (The SNP had taken part in a planning meeting in January but had withdrawn as the result of its perception of under-representation at the Convention but also because the Convention had excluded the possibility of complete independence (Kellas, 1989).) The broadly based nature of the co-alition supporting devolution emphasised that this was likely to be an issue that would not go away, although the mechanics of this constitutional arrangement remained unclear. As with so much else the political wheel had come full circle from the debates of 1979. Nationalism in Scotland, temporarily thrown into confusion by the 1978 referendum result, has revived with a broader base and has now transformed public opinion in Scotland as well as the agenda of the Labour Party there.

Pressure Group Politics

The domination of the Conservative Party at the national level over the period 1979–89 might have suggested that the interest groups in British society were in some sense becoming more cohesive or even that there was some mobilisation of interests behind the Conservative cause. In fact British society was becoming in many ways much more pluralist and the political system should have been responsive to a wider variety of interests than ever before. Indeed in addition to the growth in numbers of pressure groups over the period of Conservative government, there was a striking rise in the political profile of many of them, especially groups concerned with environmental protection (see Chapter 10) but also hitherto non-contentious groups such as the RSPCA. Equally important was the development of new forms of political action by sections of society which had so far been relatively unorganised. One manifestation of this development was the extensive disturbances which occurred in areas of Islamic population over the publication of Salman Rushdie's *Satanic Verses*. Not merely did this episode underline how the changing character of the British population might suddenly and unexpectedly respond to a salient issue. It also revealed how difficult it was even for the Labour Party to respond to the sorts of concerns which Britain's increasingly self-confident ethnic minorities were expressing. The Rushdie affair was thus a symptom of significant cultural change in British society, change which was bound to have implications for the style of British politics.

However, the manner in which the Conservative governments of Mrs Thatcher responded to these changing demands was limited. The ideological influences of neo-liberalism made the Conservative Party in the 1980s suspicious of efforts to institutionalise the representation of group interests. They wanted to move away from the corporatist values and practices of previous Labour and Conservative governments. The apologists of the free market regarded the close relations cultivated with major industrial interests in the previous decade as detrimental not merely to sound policy-making but also to the state itself. The special treatment accorded trade-union and industrial spokesmen in Whitehall was withdrawn and there was a general distancing of government from both the TUC and the CBI. This distancing was not merely the result of a refusal to become involved in the detailed construction of prices and incomes policies; it also reflected a general unwillingness to allow trade-union representatives in particular the kind of extended advisory role which the movement had gradually acquired over the twentieth century.

The evidence of this distancing could be seen most clearly in the abolition of sponsoring by departments and in the downgrading of the National Economic Development Council (NEDC) which lost many of its sectoral committees as well as a significant number of staff. The NEDC had been one of the most important institutional products of the country's movement towards a hands-on approach to running the economy. The deliberate side-lining of its activities at a time when many thought the new challenges of European integration required more industrial intervention was a symbolic statement of government values (Grant, 1989).

Trade unions and industrial representatives thus became more like other pressure groups over the period 1979–89.

Without privileged access they had to turn to other strategies and to make their case in arenas beyond Whitehall. Parliament became marginally more important for pressure group activity both in the sense of becoming a place to make a case heard and as a possible way of influencing policy. The evolution of new structures – in the form of the select committees – offered opportunities to place arguments on the record and to join the policy debate, a development underlined by the extent to which they became a magnet for outside groups and a focus for consultancy firms (Rush, 1990; Grantham, 1989). Select committees were also able to respond quickly to new causes of public concern. Thus the heightened debate about green issues saw the Environment Committee taking increased evidence from ecological pressure groups (Drewry, 1989).

Publicity campaigns – once the symptom of a lost cause – became extremely important instruments for pressure groups, although the government took powers to stop some campaigns directed against its policies from being publicly funded. Thus as a result of the highly professional campaign by the Greater London Council (GLC) against its abolition, the government introduced restrictions on running campaigns of this kind from public funds. Critics noted that there was an obvious imbalance in restricting local government's ability to make its voice heard at the same time that the government's use of information was becoming more sophisticated.

The growing importance of Europe in the whole policy process added another dimension to pressure group activity. Pressure groups found that they had to fight some parts of their battles on a wider European stage. While this was unfamiliar and costly at first, it offered an alternative outlet if access to Whitehall seemed unsatisfactory. Thus the National Farmers' Union (NFU) found itself by-passing the Ministry of Agriculture, Fisheries, and Food (MAFF), with whom it had had in the past a very close relationship, in order to join forces with French and German governments who might prove more reliable supporters of farmers than the British government. And individual regions such as Strathclyde found that they too could by-pass Whitehall to seek funds from Europe.

Parliament

The workings of Parliament were affected by the succession of Conservative governments between 1979 and 1989 in a number of ways.

First, the radical agenda of Thatcherism kept the legislative machine not merely busy but, some critics would argue, overloaded.

Second, the size of the Conservative majority in 1983 and 1987 often made debate on the floor of the House of Commons appear redundant. The personal style of the Prime Minister tended to reinforce the impression. As Dunleavy *et al.* (1990) have shown, the Prime Minister was very reluctant to appear more than necessary in the Commons. And when she did appear – for example in parliamentary question time – the well-briefed style led to a rather wooden rehearsal of statistics rather than the cut-and-thrust of interchange.

The internal battles of the Labour Party and its lacklustre leadership made the normal adversarial battle in the House of Commons decidedly uneven for much of the decade. Not until well into the 1987 Parliament did Labour's performance in the House of Commons begin to offer a real challenge to the Conservative government. Many Labour MPs during the period of demoralisation stayed away from parliamentary debates and indeed did not bother to vote in divisions.

The advent of the television cameras to the Commons in 1989 (following a successful experiment with televising the House of Lords) seemed likely to change frontbench attitudes significantly since the cut-and-thrust of debate would be transmitted directly into voters' homes. Each debate could thus be seen as part of the run-up to the next election in the sense that the overall impression given by party leaders would contribute directly to the party's standing in the polls. For backbenchers the television cameras had the effect of providing free publicity, though whether this will give incumbents an advantage over challengers, as in the United States, remains to be seen. For the frontbenches, however, it seems likely to put a greater premium on performance in debates and perhaps an additional strain on already heavily stressed politicians.

The House of Commons was an uncertain mirror of political realities in the country in one way for much of the 1980s. For although public opinion was consistently recording a high vote for the Alliance parties for much of this time, the barrier of the electoral system prevented the Liberals and the SDP from making their voice heard at anywhere near the strength they commanded electorally. Indeed the additional injustice done to the Green vote in the European elections of 1989 prompted one sitting SLD MP – Simon Hughes – to threaten to call himself a Liberal and Green MP. However, the SLD leadership was convinced that the Greens were competing with it for the same issue-oriented vote and ideas of pacts and negotiations were explicitly ruled out after Paddy Ashdown's 1989 conference speech.

On another level the House of Commons seemed unrepresentative of the political life of the country. Although the 1987 election saw four blacks returned to Parliament, it remained overwhelmingly a white, middle-aged and male assembly. All parties had in theory expressed concern for women's issues but the extent to which the parties could do very much to make sure that women's voices were heard in Parliament was limited.

The class composition of Parliament had long failed to reflect the population of the country as a whole, since Labour's parliamentary intake had ·become increasingly middle class and professional at the expense of its working-class component. And, although there were some slight shifts in the makeup of the House of Commons over the 1980s, this continued to be the case.

However, there had been subtle changes in the behaviour of the House. The select committee system had grown and established itself as an integral part of the life of the House of Commons rather than a peripheral distraction from the floor of the Chamber. The Committees themselves developed increased self-confidence and provided an opportunity to explore many of the key issues of the 1980s. Yet the operation of the committees was not entirely trouble-free. The delay in establishing the committees at the beginning of each Parliament caused an impairment in the scrutiny process in the eyes of some experts, as did the turnover of members (Drewry,

1989). Certainly, the problems associated with the Scottish Committee which could not be established because there were not enough Conservative MPs from Scotland to give the government a majority was a major embarrassment. And there were renewed efforts to find a way for the House of Commons to effect some meaningful scrutiny of European legislation.

Individual MPs had become more vocal and willing to dissent from the party line even if episodes such as the loss of the Shops Bill of 1986 (where the government was defeated in a second reading debate) are comparatively rare.

There was also a marked change in the way in which individual MPs behaved in relation to the wider political arena of policy-making. This was shown by the increased attention paid by public relations firms and political consultancies to individual MPs and to the parliamentary processes generally. In part this change was a reflection of the new and more pluralistic world of policy entrepreneurs which had introduced new actors into the political game. In addition to the established party hierarchies, think-tanks such as the Centre for Policy Studies, the Institute of Economic Affairs and the Adam Smith Institute had become important sources of new ideas. This change also reflected the distance put between Whitehall and many organisations previously consulted regularly by civil servants and ministers. As easy access to government seemed to be a thing of the past, organisations turned to Parliament for advice. A third factor was the fact that institutional developments such as the growth of supra-national influence (principally in the European Community) and new policy developments (for example in relation to privatisation) seemed to require expert guidance.

One reflection of the increased number of consultants and of lobbying activity was a rise in the number of letters to MPs and questions to ministers. Another was the expression of concern that the facilities of Parliament might be exploited by professional groups seeking to trade access to MPs for gain. Certainly there has emerged a new form of political career, as former MPs, civil servants and employees of political parties can either establish themselves with preexisting consultancy firms or organise their own (Grantham, 1989). The links between MPs and these consultancies may or may not be a threat to the integrity of democracy. But they do suggest a belief – to put it no higher than that – that Parliament and its members can again exercise some influence and that there is a policy space which those who are ahead of the game can fill.

House of Lords

Although discussions of Parliament tend to focus on the House of Commons it should be noted that there were over the period of the Thatcher government some interesting developments in the House of Lords. Most important perhaps was the willingness of the Lords to challenge the government on issues where it either thought it had special expertise or where constitutional questions were at issue. The Lords forced a series of amendments to the Education Act of 1988 following pressure from vice-chancellors and others in the Chamber, and also expressed serious reservations about the proposals to reform the legal profession.

Over the decade the House of Lords had in many ways reflected a different mix of political opinion in the country. A number of peers took the SDP whip when that party was formed. The cross-benches reflected independent non-partisan opinion. And even among peers taking the Conservative whip the government's ability to command a majority was limited not only by the natural independence of members of the upper house but also by a generational difference. Tory peers – unlike their counterparts in the Commons – were more likely to reflect in attitudes and style the 'one nation' tradition of Conservatism rather than the free market liberalism associated with Thatcherism.

Thus the House of Lords over the 1980s exercised a serious role as a check on the Conservative majority in the Commons, as well as performing more detailed but essential functions such as the scrutiny of European legislation.

Conclusion

The period of the 1980s was undoubtedly one of change at a number of levels in the British political system. There was greater pluralism and continuing electoral volatility as well as a degree of cultural change in relation to attitudes towards the state and the environment. But much of this change was masked by the apparent continuity and stability of the series of Conservative governments.

However, two important aspects of the system made the Conservatives position insecure. First, the British polity had clearly lost some of its insularity and become part of a wider political environment. European political decisions and influences could thus penetrate the system to create new configurations which cut across established party loyalties. Even the smallest and newest of parties such as the Greens might not be isolated in a European context, while large parties such as the Conservatives might find themselves without allies on the larger European stage. And indeed many of the changes in the pattern of British politics were ones which had their counterparts elsewhere in Europe, as a number of observers noted (Mair, 1989).

Second, the very success of the Conservative Party seemed to call forth a corrective as opposition parties and especially Labour adapted and responded both to the new agenda of politics and to many of the political strategies adopted by the Conservatives. Thus at the end of the 1980s Conservatives still had many important advantages in the battle for political power. But they could not be certain of permanent superiority. And it remained an open question whether the Conservatives could show sufficient flexibility to adapt more quickly than their competitors to challenges of the 1990s.

5

Government at the Centre

PATRICK DUNLEAVY

The 1980s have been widely perceived as a decade of increasing centralisation of political and administrative power away from sub-national governments and into Whitehall. And within central government itself, Margaret Thatcher's dominance as an electoral and ideological leader has apparently extended throughout the policy process. For some observers:

> She has towered over all her contemporaries, inside her party as well as outside ... It is her unwavering purpose that has kept her governments on their fixed course through the troughs as well as the crests of party and personal popularity ... She has impressed herself upon government as nobody has done since the war years of Churchill. (Finer, 1988, p. 140)

Such perceptions are systematically fostered by the Prime Minister's press office and the Conservative Party. But they also provide the opposition parties with a convenient stick to beat the government with. And for the mass media a highly personalised account of government allows them to present complex policy processes in accessible fashion to a mass public.

In practice, British government at a national level is a large and elaborate machine. First, ministers and central departments in Whitehall still supervise a large central state.

Second, at the heart of this machinery stands the Prime Minister, Cabinet, and key coordinating institutions. Third, the civil service provides bureaucratic support for about half the central state. This chapter reviews these three key elements before examining the role of the intelligence services and showing how crises have influenced policy-making.

Central Government and the Central State

For some academics the idea of a central 'state' in the United Kingdom is still controversial because of the legal separation between Crown agencies and other public sector bodies. Traditionally associated with the Left, the 'state' concept has also played a key role in New Right discourse, as in Thatcher's pledge to 'roll back the State'. Its analytic value is to draw attention not just to formally designated public institutions, but to the wide range of organisations and mechanisms which achieve the same governmental purposes.

Central government in Britain has conventionally been defined in terms of Whitehall ministries and their outstations, staffed by civil servants, and acting directly on behalf of the Crown. But other large agencies respond directly, without any intermediating board or controlling committee of their own, to the imperatives laid down by ministers and other policy influentials in the core executive – notably the three armed forces, the civil service and police force of Northern Ireland, and the Metropolitan Police. The concept of the central state refers to all these organisations as well as to the civil service proper. Table 5.1 shows what a large difference this focus makes when compared with earlier definitions. The central state is over twice as large as 'mainstream' Whitehall ministries in terms of personnel, and includes 84 per cent more running costs. It is also 72 per cent larger than the whole civil service in terms of manpower, and includes 56 per cent more running costs.

The central state plays little direct part in implementing some key public policies. The delivery of collective consumption services (housing, education, social services, transport, health care and urban development) are all allocated to local

TABLE 5.1   *The size of central government and the central state, 1987–8*

	Mainstream Whitehall ministries only	Central government (all civil service)	Whole central state
Number of agencies	18	60	76
Personnel numbers	402,600	590,400	1,016,830
Running costs (£ million)	10,320	12,160	19,000

Source: Dunleavy (1989c, p. 265).

authorities, health agencies and other bodies (see Chapter 6). Most direct employment of staffs in economic functions (such as transport) is undertaken by the dwindling public corporations and various quasi-governmental agencies. (Northern Ireland is the exception to this pattern. Because of Stormont's abolition in 1972, Westminster ministers still directly head agencies delivering consumption services and carrying out economic functions in the Province.)

Defence predominates in the central state's personnel and running costs, accounting for half of these totals (Table 5.2). Three other functional areas are important. 'Law, order and protective services' covers the London and Ulster police, the prisons, and legal and court services. The administration of the social security system absorbs large amounts of staff in two UK departments, and another in Northern Ireland. And about one in ten central state staff work in organisations delivering services or performing functions for national level government as a whole, most collecting taxes.

Another way of analysing the central state is to look at the radically different types of organisation which exist (Dunleavy, 1989c). Four types account for the bulk of central state manpower and running costs:

(1) *Delivery agencies* use virtually all the money voted to them by Parliament on employing large staffs and meeting running costs. Examples include the armed forces, the Metropolitan Police, the Royal Ulster Constabulary and the prison service.

(2) *Taxing agencies* also employ many personnel and spend almost all their budget on running costs. But the Inland

TABLE 5.2   *Distribution of central state personnel and running costs across policy areas,*
1987–8

	Running costs (£ million)	Staffing numbers	% of all staffing
Defence/overseas	9,150	511,760	50
Law and order	2,995	141,350	14
Social security	2,060	119,510	12
Central government org.	1,700	105,420	10
Employment, trade etc.	1,530	52,860	5
Collective consumption	705	32,425	3
Agriculture	375	21,700	2
Land, built environment	295	20,290	2
Mixed (Scotland/Wales)	160	9,480	1
Totals	19,000	1,016,830	99%

Source: Dunleavy (1989d, pp. 412–13).

Revenue and Customs and Excise of course raise much larger sums in revenues.

(3) *Transfer agencies* by contrast channel most of their budgets into transfer payments to private sector individuals or firms. In 1987–8 the Department of Social Security spent only 4 per cent of its £47,500 million budget on running its administration. Benefits paid to pensioners, the sick, the disabled and the unemployed absorbed 94 per cent of budget. Similarly the Intervention Board for Agricultural Produce spent all but 3 per cent of its £1,650 million expenditures to farmers supporting the prices of agricultural produce under European Community policy.

(4) *Contracts agencies* design and commission projects or services which are then implemented by private sector firms. The largest is the Procurement Executive in the Ministry of Defence which in 1987–8 spent £8,660 million on weapons systems for the armed forces, 90 per cent of which went outside the agency to large defence corporations.

There are two much smaller types of organisation which extend central state influence over other parts of society, rather than carrying out functions directly:

(1) *Control agencies* route money to other parts of the public sector, using legislation and financial controls to ensure that central government priorities are observed. For example, the

Department of Education and Science directly spends only 1.7 per cent of central government spending on education, passing on 98 per cent of its nominal budget to universities, polytechnics, local governments and now opted-out schools.

(2) *Regulatory agencies* rely on inspections and legal rules to make private sector actors comply with government policies. Some regulatory agencies (such as the transport licensing office) are medium sized, others are tiny (such as those regulating privatised public utilities).

Finally there are some other central state organisations which spend most of their budgets on their own operations. Trading agencies engage in basically commercial activities (like the Forestry Commission). Servicing agencies provide facilities to the central state as a whole (such as the Central Office of Information).

TABLE 5.3 *The distribution of personnel and running costs across agency types in the central state*

	Running costs (£ million)	Personnel numbers	Per cent of staffing
Delivery agencies	12,070	655,720	65%
Transfer/contract agencies	3,200	172,520	17
Miscellaneous agencies	1,460	59,140	6
Taxing agencies	1,290	84,050	8
Control agencies	990	45,420	4
Totals	19,010	1,016,850	100%

Note: Miscellaneous agencies here includes regulatory agencies, trading agencies, and servicing agencies.
Source: Dunleavy (1989d, p. 409).

Delivery agencies account for just under two-thirds of central state personnel and running costs (Table 5.3). Transfer agencies (especially social security) and contract agencies which route most of their funds to the private sector account for over a sixth of staffing and running costs. Taxing agencies and the miscellaneous group each account for a further twelfth of central state running costs. Although control agencies supervise large welfare state budgets being spent by sub-central governments, they absorb less than a twentieth of central state staff.

The way that the central state operates is heavily conditioned by the predominance of a few policy sectors and types of agency. The top six agencies controlling staff in 1988 were:

MOD and armed forces	503,500
Department of Social Security (plus some Employment staff)	114,250
Treasury and sub-departments	104,340
Home Office, prisons, Met police	79,550
Northern Ireland Office, NI civil service, and RUC	38,910
Department of Employment	31,850

Thus six ministers in 1988 controlled 86 per cent of all central state personnel. In a normal Cabinet of 23, this leaves the remaining 14 departmental ministers each controlling an average of 1 per cent of central state manpower and associated running costs. Almost half of all central state manpower falls within the Ministry of Defence, whose sheer size, self-contained character, and strong position *vis-a-vis* even the Treasury make it seem at times almost an independent fiefdom (Johnson, 1980; Edmunds, 1985). However, as I note below (p. 113), the current 'Next Steps' reforms of the civil service will have a major impact on all those departments controlling large staffs.

Outside these heavily staffed areas, most Whitehall departments exert influence by influencing funding or altering the legislation, circulars and regulations applying to sub-central agencies or private sector actors. Because these ministries depend on other organisations to implement their decisions they cannot quickly or unilaterally reorientate public policy. And this constraint also restricts the decision-making capabilities of the Prime Minister and Cabinet.

The Core Executive: PM and Cabinet

At the heart of British central government, the topmost 'commanding heights' of the state apparatus, there lies a complex of institutions and actors which can be labelled 'the core executive' (Dunleavy and Rhodes, 1990). Included under

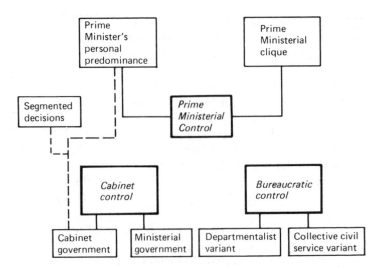

FIGURE 5.1   *Models of the PM, Cabinet and core executive*

this term are the Prime Minister, the Cabinet, Cabinet committees, the coordinating departments (number 10 Downing Street, the Treasury, Cabinet Office, the law officers, and the intelligence services), and an extensive network of interdepartmental committees. There are three fundamental ways of interpreting how this system is controlled: by the chief executive acting in a quasi-presidential fashion; by ministers as a group; or by central bureaucrats (Figure 5.1). In turn each basic position has been elaborated during Thatcher's premiership into a couple of variants, for each of which some relevant evidence can be cited in recent experience.

PM's Personal Predominance

Images of British government as dominated by Thatcher were the stock in coin of media observers in the 1980s, as the quote from Finer above illustrates (page 96). Thatcher's long unbroken period in office marked by two successful re-elections to power gave her a very strong position inside her party, a distinctive (if divisive) public persona, and an international reputation as a strong leader. Exponents of the thesis that prime-ministerial 'power' dwarfs that of the Cabinet have seen the last decade as grist to their mill. In their view Thatcher only somewhat exaggerates the normal operations of the core executive – in which the premier exercises a predominant role by virtue of her or his control over the composition, agenda, and committee structure of Cabinet. However, this argument remains vulnerable to the criticism that no single individual can hope to control the whole flow of issues through the core executive, because the PM's time and attention span will inevitably be limited. Even an exceptional personality such as Thatcher cannot push these limits very far when foreign affairs and visits absorb up to half her timetable.

Prime Ministerial Clique View

An alternative, more organisational version of this basic position stresses that Thatcher's success partly reflects her success in mobilising exceptional resources to back up her strong ideological convictions. Thatcher's ideological dominance inside the Conservative Party and across Whitehall is not a single-handed creation, but rather reflects the ability of a team around the PM to develop and project a standard policy line across diverse issues. It is this prime ministerial back-up which has so effectively converted her cabinet ministers into agents of a central purpose.

In the early 1980s expectations that Thatcher would develop a fully fledged Prime Minister's Department (Weller, 1983; Jones, 1983) were fuelled by a number of factors – her extensive use of senior advisers on economic affairs and foreign policy; her strong reliance on the Political Office at Number 10; the development of the PM's Efficiency Unit as a powerhouse of ideas for reforming the government machine; the centralisation of all Whitehall press and information services under the overall control of her powerful Press Secretary, Bernard Ingham; and the important role played by a shifting set of consultants, policy analysts, and New Right thinkers in generating detailed ideas to back up her gut feelings on policy issues. In addition a wide range of speech writers, advertising people, and 'spin-merchants' have ensured that Thatcher's personal appearances are always carefully rehearsed and scripted. The 1983 abolition of the Central Policy Review Staff, a 'think tank' nominally responsible to the whole Cabinet, and the apparently reduced 'secretarial' role of the Cabinet Office during Robert Armstrong's period as Cabinet Secretary in the 1980s (Seldon, 1990; Lee, 1990), all added to the view that influence had decisively shifted to the PM's advisers. However, Thatcher has been reluctant to create any formal new machinery of government (Fry, 1988, pp. 96–9), so that the concept of a 'Prime Ministerial clique' must suffice to describe this extensive set of different support mechanisms for the premier.

The role of the PM's advisers has always been controversial. But matters reached a head during 1988–9 when a strong disagreement developed between Thatcher and her Chancellor of the Exchequer, Nigel Lawson. Lawson believed that the fluctuations in sterling's value on the foreign exchanges should be managed so as to prepare for the UK's full entry into the Exchange Rate Mechanism of the European Monetary System (EMS) (see page 177). Thatcher disagreed, believing that governments should not try to second-guess movements in currency markets. To buttress her position she brought back as her personal economic adviser a strong monetarist supporter of this view, Professor Alan Walters. A chronic difference of view between the Treasury and 10 Downing Street opened up, fuelled by repeated incidents in which Thatcher first criticised her Chancellor's policies in public, then reaffirmed her support for him, at the same time as off-the-record Downing Street press briefings indicated that she wanted to change her Chancellor. In October 1989 the Conservative Party gathered at Blackpool for a conference whose theme was 'The Right Team', and whose centrepiece was a speech by Lawson warmly applauded by Thatcher. However, within a few days the underlying dispute about economic policy was brought to a head with the publication of an article by Walters which had in fact been written much earlier, in which he criticised the EMS as 'half-baked'. Lawson seized on this and demanded that Thatcher sack Walters or he would resign. Thatcher refused to bow to Lawson's ultimatum and the Chancellor left office immediately; within a few hours, Walters too resigned.

Lawson's dramatic resignation, and his complaints of being constantly hampered in his ministerial duties by contrary policies suggested to the PM by her advisers, projected the 'presidentialism' of Thatcher's style into the forefront of party political debate. They seemed to confirm the seriousness of previous incidents of a similar sort, such as the influence of the PM's foreign affairs adviser Charles Powell in undermining the position of Geoffrey Howe, shifted from the Foreign Office against his will in July 1989 to the nominal position of Deputy Prime Minister. Thatcher publicly reaffirmed the old doctrine that 'Advisers advise and ministers decide'. But her reaction to the Lawson resignation and the controversy over Howe, in particular her refusal to sack Walters, contradicted this stance. During the autumn of 1989 the political furore generated by these events was maintained by the backbench challenge to Thatcher's leadership, and her own conflicting signals about her willingness to stand down after the 1991–2 general election (see Chapter 4).

Cabinet Government

There are still numerous defenders of the normative ideal of collegial decision-making by the whole Cabinet, including most of the disaffected ministers who have resigned or been pushed out of Thatcher's Cabinets. But very few academic or mass media commentators believe that this ideal has worked in practice since Thatcher's 1981 decision (advised by Walters among others) to force through a severely deflationary budget opposed by a majority of her ministers, and subsequently to sack or reshuffle the key dissenting voices. Vindicated by the Falklands victory, Thatcher's style of leadership has seldom subsequently wavered. Her Cabinets have become more homogeneous, composed almost equally of pragmatists and convinced New Right politicians, but devoid of the prominent 'wets' and dissenters of the 1979–82 period. Subsequent disagreements between the PM and individual senior colleagues, such as the 1985–6 Westland Affair or the 1988–9 conflicts with Lawson over economic strategy, were marked by a complete absence of coordinated opposition by ministerial dissenters. The most that Cabinet government exponents have claimed is that the Cabinet and its committees remain an important court of appeal and a key mechanism for coordinating party policy and the legislative timetable.

Ministerial Government

Even under Thatcher, Whitehall has remained a federation of departments, each of which jealously guards its own political and administrative autonomy. Both in law and in terms of their individual political futures, ministers know that they can be held responsible for mistakes, less perhaps by the Commons than by the mass media and their party's membership. At the official level, departments have their own strongly developed policy interests, networks of 'client' interest groups, systems of inter-organisational relations, and standard operating procedures which they want their ministers to safeguard. Although the Thatcher government has made a virtue of attacking 'vested interests', in practice there has been a considerable area of agreement between senior officials and Tory ministers in most departments about the purposes and methods by which this shake-up is to be achieved. For example, both have shared a common interest in extending the scope of Whitehall control over subordinate public sector bodies such as local governments, NHS authorities, universities, and other quasi-governmental agencies. The concentration of central state personnel in a few large delivery, transfer and taxing agencies, and the importance of control agencies across most social policy areas, have tended to maintain each department's and Cabinet minister's autonomy of action.

Seen in this light, the dynamic of the 1980s has been set by Thatcher's unusually wide-ranging efforts to impose a standard policy line upon departments, and also to develop her own independent sources of advice to criticise and counteract the briefs submitted by ministers and departments. The ministerial government thesis argues not that collegial Cabinet decision-making has survived, but that individual ministers have for the most part been able to defend their own scope of action — which is what really matters to them:

The form and structure of a modern Cabinet and the diet it consumes almost oblige it to function like a group of individuals, and not as a unity. Indeed, for each minister, the test of his [*sic*] success in office lies in his ability to deliver his departmental goals . . . No minister I know of has won political distinction by his performance in Cabinet or by his contribution to collective decision-making. To the country and the House of Commons he is simply the minister for such-and-such a department and the only member of Cabinet who is not seen in this way is the Prime Minister. (Wass, 1984, p. 24)

In the late 1980s, two developments seem to have strengthened ministers' resistance to losing control of issues to Downing Street. First, in 1986–8 at least electoral politics seemed to have shifted towards a 'dominant party system' (see pages 4–5). With strong opinion poll leads at this time the Conservatives felt assured of government power. By loosening the discipline of party competition which previously kept Tory MPs tied to rigid support of the government for fear of losing power, this change strengthened tendencies for sectional lobbies inside the Conservative Parliamentary party to become more important influences on policy-making, constituting a new and very active departmental 'clientele' to whom ministers must be attentive. In this period some observers argued that a concern to keep issues away from Downing Street's interventions may also have prompted ministers to settle inter-departmental disputes more frequently by correspondence or bilateral meetings, thereby keeping issues out of the Cabinet committee system altogether.

When the Tory poll lead disappeared in 1989, the proximate causes were seen as Thatcher's style of government and promotion of divisive issues (such as poll tax and NHS reforms) – both of which convinced Conservative ministers and backbenchers concerned with different policy areas to carry on steering an independent course. The 1989 ministerial reshuffles illustrate how important individual ministers can be in overturning previous policy lines. The new Environment Secretary (Patten) scrapped decisions by his New Right predecessor (Ridley) to break the Green Belt and privatise nature reserves. And the new Energy Secretary (Wakeham) withdrew all nuclear power stations from the electricity

privatisation, contradicting strong statements by his predecessor (Parkinson) that this would never happen.

Second, the transition towards a single European market
has dramatically increased the dealings which all Whitehall
departments have with the European Community. The volume
and increasingly detailed character of this business means
that central departments such as the Foreign Office and the
Cabinet Office's European section have to work harder at
monitoring let alone determining policy (Wallace, 1990; and
see below, Chapter 7). One result has been a tendency for
each minister to develop her or his own 'foreign policy' with
EC counterparts. In addition, there are strong trends elsewhere for international forums to become critical loci of
policy-making on a host of issues such as airport security,
fishing and sea-dumping practices, the control of environmental
pollution, regulation of nuclear energy, and food, medicine,
and health and safety issues (see Chapter 10). All these trends
for the international standardisation of policy-making tend to
reinforce the boundary walls which protect one policy sector
from interference by core executive actors, whether the PM or
her or his staffs, or Cabinet as a whole.

Segmented Decisions

Claims of prime-ministerial hegemony and a stress on pressures for ministerial or departmental autonomy need not
conflict, according to this view. British PMs' influence seems
to be concentrated on strategic economic decisions (shared
with the Chancellor), foreign affairs (shared with the Foreign
Secretary), and very major defence decisions (shared with the
Ministry of Defence). At the end of the 1970s it was fashion-
able to conclude that: 'Where the Prime Minister is most
involved, Britain is now *inevitably* weak: this is true of the
management of the economy as well as foreign affairs' (Rose,
1980, p. 49: my emphasis). Thatcher's style of leadership and
effort to recreate an image of strong government has qualified
perceptions of inherent weakness. Yet the difficulties caused
for the PM by the 1989 ditching of Howe as Foreign Secretary
and Lawson's resignation, after both ministers had urged
Thatcher to be more positive towards European unification,

demonstrate that prime-ministerial dominance of these issue areas is by no means complete. And on the broader world stage whether there has been any substantive improvement in Britain's position as an economic force or a diplomatic and military influence remains contentious (see Chapters 8 and 11).

In the late 1980s, however, it was the other side of the segmented decision view which has looked the least sustainable – the claim that prime ministers can have little influence over the full range of domestic policies falling outside their three main areas of influence. Callaghan's attempts to influence several domestic policy areas (such as council house sales, education standards, reform of the professions, and broadcasting) had little impact in the late 1970s (Donoghue, 1987, p. 124). Yet in all these and many other areas Thatcher has been remarkably active and influential by the standards of previous premiers. The primary focus of government policy shifted across her three terms in office – beginning with trade-union 'reform' and economic monetarism in 1979–83; through a drive for public enterprise privatisations and a crusade against Labour local governments in 1983–7; into a phase of management reorganisations of welfare state institutions in 1987–91. Thus the 'key issues' netted and processed by the Downing Street machine, and subjected to the PM's forceful interventions, have covered a remarkably wide sweep of policy.

There is evidence that on some kinds of issues Thatcher's influence has not been sustained. For example, on one high-technology policy area it was confined to two aspects where lay politicians can most easily exert influence – how programmes are financed, and which personnel are appointed to run them (Keliher, 1990). But elsewhere Thatcher's approach has considerable strengths. She focuses on details of policy in order to assess the whole proposal; keeps a tight (almost obsessive) rein on public spending commitments, setting a deliberately high threshold for new programmes to surmount (unless departments can offer up savings on other programmes); and she always insists that programme management is run on strong, corporate management lines, preferably by a person who is reliably 'one of us'.

Bureaucratic Control Models

This view has been less influential in the 1980s, because of the apparently strong core executive control over the rest of the state apparatus and Whitehall under Thatcher. One variant of bureaucratic influence arguments stresses the importance of departmentalism, so that policy control still lies preponderently with top officials in each ministry. A second version ascribes influence to a centralised inner core of the higher civil service, dominating the central departments such as the Treasury and the Cabinet Office (Kellner and Crowther Hunt, 1980; Ponting, 1986). Traditionally supported by left-wing critics blaming the civil service for deradicalising previous Labour governments (Sedgemore, 1980), both arguments about bureaucratic control or obstruction have also attracted New Right adherents dissatisfied by the pace of policy 'reforms' in the 1980s. But while left critics have been suspicious of enhancing prime-ministerial or core executive power, New Right critics favour building up a strong PM's office as a counterweight to civil service influence and departmentalism (Hoskyns, 1983).

The Civil Service

When the Conservatives took power in 1979 they broke radically with the previous tradition of bipartisan support for the civil service. Thatcher went on a tour of Whitehall ministries, dressing-down senior civil servants for alleged failings in their departments' policies. New Right ministers made clear in public that they regarded the civil service not as a faithful and neutral instrument, but at worst a machine dedicated to wasteful public spending and at best a necessary evil. The government announced across-the-board manpower targets, which effectively amounted to a 15 per cent random cut phased over six years. Departments had no choice but to meet these targets, mainly by load-shedding and small-scale hiving off to quasi-governmental agencies and local authorities. The linking of civil service pay scales with private sector levels was broken in 1982. The abolition of the Civil Service

Department (whose head was booted unceremoniously into retirement) and a campaign to 'de-privilege' the service followed a failed 1981 pay strike by civil service unions. Business methods were lauded by ministers as the acme of progressive efficiency, and Lord Rayner (from Marks & Spencer) was drafted in to head up the Prime Minister's Efficiency Unit. The Rayner scrutinies specialised in investigating detailed issues inside departments, and demanding cost-cutting responses.

However, the Falklands War marked an important watershed in ministers' and Thatcher's relations with the civil service. Although the Foreign Office, the Secret Intelligence Service (SIS) and the Defence Intelligence staffs clearly failed to give advance warning of the Argentinian invasion in early 1982, these omissions were quickly dwarfed by the exceptional scratch mobilisation of the Falklands task force which successfully recaptured the islands. Preparations for fighting a full-scale war over islands populated by 400 families and 8,000 miles distant from the UK mainland would probably have been counted by a pre-1982 Rayner scrutiny as among the most bizarre examples of Whitehall's obsession with unproductive 'contingency planning'. But that merchants ships could be so hastily requisitioned, a task force fully supplied, and diplomatic backup maintained throughout the operation certainly made the Falklands War a logistical triumph. This point was not lost on Thatcher, for whom the war proved a political godsend, rescuing her government from a trough of unpopularity more marked than for any other post-war government (Dunleavy and Husbands, 1985, ch. 3).

Almost contemporaneously the senior civil service managed to put together a service-wide programme of management 'reforms' designed to tone down and civilise ministers' previously randomised assaults on Whitehall's methods of working. This package, known as the Financial Management Initiative (FMI), was co-authored by the Management and Personnel Office in the Cabinet Office and the Treasury public expenditure control divisions. It involved each department developing better measures for costing their 'outputs'; tighter control of sectional or unit costs, achieved by delegating more control over whole budgets to line managers in 'cost centres' (e.g. a local social security office); and the creation of 'top mangement systems' designed to allow ministers and senior civil service staff to maintain more effective and continuous scrutiny over the whole range of their departments' activities. These systems were supposed to be fairly standardised, but in practice variations across departments were considerable and diverged further during implementation. Spending departments wanted the Treasury to surrender more of its detailed control powers over staffing, budgets and computing, so as to allow more effective decentralisation to line managers. But the Treasury put less emphasis on decentralisation in favour of simply tightening up cost control systems.

Thatcher accepted FMIs, and the stabilisation of ministers' relations with the senior civil service, because she believed that the Conservatives were succeeding in populating Whitehall's higher ranks with 'managerialists' – in place of the traditional mandarins orientated towards political issues and policy advice. Critics argued, however:

> The fundamental institutions of Whitehall have survived the Thatcher government intact. Although there has been a good deal of rhetoric about changing the culture of Whitehall, in practice little has been achieved ... Whitehall has absorbed and neutered the attempt to change the culture and make it more managerial. (Ponting, 1986, pp. 223–4)

Only in one area has the crusade for managerialism clearly wrought changes. Permanent secretaries and their deputies' pay scales were safeguarded by being included along with judges, senior armed services officers, and public corporation chairmen in the top people's salaries review – which year-on-year delivered increases in line with inflation. Peters (1989) demonstrates that in 1979 top civil servants' salaries in Britain were 6 times the basic civil service pay minimum (on a par with Sweden and West Germany). But by 1987 top civil servants received 15.5 times the basic salary – a level of civil service pay inequality greater than other West European countries.

Just after the 1987 general election the Prime Minister's

advisers reconsidered the standstill on civil service reorganisation which had lasted for five years. A report by the Efficiency Unit (1988) on the progress of management reform (written largely by Kate Jenkins), delivered a damning indictment of FMIs under the conventional guise of declaring that progress had been achieved and that it should be further developed. The *Next Steps* report effectively demonstrated that the key FMI objective of getting top civil servants and ministers to concern themselves with routine organisational management had almost completely failed. It concluded that reform efforts such as the FMI had two fundamental flaws: first they tried to buck the inescapably dominant short-term and political pressures acting upon ministers and top civil servants by adding management tasks to their overburdened responsibilities. And second, they perpetuated the doomed effort to manage the civil service as a unified whole, when it was much too large and disparate to be controlled in this way by modern management techniques. This conclusion directly contradicted the findings of another report circulating in Whitehall during 1987 which gave the 'mandarins'' response to government dissatisfactions (Flynn *et al.*, 1989). Written by a former permanent secretary of the Department of Health and Social Security (DHSS), Sir Kenneth Stowe, this document recommended the creation of a new Management Board for the whole civil service on the lines of the National Health Service Board (see below, page 140).

In the event, Thatcher rejected the Stowe report as adding another layer of bureaucracy to those already existing. Instead the government accepted the Efficiency Unit report, which proposed a radical, New Right solution to management reform:

> The aim should be to establish a quite different way of conducting the business of government. The central Civil Service should consist of a relatively small core engaged in the function of servicing Ministers and managing departments, who will be the 'sponsors' of particular governmental policies and services. Responding to these departments will be a range of agencies employing their own staff, who may or may not have the status of Crown servants, and

concentrating on the delivery of their particular service, with clearly defined responsibilities between the Secretary of State and the Permanent Secretary on the one hand and the Chairmen [*sic*] or Chief Executives on the other. (Efficiency Unit, 1988, p. 15)

In February 1988 Thatcher announced the start of a radical programme of hiving-off executive responsibilities from central government proper to separate executive agencies. In subsequent Commons Select Committee hearings the permanent secretary appointed to head up the 'Next Steps' unit implementing the reforms estimated that 75 per cent of civil servants would have been hived-off within a decade, while other estimates put the figure as high as 90 per cent. In response to Commons pressure (Treasury and Civil Service Committee, 1988), the government conceded that the chief executives of agencies should answer directly to select committees and be accounting officers for their budgets, instead of these functions being vested in the permanent secretaries of their 'sponsor' ministries. A series of announcements about the transition to agency status has now encompassed major blocs of staffing in the social security system, the breaking-up of the detached parts of the Department of Employment into local Training Education Councils, and numerous small agency creations of units carrying out ancillary governmental functions. By the end of 1988 the serious candidates for agency creation already involved 129,000 staff, and by the end of 1989 some 174,000 out of a civil service core of 590,000 personnel.

The rolling programme of reorganisation has been interpreted in several different ways. The civil service and governmental view stresses that the current changes are integrally related to FMIs and a series of earlier efficiency efforts stretching back to the Fulton report of the late 1960s (which also advocated hiving-off but was never really implemented). But this 'seamless web' view is flatly contradicted by the highly critical text of the *Next Steps* report, and by the sudden transformation of government attitudes to the civil service from the quiescence of 1982–7 to the hectic progress of the agency-creation thereafter. In order not to alienate the civil service unions, the official view also stresses that hived-off staff will remain in the public sector, although with decentralised pay bargaining and remuneration arrangements – designed to allow out-of-London wage scales to be reduced below the national levels currently necessary to attract staff in the south-east.

Critics suggest that if the Conservatives remain in power the executive agency programme may well open the door for further privatisation in several ways. When functions are proposed for agency status the Treasury first asks whether this function should not be fully handed over to the private sector. Even where agencies start out as public sector bodies they could easily metamorphose into firms. A chief executive recruited from the private sector could hire in several private sector deputies, who in turn hire in their own assistants. Within a few years a management buy-out of the agency's operations or franchise could be feasible, supported by bank finance – a pattern set by several public corporation sell-offs.

The hiving-off programme has varied implications for differently placed officials. Most affected are the large heavily staffed ministries in defence, social security and other areas (see page 101 above). Delivery and transfer agencies here could be radically transformed into control or contract agencies. For managers in these departments' executive operations the change offers a welcome chance to get out from under what they experience as the stifling burden of centralised Treasury rules, to gain managerial freedom to conduct their own affairs, and almost certainly to radically upgrade their salaries. For Whitehall headquarters staffs in large ministries the prospect may also be welcome, since they can cut themselves free from a host of tiresome lower-grade administrative responsibilities, and concentrate instead on the most interesting policy-orientated work. The existing control agencies which dominate in social policy areas will be relatively little changed. But spending departments may now effectively take over many 'sponsor' functions previously the prerogative of the Treasury public expenditure control divisions. Not surprisingly the Treasury public expenditure divisions are critical of the changes proposed, warning that financial controls could weaken if centralised limits on budgets, personnel, computing and premises are dismantled. In addition, the

Treasury claims that its own heavily staffed sub-departments, the Inland Revenue and Customs and Excise (both run by boards of civil servants), are already 'executive agencies' and that no change of their status would be useful. However, support for the hiving-off solution is strong among the Treasury's economic divisions.

The precise pattern of relations between Treasury, Whitehall departments, and agencies which will be created by the 'Next Steps' process, together with the patterns of ministerial and Parliamentary control which will apply to hived-off functions, thus remain to be established (Jones, 1989). Equally the ways in which agencies will be managed and staffed are as yet only vaguely defined. But there are already grounds for believing that these changes could prove the most radical post-war reorganisation of the civil service.

The Intelligence Services

One of the most controversial areas of British central government operations remains the security and intelligence services, whose operations are shrouded in complete secrecy and are not controlled via the normal Parliamentary process. Instead the Secretaries of State at Defence, the Foreign Office and Home Office are supposed to exercise control over these agencies on behalf of the public interest (Figure 5.2). These ministers are not answerable in turn to either the Commons or the electorate for their decisions. Even the most basic details of security agencies' staffing or funding levels are withheld from the House of Commons, supposedly the guardian of public spending. Figure 5.2 shows that informed estimates of security agencies' staffing and funding levels are quite incommensurate with their parent ministries' published staffing and running costs figures. However, the Joint Intelligence Committee run from and chaired by the Cabinet Office, and the PM's overview of this area, are both designed to ensure coordination of the various security agencies' operations. Thatcher has shown a slightly increased willingness to account to the Commons for security and intelligence scandals. The only additional public protection against inefficiency,

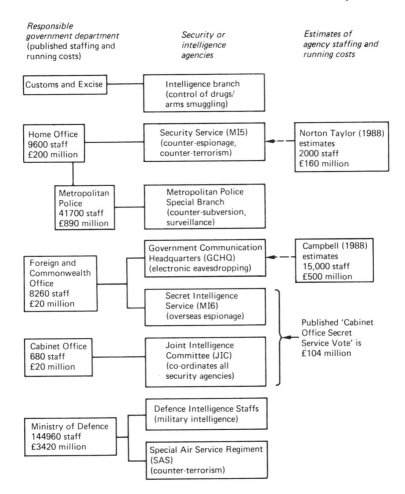

FIGURE 5.2 *UK security agencies*

Notes: All staff and running cost figures are for 1987–88.

Source: Dunleavy (1989d).

wrong-doing or the security services supplying misinformation to ministers is provided by the Security Commission – a panel of senior judges and former officials asked by the PM to investigate security lapses and potential scandals, although they have no investigating staff of their own. One of their reports produced a major reorganisation of MI5 in 1984, after an MI5 official was convicted of spying.

In the terms used by Dahl (1985), all the UK's security and intelligence services can be regarded as enclaves operating on the basis of non-democratic 'guardianship' ideals. British citizens are asked essentially to place implicit trust in the professionalism of security and intelligence personnel and in the vigilance of ministers unaccountable for their conduct to anyone else. Defenders of this system argue that to reveal anything more would negate the concept of secret security or espionage services altogether. Critics argue that Britain is now unique among liberal democracies in the paucity of public controls in this area. For example, the US Congress has a joint committee of both houses to whom the directors of all the main American intelligence services are directly but privately accountable. A similar system for the UK might create a special Commons/Lords committee, or a committee of Privy Councillors including senior representatives of all parties.

The limitations of the UK system were highlighted in the late 1980s by four developments. First, the book *Spycatcher* published by a former senior MI5 officer, Peter Wright, became a world best-seller and made its author a millionaire after a series of bungled government efforts to ban its publication. This extraordinary saga culminated in a protracted Australian court appearance by the British Cabinet Secretary Robert Armstrong, seeking in vain to ban the book's publication there. Perhaps the most sensational Wright claim was that in the 1970s a sizeable group of senior MI5 personnel convinced themselves that the then Labour leader Harold Wilson (Prime Minister 1964–70 and 1974–6) was a Soviet agent. They prepared a file on Wilson and repeatedly leaked hints of their bizarre suspicions as 'official' investigations to Tory MPs and media personnel, especially in the mid-1970s, Wilson resigned suddenly and unexpectedly in 1976, alleging soon afterwards that there had been a whispering campaign against him and his acquaintances by the security services. Wilson's claims were investigated at the time and dismissed by the MI5 Director, a denial accepted by the Labour Home Secretary of the day.

Second, it became clear that some of the British security

services operated completely outside the law and in breach of the European Convention on Human Rights, which Britain ratified in 1950 but never incorporated into domestic law. Wright alleged that MI5 had burgled premises and tapped telephones all over London in pursuit of its aims, without undertaking any formalities about warrants, etc. Various other disaffected former MI5 employees alleged systematic hostile surveillance of anti-nuclear groups and union leaders. In 1988, apparently responding most directly to fears of legal challenges at the European Court of Human Rights, the government introduced a very short Bill to legalise the activities of MI5. The agency was constituted on a statutory basis (instead of under Crown prerogative powers), and its operatives were given extensive scope to break normal UK property and privacy laws if authorised to do so by a responsible minister.

Third, almost a decade after its first attempt to reform the 1911 Official Secrets Act was withdrawn from the Commons, the government in 1988 introduced a bill to reform it. The catch-all provisions of the original Act had fallen into disrepute during the 1980s because public opinion found the ban on revealing all kinds of government information unsupportable. In 1985, for example, a jury ignored the legal summing up by a trial judge and found Clive Ponting not guilty of leaking secrets for passing confidential files about the Falklands war sinking of the Argentinian cruiser *General Belgrano* to a Labour MP. The new Bill confined the blanket ban on leaking secrets to the operations of all the UK's security and intelligence services, plus communications from foreign governments. No public interest defence against conviction was allowed in the new legislation, so that for example a newspaper publishing accurate evidence of wrong-doing by MI5 or the SIS would still fall foul of the law.

Fourth, suggestions of wrong-doing by security forces began to take on a more sinister tinge in the 1980s in the context of the fight against IRA terrorism in Ulster. In 1982 special units of the Royal Ulster Constabulary (RUC) acting on the basis of MI5 information on several occasions shot dead six un-armed Armagh men suspected of being IRA terrorists, on one occasion in a barn completely surrounded and bugged by the

RUC. A wide range of Catholic opinion in Ulster and in Eire concluded that the security forces had adopted a 'shoot to kill' policy, either unofficially or on the basis of a nod and a wink from ministers or top officials, with the object of deterring potential terrorists. An outside investigation into these claims was begun by the Deputy Chief Constable of Greater Manchester, John Stalker, who appeared to have concluded that the RUC special units had a case to answer. But in 1986 before Stalker could complete his inquiries he was suspended from duties following anonymous allegations that he had corrupt links with a Manchester property developer, allegations which were always insubstantial and quickly proved unfounded. Meanwhile the inquiry into the RUC was concluded by a replacement mainland officer, and although some prosecutions for perjury were recommended the Attorney General decided that they would not be in the public interest. Stalker meanwhile felt that he was virtually forced to resign by his Chief Constable (Stalker, 1988).

'Shoot-to-kill' allegations resurfaced strongly in 1988 when a large unit of the Special Air Services (SAS) regiment shot dead at close range three unarmed IRA members in the British colony of Gibraltar. The highly trained SAS operatives claimed that they feared the IRA members were seeking to trigger a radio bomb planted in a car which had previously been left in a square used for military parades. In fact this car contained no bomb (the IRA team's explosives were subsequently found still inside Spain) nor were the three in possession of any trigger devices. A Gibraltar inquest jury concluded by 9 votes to 2 that the killings were lawful, after hearing evidence reluctantly given by the SAS squad and by the MI5 officers in charge of the operation. However, the Labour Party, Amnesty International and several newspapers rejected the inquest as inadequate and demanded a public inquiry over four features – claims that the IRA members had been shadowed to Gibraltar by Spanish police; that the car in the square could not have contained a bomb; conflicts about the circumstances of the shootings in the evidence of civilian witnesses and the SAS; and why the Ministry of Defence misinformed the media that a Gibraltar bomb had been found for 24 hours after the killings.

Crises, Conflicts, and Policy-Making

As with previous governments, the late 1980s have been marked by the importance of inter-departmental or inter-ministerial conflicts in shaping the evolution of government policy, as three examples demonstrate.

The Westland Affair blew up in mid-1985 when Britain's only helicopter manufacturing company, the middle-sized Westland Plc became virtually bankrupt because of losses on a civilian helicopter project, endangering its main business of supplying MOD with military helicopters (see Linklater and Leigh, 1986; Dunleavy, 1990). Thatcher and the Trade and Industry Secretary Leon Brittan favoured a rescue plan linking up Westland with Sikorski, a subsidiary of the American multi-national company United Technologies. But the Defence Secretary, Michael Heseltine, became anxious that this deal would expose the MOD to strong pressure to buy US helicopters, thereby extending American domination of the defence industries. To prevent this outcome he assembled a Euro-consortium of medium-sized aviation firms to put forward an alternative rescue package, and negotiated backing from the French, Italian and German governments. His effort to tie Britain into the deal was thwarted in Cabinet committee by Thatcher, who insisted that Westland shareholders should choose which package to adopt without UK government interference. Heseltine nonetheless waged a strong semi-public dissenting campaign, designed to bolster the Euro-consortium solution. In their bid to defeat him Thatcher and Brittan first arranged for the Solicitor General to write a letter criticising some of Heseltine's statements for containing 'material inaccuracies', which the DTI and Number 10 staffs then leaked to the press. Finally in early 1986 Thatcher peremptorily banned all public statements by ministers on Westland's affairs not authorised by the Cabinet Office, a surprise move which provoked Heseltine to resign from the Cabinet (Young, 1989).

The open conflict between Downing Street and MOD over Westland was damaging enough in itself to the government, but Thatcher and Brittan's tactics had more immediate backlash effects. Brittan first had to apologise to the Commons for misleading MPs over complaints by British Aerospace that he had leant on them to withdraw from supporting the Euro-consortium rescue package. And when the Law Officers complained about the leaking of the Solicitor General's letter, a leak inquiry by the Cabinet Secretary pinned the blame on DTI and Downing Street civil servants. Leon Brittan was forced to resign as a Cabinet minister, drawing most of the flak which might otherwise have attached to Thatcher.

The impact of the Westland affair apparently petered out by the autumn of 1986 when Thatcher's poll ratings recoverd from their previous depressed position, and the Conservatives went on to win the 1987 election comfortably. But in fact the crisis reverberated on through British politics in several ways. Heseltine became the main alternative Tory 'leader in exile', whose assiduous wooing of the Conservative grass roots by 1989 posed a serious implicit challenge to Thatcher's leadership. Strong echoes of the Westland affair also resurfaced in 1988–9 in the chronic semi-public conflict between Thatcher and Lawson, eroding the premier's poll standing. And the conflict between US-orientated and British- or Euro-orientated solutions recurred in a number of other defence procurement controversies – such as the cancellation of the Nimrod early warning aircraft in early 1987, and the choice of a new army battle-tank in 1989–90.

Salmonella in eggs was a second acute case of inter-departmental conflict, this time between the Department of Health (DoH) and the Ministry of Agriculture, Fisheries and Food (MAFF) in late 1988. DoH concerns about lax standards of food production, regulated by MAFF, surfaced suddenly over unscripted public remarks by the junior Health Minister, Edwina Currie, that: 'Sadly, most of the egg production in this country is contaminated with salmonella.' The mass media interpreted this comment to mean that eating raw eggs was unsafe, sparking an acute crisis of public confidence in the food safety regulations generally and a large-scale drop in consumer demand for eggs. Farming lobbies demanded Currie's resignation, eventually conceded after over a month of ineffectual and muddled government responses to public anxiety and escalating media inquiries about other health risks. The acute phase of the controversy was only resolved by the creation of a

Cabinet committee chaired by Thatcher to put across a standard government line, followed shortly afterwards by promises of tougher regulation, new legislation, and (eventually) a reshuffling of the Agriculture minister.

Control over education and training was a more long-term example of an 'incubated' and unpublicised conflict between the Education ministry (DES), which traditionally controlled all aspects of education via its influence over local authority schools and colleges, and the Department of Employment (DE). In the mid-1980s under Lord Young the DE used its employment services agency, the Manpower Services Commission (MSC), to build up its involvement in training and to influence the curriculum in local authority colleges and even secondary schools by paying special grants for more business- and technology-orientated education. Under Sir Keith Joseph the DES seemed in danger of losing substantial control over its education brief. The department was completely dependent on local authorities for policy implementation, and by this stage the Thatcher government had become resolutely hostile to municipal provision in many respects (see Chapter 6). By 1985 over £110 million of money previously controlled by the DES had been transferred to the MSC schemes.

The DES fightback started in 1986 with the arrival of a new Secretary of State, Kenneth Baker. His initiatives to stabilise the DES's role all involved cutting its dependence on local government. Special, business-funded schools (City Technology Colleges) with more vocational and technology elements were set up. Polytechnics were moved out from local authority control, with new business-dominated boards of governors responsible directly to DES. Legislation was passed to allow state schools similarly to opt out of local authority control. And a new National Curriculum for all publicly funded schools was introduced. By the time of the 1987 election Baker's schemes had buried the DE/MSC challenge for control over secondary and tertiary education, and restored DES's influence and budgets. Lord Young moved from DE to Trade and Industry, where his efforts to centralise control of all the government's 'economic' ministries (including DE and Energy) in his new department were also rebuffed – contributing to his eventual retirement from the Cabinet. In 1989

Baker moved on from DES to become Conservative Party Chairman and a possible future Conservative leadership candidate.

Conclusions: Thatcherism and the Central State

Margaret Thatcher's impact upon British government reflects the combined impact of three factors. First there is her own personality, combining workaholic zeal, a slightly manic concern to meddle in any area of public affairs which attracts right-wing media attention, and the conviction that most problems invite simple, authoritative resolution. Second, Thatcher has made skilful use of cliques to extend her influence, especially advisers at 10 Downing Street and policy analysts from the Conservative party, New Right think-tanks, and intellectuals. The circle around her has provided a network in Whitehall and Westminster capable of pulling in issues for central examination and recognising opportunities for influence. And Downing Street's centralised control over government public relations has stamped prime-ministerial authority on most issues in public debate.

Third, Thatcher differs from previous premiers – especially Wilson and Callaghan – in both believing and relentlessly disseminating a coherent ideology. These views can be simply formulated, almost resembling Orwellian slogans (e.g. market processes good, state intervention bad). However crude such doctrines seem, their virtue is that Thatcher's Cabinet colleagues, senior civil servants across Whitehall, and managers of sub-central agencies can reliably predict which issues or policy proposals will attract Number 10's attention and displeasure, and hence can steer their course accordingly. Thus the New Right ideology acts like a multiplier, extending the influence of the PM's clique into areas which previous premiers had little success in penetrating.

The flipside of this successful formula for dominating the core executive can be charted in the continuing importance of Thatcher's authoritarian image in focusing public discontents with her government. And as a decade of unbroken Conservative rule opens out into a new political period, the value to be placed on a strong, coherent, non-collegial approach to government remains deeply controversial. Defenders of Thatcherism claim that the radical changes of policy style and centralisation of power involved can be justified by the achievement of 'watershed' effects in British social and economic affairs. Critics respond that fundamental social and economic problems have not been solved, perhaps only exacerbated, while the slender apparatus of conventions and constraints protecting the British system of government from creating arbitrary or uncontrolled centres of power has been severely damaged.

6

Government Beyond Whitehall

GERRY STOKER

Media discussion of our political system is focused on the debates of Westminster and the intrigues of Whitehall. But there is a world of government and politics beyond the elite circles of government ministers and civil servants, a world of sub-central government. The institutions of sub-central government include local authorities, the NHS and various quasi-governmental agencies (QGAs). They have a profound effect on everyday life, not only through their provision of an extensive range of public services but also through their economic impact as large-scale employers, landlords and spenders of public money. During the 1980s sub-central government has experienced a number of major changes and looks set for a profound restructuring on entering the 1990s. This chapter first examines the basic features of the institutions of sub-central government; second, the process of change and restructuring that is occurring; and third, different explanations of the driving forces behind and likely impact of these shifts.

The Main Agencies of Sub-Central Government

It is important to break out of a legalistic focus which portrays governmental relations in simple hierarchical terms. British

126

central government may legislate, regulate and exhort but it does so in the context of a system of sub-central government in which day-to-day control and the scope for innovation and initiative is in the hands of a range of other elected representatives, appointees and full-time officials and managers (see Chapter 5). The centre may seek to control the system but its influence is limited by the scale and fragmented character of the governmental system it oversees.

Sub-central government is here taken to include those governmental and quasi-governmental institutions which stand beyond central government, its territorial ministries, regional offices and departmental agencies. Two core elements of this world are the systems of elected local government and the institutions of the National Health Service. Two further broad groupings of organisations can be identified: nationally based quasi-governmental agencies and locally or regionally based quasi-governmental agencies. In both cases these quasi-governmental agencies shade into literally hundreds of QUANGOS or quasi-non governmental organisations that involve voluntary and private enterprise resources but which nevertheless receive public funding and undertake tasks crucial to public policy.

Local Authorities

Local councils constitute the only form of direct representative government in Britain apart from Parliament. Authorities are accountable to councillors who are elected and who usually organise themselves along party political lines. The influence and intensity of party politics within local government has grown substantially since the 1970s (Widdicombe, 1986; Gyford *et al.*, 1989) and in the late 1980s over 80 per cent of councils were controlled by a majority political party or a coalition of parties.

Local authorities in 1988/9 spent approximately £43 billion. This accounted for about a quarter of all public expenditure and a tenth of the gross domestic product. This spending was financed by grants from central government, rates levied by local authorities, and other miscellaneous sources. From 1990, as will become clear, this system has been fundamentally changed.

Local authorities employ a considerable number of professional, administrative and manual staff in order to carry out a complex mix of functions. In 1988/9 there were about 3 million full and part-time local authority employees. Upper-tier authorities (9 regions in Scotland and 48 counties in England and Wales) have responsibility for strategic planning, transport, fire, education and social services. Lower-tier authorities (53 districts in Scotland and 433 districts in non-metropolitan areas in England and Wales) have responsibility for housing, local planning, environmental health and leisure services.

In London, the abolition of the Greater London Council in 1986 and the Inner London Education Authority in 1990 has led to a complex split of tasks with 32 London boroughs having individual responsibility for education, housing, social services, local planning, leisure and environmental health. The boroughs share combined responsibility for fire and civil protection services, strategic planning, waste disposal, grants to voluntary organisations. In the metropolitan areas of West Midlands, South Yorkshire, West Yorkshire, Tyne and Wear, Greater Manchester and Merseyside 36 metropolitan district councils undertake a range of functions similar to that of the London boroughs. After the abolition of the Metropolitan Counties in 1986 these districts share joint responsibility for a range of services including transport, fire and civil defence, strategic planning, waste disposal and grants to voluntary organisations. The shared responsibilities of London and metropolitan authorities are organised either through joint boards composed of representatives appointed by the authorities or by way of other joint organisational arrangements set up by the authorities. Arrangements for overseeing the police service are distinctive, with police committees or boards in metropolitan areas comprising a mixture of local authority representatives and nominations from the magistrates bench. In London, policing is the responsibility of the Home Secretary.

While the main functions of elected local government have been listed above, they do not capture the breadth of the activities undertaken by local authorities. Manchester City

Council's *A–Z Guide*, for example, contains information about its services under more than 700 separate headings, starting with advice about abandoned motor vehicles and ending with a reference to zebra crossings.

The National Health Service

The National Health Service (NHS) has responsibility for hospitals, primary health care and some community care. In undertaking this provision it employed nearly 1¼ million people in 1986/7 and spent just under £20 billion, about half as much as the total spent by local authorities. The expenditure of the NHS, therefore, constitutes about one-eighth of all public spending. The administration of this vast system is decentralised. In England, which has a two-tier structure of 14 Regions and 192 Districts, Regional Health Authority (RHA) members are appointed by the Secretary of State for Health. The membership of District Health Authorities (DHAs) is under review as part of the government's broader plans to restructure the NHS. At present the majority of members are appointed by the RHA including four to six professional members and eight generalists. Local authorities in the relevant area have nomination rights over the remaining four to five places on the board while the Secretary of State appoints a chairman. In Scotland and Wales, which have a single-tier system of management boards, a similar allocation system for their membership has operated, with the Scottish Office and Welsh Office allocating funds between the boards.

Health authorities, under established arrangements, have no significant independent sources of finance. Health services are funded directly by central government. In addition to services run by health authorities, central government also funds Family Practitioner Committees which oversee and regulate the provision of primary health care by GPs and some other semi-autonomous health professionals.

National Quasi-Governmental Agencies

At a national level, quasi-governmental agencies account for about a quarter of public sector manpower. Public corporations are a dwindling element of this world as the government's privatisation plans have transferred nationalised industries and publicly owned corporations to the private sector, although a degree of government involvement in and regulation of such enterprises has continued (see Chapter 13). Remaining corporations, such as British Coal and British Rail could be sold off if there is a fourth term of Conservative government. Other QGAs fall into a broad category of single-purpose bodies. They are generally controlled by a Whitehall-appointed board, and funded to a large extent from the Exchequer. They are subject to some indirect Parliamentary scrutiny and some degree of ministerial supervision, but otherwise retain day-to-day control of their own activities. Bodies such as the Arts Council, the University Funding Council and the Commission for Racial Equality are good examples.

Local and Regional QGAs

During the 1980s the range and variety of local and regional QGAs has increased considerably (Stoker, 1988, ch. 3). Central government under Thatcher has created and funded a number of powerful implementation agencies more suited to its purposes which by-passed the established system of elected local government. Eleven Urban Development Corporations (UDCs) have been launched, each with their board appointed by Whitehall, but with considerable day-to-day control over their operations (Stoker, 1989a). In order to stimulate urban renewal in depressed areas UDCs have taken over development control powers from local authorities for parts of their urban areas and have a range of land assembly and grant-giving powers to attract private sector investment. In 1988–9 they spent about £250m of public money which is the equivalent to the total Urban Programme funding provided to over 50 inner-city local authorities during the same period. The London Docklands Development Corporation (LDDC) is the prime example of a successful UDC from the government's perspective. Since its establishment in 1981, it has attracted nearly £1 billion of private investment and has transformed the docklands area of East London bringing new economic activity and residents. Its critics argue that LDDC has undermined established industries and done little for the disadvantaged groups within the existing population (Brindley *et al.*, 1989, ch. 6).

During the 1980s the Manpower Services Commission provided central government with a powerful tool to promote training and new education initiatives. In the 1990s much of the work of the MSC will be undertaken by a network of around 100 Training and Enterprise Councils (TECs) in England and Wales and a smaller group of Local Agencies in Scotland that will not only take on functions from the training field, but also from the Scottish Development Agency which is to be disbanded. These new TECs and Local Agencies will be employer-led with two-thirds of their directors being private sector managers or businessmen. Each will have an annual budget of about £20m of public money and have responsibility for implementing government employment and training schemes as well as a strategy responsibility for training and business development in their area.

Local authorities have also established a number of local and regional QGAs during the 1980s, especially in the area of economic development. Over 500 such agencies were identified in a 1988 survey, mostly in the fields of economic development, tourism, arts, and recreation (Department of the Environment, 1988). Arm's-length agencies such as Enterprise Boards and cooperative development agencies have been established because they have a flexibility and speed of reaction which normal local authority committee and departmental processes do not allow.

Local and regional QGAs have also been used to encourage private sector corporations to get involved in the management of the social and economic problems of their areas, for example through the network of nearly 300 local enterprise agencies or trusts recognised by Business in the Community which provide a range of business advice and development services. Since their establishment during the 1980s, these agencies have received some £50m in private funding, matched by a similar amount from the public sector. Many government nominations to UDC boards, TECs and Local Agencies are drawn from a pool of private sector businessmen and managers.

Developments in Sub-Central Government

During its first two terms the Thatcher government passed some forty Acts, dealing with various elements of local authority work, virtually all constraining local authority expenditure. Withdrawing central government grant, a system of targets and penalties and ratecapping were among the measures fashioned to encourage local authorities to conform to central government's preference for a reduction in public spending on welfare services (Stoker, 1988, chs 6, 7). Funding issues also figured prominently in debate about the NHS during this period. The government pointed to more public spending on health and the rise in the number of patients treated. Opponents highlighted escalating needs, the increased cost of treatment, ward closures, lengthening waiting list and staff shortages (Klein, 1989, pp. 228–35).

As one initiative or piece of legislation only partially succeeded, or met with resistance, so another would be drafted and brought forward. Central intervention in sub-central government clearly increased but central control in terms of achieving the purposes of central government was by no means always enhanced. For example, local authority current expenditure despite all the government's efforts grew in real terms during the administration's first two terms. Indeed, Dunleavy and Rhodes (1986, pp. 142–3) argue that the government failed to comprehend the complexity and capacity for resistance embodied within the system of sub-central government (see also Rhodes, 1988).

In the case of local government, by the mid-1980s ministers were beginning to admit the limitations of simplistic and reactive measures and the narrow focus on restraining public spending. The search for a different way forward began with a series of measures announced in the run-up to the 1987 general election. In the case of the NHS, pressure over its funding crisis encouraged the announcement of a review in January 1988 and the immediate release of additional funding. The subsequent White Paper *Working for Patients* marked a substantial new departure in government thinking (HM Government, 1989b).

The dominant theme in the reform of sub-central government

can be labelled 'marketisation'. The aim is to fragment public sector institutions and stimulate private and voluntary sector alternatives in order to create a market place of service providers. The production and allocation of state-supported provision will be increasingly conditioned by market or quasi-market systems as opposed to the established political, bureaucratic and professional forms of mediation. Who produces what and who gets what will become less a matter of political, professional or bureaucratic judgement and will depend more on the operation of quasi-market mechanisms. Competition between public sector agencies, and with the private sector, is seen as ensuring efficiency and responsiveness to the customer. Choice is to be made available to the customer in its market form of an option to exit to another provider. A greater awareness of the opportunity costs involved in public spending decisions is to be stimulated by ensuring that both service providers and receivers have a sharper understanding of the costs of their choices.

A second and related theme of the programme is a clearer separation of the roles of authorisation and production among the institutions of sub-central government. The responsibility for provision is to an increased degree to be divorced from the process of doing. 'Enabling' sub-central agencies will carry prime responsibility for authorisation, making judgements about the scale and scope of provision and regulating the activities of direct service providers. The daily responsibility for service provision will rest with a fragmented range of public, private and voluntary sector service agencies. They, rather than the enabling bodies, will employ the necessary staff and resources to provide services. The service agencies will provide a market place of competing suppliers which enabling agencies will engage to meet the needs and policy priorities they identify. In the long run it is claimed that all these changes will help to discipline public service provision to ensure 'value for money' and undermine the tendency for public spending to grow.

Restructuring Local Government

Finance The reform of revenue financing in local government has at its core the introduction of community charge to replace domestic rates. Community charge is, in effect, a poll tax to be set by each authority and levied on all adults, with a small number of exemptions. The overwhelming majority of Britain's 38 million adults will pay the tax, as compared with the existing total of 18 million domestic ratepayers. A rebate system will operate, though there will be a maximum level of rebate so that no one will pay less than 20 per cent of their local charge.

National Non-Domestic Rate (NNDR) will replace the existing local non-domestic rate levied on industrial and commercial premises. What was a locally determined tax will in the future be set at a rate determined by national government with a single, common rate poundage charged on all non-domestic properties. The yield of NNDR will be allocated by central government to local authorities on the basis of their adult population.

The existing system of central government support is also to be restructured with Revenue Support Grant (RSG) replacing Rate Support Grant. This new grant, which it is hoped will be simpler and stabler in its operation than the previous system, will provide support to local authorities on the basis of central government's assessment of their need to spend.

Finally the government has taken the opportunity of this comprehensive reform of revenue financing to also introduce a new system of capital spending controls. The new system will give the government power to make credit approvals to local authorities which will cover all transactions undertaken during the year concerning agreements to acquire capital goods. The government will be free to set these allocations taking into account the level of capital receipts available to the authority. Where the level of receipts is high, little or no credit approval may be granted and indeed the authority may be required to use a proportion of the receipts to pay off its accumulated debt.

The reforms will be in place throughout Britain by 1990. However, there will be a phasing-in period so that the impact of the change-over from one system to another can be softened. For example, with respect to community charge, 'safety net' provisions will operate between 1990 and 1994 so that those authorities whose high spending will require them to raise a very high community charge will receive additional financial support in the short run.

In the long run, however, the government claim that its reforms will enhance the accountability of local government. By removing the 'soft' option of relying on non-domestic rates and by spreading the local tax burden to a wider proportion of the population a more realistic assessment of the virtues of local spending will be made. If local decision-makers want to provide services at a level above that determined by the centre they will be free to do so but they will have to find the additional resources through community charge.

Critics of the government counter these arguments by noting that under the new arrangements on average three-quarters of the revenue income of local authorities will be derived from central sources (i.e. NNDR and RSG) compared to roughly half under the old system. An increased reliance on centrally controlled funding is hardly a recipe for greater local accountability. Moreover, given the flat-rate nature of community charge and the complex arrangements for its collection, it may prove a very difficult tax to raise. This in turn may make local authorities more dependent on central sources even to maintain basic services. The combination of the new capital spending controls and the weakening of the local financial base of authorities is likely to lead to a significant increase in central control.

The financial measures proposed by the government imply a concern with linking more closely the consumption of local services with their cost. In this sense they do develop the theme of 'marketisation' associated with the reform package. However, the increased dependence on centrally determined finance together with the reserve powers to 'cap' the community charges levied by authorities, suggest the sustained influence of the government's more long-standing concerns with restraining and directing public spending.

Competitive Tendering Subjecting an increased range of services to competitive tendering illustrates the reform themes of marketisation and the separation of authorisation and production. The services subject to tendering include refuse collection, cleaning, catering, vehicle maintenance and the management of leisure services. The legislation enables central government to add other services to this list and builds on existing provisions for putting construction, maintenance and building control work out to tender. A requirement to put NHS catering, domestic and laundry services out to competitive tender has been in place since the mid-1980s (Ascher, 1987). Other quasi-governmental agencies are also required to subject some of their activities to competitive tendering.

In the case of the NHS, private contractors won only 18 per cent of services, and less than ten per cent of contracts. The bids from 'in-house' staff to undertake the work were generally successful. In the case of local government, earlier indications are that in the short run most contracts will stay 'in-house'. Of the first 265 contracts allocated under the new procedures some 80 per cent were won by 'in-house' workforces (*Guardian*, 14 July 1989).

However, the requirement that the 'in-house' workforce operate on a trading basis is likely to encourage the 'marketisation' of relations within the authority. Service staff and others within the authority are obliged to adopt a client role (as authorisers) treating the 'in-house' staff as contractors (or providers). The 'in-house' staff in turn will have to work to the contract and will receive their income on the basis of fulfilling its requirements. There are already clear signs that this has encouraged an ethos of commercialism within local authorities. Trading workforces have set up their own management arrangements and developed new accounting and marketing skills. They have, in effect, become medium-sized businesses operating within local authorities. A knock-on effect has been felt by central staff providing legal, financial and personnel services. Since 'in-house' staff have to levy a charge against their trading account for these services, the changes have put considerable pressure on central staff to provide cost-effective and competitive arrangements. In short, even where the task of service provision remains within the local authority, commercial criteria and market relationships are introduced.

Competition and Choice in Service Delivery The government have also launched major reforms in three of the core, high-spending areas of local authority provision: Education,

Housing and Community Care. (For a fuller discussion of these and other reforms, see Stewart and Stoker, 1989.) Again, the restructuring of each reflects the themes of the reform programme identified earlier.

The impact of the changes will be to create a market place of service providers. Education reforms involve local authority schools being given more financial and managerial discretion and encouraged to compete for pupils. Standing beyond local authority control a range of City Technology Colleges and Grant Maintained Schools will provide competition for those schools remaining within the local authority orbit. The authorisation/provision split can also be observed. Local education authorities rather than organising direct provision will take on the task of monitoring and evaluating the quality of the national curriculum as it is being delivered in school. They will also have a key role in laying down procedures and guidelines in the development and operation of the local management of schools.

In housing, local authority near-monopoly provision of social housing for rent is to be challenged by the encouragement of other approved social landlords, including housing associations, to compete for the management of existing estates and in new provision. The Housing Corporation, a national QGA, has been given a key role in stimulating alternative social landlords. In some areas, centrally funded Housing Action Trusts will provide an alternative. Tenants are allowed to 'opt out' of local authority control and have their housing managed by another landlord, or through a tenants' management co-op. With respect to community care for elderly, handicapped and mentally ill people, a complex market of public, private and voluntary sector providers is also to be actively encouraged. The housing reforms illustrate other features of the marketisation strategy. The income and investment associated with local authority housing is to be 'ring-fenced' so that housing departments will act on a trading basis – a business within the local authority. Central government financial support will continue but it will reflect regional rent levels and will depend on the authority achieving efficiency targets on levels of rent arrears and other concerns. The initial aim is to push rents up and to reflect differences between regions in terms of house prices. In the long term the aim is to achieve market rents for all housing that remains in the council sector. Again the local housing authority is being encouraged to take on an enabling role. The White Paper *Housing* (HM Government, 1987) puts it explicitly: 'Local authorities should see themselves as enablers who ensure that everyone in their area is adequately housed; but not necessarily by them.'

The proposals in relation to community care also give local authorities a central strategic role. The White Paper *Caring for People* (HM Government, 1989a) argues that local councils should take the main responsibility for assessing individual need and designing care arrangements for the elderly and disabled people in the community. They are, however, expected to make full use of private and voluntary sector providers in designing their care packages. The proposed changes in the funding system are likely to put pressure on council-run homes but also undermine the rapid growth of private profit-making residential and nursing homes. It is primarily 'not for profit' independent providers and other elements of the voluntary sector that are likely to see a growth in their role in the future. In addition local authorities will be required to set up arm's-length inspection and registration units responsible for checking standards in council, private and voluntary homes.

In each of the service areas we have considered, local authorities are left with a mixture of 'authorisation' and 'production' functions. It is difficult to predict how the balance between the different elements will unfold. In housing and community care considerable levels of hands-on provision seem likely to remain in the short run, and in education the main plank of delivery is likely to be site-managed local authority schools. As to the broader authorising/enabling role it seems most likely to develop strongly in the case of community care and remain at its weakest in housing, where local authorities lack the resources and powers to intervene in the general housing market, as suggested by the 1987 White Paper.

The Reform of the NHS

The themes of marketisation and the separation of authorisation and provision emerge clearly in the reform plans for the

NHS proposed in The White Paper *Working for Patients* (HM Government, 1989b). In the case of the hospital service, the creation of an 'internal market' is at the core of the reform package. On the demand side of the market there will be three purchasers: District Health Authorities, GPs with lists of more than 11,000 patients, and private sector insurance companies. They will 'purchase' health care on the part of their population, patients and customers. On the provision side, there will be DHA-managed hospitals. In addition there will be self-governing hospitals which will opt out of the NHS and be run through independent trusts. Finally, on the provision side, private sector hospitals, which have an over-capacity in beds, will also compete to provide NHS-funded care. The whole system will require a massive investment in information technology and training in order that the various purchasers have the necessary information on bed availability and comparative costs of treatment and suppliers of services can levy charges for the work they have undertaken in order to maintain their income. The aim is to introduce market relationships and criteria into the decision-making and management processes of the NHS.

In the case of primary health care, the government plans to give GPs an increased incentive to attract patients by linking more of their funding to the size of their lists. Each patient enrolled will carry with them a state-provided fee. At the same time, procedures for patients to change their GP are to be made easier so that following the logic of the market 'good' practices will expand and 'poor' ones will contract as patients vote with their feet. GPs in larger practices are also, as noted earlier, going to have budgets to spend in referring-on patients to hospitals which will be competing for these referrals. Finally, in their own treatment of patients, further financial disciplines are going to be placed on GPs in terms of judgements about the cost of alternative forms of treatment and prescriptions for drugs.

As well as the introduction of an 'internal market' the White Paper also encourages a focus on an enabling or authorising role for health authorities. It proposes that health authorities should be given budgets determined exclusively by the characteristics of their population, rather than (as at present) by the number and nature of the institutions which they own. The health authority will retain responsibility for health care in its area but will contract with public, private and independent hospitals both in and outside the area in order to meet the needs it identifies. The flexibility of the NHS is also to be enhanced by a proposal that individual health authorities could negotiate wage and salary levels in the light of local demands and labour markets rather than through the established system of national negotiation. The White Paper further enhances the regulatory role for Family Practitioner Committees (FPCs) over GPs established by earlier reforms, through, for example, proposing that FPCs should have the power to impose financial penalties on those GPs that over-prescribe certain drugs.

One of the contradictions of the White Paper is that the increased emphasis on markets and flexibility is accompanied by a more streamlined system of centralised managerial controls (Klein, 1989, pp. 238–41). The White Paper proposes the removal of all professional and local authority representatives from district health authorities. Family Practitioner Committees are also to be reduced in size and reformed on business lines so that they are run by a mixture of executive and non-executive managing directors. The system is driven by the vision of a managerial hierarchy operating from top to bottom of the NHS and abandons the concern with local representativeness. At the top of the system is a Policy Board and a Management Executive. Increased accountability to central government, and in particular the health minister, is clearly a prime aim of the reform package.

Interpreting the Changes in Sub-Central Government

The Centralisation Thesis

The most popular interpretation views the restructuring of sub-central government as part of a consistent and pernicious policy of centralisation pursued by the Conservatives since their election in 1979. Even before the third term agenda was drawn up, a queue of British academics lined up to damn the government for its 'assault' on local democracy and its all-pervading centralism (Jones and Stewart, 1985; Loughlin 1986; Parkinson 1987; Newton and Karran 1985, p. 128). Commenting on the post-1987 position, Bogdanor (1988, p. 7) argues:

> The Conservative government elected in 1979 has been the most centralist since the Stuart monarchs of the 17th century. The government appears to have taken the view that other centres of power in society, such as local authorities, are somehow illegitimate, and must be curbed. For the Conservatives, there seems to be only one power centre which is truly legitimate, and that is central government.

Jones (1988) claims that the last decade has seen a major constitutional change in five fundamental respects. First, the Conservatives have interpreted parliamentary sovereignty as governmental supremacy and have sought to impose government's policies even when they have not been enshrined in statute (as in the case of the financial targets and penalties of the early 1980s). Second, the Thatcher government increasingly sought to specify and define the functions of local government, reducing local authorities to implementing arms of the centre with no policy-making role of their own. Third, since 1979 the government has taken upon itself the right to decide what should be the level of local spending. Fourth, the independent tax and revenue raising powers of local authorities have been interfered with (through ratecapping) and ultimately undermined through the introduction of community charge. Finally, the government has since 1979 ridden rough-shod over the mandate given to local authorities through local elections.

A paradox for writers within this approach is that traditional Conservatism has generally been supportive of local democracy, with its emphasis upon individuals and communities being encouraged to take responsibility for their own affairs. The paradox is explained by noting how a concern with public spending in the context of international economic developments led government ministers through a process of action and reaction to develop more and more centralist instruments. The Prime Minister's increased frustration with local government and the arrival of key personalities such as Nicholas Ridley are seen as explaining the even more radical, market-orientated restructuring that emerged in the mid-1980s. The Conservative government have since 1979 maintained a consistent, if not predetermined, drift towards centralism.

The centralisation thesis has many powerful arguments to muster and it is difficult to resist the main thrust of the interpretation, especially in terms of local government finance. It is also clearly part of the government's agenda to establish greater accountability to the centre within the NHS. Defenders of the government's record (Pirie, 1988) have argued that the process of centralisation is only a temporary element in a wider transition that will eventually lead to greater autonomy and choice for local citizens and consumers, if not necessarily local authorities. Government critics, however, have countered such justifications by arguing that they look 'dangerously like the dictatorship of the proletariat in reverse; if the public do not rejoice at the results, authoritarianism could become still more necessary to sustain a much enlarged but inegalitarian and unstable market system' (Self, 1989, p. 5).

A stronger line of attack on the centralisation thesis is developed by Bulpitt (1990) who questions the idea that local interests and the interests of elected local authorities are the same. Parrot-like repetition has simply led to local democracy being hailed as a 'good thing', yet in practice in terms of voter turn-out and the actions of local authorities, local democracy seems to meet apathy and lack of critical attention. Bulpitt claims that the centralisation thesis rests on an idealised and Utopian vision of local democracy based on consensus and a depoliticised decision-making process. Behind the rhetoric of the interests of the local community is a reality of gainers and losers from different state policies and actions. Local government cannot be run as some protected reserve where politics is forbidden. If central government seeks to protect and promote certain local interests it favours, is it any more than 'humbug' to accuse it of attacking local democracy?

A Matter of Party Advantage

A number of writers have interpreted the restructuring in terms of party interest and advantage. The intensity of party politics in local government together with the simple plurality rule electoral system has delivered huge majorities for the Conservative Party nationally but left substantial areas in local government outside Conservative control. In July 1985, for example, only 35 per cent of local authorities had a Conservative majority.

Hence some writers see a Tory central government drive to reward its supporters and undermine its opponents (Hambleton, 1989; Parkinson, 1987). In examining the impact of community charge, Travers (1989, p. 17) notes that following the 'phasing in' period, 'it has been predicted that local taxpayers in the South East, South West, the West Midlands and outer London will gain, while those in the North, North West, Yorkshire and Humberside and inner London will lose'. Areas of Conservative control predominate in the former areas, while most Labour councils are in losing regions. Other measures in education, competitive tendering, housing and health can be seen as attempts to bolster the Conservatives' natural supporters and undermine the political base of their opponents.

The Labour Party is seen as a particular target. According to Hambleton (1989, p. 382), 'the government's current strategy is clearly more concerned with destroying the remaining institutions controlled by Labour than bringing about any fundamental reform of local government'. Some authors argue that ministers want to destroy the political platform of the urban left in local government because their radical alternative policies were perceived as a threat to the ideological dominance of Thatcherism (Duncan and Goodwin, 1988). Their critics argue that the 'Loony Left' was more of an electoral advantage to the Conservatives than a threat.

Bulpitt (1983, 1990) argues that for much of the post-war period, national politicians largely regarded sub-central government as a matter of administration, with which they wished to have little to do. However, economic crisis and the encroachment of some left-wing councils on the traditional national concerns of economic policy led to breakdown of national political indifference. A number of specific triggers led to actions: ministerial frustration at the high spending of authorities controlled by opponents and the convenience of using local authorities as a scapegoat for the failure to radically cut back on public spending. Thereafter a process of action and reaction set in until the summer of 1986, when the combination of a growing ministerial taste for the range of detailed controls exercised over local spending, and the arrival of Baker, Ridley and Hurd – all committed to putting an ideological gloss on the government's programme – helped to create the climate for the market-orientated post-1987 programme. The main outcome of the restructuring of sub-central government according to this interpretation would be a positive gain especially in electoral terms for the Conservative Party.

The immediate evidence appears to contradict such a prediction, since the community charge and health reforms, according to opinion polls, have lost rather than won support for the government. It could be argued that the government has miscalculated. Alternatively, over the long run, community charge, competitive tendering and the health, housing and education reforms may bring political credit by creating new 'constituencies' of people who have gained under the programme. Paradoxically, this interpretation implies that the post-1987 restructuring of sub-central government is far from permanent. If statecraft considerations imply party advantage in undertaking further reforms or withdrawing parts of the package, then policy will change. If another party comes to power, at the national level, then the 'merry-go-round' of reform will start again.

A Triumph of New Right Ideology

A widely propagated idea among government supporters (Pirie, 1988; Mather, 1989), opponents (Self, 1989), and those who present themselves as neutral observers (Flynn, 1989; Hood, 1987), is that the restructuring of sub-central government follows 'New Right' thinking. The programme of reform represents a coherent attempt by the Thatcher government to apply a particular set of assumptions and principles to the diagnosis and treatment of the ills of the public sector. The growth, influence and indeed dominance of New Right thinking (Green, 1987; King, 1987) among academics and practitioners alike is noted and is seen as the driving force for change. According to Pirie (1988) the 1970s and 1980s have seen prevailing paradigms collapse under the weight of contradictions and anomalies and a New Right paradigm rise because of the quality of its perspective and the coherence of its prescriptions influenced by the 'public choice' school (Jackson, 1982; Mueller. 1979). This approach applies to political and administrative questions the basic behavioural postulate of neo-classical economics, 'that man is an egoistic, rational utility maximiser' (Mueller, 1979, p. 1). From this simple assumption a range of critical analyses of the operation of both modern democracy and bureaucracy have been derived (Buchanan and Tullock, 1962; Niskanen, 1971).

For public choice theorists the optimal mechanism for allocating goods and making decisions is the market. Existing public bureaucracies and representative democratic institutions are inherently prone to over-supply public services and insufficiently responsive to the needs of individual consumers. The self-interest of politicians seeking votes leads them to make promises and inflate public expectations above what the state can provide. Sectional interest groups pursue their own narrow interests by pushing for more and better provision. The losers are the disorganised and silent majority who finance the public expenditure to support expanded services. Bureaucrats, too, pursue the self-interested goal of budget maximisation through the expansion of their departmental programmes.

The public choice theorists offer a number of remedies aimed at tackling these problems. Hood (1987, p. 147) argues that they favour:

– small-scale rather than large-scale enterprise in public service provision;
– performance contracting rather than direct labour through open-ended employment contracts;

- multiple-provider structures of public service provision (preferably involving rivalry among competing providers) rather than single-provider structures;
- user charges (or at least earmarked taxes) rather than general tax funds as the basis of funding public services; and private or independent enterprise rather than public bureaucracy as the instrument of service provision.

Plainly many of the elements of the Conservatives' early and post-1987 legislative and reform programme follow these public choice prescriptions. With the support of 'think-tanks' such as the Adam Smith Institute, the Institute of Economic Affairs and the Centre for Policy Studies, a micro-level politics has been developed which recognises the self-interested dynamics of the political system (see Chapter 2). In a number of the proposals for restructuring local government the Thatcher government has not favoured 'pure' market solutions but instead adopted policies which make sense in terms of micro-political calculations. For example, contracting-out is promoted rather than a full-blown system of user-specific charges. The latter would meet insurmountable opposition but the former can be designed to offer new opportunities for contractors, and new highly skilled jobs for local authority managers overseeing contracts. For the manual workforce who are retained there is continuing employment and the possibility of better wages and conditions, and for those who take early retirement there is the option of a 'generous' financial settlement.

> An analysis identifies all of the groups in the political market in question, and traces the perceived benefit they receive. A policy is then constructed to offer as many of them as possible a bigger gain from the new method than they enjoyed before. (Pirie, 1988, pp. 143–4)

Micropolitics is about making 'trade-offs to interest groups' in order to achieve the transformation in the political and bureaucratic systems favoured by public choice theorists.

The outcome of the restructuring will be a reduction in the power of producers and a lesser role for the intermediaries of the system: professionals, trade-union leaders and political representatives. Market methods of production and allocation will deliver more efficient services tailored to meet the needs of individual consumers.

However, Pirie might be accused of a combination of 'self-trumpeting' and 'post-hoc' rationalisation. New Right 'think tanks' have produced a number of reports that have pre-figured later legislative changes but few have displayed the kind of micro-political analysis advocated by Pirie. Further, the nagging question remains: do the ideas drive the reforms or do they simply provide a rhetorical window-dressing used by ministers to justify the actions they are taking?

More 'fatalist' public choice accounts (Dunleavy, 1986) fear that the stranglehold of self-interested politicians, professionals and bureaucrats will be very difficult to break – so much so that the reforms are unlikely to fundamentally change the system. Rather, powerful and established self-interested groups will reorganise and reorientate themselves to maximise their gains out of the emerging new system. Thus, for ex-ample, the rhetoric about 'service to the customer' may be used by professionals and bureaucrats to justify greater auton-omy for themselves from the interference of politicians and better working environments in order to have the necessary 'flexibility' and the 'right conditions' to respond to customers. In this perspective, Pirie's micropolitics looks as if it provides a rationale for sustaining the strong and undermining still further the weak. Skilled professionals and highly organised male rubbish collectors may need to be 'bought off'. But why bother with the more vulnerable, largely female, cleaning and catering workforce; let alone groups of consumers such as the homeless? The triumph of New Right ideology, if that is what we are witnessing, looks less like individual choice conquering bureaucratic red-tape and more like the intellectual under-pinning to a system of increased inequality and unfairness.

Conclusion

The system of sub-central government is undergoing a radical restructuring. None of the broad interpretations which dominate discussion were found to be wholly convincing. The centralisation thesis rests on an overly cosy view of local democracy and conducts its debate in the abstract terms of a shift in the balance of power between central and local government, making it more difficult to grasp which social and economic interests are losing power and which are gaining. The party advantage model is more happy with the language of winners and losers. But the implication that sub-central government is just a political machine to be moulded at the whim of party advantage belies both the complexity of the restructuring proposed and the depth of the transformation that is taking place. Those who see the restructuring as a product of the increased influence of New Right thinking recognise that a sea-change is occurring but provide unconvincing explanations of both why some New Right ideas have found favour and what the likely outcome of the process of restructuring will be.

A final approach has developed an argument that the challenges facing sub-central government can only be fully understood in the context of a broader pattern of social and economic change (Stoker, 1989b; Klein, 1989, pp. 196–200). A profound shift in the patterns of production and consumption in our society is occurring which can be labelled as a transition from Fordism towards Post-Fordism. From the 1930s to the 1970s a system of mass production and consumption dominated. The leading industries were those using assembly-line techniques to produce long production runs of standardised products. In this process previously luxury items such as motor cars, refrigerators, etc. became available to the mass of consumers. In the 1970s a combination of market saturation, industrial unrest and economic crisis signalled a challenge to this system. At the same time developments in technology (robotics, computerised production aids, information management) and changing consumer aspirations opened up opportunities for more flexible forms of production and differentiated marketing to consumers. In the service sector, in particular, information technology created opportunities for increased productivity, new services and new forms of management control.

The large-scale, bureaucratic, hierarchical organisational

forms of the period of mass production and consumption have in this process of change been increasingly challenged. There has been a search for more flexible and responsive organisational forms, in which a central core retains key strategic powers, but in which greater use is made of contracting, franchising and more generally a fragmented system of 'independent' units and sections. The argument is that this organisational revolution is passing from private to public sector. Beyond this, however, it can be claimed that for the transformation to be fulfilled in the private sector alone a fundamental shift in the pattern of governmental organisations is required. The development of flexible production systems, consumption patterns and labour markets cannot unfold without challenging those public sector organisations which through their role as spenders, employers and landlords are central institutions within the UK's mixed economy.

This explanation too has its weaknesses (in particular the process of change is far less clear-cut than that implied by the simple statement of key trends made above) and needs to be developed and refined. But it does have the prime advantage of putting the debate about the restructuring of sub-central government back into a broader social and economic context.

7

Britain and Europe

HELEN WALLACE

It has taken a long time for British politics to become 'Europeanised', in the terms that have for a long time been recognised in most of the other member states of the European Community (EC). For some ten years after British accession to the EC on 1 January 1973 the characteristic profile of British political debate remained locked in the conditional mood, that is to say focused still on the underlying question of whether membership itself was the appropriate policy for any British government to pursue.

The Conservative Party, both in government and opposition, had worked on the assumption since the early 1960s that on balance membership was the right course. But two inhibitions remained: first, a continuingly vocal group, albeit a minority, persisted in arguing that the policy was misguided; and, second, the Thatcher government remained reserved about the implications of membership, unless and until it could be sure that the basic terms of the deal as regards agriculture and the budget were adequate to permit other issues to be addressed. The Labour Party remained formally committed to withdrawal from the EC. At least as far as organised party opinion was concerned, only the Liberals and Social Democrats were unequivocally attached to membership, warts and all, as the necessary status quo.

The consequence was that much of the public discussion on EC issues was confined to 'Anglo-British' introversion, with a vocabulary and themes that were virtually incomprehensible to commentators in other member states, apart from Denmark and Greece, where similar factors were in evidence. Perversely even at the level of the fine print of EC proposals and legislation, where in principle at least a sophisticated exchange of views might have been expected, the British debate more often consisted of shadow-boxing than of either careful analysis of options or well-articulated arguments about competing value preferences. Such informed debate and appraisal of choices as took place was either behind closed doors in Whitehall or in the specialised networks of interest representation and lobbying.

On the continent it had long been evident that the European dimension was well inserted into the domestic political process as a given for policy-makers, political parties, interest groups and commentators. Sometimes exciting, often excruciatingly dull, but unavoidably present, this European dimension had become one of the many strands of the fabric of politics. Europe was not necessarily always a lively subject of debate nor at the top of the domestic political agenda; indeed it could be argued that Europe was often taken for granted. But from time to time political and economic actors would turn their attention to big questions about the future of Europe, or at least the EC, in terms of both the substantive policy agenda and the overall political framework and goals to be pursued. Not surprisingly EC initiatives rarely emanated from the UK and the British were ill-at-ease with proposals that went beyond the manageable bread-and-butter issues. Slightly surprisingly it was only in the sphere of foreign policy cooperation that the British found themselves making early initiatives to reinforce collective European positions.

The European Political Context

Some explanation of the political features of the EC is needed to put into context the ways in which it permeates British politics. The section which follows summarises, with inevitably some over-simplification, the main features of the structures, functions and processes of the EC (see Figure 7.1). It

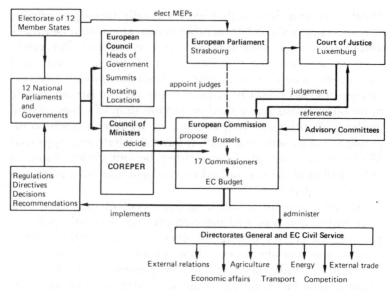

FIGURE 7.1   *The Eurocracy*   *(Source: Brendan O'Leary)*

Britain's influence in Europe is exercised through the various EC institutions and depends on the extent and quality of UK representation in them.

The European Commission is a college of 17 Commissioners appointed by common accord of EC member governments. The Commission is responsible for policy proposals and policy execution, assisted by the Directorates General, the bureaucratic arm of the EC. There are by convention two Commissioners from the UK (and from France, Italy, Germany and Spain), and one each from all other member states.

cannot, however, be overstated that the EC is, politically speaking, a half-built house.

Its basic characteristics were set by the founding Treaties – of Paris, establishing the European Coal and Steel Community in 1951, and of Rome, establishing the European Economic Community and the European Atomic Energy Community (better known as Euratom) in 1958. But periodically since then these Treaties have been amended and supplemented to take account of new members, to change institutional rules and to add policy powers. In addition, practice has evolved and interpretations of treaty provisions have altered, with the result that the EC is now a very different animal from the initial design. Nor is the process of revision complete: the operations of the EC are peculiarly susceptible to the swings of

The European Council of Ministers is the principal forum for detailed negotiation and legislation by the member states. The Council of Ministers has different compositions according to the policy areas under discussion. Countries are allocated varying voting strengths. Out of 76 votes in all, the UK disposes of 10 votes (along with Germany, France and Italy) and all other countries of between two and eight votes. A qualified majority requires 54 votes.

COREPER, the Committee of Permanent Representatives, does much of the detailed work of servicing and coordinating the work of the Council. Its working groups, with Commission participation, are especially influential. Each member state has one permanent representative.

The European Council consists of all 12 EC Heads of Government, meeting two or three times a year. The European Council has assumed greater importance in EC affairs as the locus of ultimate authority since the late 1970s. Its meetings are informal but much preparatory work precedes them.

The European Parliament consists of 518 MEPs elected directly every four years from all 12 countries, although at present under different systems of voting. The UK sends 81 MEPs to Strasbourg (along with Germany, France and Italy). All other countries send between six and 60 members. The Parliament's initial role was rather restricted, as an advisory and consultative body, though with major budgetary powers since the 1970s. However, its scrutiny and legislative powers have increased somewhat under the term of the Single European Act, and its political salience in member countries has slowly grown. Labour won the majority of the UK's seats at the 1989 elections.

The European Court of Justice consists of judges chosen by common accord of member governments, in practice one per member state plus one other. Its role is to interpret and apply the various EC treaties and legislation and to act as a Court of Appeal. The Commission or a member state can ask the Court to consider issues such as non-compliance with EC legislation by a particular member state. Member states can also challenge the validity of EC legislation. The European Court of Justice is not to be confused with the European Court of Human Rights, which is attached to the Council of Europe.

---

politics and economics within the member states and in the external environment; and there are evident dynamic forces of political transformation at work which subtly and often opaquely alter the interrelationships between the EC and national levels of politics.

The political structures of the EC owe more to the inspiration of federal systems than they do to unitary states of the British kind. The EC explicitly rests on a division of powers between the EC and member state levels, with some policy powers assigned in full to the EC level, e.g. for tariffs and tariff negotiations, and others shared between the two. The EC also separates powers between different institutions on lines broadly analogous to those found in the American constitution, with the consequential tensions and conflicts between institutions that are typical of American politics. None of this is to suggest that the EC is yet or will necessarily ever be a federal system, but rather to make clear that its institutional and political style is easier to understand in American terms than in conventional British terms.

Yet the American analogy should not be over-drawn – the EC is after all a European creature, devised by politicians from countries which were accustomed to coalition politics as normal and the pursuit of compromise as the means to build a kind of consensus for policy changes. In the continental countries which shaped the EC it is commonplace for parties to cooperate and to involve the 'social partners' (i.e. employers and organised labour) in decision-making. It is also usual for the lines between the politician and the senior official to be blurred – officials can, for example, stand for elected office or admit to political affiliations. In these respects Britain is atypical by West European standards and thus the British find themselves operating in unfamiliar political structures.

The main decision-making body of the EC is the Council of Ministers, which brings together the relevant ministers from the member states to negotiate *and* legislate. Membership depends on the subject under discussion – agricultural ministers for agricultural policy and likewise for trade, financial issues, employment, environment and so on. In addition foreign ministers meet at least once a month both to deal with their own regular fields of responsibility and to coordinate the work of the EC as a whole. For those issues of high political significance or controversy heads of government meet in the European Council, usually twice a year. Meetings of ministers are prepared by committees of officials, very much as Cabinet and its committees are serviced in Britain by interdepartmental committees. Member governments take it in turns to preside over Council sessions with the help of the Council Secretariat in Brussels.

The agenda of the Council is largely shaped by the European Commission, the main executive arm of the EC. It has a triple role: to initiate legislative proposals, to mediate among member states in pursuit of the collective interest and to carry out policies once agreed. The Commission is led by the college of Commissioners (two from the larger and one from each of the smaller member states) who are independent political figures in their own right. They supervise the 'services' of the Commission, the European officials (some 12,000 in total) who do the detailed policy preparation and implementation, always working in consultation with member governments, interest groups and independent experts.

The lifeblood of the EC is the legislation that it produces on the basis of treaty provisions. Regulations are directly binding in the national law of the member states; directives set a framework and objectives that each member state has to implement in national law: decisions are selectively binding; and all other forms of agreement are advisory.[1] National courts are required to follow the precepts of EC law and to take cases under it. However, they are subject to the jurisprudence of the European Court of Justice (ECJ), which operates on lines very similar to the Supreme Court in the USA. It develops EC jurisprudence by case law, by interpreting for national courts, by acting as the court of appeal on cases from national courts and as the court in which cases are brought by one or other EC institution or member government. It is widely recognised that the ECJ has had a powerful impact on the development and reinforcement of the EC. Here again is an institutional feature that differs from the British system.

The links to the wider political arena are provided by the European Parliament (EP) and the Economic and Social Committee (ESC). The EP is composed of members elected by EC voters as their representatives on party lines, although from a smaller electoral base than is usual in most national elections. It is not a legislature in the direct sense, but has an advisory role in most areas of legislation and a power of amendment for certain kinds of legislation – notably financial and market unification measures. The EP also has considerable powers over EC expenditure, which it exercises, and the right to dismiss the Commission, which it never has. The organisation of the EP is in party, not national, groups and the main work is done in committees not plenary session. The ESC is composed of interest group representatives and it has an advisory role in legislation. In practice, however, other channels of less stylised influence are used by interest groups to express their preferences. In addition the EC has acquired a variety of less institutionalised mechanisms for regular policy consultations with the social partners.

The policy functions of the EC are broad. The founding treaties endowed the EC with a number of very specific powers for the coal, steel and nuclear industries, for the customs union, eventual internal market and competition policy and for agriculture, transport and overseas development policies. The EEC Treaty also set out a wide range of broad economic and social objectives, sometimes accompanied by detailed provisions on issues as diverse as equal pay and government subsidies to industry. Over the years the policy gamut has steadily expanded and a substantial independent budget has developed, financed by direct revenue-raising. In addition the member states have agreed most significantly to establish a European Monetary System (EMS) and to engage in regular foreign policy consultations through European Political Cooperation (EPC). The net result is that the EC directly or indirectly has a foot in the door of most major areas of governmental activity.

The policy process of the EC rests on bargaining within and between EC institutions and between the EC and national levels. Again the Washington analogy is helpful. The EC has a competitive and often long-drawn-out way of reaching decisions. Support for new policies has to be mobilised from a variety of elites and agencies and cross-cutting coalitions have to be constructed. There is always a tussle between the central EC institutions and the member states, and policies as they operate on the ground do not always coincide with the legislators' intentions. The power structure is diffuse and allows multiple opportunities for the exercise of influence and counter-influence. The processes of building coalitions and log-rolling prevail rather than clear-cut ideological competition, which tends to be buried under the technical detail of legislative proposals.

Thus the EC has political characteristics that not only differ in kind from the embedded habits of British politics, but sharply contrast with the radical style of Mrs Thatcher's government. It is simply not possible to disregard other opinions or to adopt policies in a pure version. On the other hand, the EC process is open and transparent, leaving the British, through the various EC institutions and its informal channels, plenty of opportunity for exercising influence on the outcomes of negotiation.

British Adaptation to Europe in the Mid-1980s

Britain's profile as an EC member changed almost beyond recognition in the second half of the 1980s. Three sets of factors combined to make Britain a more 'normal' EC member. First, the steady accretion of experience has bred familiarity, respect and a willingness to exploit the new European arena. Those most ready to ride with this tide of involvement have been the leading elites – the discernible European *cadre* within the bureaucracy along with those ministers unavoidably immersed in day-to-day negotiations with EC partners (across the range from diplomacy to agriculture and customs and excise); the business and financial groups, whose direct concerns were routinely the subject of EC legislation and who believed their interests would be well served by EC policies; and much of the political and intellectual establishment.

Second, the agreements so vigorously pursued on the 'agro-budgetary' cluster of issues came to constitute a structural righting of the grievances which had for so long kept the British as heretics battling against the orthodoxy of an *acquis communautaire* that had failed to weave British interests into the basic deal struck between EC members. With these issues resolved (by 1984) British attention and energy could be turned to both the other subjects already on the table in Brussels and ideas about the potential future agenda.

Third, the changing ideological constellation in British politics began to find expression in European terms. Neo-liberalism in the Thatcherite version began to be articulated as a recipe for the European, and not just the British, economy, both by the government and by exponents of an even purer variant of economic liberalism. On the left, first many of the intellectuals and then the leadership of the

Labour Party and the trade unions started to look to Europe for vehicles to promote their alternative values.

To these domestic developments must be added the other catalyst of Europeanisation; in the early to mid-1980s the EC itself underwent a major transformation after the doldrums of the 1970s and the hard years of recession and retrenchment. The first decade following British accession had provided numerous reasons for containing and discounting the European dimension to British politics and policy. The policy repertoire of the EC seemed locked into the mind-set of the 1960s and the performance of EC institutions had been lacklustre. Just as the British debate began to emerge from its introspective preoccupations, so the EC changed gear to become an altogether more credible and pervasive frame of reference. Whether these shifts rested on mere coincidence of timing or were causally related is a matter of judgement, to which we shall return. Either way the scene was set for the European dimension to bite deeply into British politics.

The Sovereignty Issues

One further theme has to be sketched into the picture of Britain in Europe, namely sovereignty. On each of the various occasions that British membership of the EC had been mooted, a recurrent issue was the extent to which it was acceptable for British sovereignty to be eroded by the obligations of EC membership and the tentacles of EC legislation and jurisprudence. The absence of a written constitution for the UK always made it infinitely more difficult for the British than for other EC members to define precisely what the erosion of sovereignty would actually imply or to determine on what basis political authority might be reassigned to European institutions. The Germans, for example, in contrast had a Basic Law which gave clear status to international obligations and law and thus a framework for managing the consequences. In the British case a combination of constitutional imprecision and political argument ensured that the sovereignty issue remained a persistent source of controversy. Nor did the controversy die away, once British accession had been ratified or even after the 1975 referendum. On the contrary, periodically the issue has reemerged as a bone of continuing contention.

In the British debate sovereignty has been polymorphic. A primary focus has been the difficulty of reconciling the sovereignty of Westminster with permanent EC membership and binding EC law, of which a sub-theme has been whether parliament could exercise any effective scrutiny over directly binding EC law or distant bargaining sessions in Brussels. Thus the precise formulation of the European Communities' Act of 1972 was a challenge at the time and has subsequently been the object of calls for amendment.

Secondly, the role of government of the UK in relation to its component territories, both regional and national, has been a source of debate, with the powers of the establishment in London always at pains to ensure that the complications of Brussels would not lead to undue interference in the domestic political order of the UK. This was explicitly an issue during the devolution debate of the 1970s. It has surfaced again with the reemergence of the Scottish National Party as a serious political force, operating since 1988 under the slogan 'Scotland free in 93'.

Thirdly, concerns about sovereignty have frequently provided the rhetorical cover for those in the UK who feared the erosion of British, or more correctly English, identity under the weight of continental, and for some catholic, influences. Seventeen years of British membership have not overcome these doubts, or at least a powerful emotional appeal for the retention of an independent British identity remains one of the features which distinguishes British political debate on Europe from that in most other member states, especially vocally articulated by Margaret Thatcher.

The European Community Changes Gear

The early years of British membership of the EC were troubled by the uneasy combination of continuing British hesitations, the conflict over the Community budget and the oil-price-induced recession. British politics were unsettled and the British economy was under severe strain. However, by the mid-1980s the picture was transformed. After a series of interim remedies the Fontainebleau agreement of 1984 had at last produced the outline of a structural solution to the budget problem. The British government, full of confidence in the radical economic experiments of Thatcherism, was keen to propagate the prescription of market and deregulatory solutions for the rest of Europe. The European Community as a whole was fretting over the unfortunate consequences of a policy repertoire too heavily distorted by its agricultural commitments and rigidities. Moreover, the accession of Spain and Portugal risked producing total immobilism in the collective decision-making processes.

A European Agenda Defined in London

At this point the British government found itself in the unprecedented situation of being ahead of the Community game. It had been quicker than its partners to identify some of the underlying factors of change in the international economy and had at hand some tested antidotes for wider consumption. Though it would be wrong to credit the British with the entire responsibility for the change of gear in Brussels, it is beyond question that the British played a key role in refashioning the Community's agenda. Other factors also played important parts, notably the radical shift in the entrepreneurial climate across Western Europe and the dexterity of the Commission in developing new and well-targeted proposals. But by 1985 the Community as a whole had endorsed a programme to complete the internal market and to do so by liberalising measures rather than by the traditionally heavy-handed harmonisation. Nor was it a coincidence that the architect of the programme in the European Commission, Lord Cockfield, had been both one of Thatcher's ministers and a senior businessman. After years of efforts to adjust the *acquis communautaire* to incorporate British interests the British were beginning to set the terms of the forward debate and were regarded with a new respect by their partners.

However, the leaders of the EC had made brave pronouncements before about their ambitions to take a great leap forward, only for their plans to founder on the rocks of resistance in one or other member state. A thoroughly unified market with a deregulatory regime would not be in everyone's interest or to everyone's taste and the less prosperous and more socialist Mediterranean members were obviously potential sources of dissent.

This prospect alarmed Thatcher enough for her to propose at a European Council meeting in Dublin in late 1984 that perhaps there should be a 'gentlemen's [*sic*] agreement' not to use national vetos on legislation under Article 100 (EEC) to remove barriers to trade. The other heads of government at the time were too bemused to hear the astounding offer which they curtly refused. However, in terms of British politics it was indeed a remarkable move. Thatcher's objective was to prevent backsliding by the Greeks and others in the face of sound but tough market prescriptions; but in so doing she admitted that the views of the sensible *majority* should be seen to prevail.

The Institutional Price of Policy Victory

It was a year before the Community adopted new decision rules and then only after second and third thoughts by the British. For some time the issue of constitutional reform had been on the Brussels table, prompted partly by Iberian enlargement and partly by the Draft Treaty on European Union, adopted in February 1984 by the European Parliament. The British government was deeply reluctant to engage in constitutional amendments, partly because of their less formal approach to institutional issues and partly out of dislike for expanding the powers of the Community's institutions *vis-à-vis* the member states. The British government recognised that powers once conceded to the EC would be difficult to claw back. In only one area – European Political Cooperation – was the British government keen to codify the pre-existing loose arrangements for foreign policy consultations. Yet at the Milan European Council in June 1985 Thatcher found herself outvoted and caught up in an Intergovernmental Conference.

Over the preceding six months a special group – the Dooge Committee – had been wrestling with the issues, and Malcolm

Rifkind, the British member and Minister of State in the Foreign and Commonwealth Office, had found himself in an uncomfortable minority of 'footnote' countries expressing reservations against substantive constitutional changes. The discussion began to turn to the possibility of a 'two-tier' Community, in which some members, by implication including the UK, would be in the second and less influential tier. As the issues moved up the political hierarchy Thatcher found herself in a real quandary: she was genuinely keen on the internal market, determined not to be held to ransom by the Mediterraneans and quite clear that Britain should sit at the top table; but she did not like at all the notion of a new Treaty, least of all one which talked of European Union, both emotively reminiscent of the Act of Union with Scotland and dangerously over-weaning as to the future of the EC.

The arguments were finely balanced; yet in December 1985 Thatcher signed the Single European Act (SEA), which extended majority voting in the Council of Ministers, gave the European Parliament more say in legislation, endorsed the single market, extended the policy competences of the EC, embraced the concept of economic and social 'cohesion' (and thus inter-regional transfers) and codified EPC. At the time the government judged that the key point was to entrench 'correct' economic doctrines in EC legislation and that the new institutional mechanisms would make a marginal difference to the division of powers between the EC and the member states.

European Policies and British Interests

The EC gave itself seven and a half years to complete the internal market with some 280 pieces of legislation to set in place, ranging from the 'macro' issues of capital liberalisation, tax approximation and dismantled border controls to the minutiae of toy safety, food standards and customs documentation. By any test of decision-making effectiveness the EC has made remarkable progress with this legislative mountain, agreeing over half of the measures by mid-1989 and using majority votes in the Council of Ministers as a matter of routine.

The result, of course, is that collective European legislation penetrates widely and deeply into the economic life of the member states, so much so that Jacques Delors, President of the Commission, went so far as to claim in June 1988 that some 80 per cent of economic and social legislation in EC countries would be determined by reference to EC law. It should, however, be noted that most of this legislation is in the form of EC directives, i.e. framework law which has then to be translated into domestic law, and that the implementation of the ensuing commitments rests on a partnership between the Commission in Brussels and national agencies, under the surveillance of the national courts and ultimately the European Court of Justice.

How then have the British fared in promoting their interests? Here we must begin to distinguish different segments of British opinion. From the government's point of view good progress has been made with some of the key items which it advocated – the single most important by far being the agreement to liberalise capital movements throughout the EC by mid-1990, in line with British practice since 1979. In addition the real shift into the service sectors, both transport and financial, coincides with British policy objectives and stands to benefit relatively efficient and competitive British firms. Broadly the government has worked hard to ensure that there is as strong a deregulatory thrust as possible to the character of legislation in all of these fields and, by and large, this has coincided with the expressed preferences of British firms.

Indeed the Department of Trade and Industry has since March 1988 mounted an ambitious and costly awareness and advertising campaign to encourage all British firms to be prepared to take advantage of the new market opportunities as they open up. The DTI has worked closely with both the CBI and chosen business leaders more informally. The strong support of the business and financial elites in the UK for continued EC activism in determining legislation has become remarkable.

Conservative Reservations

There are, however, limits to the government's enthusiasm for the 1992 programme; 'market opening', their preferred term for deregulation in the EC, is their key aim, but market homogenisation is not, especially where it would make incursions into sensitive areas of domestic policy. Two issue areas stand out as sources of conflict for the government – tax approximation and border dismantling. On tax, the Commission initially proposed the alignment of tax rates for value added tax and excise duties, the second of which was widely considered premature, while VAT seemed a more plausible candidate for some form of agreement.

The British government consistently argued that the approximation of VAT was unnecessary and unacceptable, resting their case on a mixture of economic and political arguments. According to the Treasury the 'market approach' could be applied just as well to VAT as to capital flows; with open tax borders, a technically feasible proposition, companies and individuals could exercise choice as to where to pay which level of tax for the goods they purchased. There is indeed a respectable economic logic in this case. However, the more serious objection from the government was that the alignment of VAT rates would interfere with domestic tax autonomy, both objectionable in principle and awkward in practice given their electoral commitment not to tamper with the zero VAT rate on food and a few other basic items.

The second sensitive policy issue concerns the reference in the SEA to the creation of an 'area without internal frontiers' by dismantling border controls on people as well as goods. The subject is difficult for the EC as a whole, but the British have been more explicit than most about the extent of the difficulties and the special concerns of a country with mainly sea frontiers. British preoccupations cover the gamut from terrorism and drugs to rabies. Five EC members are pressing ahead under the Schengen agreement to dismantle borders in 1990, thus again raising the suggestion of the British in a second and slower tier.

These two issues should not be over-exaggerated in that neither is vital for the establishment of an effective single market for economic purposes. However, British resistance has been widely interpreted on the continent as disaffection and at home as evidence of an over-ambitious Community.

The EC agenda spreads considerably further than the

single market as such. Even to achieve its core economic objectives, many have argued, requires a reformulation of competition policy and company law, a serious investment in European R&D and further strengthening of monetary cooperation beyond the European Monetary System (EMS). The EC is also a political construction and, at a minimum, political support has to be sustained for the 1992 programme. The Commission and most other member governments have joined in agreeing that the social partners must be engaged in the process. Proposals have begun to come on stream for the development of a social dimension and the honouring of the SEA commitment to cohesion.

On all of these issues the British debate has become highly differentiated. The Conservative government found itself at odds with much of the rest of the EC on most of these issues (the differences on competition policy being largely over some of the details). British negotiators argued that neither the social nor the monetary dimensions were necessary corollaries of the 1992 process, and that in any case the EC proposals were misconceived. However, these were not monolithic British opinions, as was revealed by the emergence of a debate among different political and economic groups, each with competing definitions of British interests and contending ideological positions.

Monetary Dilemmas and British Policy

The running debate about economic and monetary debate is an apt example. Margaret Thatcher remained resolutely opposed to full British membership of EMS, though the Bank of England and the Treasury have in practice frequently shadowed the Deutschmark and the EMS basket of currencies. Nigel Lawson, as Chancellor of the Exchequer, and Sir Geoffrey Howe, as Foreign Secretary until July 1989, along with much of the business and financial establishment, were arguing in mid-1989 that the time was already over-ripe for EMS to include sterling and were willing to enter into serious dialogue about successor arrangements. Here then was a case of a divided government and a split between government policy and one of its main constituencies of domestic support.

One immediate result of these divisions becoming evident at the Madrid European Council in June 1989 was that Thatcher was persuaded to moderate her hostility to EC plans for further discussion of a European Central Bank. A second result was that Sir Geoffrey Howe lost his post as Foreign Secretary. As the pound sterling began to falter in exchange markets in summer 1989 and the government's economic policy became exposed to increasing criticism at home, the interaction of EC and British levels of politics became acutely visible.

The Social Dimension and Party Attitudes

The debate on the social dimension illustrates a different strand in the changing configuration of domestic politics in the UK. The Conservative government was united in resisting the calls for a European social charter or any further social legislation and had apparently the solid support of British business opinion. The insistence of both Thatcherite policy and business leaders' preferences on removing rigidities in the labour market and limiting obligations to employees has marked out the British from their continental equivalents, who by and large take a structured social dialogue as a given. Also the Conservatives tended to dub the social charter as an attempt to inculcate EC activities with socialist ideology, finding Jacques Delors, an active trade unionist by back-ground, an easy target. It should, however, be stressed that continental Christian democratic parties do not reach the same conclusion, but rather accept the case for social partnership to go hand in hand with sound economic policies. In this gulf between Conservatives and Christian Democrats we can observe the absence of Europeanisation in the party politics of the right in Britain.

On the other hand the new interest of the British left, both the Labour Party and the trade unions, in the European dimension has produced real enthusiasm for the social dimension of the EC. The approach spearheaded by Jacques Delors and the European Commission held out to the British left some prospect of counteracting the harsher edges of market doctrines currently being pursued by Conservatives in the UK.

Thus an important European debate has begun to generate a

serious political debate within the UK and to act as a catalyst of rather rapid integration of the left into European politics.

Shifting External Policy Interests

As for the external agenda of the EC, British efforts became focused mainly on persuading their EC partners to take account of British ideas and concerns, rather than on presenting an alternative approach. This in itself marked a real shift away from the notion that Britain had to retain a sharply distinctive foreign policy profile. Though the rhetoric of a special British relationship with the US remained, it became increasingly difficult to find it being given substantive expression. Three areas of European policy emerged as areas of debate: the external impact of 1992; the continuing process of EPC; and the emergent debate on a collective West European defence identity.

On the first point the British government policy was firmly to identify British industrial interests with a liberal external trade stance for the EC, a view which coincides with much industrial and financial opinion, except inevitably those in industry who prefer the cushions of protection. Significantly the move of the left away from a defensive trade posture made this subject much less controversial than would have been the case even a few years ago.

Secondly, EPC has from the outset proved a much more comfortable framework for the British than they had expected and certainly at the level of professional diplomacy has become a rewarding area of European cooperation. This was most vividly exemplified by the firm European support of the British response to the Argentine invasion of the Falklands. There were some differences between British policies and those of EC partners, for example on how the European and transatlantic dimensions should be reconciled or on the challenge of change in the USSR and Eastern Europe. Interestingly, however, the British debate on such issues was increasingly cast in terms of what should be the appropriate European policy rather than the defence of a peculiarly British policy.

The same observation can be made on the parameters of

British defence policy. For the Conservative government the question became less and less about a distinctive British policy and more and more what European stance should be adopted and through which of the various frameworks for European cooperation, including for these purposes NATO as a quasi-European framework. It was not quite so clear how Labour Party policy would develop, given the cross-cutting pressures within the party on the issue of unilateralism versus multilateralism and the desire of the leadership to edge towards a policy that would be in tune with similar parties on the continent.

The Implications for British Policy

Cumulatively over the years since accession membership of the EC has thus wrought a real transformation in the parameters, conduct and substance of British policy in many fields. The examples cited above give some solid evidence in several important areas, although they represent only the tip of a much larger iceberg. Almost any field of policy with international ramifications automatically includes a European dimension and EC activities then begin to shape the parameters of British policy, as well as to allow scope for British influence to be brought to bear on EC partners. One particularly telling case arises from the issues of environmental protection, to which Margaret Thatcher became a late convert. The development of EC environmental legislation was long resisted by the Conservative government until both the force of the evidence and the emergence of the Green vote in the European elections of 1989 began to impel ministers to look for ways of playing European politics for domestic political advantage.

How well has the British policy process responded to this transformation? The short answer is that as familiarity and expertise have been acquired, so the policy process has adapted relatively effectively. At the core of the central government system, with a sophisticated cabinet coordination machinery as the pivot, Whitehall performs well by the standards of its peers elsewhere in the EC. There has, too, been a generational shift such that those now in mid-career by and large regard the European dimension as a 'normal' element in their day-to-day work. Problems of course arise as Europeanisation spreads to previously untouched areas, where not surprisingly traditional practices have to give way to new frames of reference and different legislation.

The 1992 programme bites deeply into domestic policy and is thus a particular challenge to the adaptiveness of the policy process. The market philosophy of the Conservative government does not necessarily lead all parts of central government to welcome the abandonment of idiosyncratic British regulation to collective European rules, as some of the British reservations on, for instance, European competition and public procurement policies reveal. Sometimes, inconveniently, EC legislation seriously limits British policy options, as the government has found in its struggle to reconcile its obligations under EC law on water quality standards with its desire to privatise the water authorities. Europeanisation is thus not cost-free either in terms of policy substance or the green profile that the government sought to acquire.

Nor is the EC of relevance only to central government. There has been a spectacular growth in European policy units in local authorities and many other agencies, both public and private. Police authorities, for example, began to become deeply engaged in considering the impact of the EC on their work. All major interest groups have established European offices of varying but increasing degrees of sophistication. At both the policy formulation and the policy implementation phases it is possible to identify intense interactions not just between these groups and the British government but also with counterparts in other European countries. Continental comparisons are better understood and more often used in discussions within the UK. In the business and financial communities 1992 in particular has focused attention on the need for a better understanding of the rest of Europe and it is becoming increasingly difficult to identify either British companies or British industrial interests in a parochial way.

The Impact on British Politics

As was argued above, for a long time the British political response to the EC was frozen in a time-warp of nostalgia for an era in which British politics was self-contained. The policy process was much quicker to adapt to the new environment, perforce as substantive issues arose on which British inputs, both public and private, had to be fed into the collective framework of making and implementing EC legislation. This discontinuity between politics and policy carried costs. Much of policy was conducted well outside the normal framework of political debate; parliamentary attention was spasmodic and often targeted on shadows not substance, with the notable exception of the revival of the House of Lords as a forum for expert analysis of current EC proposals; and interest group engagement was concentrated in the business sectors, leaving substantial segments of British society 'under-represented'.

The technocratic bias which resulted meant that pragmatism almost inevitably set the tone of the management of day-to-day policy, interspersed with the heavy and often acrimonious rhetoric that resulted from a British debate that was somewhat insular on the overall character of European integration. The disjunction between British and continental party politics on the centre and right kept the British adrift from many of the informal arenas in which transnational debate on longer-term goals took place. Like General de Gaulle in the 1960s, Margaret Thatcher in the late 1980s fell back on nationalism as her protective armoury, with the ready support of those who shared her neo-liberal or insular preferences. By mid-1989 a curiously old-fashioned version of sovereignty pervaded government rhetoric, as ministers sought to hold back what they saw as the creeping onslaught of EC powers, tinged with unacceptably socialist colours in some policy areas. The stage was set for a lively period of adversarial exchanges on monetary policy and the social dimension, with a few skirmishes almost at random on other policy issues as they surfaced in Brussels negotiations.

On the other hand, in the wider process of British politics in recent years European issues have become embedded in the 'normal' political process. All the political parties are now locked into the debate about current and projected European policies and even about what kind of European Community they would prefer. Opinion poll evidence has begun to suggest, for example, that British citizens, including Labour voters for the first time, are relatively relaxed about transfers of sovereignty from the national to the EC level. Moreover, there is, too, emerging a debate within parties on the same questions, notably within the Conservative Party, where positions are beginning to be staked out on the succession to Thatcher partly by reference to the European dimension. Interestingly, too, the Labour Party is beginning to look to the European arena as a means of pursuing ideological and policy preferences that may be helped by proposals emanating from elsewhere in the EC.

Above and beyond the emergent political debate on substantive policy issues and ideological preferences remains the overarching question of the permeability of British state power, faced with the encroachment of European legislation and the possible scenarios for the political development of the EC. Ratification of the SEA committed the UK to a considerable extension of EC action and to the acceptance that from time to time British governments would have to live with being out-voted. British constitutional conventions and political habits still fit somewhat uneasily into the EC pattern. The reflexes of single party government, especially the Thatcherite variant, are at odds with the coalition behaviour of the EC as a whole, where gradual consensus-building is crucial. Nor does the centralisation of state power within the UK mix well with the fluid allocation of policy competences to the range of European, national and sub-national that comes more easily to most other EC members. It is thus not surprising that the sovereignty issue remains prominent in the debate between the UK and other EC members, since it symbolises a point of continuing difference. We can therefore expect to see a persisting tension between on the one hand, the practical imperatives of policy interests and party advantage and, on the other, the seductive reflex of British particularism.

Note

1. The terms used here hold for the European Economic Community (EEC) and Euratom. The terms under the European Coal and Steel Community (ECSC) treaty differ, with decisions being the strong form of direct legislation.

PART TWO
Public Policy

8

Economic Policy

PAUL WHITELEY

Many observers attributed the Thatcher government's third election victory in 1987 to widespread public perception that the government had solved the so-called 'British disease' of low growth and high inflation, and ushered in a new era of enterprise culture, transforming Britain into a model for other countries to follow. The Conservative government was said to have pursued a consistent well-thought-out strategy which aimed to slay the dragon of inflation, regenerate enterprise, defeat entrenched special interest groups such as trade unions, promote profits and investment, and generally infuse the economy with a commitment to the market as the supreme arbiter of economic performance.

The most succinct summary statement of Conservative economic strategy was given by Nigel Lawson in his City of London Mais lecture in June 1984. He argued that post-war economic policy had been wrong in trying to use microeconomic policies such as incomes policy to restrain inflation, and macroeconomic policy to stimulate growth. Instead the priorities of economic policy should be the exact reverse. Macroeconomic policy (especially financial policy) should be used to control inflation. And the supply-side incentives for growth should come from privatisation, industrial relations reforms, tax cuts and the general promotion of free markets.

To evaluate the success of these policies, especially in the light of developments since 1987, this chapter will look at three topics: the general characteristics of economic policy-making by government; the evolution of Conservative macro-economic policies in terms of their policy objectives and implementation; and the impact on the economy of various microeconomic policies.

The Characteristics of Economic Policy-Making

There are enormous difficulties facing decision-makers who seek to make fundamental changes in any area of policy-making (Pressman and Wildavsky, 1973; Wildavsky, 1980; Rose, 1980). Objectives in policy-making are often ill-defined or in conflict with each other; there is often no well-defined theory to explain how goals can be achieved; decision-makers face great uncertainties and frequently a pervasive shortage of information and feedback about their own performance; there are often no suitable policy instruments which can be used to attain objectives; and when many actors are involved, there are fundamental problems of collective action to deal with, which can produce irrational outcomes.

One of the most interesting features of macroeconomic policy-making after 1979 was that for a time many of these problems did not appear to apply. The Thatcher government accepted neo-classical economic theories which emphasise the importance of market solutions to macroeconomic problems. It had a well-defined theoretical analysis of how the economy worked, and an apparently efficient policy instrument, the market, for steering it in a new direction. Objectives were clear-cut, with the control on inflation the prime macroeconomic aim, and deregulation the main microeconomic aim. There was little goal conflict, since maintaining full employment was dropped as a policy objective.

Secondly, shortage of information was not a problem, since up-to-date measures of economic performance and of the policy instruments used to influence it are available. Thirdly, by handing large areas of microeconomic policy-making over to the market the Government could disclaim responsibility for what happened in many areas of the economy. In macroeconomic policy the Government continued to accept responsibility for the rate of inflation, but since the key to inflation was control of the money supply, policy could be entrusted to a small group of officials in the Treasury and the Bank of England. There was no need to negotiate with powerful producer groups. Despite these advantages Conservative economic strategy has undergone a number of radical changes in the last decade. In part these reflect problems in the making of economic policy. Firstly, there are major disagreements among economists about how the economy works. The monetarist strategy was attacked from the beginning by a number of economists (Kaldor, 1982; Goodhart, 1984) both on theoretical and empirical grounds. There is currently little agreement among macroeconomists about the structure of the economy (Fair, 1984), and though the neo-classical paradigm remains dominant in microeconomic theory it has been strongly challenged by several leading economists and is in considerable disarray (Balogh, 1982; Thurow, 1983; Wiles and North, 1984). With such a confusing variety of different opinions and advice, policy-makers find it harder to know if they are pursuing the right strategy.

Secondly, in an increasingly interdependent world the openness of the British economy makes it more difficult to operate an independent economic policy. Some writers have complained of a deflationary bias in the operation of international financial institutions such as the World Bank and the International Monetary Fund (IMF) (Browning, 1983). If it is impossible to operate a policy running counter to the opinions of international financial markets, national governments may well end up accepting this deflationary bias.

Current debates in the British government over the issue of joining the European Monetary System highlight this problem. Some argue that the loss of control of a policy instrument, the exchange rate, makes a decision to join the EMS unwise; others say that international interdependence makes it impossible to run an independent exchange rate policy in any case, and membership of the EMS brings security by creating stable expectations, and generates support from EC governments for sustaining a stable currency.

Thirdly, the key policy instrument in the monetarist strategy, the money supply, has been sending confusing and contradictory messages during the 1980s. There are a variety of different measures of the money supply, distinguished from one another by the types of credit included in their definition (Bain, 1982). A broad measure of money like M3, which contains a number of measures of short-term credit, has behaved very differently from a narrow measure like M0, which consists purely of cash. The government has switched between different measures at different points of time, and has been unable to find an adequate policy instrument with which to implement its policy goals.

Experience in the 1980s shows that there is no stable and predictable relationship between the supply of money and inflation which is consistent with monetarist theories. The essence of monetarism is the proposition that the money supply causally determines the behaviour of the money economy, but has no long-term influence on the real economy (Laidler, 1981). Increases in the money supply will cause increases in nominal income (national income measured in money terms) after an uncertain and variable lag. But this will not influence real income, which is income measured after taking account of inflation. The theory assumes that real growth is determined by institutional and technological forces unrelated to the money supply.

For monetarists, monetary policy has to ensure that the money supply expands fast enough to finance real growth, but not so fast that it stimulates spending above the 'natural' rate of growth of the economy, since this increases inflation (Friedman, 1968). At the core of the theory is the assumption of a stable relationship between the money supply and nominal income, the so-called quantity theory of money. But the evidence suggests that this does not appear to hold (see Hendry and Ericsson, 1983).

Fourthly, deregulation has had unanticipated consequences, particularly in the financial sector. It has produced a situation where the Chancellor has only one rather blunt and indiscriminate policy instrument, interest rates, for controlling the demand for credit. The current lack of direct controls on credit of the type common in other West European countries, helped fuel an explosion in private credit after the election of 1987, which added to inflationary pressures. Between 1987 and 1989 interest rates doubled but still did not restrain this credit expansion in line with the Chancellor's expectations. The rise in interest rates threatens to increase the Balance of Payments deficit, and stimulate inflation in the run-up to the next general election. By relying on potentially misleading theories and inadequate policy instruments the Thatcher 'experiment' has made many of the long-term structural problems of the economy considerably worse. Ultimately conventional fiscal and monetary policy are limited in what they can achieve, and the key requirement of economic success remains supply-side policies which promote growth and productivity. In the crucial areas of promoting manufacturing investment, improving the infrastructure and developing human capital, Conservative economic policies have not helped to promote long-term sustainable growth.

Macroeconomic Policy, 1979–89

Macroeconomic policies during the Thatcher years can be divided into four distinct phases. Firstly, there was a period of early or 'hubristic' monetarism up to 1982, which faithfully tried to follow Friedmanite prescriptions, with very damaging consequences for the real economy. Secondly, there was a period of pragmatic monetarism up to 1985, during which the primary focus of attention was the exchange rate rather than the money supply. This was followed by a period of 'reverse' monetarism in which the original policy was not merely abandoned but reversed, largely in order to stimulate the economy for electoral purposes. Finally, there has been a post-election period, which has produced severe withdrawal symptoms from the excesses of the pre-election boom. Thus, far from there being a well-defined economic strategy during the Thatcher years there have been inconsistent policies which have often ignored the underlying problems of deindustrialisation.

Early Monetarism

The first phase of policy was the attempt to apply a monetarist strategy to bring down inflation. Monetarist theory played a key role in the rise of Thatcherism in the Conservative party, and in the early years of the Conservative administration. The theory had come to the fore in the economics profession and among financial journalists in the 1970s because it provided a theoretical explanation of 'stagflation' or the combination of inflation and stagnation which dogged the economies of many western nations in those years. The Keynesian orthodoxy, which to varying degrees had previously dominated post-war economic policy-making, was discredited principally because it could not explain stagflation.

Monetarism embraces fixed rules of monetary management and eschews counter-cyclical policies which argue that monetary policy should be relaxed in time of recession and tightened in time of boom. In Britain an emphasis on monetary targeting first arose during the sterling crisis of 1976, when the Labour government was obliged to call in the International Monetary Fund (IMF) for a loan. The IMF imposed the condition that the government accept monetary targets as part of the loan package.

The newly elected Thatcher government went considerably further than its predecessor in embracing monetary targets. This was demonstrated by the publication of the Medium Term Financial Strategy (MTFS) in 1980 (HMSO, 1980), which set out target growth ranges for the money supply up to 1984. The strategy envisaged a planned growth of M3, a broad measure of the money supply, of between 7 per cent and 11 per cent in the financial year 1980–1, culminating in a planned growth of between 4 per cent and 8 per cent in 1983–4. This was the 'step-down' fixed rule of monetary policy advocated by Friedman and others. The theory behind this is that decision-makers will change their expectations of future inflation once they become convinced that a government will stick rigidly to a declining rate of monetary growth, and this in turn will make it possible to reduce inflation at a lower cost in terms of rising unemployment.

Plans for the Public Sector Borrowing Requirement (PSBR) – the difference between government borrowing and spending – in the MTFS were even more ambitious than the monetary targets. The aim was to reduce the PSBR from 4.6 per cent of Gross Domestic Product in 1980–1 to 1.5 per cent by 1983–4.

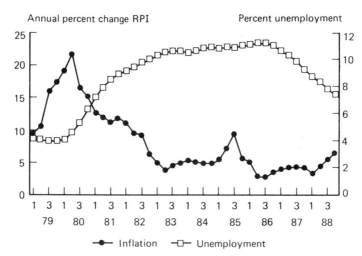

FIGURE 8.1   *Inflation and unemployment 1979–88*
Source: *Economic Trends* (various).

Keynesian orthodoxy would advocate a growth in the budget
deficit at a time when unemployment was over 6 per cent of
the workforce and rising, so this was a decisive break with past
practice.

The results of this policy can be seen in Figure 8.1 which
contains quarterly observations of the annual inflation and
unemployment rates between 1979 and 1988. The inflation
rate was rising at the time of the general election of 1979, and
it continued to rise rapidly reaching a rate of 22 per cent in the
second quarter of 1980. Some of the post-election inflation
reflected supply shocks associated with OPEC oil price rises,
and the effects of the breakdown of the Labour government's
incomes policies, but a major portion of it was the direct result
of policies pursued by the Conservatives such as the relaxation
of price and exchange controls and the raising of public-sector
prices. From the third quarter of 1980 onwards the inflation
rate began to decline, falling eventually to below 4 per cent
per annum just prior to the 1983 general election.

In his evidence to the House of Commons Select Committee
on the Treasury given in 1980, Friedman had predicted 'a
modest reduction in output and employment ... [as] a side

effect of reducing inflation to single figures by 1982' (House of Commons, 1980). The reality was very different as the figures on unemployment in Figure 8.1 demonstrate. Within eighteen months of the start of 1980, the first full year of the Conservative government, unemployment nearly doubled. In a respected analysis of economic policy during this period Buiter and Miller (1981) likened the collapse in employment and industrial production to the onset of the Great Depression of the 1920s.

At first sight it might appear that the squeeze during this period was a testament to the effectiveness of monetary policy in constraining inflation, even if the employment consequences of the policy were much worse than monetarists had anticipated. But this was not so, since up to the start of 1981 when inflation rates were falling, the then preferred indicator of the money supply, M3 was rising. Over the entire ten-year period the correlation between M3 and inflation was negative, which in direct contradiction to monetarist theory implies that increases in the money supply are associated with decreases in inflation.[1]

In fact monetary policy did play an important role in creating the recession of 1980 to 1982, but it did not operate by means of a reduction in the money supply, but rather via the exchange rate, a mechanism not widely understood at the time. In 1979 the newly elected Chancellor of the Exchequer attempted to control the money supply by rapidly driving up interest rates. The idea is that since interest rates are the price for borrowing money, increases in base rates tend to choke off the demand for credit, which is an important component of broad money. Thus manipulation of interest rates is the main mechanism for influencing the money supply.

However, high interest rates also attract foreign currency or 'hot money' to Britain seeking a higher rate of return than elsewhere, which in turn drives up the value of sterling. In 1980 this served to increase the value of sterling at a time when it was high anyway because of North Sea Oil. Minimum lending rate reached 17 per cent by the end of 1979, and sterling–dollar exchange rate increased by nearly 20 per cent between the first quarter of 1979 and the third quarter of 1980, thus increasing the price of exports and reducing the price of imports. Not surprisingly, this damaged exports and stimulated imports, and this in turn, in effect, imported unemployment. The other major consequences of the penal rates of interest was that they choked off industrial investment, creating rapid increases in unemployment in the capital goods and construction industries. At the same time high interest rates failed to reduce the money supply in line with theory. This was partly because firms were obliged to undertake 'distress' borrowing, that is they had to borrow regardless of the cost, just to stay in business.

A second factor in the recession were the large cuts in public sector investment designed to meet target reductions in public expenditure. General government capital formation, which includes investment by public corporations, fell by nearly 20 per cent during 1980. Such cuts are ultimately short-sighted because they reduce the efficiency of essential infrastructure, and investment in human capital which is necessary to sustain long-run growth. However, they are an attractive short-term option for a government seeking quick reductions in public expenditure.

A third factor discussed by Buiter and Miller (1981, 1983) was a fiscal squeeze. This took the form of trying to reduce the Public Sector Borrowing Requirement (PSBR) at a time when a decline in world trade resulting from the oil shock, together with the appreciation of the exchange rate, reduced economic activity. Normally during a recession the PSBR would automatically rise as tax revenues declined and public expenditure on items like unemployment benefit increased. This acts as an automatic stabiliser of the economy by helping to sustain aggregate demand. Reducing the PSBR in a recession will therefore tend to make the recession worse. The government, in the event, failed to reach its targets for reductions in the PSBR in its first Parliamentary term, though the PSBR did fall marginally during this period. The failure to achieve the planned reductions was in retrospect fortunate, since if the targets had been reached the recession would have done even more damage to the economy than actually occurred.

Overall the aim of the 'monetarist experiment' was to fight inflation and establish 'credibility' among bargainers that inflationary wage claims would not be underwritten by the

TABLE 8.1   *Indicators of the real economy 1979–88*

	Gross Domestic Product (1985 prices)	Gross investment in machinery (constant £bn)
1979	93.0	7.7
1980	90.8	6.9
1981	89.7	6.2
1982	91.3	6.1
1983	94.6	5.2
1984	96.6	6.2
1985	100.0	7.0
1986	103.2	6.9
1987	107.7	7.3
1988	111.9	8.1
	Output per person employed	UK competitiveness– relative export prices
1979	89.4	98.6
1980	87.4	109.1
1981	89.3	108.3
1982	93.1	102.5
1983	97.0	99.4
1984	98.0	97.2
1985	100.0	100.0
1986	102.3	96.4
1987	105.3	100.7
1988	106.0	108.9

Source: *Economic Trends*, annual supplement 1989.

government. But the cost in terms of the performance of the real economy was extremely high. Table 8.1 shows that Gross Domestic Product fell sharply in 1980 in comparison with the previous year, and on an annualised basis did not reach 1979 levels until 1983, four years into the Thatcher government. Gross Investment in machinery in constant prices, one of the prime determinants of long-run economic growth, did not attain 1979 levels until 1988. Output per person employed, the key measure of productivity, responded more rapidly and exceeded pre-Thatcher levels by 1982. But that reflected a rapid rise in unemployment (since it is the ratio of output to employment) as much as a rise in competitiveness, as the index of relative export prices in Table 8.1 shows. A rise in the export price index implies a loss of competitiveness, reflecting an increase in the value of the pound. This loss of overseas

TABLE 8.2 *Indicators of the money economy 1979–88*

	Balance of Payments (constant £bn)	Broad Money Supply (M3) (constant £bn)
1979	−0.49	6.5
1980	3.12	10.6
1981	6.94	9.3
1982	4.68	7.5
1983	3.84	9.5
1984	2.08	9.9
1985	3.36	15.0
1986	0.15	23.1
1987	−2.91	34.7
1988	−14.67	40.2
	PSBR (constant £bn)	Savings Ratio
1979	12.6	12.6
1980	11.8	13.8
1981	10.5	12.8
1982	4.9	11.8
1983	11.6	10.4
1984	10.3	10.5
1985	7.5	9.5
1986	2.4	7.3
1987	−1.5	5.4
1988	−11.6	1.1

Source: *Economic Trends*, annual supplement 1989.

competitiveness was severe, particularly in 1981, and the index did not return to 1979 levels until 1984, a full five years after the start of the Thatcher administration.

Table 8.2 focuses on additional indicators of the performance of the *money* economy during the Thatcher era. It can be seen that the Public Sector Borrowing Requirement declined very slowly until well into the second term of the Thatcher government, at which point it declined rapidly. This rapid decline after 1985 coincided with a rise of the balance of payments deficit, which is currently the most serious problem facing the British economy. A third trend, which is related to the rising balance of payments deficit, is the decline in the savings ratio, or the percentage of income which consumers save. By the end of our period the savings ratio was roughly one-third its value at the start of the period. This produced a veritable credit explosion in the run-up to the 1987 election which in turn produced a surge in imports, and balance of payments problems.

In retrospect, the newly elected administration pursued policies which in the first two or three years did great damage to productive industry and competitiveness. It did achieve a reduction in inflation, but a less restrictive policy could have done that, perhaps over a longer period, without so damaging the real economy that it was chronically unable to respond to the changes of policy which occurred after 1982.

In the words of David Smith, who wrote a lively journalistic account of this period, 'By the end of 1981, Britain's monetarist experiment appeared to have been an unmitigated disaster. Inflation, at nearly 12 per cent, was higher than when Mrs Thatcher took office, despite the worst recession since the 1930s' (Smith, 1987, p. 105). Attempts to substitute fixed rules of monetary management for discretionary rules had clearly failed; control of the money supply had proved much more intractable than the simple textbook models suggested.

Pragmatic Monetarism

The response of the government was to abandon fixed rules and adopt a discretionary policy which focused on several indicators of monetary policy, rather than just M3. This was signalled in the redrafted Medium Term Financial Strategy of March 1982 (HMSO, 1982). A key feature of the redrafted MTFS was that it revised the monetary targets upwards by a large margin in comparison with the 1980 version. Whereas the earlier version had set out a target range of 5–9 per cent for the growth of M3 in 1982/3, the revised version set a target of 8–12 per cent. In addition in the Financial and Budget Report (HMSO, 1982) the Treasury stated its willingness to adjust targets in the light of circumstances, a change of line in comparison with the earlier version where it had stated that 'there would be no question of departing from the money supply policy' (HMSO, 1980, p. 19).

Undoubtedly towards the end of 1981 the prospects for a possible election in 1983 began to loom large in ministerial minds, when the popularity of the government in the polls reached very low levels. Thus from the end of 1981 the government began to reduce interest rates, which has the effect of easing monetary policy. In the 1982 March budget it reduced national insurance payments by employers, and despite the increase in the money supply over the previous two years inflation rates began to fall. The abolition of hire purchase controls in July 1982 during a period of falling interest rates paved the way for a consumer boom in time for the 1983 election.

The arrival of pragmatism meant that the government now began to recognise the damaging effect of a soaring pound in 1980/1 and began to ease the pound down by means of the reduction in interest rates. The proliferation of monetary measures and the new pragmatism about targets meant that control of the exchange rate took over as the primary mechanism of monetary policy rather than control of the money supply. Econometric evidence suggests that the exchange rate has a bigger impact on economic activity in the UK than the domestic money supply (Fisher, 1987), and so this increasingly became the focus of concern. The index of UK competitiveness in Table 8.1 shows that from 1981 to the time of the election the prospects for UK exports improved as export prices fell.

In the post-election reshuffle Nigel Lawson, the architect of the Medium Term Financial Strategy, was appointed Chancellor to replace Geoffrey Howe, who moved to the Foreign Office. Initial feelings among financial commentators was that Lawson would move back in the direction of fixed rules and away from the pragmatism which had evolved under Geoffrey Howe. Immediately after his appointment he undertook a review of monetary policy, which resulted in the introduction of yet another target measure of the money supply, M0, the narrowest measure of all. This is a measure of the cash base, which up to that point had tracked inflation with more success than the ill-fated M3. However, Lawson never succeeded in getting outside commentators to take this seriously, since a measure of money which excludes all forms of credit is hardly reliable in a modern industrial society with a sophisticated credit system. Apart from a package of spending cuts designed to damp the electoral credit boom, the new Chancellor faced a relatively stable economic environment until 1984.

Shortly after his Mais speech to the City, a sterling crisis began to unfold, and the Chancellor reacted by raising interest rates to defend the value of the currency. The policy dilemma he faced was that a rapid devaluation of the currency would accelerate inflation by driving up the cost of imports, whereas a rapid rise in interest rates would undermine investment and ultimately slow economic growth. The essential aim of policy during this period was to keep interest rates as low as possible consistent with a slow devaluation of the currency. But this proved very difficult to achieve; when the pound dropped to $1.12 in January 1985 interest rates were raised by no less than 4.5 per cent in the space of a fortnight. In a television interview at the same time the Prime Minister was asked if she thought the economy had reached the natural rate of unemployment, and she dismissed this key concept of monetarist theory by saying that it was not a doctrine to which she subscribed. Thus monetarism as an ideological underpinning for Conservative economic strategy was dead. Its epitaph was written by Chancellor Lawson in his Mansion House speech of 17 October 1985 when he suspended the target range for M3, thus effectively abandoning the increasingly threadbare policy. At the time M3 was growing at an annual rate of 14 per cent, well above the designated target range of 5 to 9 per cent.

Overall, the arrival of pragmatism had enabled the Chancellor to avoid the mistakes of the first two years, and to begin to stimulate growth so that some of the lost ground of that earlier period could be recouped. But essentially the policy had returned to the traditional stop–go strategy, characteristic of economic policy for most of the post-war years; this involved the government stimulating the economy in order to produce growth and reduce unemployment, and following this with periodic deflations designed to deal with the balance of payments and currency problems which resulted from the initial stimulus (Pollard, 1982).

'Reverse' Monetarism

From early 1986 a third phase of policy ensued, as a direct consequence of the approaching election. Conditions were relatively favourable for creating a pre-election boom. The Chancellor had considerable political 'space' within which to operate. The balance of payments surplus derived from North Sea Oil revenues, though rapidly dwindling, made it possible to stimulate the economy without risking a run on the pound, a serious danger when the balance of payments is in deficit. Inflation was below 5 per cent, and estimates show that the inflation–unemployment tradeoff was relatively favourable at that time (Clarke and Whiteley, 1989). In March 1986 no less than 81 per cent of the electorate thought that unemployment was the most urgent problem facing the government (Gallup, 1986). Thus a stimulus to the economy designed to bring down unemployment which would have only a small impact on inflation in the short run was an attractive political option.

From the start of 1986 the government presided over a rapid rise in the money supply, which was well in excess of that required to support economic growth. According to one estimate the Chancellor reflated the money supply at a rate of 1.6 per cent per month faster than was warranted by the behaviour of the economy (Clarke and Whiteley, 1989). The effect of this can be seen in Table 8.2 where a large increase in M3 occurred in 1986 in comparison with earlier years. The change of policy was not confirmed to monetary policy. In November 1986 the previous targets for public spending were scrapped and some £7.5 billion was added to public spending programmes for the 1987/8 fiscal year.

The fiscal stimulus to the economy in the period prior to the election was defended in public on the grounds that the Public Sector Borrowing Requirement was at a historic low level in 1986 and actually went into surplus by 1987. However, another development which changed the traditional way of looking at fiscal policy was the huge rise in consumer debt, what might be termed the 'Private Sector Borrowing Requirement'. Deregulation of the financial sector together with ferocious competition among banks and retailers to promote high-cost credit, produced a rapid decline in the savings ratio. As the figures in Table 8.2 show by 1988 the ratio was only about a third its 1982 value. This change enormously benefited the Conservatives' election prospects since the consequences of this credit boom were not felt until after the election. In 1987 economic growth and consumer spending were accelerating, investment reached levels not seen since the late 1970s, unemployment though still very high began to decline, and the balance of payments deficit was not yet serious enough to influence the pound. In the light of this it was not surprising that the Conservatives won a third election victory.

Just as in the first period of Conservative incumbency economic management was mishandled in comparison with the period up to the 1987 election, the same is true for the post-election period. It may be that the hubris of the early 1980s returned to disguise the true consequences of its economic policies from the government. Instead of reining back the monetary and fiscal stimulus to the economy after the election, an essential tactic for operating a successful political business cycle, the government further stimulated an already overloaded economy. This was done in two ways. First the rapid and accelerating increase in the money supply continued, so that by 1988 M3 was increasing at an unprecedented rate of 40 per cent per annum. Monetary abstinence had given way to monetary promiscuity. Second, and more important, there was an enormous fiscal stimulus to the economy provided by the tax cuts of March 1988.

In the March budget the Chancellor reduced the basic rate of income tax to 25 per cent, and the maximum rate to 40 per cent. He raised all personal allowances by twice the rate of inflation, and reduced Corporation tax for small companies to 25 per cent, as well as making a number of other changes to inheritance and indirect taxation. This was the most radical change to personal taxation for a generation, and from the beginning it looked very risky, since it gave a very large stimulus to private consumption. Again a narrow focus on the PSBR allowed the government to rationalise the tax cuts as a necessary supply-side stimulus to reward initiative and enterprise. Ministers argued that the Exchequer could afford such cuts at a time when there was a surplus of revenues. However, this argument ignored the effect on aggregate demand of a big fiscal stimulus. A budget surplus is irrelevant if government policies stimulate aggregate demand in the private sector to the point where it produces a balance of payments deficit.

After Lawson

The results of the 1986–8 policy line can be seen in the burgeoning balance of payments deficit, which reached nearly £15 billion in 1988, and £20 billion in 1989. By early 1989 the pound was experiencing serious problems in the foreign exchange markets, and the Chancellor began a series of increases in interest rates which took them to crisis levels by the middle of the year. Ultimately the mishandling of the economy after the General Election led to the resignation of Nigel Lawson as Chancellor in October 1989, although the ostensible reason given for this was policy disagreements about the role of Sir Alan Walters, the Prime Minister's economic adviser (see Chapter 5).

He left the government, and his successor as Chancellor, John Major, on the horns of a dilemma. If the pound is allowed to devalue *vis-à-vis* the other major currencies, this stimulates inflation resulting from the higher costs of imported goods. On the other hand if the pound is not allowed to devalue it has to be defended by direct intervention to buy sterling in the foreign exchange markets, which is limited by the availability of foreign currency reserves. They can run out rapidly if the balance of payments deficit persists. One complication of the latter strategy is that as long as Britain remains outside the European Monetary System, central banks in the EC, particularly the German Central Bank, are unlikely to give significant help to the Bank of England in supporting the pound. This fact, of course, makes speculative pressures on the currency worse, since the pound is seen as being more vulnerable to speculative attack.

Macro-Effects of Microeconomic Policy, 1979–88

Microeconomic policy is much more diverse and complex than macroeconomic policy. At its broadest it takes in many aspects of government activity including taxation, industrial policy, education and training, regional policy, trade-union law and industrial relations, trade policy and even social security policy. Some of these policy areas are discussed more fully in other chapters of this book, and it is beyond the scope of the present chapter to examine all these issues in detail. But we can address an important question which has loomed large in the eyes of many commentators: has the microeconomy been fundamentally transformed in the last ten years, in comparison with the 1970s and earlier?

We begin this chapter by arguing that the key microeconomic objective of the Thatcher government in 1979 was to introduce and develop free market solutions to industrial problems. In policies like privatisation, deregulation and industrial relations, there have been roughly three phases of policy development. Initially, the government moved slowly and rather tentatively, and then early success made it accelerate the implementation of the policies after the 1983 election. However, a third phase is increasingly becoming apparent after the 1987 election victory, a phase of 'going too far'. This is evident, for example, in the policy of privatisation, which was initially popular, and in the case of companies like Jaguar and British Steel, very successful in promoting growth and profitability. However, the privatisation of basic utilities such as water and electricity has proved more of a political minefield, as consumers face rapid price increases from private companies eager to take advantage of the earning power of these natural monopolies.

The free-market thrust of government microeconomic policy has at least been consistent (see Chapters 13 and 15). Privatisation has transformed large parts of British industry to private sector ownership. The industrial relations legislation has been designed to curb the bargaining power of trade unions to make claims over wages and conditions of service. The creation of 'enterprise zones' is a distinctive free-market approach to regional policy, and is premised on the idea that deregulation and the removal of the burdens of local taxation will liberate enterprise and productivity. The big tax cuts of the 1988 budget were justified by the argument that taxation rates were too high in Britain, and inhibited growth and enterprise. In other words the proposition is that tax cuts make people work harder and more productively.

Finally, deregulation has taken a number of different forms. Immediately after the 1979 election the government abolished controls on the free movement of capital out of the UK. Financial deregulation in the City, which became known as the 'Big Bang' has swept away many former restrictions, such as the distinction between jobbers and brokers in the stock market. It has allowed the building societies to expand their activities beyond the traditional limits, to provide much of the same services as the banks. Similarly, part of the rhetoric behind the introduction of the poll tax is the argument that local businesses would be freed from the heavy burden of the rates which, it was alleged, restricted growth and created unemployment in many inner city areas (see Chapter 6).

In a well-known study published in 1980, a team of economists from the Brookings Institution, a prestigious 'think tank' based in Washington, carried out a detailed analysis of the British economy looking at taxation, productivity, trade unions and industrial relations, and the management of North Sea Oil. They concluded that 'Britain economic malaise stems largely from its productivity problem, whose origins lie deep in the social system' (Caves and Krause, 1980, p. 18). Part of the study involved comparing British economic growth with that in other advanced industrial countries over varying periods of time. It is interesting to bring their analysis of growth rates which ended in 1978 up to date, as a way of evaluating the Thatcher years in comparison with earlier periods, and other countries.

The first two columns of Table 8.3 are taken from Caves and Krause's original study, and column three updates them for the period 1980 to 1988. The first point to make about this table is that growth rates in the 1980s have been slower than rates in the 1960s and 1970s in all countries. In the earlier

TABLE 8.3   *Growth rates of OECD countries 1957–88*

Country	*1957–67*	*1967–78*	*1980–88*
Japan	10.4	7.2	3.4
All OECD	*4.8*	*3.8*	*2.0*
USA	4.1	3.0	1.9
West Germany	5.5	3.8	1.7
France	5.6	4.4	1.4
Britain	3.1	2.3	1.7

Sources: Caves and Krause (1980) p. 3. OECD Main Economic Indicators.

periods Britain had slower growth than the other OECD countries, particularly the United States, West Germany and Japan. This situation has continued throughout the Thatcher years, although the gap between growth rates has narrowed. Historically, Britain's growth rate has been much lower in the 1980s than it was in the 1960s and 1970s. In particular, growth rates in the period 1957 to 1967 were nearly twice as fast as in the period 1980 to 1988.

In the 1980s Britain did some modest catching-up with the growth rates of other countries, such as France and West Germany, though not relative to Japan and the United States. If Britain is doing better relative to some other countries during the Thatcher years, that might be described as an improvement, but it is hardly an economic miracle. However, such a conclusion would be premature, since as the balance of payments figures in Table 8.2 indicate, these growth rates are not sustainable in the long run. To claim economic success, and a break with 'stop–go' policies it is necessary to show that higher growth rates are sustainable over time. There have been periods when UK growth rates were high in relation to competitors, but unfortunately these were short-lived.

The 1989 annual statement on economic policy and public spending provided a very gloomy forecast of the growth prospects for the British economy in the early 1990s. The forecast is for a meagre 0.75 per cent in non-oil growth, rising unemployment, and a balance of payments deficit of £15 billion in 1990. As bad as the latter figure is, it would be much worse if the Treasury did not make very optimistic assumptions about the forecast growth of exports in relation to imports. In view of this there is the real prospect of a serious recession combined with a devaluation of the pound and a rise in imported inflation over the next few years.

The Thatcher Experiment – Conclusions and Prospects

A balanced assessment of the Thatcher years would look at the entire period of her government. By common consent disastrous mistakes were made in the first period when many productive jobs in manufacturing industry were destroyed by the excessive recession. Between 1982 and 1986 the govern-

ment did as well as any government could do in the circumstances in promoting growth without inflation. Real gains in
productivity and the profitability of industry were made in
these years, but in the entire Thatcher period investment was
significantly below rates achieved in the late 1970s.

Unfortunately as the 1987 election approached the revised
policy was abandoned as the government sought to stimulate
the economy for electoral purposes. Moreover, seduced by its
own rhetoric and apparent success the government continued
the reflationary policy long after the election was over. With
the prospects of low rates of economic growth and a burgeoning balance of payments deficit over the next few years, it is
very unlikely that the government can engineer another
pre-election boom in time for an election in 1991 or 1992.
With signs of a slow-down in the US economy adding to the
economic difficulties, and a return to two-party politics in
Britain, there is a real prospect that the Conservatives will be
defeated in the next general election, since the performance of
the economy plays a very important role in influencing voting
behaviour (Miller *et al.*, 1990).

Ultimately, economic policy should be judged by the long-
run performance of the real economy, that is of productivity
and growth. While progress has been made at stimulating
productivity, this has been achieved at great cost in terms of
unemployment, and taking the period as a whole, growth
rates have been lower than in the 1960s and 1970s. Moreover,
the inadequacy of investment in education and training can be
seen by the problems of skill shortages in key industries and
rising wage inflation at a time of high unemployment. A
related problem is the low levels of commercial research and
development expenditures in Britain in comparison with
competitor nations.

At the end of the day perhaps the most telling fact of the
Thatcher era is that for the first time in two centuries, Britain
has become a net importer of manufactured goods. Since
production volumes of North Sea oil have already peaked,
and are now on a declining trend, the supply-side weaknesses
of the British economy will become more and more apparent
as time goes on in terms of balance of payments and currency
problems. That is the most telling legacy of the 1980s.

Note

1. The correlation between the log of broad money M3 and the log of inflation is -0.38, using quarterly observations from the start of 1979 to the end of 1988. Monetarists, of course, argue that the money supply determines inflation after a 'long and variable lag', and so would argue that contemporaneous correlations say little about the relationship between money and inflation. However, there are no statistically significant positive correlations between inflation and broad or narrow money lagged up to three years, during this period. Empirical social scientists not committed to ideological dogma would accept that monetarism, at least in the form advocated by Friedman, is clearly invalidated by the evidence. See also Hendry and Ericsson (1983).

9

Social Policy

ALBERT WEALE

The United Kingdom is a welfare state. A fundamental assumption in a welfare state is that citizens should not be denied health care or education or suffer poverty merely because their labour market position deprives them of the earnings capacity to cover these basic needs. To secure these ends governments have developed public programmes and policies whose effect is to insure citizens against the income losses of sickness, injury and unemployment, to provide income in old age and to make available a range of services, most notably health care, on test of need rather than ability to pay. During the 1980s political ideologies and interests came increasingly to coalesce around attitudes to the welfare state and it has been clear since the 1987 election that the politics of the welfare state would be one of the central issues of Mrs Thatcher's third term of office.

It is often said that the period 1945 to 1974 was one of consensus about the welfare state which has been disrupted by policies of economic stringency in the wake of the OPEC oil embargo at the end of 1973 and the rise of New Right ideological movements. This is an oversimplification. Historically, few programmes or policies within the welfare state have escaped political controversy (Weale, 1986). The Conservative Party voted against the introduction of the National Health Service in 1946; trade-union resistance had to be overcome before family allowances (now child benefit) could be introduced in

1945; throughout the 1950s and 1960s there was controversy about the growth of state pension provision; and the existence and scope of means-tested benefits has remained a topic of partisan controversy between Labour and the Conservatives. Yet, despite these political differences and controversies during the heyday of the welfare state consensus, it can be argued that the last fifteen years have witnessed a crystallising of two opposing views on the welfare state, of which one is usually termed the 'residualist' position and the other the 'institutionalist' position (see Chapter 2).

According to the residualist view government programmes and policies in the fields of income maintenance, health and education should be aimed at those who otherwise could not afford to make provision for themselves. In this view, it is accepted that the state has a responsibility to protect the poorest and most vulnerable members of society, but it is further assumed that the vast majority of the population are capable of looking after themselves by means of private or occupational insurance provision, covering health and income deficiency. Moreover, private provision is regarded as superior on this view because it allows for greater choice and diversity and a more efficient matching of resources to preferences. On this view, the purpose of the welfare state is to enable people to do without it.

The institutionalist conception of the welfare state by contrast sees public programmes as a means of providing welfare to the whole of the population. In this conception, citizenship is the crucial principle (Marshall, 1950). For the institutionalist a national health service should be aimed at the vast bulk of the population, and income benefits should not be restricted merely to those who would otherwise be in poverty. The arguments supporting this conception are varied, but they essentially turn on the claim that membership of a political community bestows certain social rights upon citizens, and these rights should be enjoyed by all under conditions of equal status. If the residualist stresses choice and diversity, the institutionalist stresses solidarity and community. Health services should thus provide the best available for all citizens, not a two-tier service with only adequate provision for the poor. Child support should be universal, not simply part of an anti-poverty policy. Pensions should be primarily a matter for the state, and private provision is supplementary.

The contrast between residualist and institutionalist conceptions of the welfare state is an oversimplification, but is still useful. Although the contrast should not be identified with the ideological differences between the Labour Party and the Conservatives, or the Liberal Democrats and the SDP, it is true that those who favour the residualist version of the welfare state are concentrated in the Conservative Party, or those think-tanks – like the Institute for Economic Affairs, the Adam Smith Institute or the Centre for Policy Studies – that have as their prime objective a desire to influence the agenda of government in a market-oriented direction. Many of those favouring an institutionalist conception of welfare by contrast are clustered in the Labour Party, or its think-tanks, most notably the Fabian Society. Moreover, in public services, like the health service, the vast majority of professionals and other workers favour an institutionalist conception of the welfare state. Selectivity versus universalism in welfare benefits is therefore a fundamental point of controversy in UK politics.

Universal programmes are expensive in terms of public expenditure. Since 1979 one of the government's priorities in economic policy has been to reduce the share of the national income going in the form of public expenditure. One way of doing this is to move from universal to selective provision. But such a move, as we shall see, is both politically unpopular and technically difficult. Hence, a new point of controversy has arisen, particularly in relation to health services. This is the question of how far, within a universal system, it is possible to achieve greater efficiency in public programmes, and hence greater benefit for the population, without increases in public expenditure. The issue here has turned partly upon the state's responsibility to *provide* as well as *finance* welfare. The distinction between provision and finance is best illustrated in the case of health care. At present the National Health Service (NHS) has over 800,000 employees. This is because the UK state not only finances the consumption of health care for its citizens, but also owns the hospitals and employs the doctors, nurses and ancillary staff that work in them. There is no technical reason for organising comprehensive health care in this way. Countries like Canada have managed to supply high-quality health care on a universal basis by means of a national insurance system without nationalising the hospitals and their staff. So it is perfectly possible to embody an institutionalist version of the welfare state without being committed to the view that the state should be the primary provider.

The politics of social policy in the 1980s was dominated by the debates between residualist and institutionalist on the one hand, and advocates of splitting finance and provision and their opponents on the other. The terms of this twin debate are not always clear, and it is one of the tactics of political controversy often to obscure them. Yet, as always in politics, although people make their own history they do so only under constraints, in this case the constraint generated by the nature of welfare state programmes themselves and the penumbra of interests that surround them.

The Programmes

Table 9.1 summarises the main programmes that constitute the core of the welfare state, gives some indication of their scope and provides figures for the amount they consume in public expenditure. There are really three features of these programmes that condition the capacity of governments to change social policy and alter the character of the welfare state: their expense; their popularity; and the support they enjoy from service providers.

The figures for public expenditure show how expensive these programmes are. For the financial year 1988–9 the estimated planned total of public spending, before proceeds from privatisation, is £159,063m. Of this £76,081m was allocated to the health service and social security system alone. In other words, nearly 48 per cent of planned programme expenditure would be in these two areas of public policy alone. (By contrast defence spending was planned to absorb only £19,200m or 12 per cent of planned programme expenditure.) Moreover, the programmes are not only expensive, but they have a tendency to become relatively more expensive

TABLE 9.1   *Main components and cost of welfare programmes*

Income maintenance programmes:		*Scope*	*Cost, 1988/9 (£m)*
Pensions, including widows' benefits	To provide a basic income to those who have retired from work	Virtually universal, except for the earnings-related component, provided there is a National Insurance record	20,289
Unemployment benefit	To provide short-term (1-year) basic income to those out of work	Confined to those with relevant National Insurance record	1,143
Invalidity/industrial injury benefits	To provide basic income to those disabled or injured at work	Confined to those with relevant National Insurance record	4,131
Disability benefit	To provide income for the disabled and those looking after them	Those who fulfil disability conditions	2,178
Income support/ family credit	To supplement incomes of those with inadequate income, including those on above benefits	Means-tested benefits, and so depends upon scheme	8,236
Child benefit	To provide a payment towards the costs of · rearing children	Universal benefit for all families with children under 16 or at school	4,696
Housing benefit	To supplement the incomes of low-income householders	Means-tested benefit	3,817
		Total	45,173
Health care programmes:			
Hospital and community services	To provide hospital care for ill, and community care for selected groups	Free services for resident nationals, some charges for community care	16,791
Family practitioner services	To provide for general practitioners, dentists and opticians	GPs free except for some charges. Dentists/ opticians heavier charges	5,214
Central health	To provide for central research and services	(Not applicable)	810
		Total	22,715
		Grand total Health and Income Maintenance	£67,898m

Source: *The Government's Expenditure Plans 1989/90 to 1991/92* (London: HMSO) Cm 615, table 15, pp. 1–2, and CM 621, table 21.2.7, pp. 14–17.

over time. For the 1983–4 financial year the sum spent on health and personal social services was £18,310m, whereas five years later the same programme was planned to absorb £26,940m, a growth of 47 per cent after allowing for the effects of inflation. Similarly, the social security budget for the same period shows an increase of 35 per cent. Any government would need to give high political priority to such trends, and this is especially true for a party that is committed to controlling public expenditure as a central feature of its economic policy.

The second feature of the welfare programmes is that in general they are extremely popular (see Jowell and Witherspoon, 1985). This is particularly so with the NHS which has consistently scored high satisfaction ratings in opinion polls conducted over a number of years. More surprisingly, perhaps, particularly in view of its portrayal by the tabloid press, social security is generally highly regarded. There are significant variations in approval ratings between different parts of social security, with pensions and disability benefits receiving higher levels of approval than child benefit, unemployment benefit and supplementary benefit (now incomes support). Even so, there is significant support for the principle of public provision of social security, and dissent merely on the issue of whether it is sufficiently well policed to deter 'scroungers'. It is also worth bearing in mind that this support is high across all age groups, social classes and political preferences. To this extent, any government that is seeking to shift the balance of programmes towards a residualist pattern is likely to meet strong political opposition.

The third feature of welfare state programmes is that they create classes of people who have an interest in the continuation and development of those programmes. This is most clearly seen in the NHS where doctors, nurses and ancillary staff derive their incomes and sense of job fulfilment from being members of the service.

The welfare state therefore creates a series of producer interests whose income is dependent upon the continual functioning of its programmes. This is not to suggest that in a mechanistic way the welfare state creates a 'welfare bureaucracy' whose prime interest is to maintain its own economic position. It is to suggest, however, that the politics of welfare will reflect the way in which producer groups are organised, so it is not surprising to find that the terms and conditions under which people work in the public services is of fundamental importance.

The upshot of these three features is that any government that is anxious to reduce the scope of the state in people's lives

faces a number of constraints. Where the core areas of the
welfare state are concerned, there is likely to be widespread
public opposition, supported by the interests of those whose
income and sense of professional self-esteem derives from
working in the system. Moreover, the pressure of service
developments will be against reduction. Public expectations
about the amount of income they need when ill or old will rise,
as will their expectations about the standard of medical care
they will receive. Demographic change, in particular arising
from an elderly population, will put an automatic pressure on
expenditure. And new advances in medical technology will
put health budgets under pressure. Any government with
residualist aspirations, therefore, will find its freedom of
manoeuvre severely constrained. To hold public spending
constant, let alone reduce it, means restraining the expansion-
ist momentum of the programmes themselves. It also risks
political unpopularity with service providers and the general
public. What happens when a residualist political project
meets the forces for welfare state growth? To understand the
answer to this question, we shall find it useful to examine
some important processes of decision-making that have taken
place in the last few years, both in the field of income
maintenance and in the field of health care. This examination
will also help us understand how issues of finance and
provision become entangled with broader political issues.

The Politics of Income Maintenance

The basis of the present income maintenance system goes
back to the post-war reforms inspired by the Beveridge Report
of 1942 (Beveridge, 1942). The key to the Beveridge proposals
was a system of social security benefits paid to those who had
contributed to a National Insurance fund. Because these
benefits were supposed to resemble insurance, Beveridge
insisted that they should not be means-tested, but paid as of
right to those who were eligible on grounds of sickness,
industrial injury, unemployment or retirement. The important principle according to Beveridge was that everyone who
had contributed to the scheme should receive benefits that

were sufficient to avoid the stigma of poverty. He also recognised that there were some people who for various reasons would not meet the contribution conditions, and for these people he advocated a back-up means-tested scheme of social assistance that would provide income support in cases of need. Finally, since the insurance proposals were not aimed at households whose heads were in full-time work, Beveridge also advocated a system of universal family allowances, payment of which was intended to defray the costs of bringing up children.

The Beveridge principle of making a clear separation between contributory, non-means tested social insurance, and non-contributory, means-tested social assistance remains to this day, and the only substantial modification to the distinction came in the 1970s when a series of non-contributory disability benefits were introduced without a means test. However, the resemblance between the present structure of benefits and the terms of the Beveridge plan disguises the fact that there is a marked discrepancy between the way Beveridge intended his scheme to work and the way it has worked in practice since the war. Three points are worth making about this discrepancy.

In the first place, the Beveridge insurance benefits were never paid at a level to avoid poverty once housing costs were taken into account. The reason for this was that housing costs vary from area to area, and there was considerable Treasury resistance to paying the benefits at a level that would cover costs in the most expensive areas. Secondly, in the post-war period family allowances have never been paid at a high enough level to avoid a persistent problem of family poverty among low wage-earners.

Thirdly the growth of private insurance cover over and above the Beveridge minimum was haphazard and patchy. This was a particular problem in respect of pensions. Professional, clerical and the better-organised manual workers secured increasing occupational pension coverage during the post-war period through collective bargaining, but by the 1970s this still left about half the working population with poor or no additional coverage. The Conservatives legislated for compulsory occupational cover with a back-up state scheme in 1973, and the Labour Party altered this legislation in 1975 to strengthen the state scheme, known as the State Earnings Related Pension Scheme (SERPS). SERPS was intended to be the answer to poverty in old age among the less skilled and poorly organised.

When the Conservatives came to power in 1979, the system of social security they faced was as follows. The Beveridge system was in place, but not in the way intended. Many recipients of social insurance benefits, particularly the retired and the unemployed, still had to depend upon top-up social assistance benefits. Family poverty still existed because child benefits, the former family allowances, were low and Family Income Supplement introduced in the early 1970s was inadequate to cope with the problem. And new groups, particularly the disabled and lone parent families, were liable to be in poverty or receive inadequate income.

Despite the strong pressure to contain public expenditure, little was done to alter the structure of social security during the first Thatcher term. The earnings-related portion of unemployment benefit, created in 1966, was abolished and the rules on claiming benefit tightened. The uprating of benefits in line with prices or wages, whichever was the higher, was ended, and uprating in line with prices was introduced. Child benefits were not uprated in line with inflation. But the overall structure remained in place. The result was that expenditure continued to rise, particularly as unemployment increased in the wake of the depression induced by the second explosion in oil prices in 1979 and the deflationary budget of 1981. When the Conservatives came to power in 1979 social security absorbed a quarter of public spending; by 1983 it absorbed over one-third.

The 1985 Social Security Review

There was, moreover, a timebomb hidden in the system. In addition to the growing expenditure on social security, the pension arrangements of the 1975 legislation were building up substantial future claims. Shortly after the 1983 election, the government, with Norman Fowler as Secretary of State, instigated a review of social security with the aim of containing future expenditure growth. The review was notable for three things: it aimed at a comprehensive review of all benefits; it was conducted by ministers and their personal advisers; and it came to the conclusion that SERPS should be abolished, and replaced with a compulsory system of private or occupational cover. These conclusions were published in a government Green Paper at the beginning of 1985 (*Reform of Social Security*, 1985). They were intended to provide the basis for legislation in 1986 for a new benefit scheme to come into effect in 1988.

The manner in which the review was conducted between 1983 and 1985 was unusual. In government documents the review was trumpeted as the most comprehensive reform of social security since Beveridge. Under previous governments such an important process would have been undertaken by a royal commission or interdepartmental committee of enquiry, taking evidence from a wide range of witnesses and seeking to strike a balance of competing views. Under Thatcher the style of reform is more single-minded. The review was conducted by ministers with a few outside advisers and a small team of civil servants. There was some public consultation, but it was limited in scope and lasted only ten weeks (Adler, 1988, p. 168). It is clear that this process was not intended to determine broad objectives for the system of social security, but instead to decide upon the best means for reducing the state's involvement. The main way of achieving this was the proposal to abolish SERPS.

There had been a great deal of opposition to SERPS among those in the right-wing think-tanks who distrusted the state's involvement in superannuation. These views, combined with the rather daunting calculations of the Government Actuary about how much the scheme would cost by 2020, led the review team towards abolition. No doubt other expedients could have been proposed, for example altering the retirement age, but the closed nature of the review lent itself to an ideological predisposition towards abolition, and in favour of private and occupational provision compulsorily enforced. This lack of consultation probably meant that the government completely underestimated the strength of opposition to the proposed abolition. As well as the predictable opposition from the trade unions and the anti-poverty pressure groups, abolition was also opposed by the insurance industry and the CBI, neither of whom wanted the financial and administrative problems of dealing with the long-term pension arrangements of the less well-off and poor insurance risks. The only vocal support came from the free-marketeers at the Institute of Directors. Consequently, in the White Paper published eight months later, the government dropped the proposed abolition (DHSS, 1985).

The scale of this reversal should not be underestimated. In the Green Paper the government had predicted financial Armageddon if SERPS were not abolished. In the White Paper the political opposition led them to speak of the issue as though it were one of detail. To that extent there had been strong political support for an institutionalist version of the welfare state rather than a residualist notion. However, that is not the end of the story. Although SERPS was not abolished, important conditions were changed in the way in which it was to be operated. For example, pension entitlements were to be calculated on an average of lifetime earnings, not the twenty best years. This may seem a small, technical change. In fact, it has significant implications for those whose earnings fluctuate systematically, of whom the most important group are women who re-enter the labour market at relatively low earnings after taking time off from their careers to bring up children. By this apparently small rule change, the government has effected a substantial reduction in the pension benefits of women after the year 2000. This decision will be expensive, and therefore politically difficult, for any future government to reverse. This illustrates an important aspect of the politics of welfare: even when wholesale change cannot be effected for political reasons, it is still possible for determined governments to secure part of their objective by manipulation of the administrative and technical details of policy. For political opponents to scrutinize, let alone effectively oppose such changes is difficult precisely because the issues require considerable expertise, resources for which are absent outside of Whitehall.

The same principle was illustrated with the main body of the reforms that were carried through. The reforms were

implemented on the assumption that there would be no net cost
on the social security budget, so that if one group of claimants
gained, another group had to lose. The device that was hit upon
to help achieve this balance was to merge the varying scale-rates
for different benefits, by which entitlement was to be assessed,
into one scale, with 'premiums' being offered on top of the
scale-rates for different categories of household.

In rejigging these scale-rates and the associated conditions
of eligibility, it was inevitable that some claimant groups
would have to lose if others were to gain. One main group
of losers has been the unemployed, particularly the teenage
unemployed. As we have seen in the public opinion poll
evidence, unemployment benefit is one part of the welfare
state that does not secure strong public support. Moreover,
the government since 1979 has had a strong ideological
commitment to making wage rates more flexible in the belief
that workers have been pricing themselves out of jobs. To this
end they have progressively tightened conditions for unemployment benefit so as to improve the relative attractiveness of
paid employment. Indeed, analysis shows that the unemployed have suffered a sharp deterioration in their standard of
living since 1979 (Atkinson, 1988). It was not surprising
therefore that 16- and 17-year-olds were debarred from income support under the new rules and required to register for
the Youth Training Scheme. One of the effects of this policy
has been to increase the number of homeless young people,
particularly in London, who, seeking to escape into independence (sometimes because they are badly treated at home),
discover that they are unable to obtain the social security
benefits that would enable them to find housing.

Effects of the Reform

Many of the effects of the reform will take time to emerge since
its implementation in 1988, but some were immediately
apparent. One was the change in the rules for housing benefit.
The review had imposed a capital ceiling of £6,000 on savings,
which made individuals ineligible for benefit if they had
savings in excess of that sum. Housing benefit is one of the
means-tested benefits taken up extensively by the 'respectable

poor'. When the scheme was introduced in April 1988, Conservative MPs suddenly found themselves deluged with letters from constituents who found the new capital rule had debarred them from further benefits. The government quickly acted to increase the capital limit. The incident illustrates another important feature of the politics of social security, namely the fact that the timescale of policy is a matter of years rather than months. The reforms had been put in train by Norman Fowler as Secretary of State in 1986. It was his hapless successor, John Moore, already struggling with a crisis in the NHS, who had to deal with the problems arising from their implementation. Fowler had eaten the sour grapes; it was Moore's teeth that were set on edge.

The process of reform also illustrates a feature of UK public policy that is widespread across a number of policy sectors, namely the absence of openness and government accountability. A central feature of the reform is the amalgamation of the differing means-tested benefits into a single scale-rate. However, it should not be thought that there is any logical or principled basis to the way in which this scale-rate is constructed. It is not related explicitly, for example, to studies of household budgets or estimates of how much families need to spend in order to maintain an adequate standard of living. When independent analysts have tried to relate the scale-rates to estimates of how much was needed by a family to maintain an adequate standard of living, the scale-rates have been found to be deficient (Piachaud, 1979). The government refuses to reveal its view of the relationship between scale-rates and adequacy, arguing that any such judgement would be 'subjective'. Moreover machinery has been put in place to alter policy when aspiration is not matched by performance. Independent research suggests that many families will have lost out as a result of the reform, when the opposite result was intended (Bradshaw and Holmes, 1989). Without systematic monitoring of the implementation of the reform, it will be impossible to know whether the intended goals have been achieved, and it will be correspondingly more difficult for Parliament to call the government to account. Similar issues, but on a larger scale, arise in connection with reforms to the NHS, as we shall see in the next section.

The Politics of Health Care

All developed countries have some system for ensuring that their citizens have access to health care. The UK has a health care system in which the state both finances health care for citizens and manages its provision.

To understand the politics of the NHS, it is necessary to understand the processes by which public expenditure is allocated to health care. The Department of Health does not itself administer the NHS but allocates money to health authorities which have the chief operational responsibility for the service (see Chapter 6). The funds so allocated emerge from the annual public expenditure round in which the spending departments agree with the Treasury how much can be allocated to particular programmes, and are largely derived from general taxation. They are cash limited and health authorities are expected not to exceed their budgets. If they do so, they lose a corresponding amount in the subsequent year's allocation. The essence of the system is therefore a global budget from which a full range of services has to be supplied to a population in a health district (Weale, 1988, pp. 30–6).

In the early 1980s the government, in line with its residualist ambitions, commissioned a review of alternative sources of funding for the NHS to see whether it was possible to ease the tax costs by shifting to some form of insurance or greater private cover. After it became clear that cost escalation was likely to be much more serious under alternative sources of funding than under the system of general tax financing and global budgets, the thrust of government policy changed. The prime aim became the search for greater efficiency in the use of resources and greater cost effectiveness of treatment within the scope of publicly supplied health care. Since 1982 a series of measures have been introduced with the intention of improving health service efficiency. The assumption behind all of these measures was that it would be possible to secure gains in health care through greater efficiency and effectiveness than through simply adding more money to the service. The politics of health care since the mid-1980s has almost entirely been dominated by the issue of how far greater efficiency and effectiveness in the use of existing resources can substitute for the allocation of further resources.

NHS Expenditure

To understand these issues, it is necessary to understand a number of specific features of health care spending. The first, and most important, is that over 70 per cent of expenditure is on wages and salaries. This means that large cash increases in expenditure may result in only small improvements in service, since most of the money may simply add to the incomes of service providers. The second point is that productivity improvements in health are usually more difficult to achieve than in manufacturing, since there is less room in services than in manufacture for substituting machinery for labour. Consequently, if pay keeps up with increases in the manufacturing sector, productivity (and hence real increases in health care delivered) will lag behind. The effect of these two factors on the volume of resources going to the NHS is shown in Figure 9.1. The third point is that the system of global budgeting for health districts and hospitals means that any efficiency gains that are secured will often add to costs, not save them. If more patients are treated in a ward (an efficiency gain) the cost of peripherals (for example drugs and bed linen) will also increase. Since the extra patients do not bring any extra income to the unit with them, the relatively efficient units find that their costs are increased, not decreased. The House of Commons Select Committee on the Social Services has dubbed this the 'efficiency trap' (Social Services Committee, 1987–8, para. 24).

These features combined explain the apparent paradox that by 1987 the government could claim to have been spending more in real terms on health care, and yet wards and hospitals were being closed. As Figure 9.1 shows, there is a considerable difference between money increases and real increases in expenditure. The health authorities were trying to balance their books within cash limits and subject to the above pressures, whilst trying to improve services in response to an ageing population, improvements in medical techniques and rising expectations among members of the population.

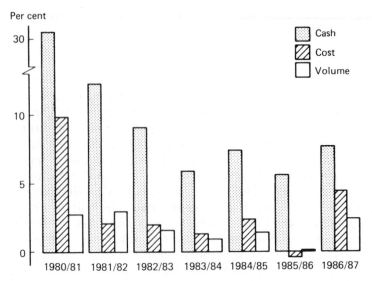

FIGURE 9.1   *Growth in NHS expenditure, 1980/81–1986/87 (per cent per year)*

Source: R. Robinson and Ken Judge, *Public Expenditure and the NHS: Trends and Prospects* (London: King's Fund Institute, 1987) p. 2.

Moreover, the government was always over-optimistic in the public statements about the amounts it was spending, as is seen in the example of the cost improvement programmes. Since 1984 health authorities were required to pursue cost improvement programmes to release cash for service developments. These programmes were intended not to affect the quality of the service, but to be genuine efficiency improvements. They included measures like the competitive tendering-out of cleaning services. The government in its public pronouncements always presented savings from cost improvement programmes as increases in spending. Not only was this misleading from the point of view of public perceptions, it almost certainly underestimated the extent to which many so-called cost improvements were achieved at the expense of medical services. The most recent research shows that there is often only a fine line between claimed cost improvements and actual cuts in services (King's Fund Institute, 1989). Moreover, doctors', nurses' and ancillary workers' pay is negotiated by central government, not by the health authorities. In an attempt to control the extra costs arising from pay awards, the government underfunded the pay awards in the cash-limited budgets given to health authorities, in effect leaving the health authorities the responsibility for picking up the short-fall.

By the end of 1987 the issue of NHS spending came to a head. Already it had been a topic of debate in the general election in June, and ward closures and delays in securing treatment brought the issue to the attention of the national press. But the crisis had been mounting as patients sought legal protection for their right to treatment, finance officers in health authorities wondered how they were to balance their books, and the Presidents of three of the Royal Colleges, the most prestigious professional bodies in medicine, publicly claimed that the health service was being underfunded.

The NHS Review

It is at this point that the role of political personality enters the story. The Secretary of State was the newly appointed John Moore, who at the Conservative Party conference in September had shown himself to be on the residualist wing of the party in a speech in which he attacked the welfare state as breeding a culture of dependency and praised the 'sheer exhilaration of personal achievement'. His own political achievements were limited, however. He had found it difficult to fend off the attacks on the government's spending record; and he coincidentally went down with pneumonia. On one occasion he collapsed at the end of a Cabinet meeting (Peter Jenkins, the *Independent*'s political columnist mischievously remarked about the event that it was not known whether Mrs Thatcher administered the kiss of life or not). The crisis continued into the new year, helped neither by a nurses' strike in Manchester nor by Edwina Currie, a junior minister, suggesting that those waiting for operations should buy them privately rather than take a second holiday. Eventually on 26 January 1988 Margaret Thatcher announced in an interview on *Panorama* that she was establishing a review of the NHS.

There are varying interpretations of the establishment of the review. Some see it simply as a muddled response to a crisis made worse by the fact that Thatcher's trusted lieutenant had failed to rout the opposition. Others see it as a piece of calculated strategy on the part of the Prime Minister by which the NHS was to be allowed to run into crisis making the residualist radical alternative of a much greater reliance on private care that much more attractive. Probably an interpretation mid-way between the two is correct. What was calculated was the policy of emphasising efficiency improvements rather than increased funding. Thatcher's political instincts enabled her to seize the opportunity of the crisis and institute a review that might provide a focus for radical reform. Residualising the NHS was now at least a possibility.

The NHS review worked in secret. Not even the membership of the review team was known. Well-informed sources suggest that Treasury ministers, in particular John Major the Chief Secretary, were closely involved, spending some six hours per week on the process. Rumours circulated that John Moore was making only a peripheral contribution, and these were confirmed when in July 1988 his department was split into two, with Kenneth Clarke taking responsibility for the new Department of Health and Moore keeping the Department of Social Security. Originally the review had been planned to be complete by mid-summer in order that its findings could be announced at the Conservative Party conference in September. That Clarke wanted to make his own impression on its conclusions is evidenced by the review findings not appearing until a White Paper in January 1989, some four months after the trailed earlier date.

When the findings of the review appeared in January 1989 they contained a mixture of radical and consensus measures (HM Government, 1989b). The two most radical proposals were to enable hospitals to manage their affairs independently of the health authorities of which they were a part, and to give general practitioners practice budgets which they could spend on purchasing care for their patients. Both of these proposals accept the point that there is a distinction between financing and provision, and seek to move hospitals away from global budgets towards income related to services performed. They aimed to create an 'internal market' in the NHS, making health authorities purchasers, rather than providers, of care.

Consensus proposals were contained in the recommendation that care should continue to be free at point of use and should be funded from general taxation. They were also contained in the proposal to instigate a system of professional audit to check the performance of medical practitioners. (It is a measure of the degree of change in the medical profession, largely connected with the turnover of generations, that this is now a consensus proposal.)

Opposition to NHS Reforms

Opposition to the White Paper proposals has taken one of two forms. On the one hand there are those who are sympathetic to their underlying intention, but are sceptical about the pace and scale of the reforms as proposed. They argue that there should be more caution and experimentation before the financial basis of the system is changed. They point, for example, to the fact that an internal market in the NHS will require medical procedures to be costed and the information and technology is not in place to do this. On the other hand, opposition to the proposals takes a more fundamental form from some quarters, most notably the general practitioners who are able to use their predominant influence in the British Medical Association to oppose the changes. One reason why GPs are opposed is connected with practice budgets. At present GP services are not cash limited, and they see practice budgets as a slippery slope down which general practice will slide to the tight financial regime of the hospital sector.

Famous battles have been fought in British politics between the BMA and health ministers, although usually it has involved Labour governments. Kenneth Clarke's tactic has been to be uncompromising in pushing the reforms through, even against his more moderate opponents. In an appearance before the Social Services Select Committee in March 1989 he was clearly determined to push ahead with the internal market even though he freely admitted that he had no idea of how much it would cost. Referring to the doctors' opposition on one occasion he said that reforms always led doctors to reach for their wallets, and recalled that Aneurin Bevan claimed only to have quietened the BMA's opposition to the

NHS by stuffing the doctors' mouths with silver. Probably this blunt style of political combat is due to Clarke's experience as Minister of Health in 1984 when he succeeded in securing a limited list for medicines prescribed by doctors against the organised opposition of the BMA. With the White Paper proposals, however, the issues are more emotive. General practitioners, already angered by the separate issue of the renegotiation of their own contracts under the existing system, can use their unique relationship with the British public to provide a forum for their grievances.

Despite this opposition, the government will be able to carry through reforms implementing some form of internal market in the NHS, since its parliamentary majority is large enough to secure the necessary legislation. The effects of the reforms both on the quality of health care and on the government's popularity are more difficult to predict. In theory an internal market should increase the responsiveness of the health care system to the needs of patients, by rewarding the more efficient hospitals and consultants. Logically, however, this implies that inefficient units will have to close. The effects of such closures, or even the threat of closure, upon patient care and political popularity is likely to lead any government to be cautious about following the principles of an internal market to their logical conclusion.

What do these events tell us about the character of health care politics in the UK? One difference between the case of social security and that of health lies in the structure of relevant interest groups. In the field of social security the main interest groups are the potential beneficiaries, most notably the pensioners, and the insurance companies and industry. Although social security officers have their own grievances and interests in pay and conditions, they do not act principally to defend the quality of the service they deliver. The same is not true in the field of health care. Doctors, nurses and ancillary workers can all be claiming to defend the NHS when defending their own terms and conditions. Some indeed can point to considerable personal sacrifices they have made for the service. Moreover, they enjoy high public esteem and this is a considerable advantage in terms of pressure group tactics.

An important aspect of both the health service and the

social security reviews is that the residualist challenge has been largely resisted. SERPS was not abolished and the principle of a health service free at point of delivery remains firmly entrenched. Welfare state spending is growing both absolutely and proportionately within the public expenditure total. This is not to say that institutionalised welfare provision has remained intact, especially in the field of social security. A government committed to an institutionalist version of welfare would have sought to increase child benefit and to reduce dependence upon means-tested benefits, whereas such dependence has increased since 1979. Residualism by attrition has led to the 'technical' changes that have adversely affected the unemployed and will worsen pension provision for women under SERPS. But the UK is still a long way from a social security system aimed exclusively at the poor. In this sense it is still a welfare state rather than a workhouse state.

With health care it is possible to say that not only has the residualist challenge been resisted but that a new set of debates has emerged in its place. Once the principle of public financing of health care for the mass of the population has been accepted, the issue is then how far it is possible to pursue the goals of greater efficiency, value for money and choice whilst at the same time preserving a system in which equality of access to a comprehensive range of high-quality services is still a feature. The experience of the 1980s suggests that there are genuine tensions between egalitarian comprehensiveness and efficiently run services that secure freedom of choice. It also suggests that British government lacks the machinery of decision-making to make the trade-off between equality, efficiency and freedom in a socially responsible and politically responsive manner. Moreover, there are other challenges that fall outside these traditional areas of public responsibility, but which, it can be argued, are equally important for the politics of welfare.

Other Dimensions of Welfare

So far we have looked at a limited, if important, range of public programmes that we have identified as the core of the

welfare state. However, citizenship rights and benefits are
affected in ways that fall outside the scope of these programmes.
In conclusion it will be useful to indicate three ways in which
welfare needs to be conceptualised outside these traditional
boundaries.

First, we need to enlarge our understanding of what has
been termed the 'fiscal division of welfare'. As well as spending directly, the state also spends by creating tax exemptions
that allow persons to keep a higher proportion of their
incomes than otherwise. The most conspicuous examples in
the present context are tax allowances on mortgage interest
payments and on occupational pension contributions. The
sums allowed under these exemptions are considerable, and in
the 1988–9 year the estimate was that the two together cost
the Exchequer £16,105m, virtually equivalent to the total cost
of the hospital and community health services. Since these tax
allowances are of greatest benefit to higher income earners,
they constitute the heartland of the middle-class welfare state,
and it is a striking commentary upon Margaret Thatcher's
political instincts that she is known personally to have vetoed
any possibility of ending mortgage interest tax relief. This is
partly a matter of misperception, since it has always proved
difficult to convince Thatcher that the effect is not to help the
hard-working suburban first-time buyers but instead to drive
up house prices (Brittan, 1988, p. 266). It is also partly an
honest recognition that this tax privilege is perceived by
owner occupiers as a considerable advantage. Ending these
privileges would enable a government to offer very substantial
cuts in the standard rate of income tax. There is at least the
possibility, then, that at some stage in the future the Conservatives will be outflanked by another party offering itself as *the*
tax-cutting alternative.

The second respect in which we need to expand our
understanding of the boundaries of welfare is in terms of the
future impact of developments within the European Community. So far the impact of the EC has been limited both in
social security and in terms of health care. Probably the
principal effect has been the ending of some aspects of sex
discrimination in the social security system. Important
though this is, it has not affected key areas like benefit levels or

coverage; it simply means that whatever benefits are paid they should not rest upon discriminatory principles of allocation. However, it is possible that, in the wake of the trade liberalisation associated with the '1992' single market programme, the European Community will become more important. One reason for this is that the West German system of welfare is occupationally based. This means that health insurance coverage, for example, is organised through trade and industry based associations rather than by the state. Since benefit levels are generous in international terms, German industry is anxious not to see its competitiveness eroded by lower benefit and welfare levels in other EC countries. This creates a powerful pressure to equalise social standards across the Community. At present the primary thrust of the 'social charter' is to create more workers' rights over such matters as participation in decision-making and information on company policy. But it is possible to envisage developments under which benefit levels and coverage in different countries become a matter for decision at European, rather than national, level (see Chapters 7 and 15).

The third respect in which social policies extend beyond traditional boundaries is illustrated by the case of health care. Although the NHS receives a great deal of political attention, there is much evidence to suggest that improvements in health care depend upon changes outside of the formal health service, for example in life-style, environmental quality and transport. British governments do not currently undertake assessments of the health effects of changes in policy, even though it is known that some policy developments will be better for health trends than others. Thus, tax harmonisation of the duty paid on alcohol and tobacco within the EC is likely to have considerable implications for consumption, and hence for long-term health. Similarly, a policy favouring private transport rather than public transport will carry health consequences, involving more accidents and higher levels of pollution. There is currently no machinery for integrating these considerations into the broad range of public policies. This is likely to change. There is now emerging a new public health movement, located among community physicians, some local authorities and epidemiological experts. One consequence of the creation of the NHS was a demise of the nineteenth-century machinery of public health. As new public health concerns grow, the UK is likely to see a revival of these nineteenth-century concerns. With its stress upon public responsibility for the health of the nation, the Victorian sanitary reformers were expressing one aspect of Victorian values. As the twenty-first century approaches, it is these Victorian values that are likely to receive greater emphasis than their nightwatchman state cousins that have been so prevalent in recent years.

10

Environmental Politics and Policy

HUGH WARD
WITH DAVID SAMWAYS AND TED BENTON

Since 1987, the environment has exploded onto the national and international agendas in a way which few would have predicted. The environment is now seen as a crucial electoral issue, ranking alongside the economy, defence and the health service. A token of its newfound political importance is the emphasis now placed upon it by Margaret Thatcher. Her Royal Society speech in September 1988 described the protection of the balance of nature as 'one of the challenges of the rest of the century', and she has gone on to attempt to build a green image, both domestically and internationally, especially over the issue of the depletion of the ozone layer.

In part, the increasing prominence of issues such as acid rain, global warming, depletion of the ozone layer, water pollution and residues of pesticides and other agrichemicals in food, was a result of an emerging scientific consensus. Besides this, environmental pressure groups, together with the media, have been extremely successful in raising awareness of the issues. As campaigns snowballed, increasing media coverage led to greater concern, higher membership figures, stronger cash flows for pressure groups and slicker campaigning. The Conservative government signalled its readiness to reassure the electorate over environmental issues when Thatcher replaced Nicholas Ridley as Secretary of State for the Environment in the cabinet reshuffle of July 1989 with Christopher Patten, who projected a less hardline image. Patten's 'Green Bill' published in December 1989 is probably the most important piece of environmental legislation of the 1980s, despite the fact that it lacks overall cohesion and fails to include any measure relating to global warming or the ozone layer.

Environmental Politics

The Arrival of the Greens

If the 'greening' of Thatcher was a surprising development, the success of the Green Party in the European Parliament elections in June 1989 was even more unexpected. The Greens polled 15 per cent of the vote nationally, and over 20 per cent in parts of the South East; making gains at the expense of the Conservative Party and pushing the Democrats into fourth place. After years in the political wilderness, the Greens seemed at last to be emulating the success of some continental Green parties.

Despite several changes of name and major internal reorganisations, often associated with bitter internal disputes, the Green Party failed electorally, at both national and local level, between 1973 and 1988. In seats contested in the 1984 and the 1987 general elections, the Greens typically polled between 1 and 2 per cent of the vote. Although they have held a handful of seats on local councils, they were also weak at this level. The contrast with continental Green Parties, especially the German Greens who passed the 5 per cent threshold for representation in the Bundestag in 1983 and polled 8.3 per cent of the vote in the 1987 federal elections, is striking. Given that there is little empirical evidence that the British are more materialistic or less environmentally concerned than continental voters, academic commentators invoked a number of specific factors to explain the 'withered British Greens': the first-past-the-post electoral system; the desire of many British environmental groups to enjoy insider status, which might be prejudiced by party political associations; the lack of a strong focus for local-level organisations, such as a major new nuclear programme; the ability of the Labour Party to incorporate fringe left groups, including those beginning to express environmental concerns (Rüdig and Lowe, 1986).

However one explains the Greens' performance in the Euro-elections in June 1989 (see Chapter 3) it represented a remarkable transformation of their electoral fortunes. Although the Greens' opinion poll ratings have fallen from about 8 per cent in mid-summer 1989 to 3–5 per cent by early 1990, there is evidence of an underlying shift in public attitudes, and this might suggest a continued electoral presence for the Greens. For instance, MORI found that between May and June 1989 the percentage of respondents rating the environment as the most, or another, important issue rose from 17 to 35 per cent (the related figures for July were 29 per cent for the NHS, 8 per cent for disarmament and 57 per cent for all economic issues). Over the same period the percentage of people willing to pay 5p-in-the-£ more for pesticide-free food increased from 26 per cent to 49 per cent, and the number of people willing to see a 1p-in-the-£ increase in income tax if this were spent on the environment went up from 34 to 49 per cent (MORI, 1989). Of course, these figures are a symptom of media attention to the environment and to the Greens. 'Green consumerism' is probably as much a function of the attempts of major food processors and supermarket chains to create a new profitable, niche market as it is of a consumer-led shift in production patterns. However, there are other indications of a longer-term trend: depending upon definitions, membership of environmental pressure groups may have grown by as much as 58 per cent since 1980, and extrapolating from the present membership figure of 4.8 million suggests that such groups may have a larger membership than the unions by the early 1990s (*Times*, 5 June 1989).

The Greens will continue to draw some electoral support from the growing environmental movement. However, despite some concentration in the south east, the Green Party lacks a strong geographical focus. The experience of better established continental Green parties suggests that, in the short to medium term, 10 per cent is a plausible upper limit to their share of the vote at national elections (Eckersley, 1989). Short of electoral reform, the Greens will continue to be penalised by the electoral system. Current debates within the party also suggest that they might be split by any attempt at electoral alliance. There are many varieties of environmentalism represented within the Green Party. The fundamentalist or 'dark green' wing of the party will have no truck with coalitions.

Environmentalism in Other Parties

The environment is a 'valence issue': in the abstract nobody is in favour of a bad environment. At the level of broad party positions and political symbolism, the logic of electoral competition, then, suggests a convergence of established parties on a 'greener' discourse. Many movements in this direction can already be discerned. Clearly, the images of the Labour and Conservative parties have strong associations with industrialism. Despite the ideological drag caused by these images, much of the electorate will probably be little affected by the environment as an issue, and easily reassured by 'symbolic' policy changes which do not touch the root causes of environmental problems. Although environmental activists have attempted to alter Labour Party policies in areas such as nuclear power and transport, they were often frustrated by the power of the unions with special interests in 'smokestack' industries. Constitutional changes within the Labour Party make it easier for such unions to be ignored in pursuit of middle-class green votes. However, the current commitment of the party to economic growth, however modified by environmental concerns, is too strong to allow for substantial policy innovation or an easy electoral alliance with the Greens (Jacobs, 1989).

How Environmental Policy is Made

In Britain, the most critical decisions and non-decisions with environmental consequences have typically been made within 'policy communities' (Rhodes, 1988) such as those discussed below in electricity, transport, agriculture, and water. Policy communities are defined by the relatively closed and stable membership, and by a shared set of underlying values and predispositions among their members which tend to damp down and constrain conflict within the community. Although there are some asymmetries of power, the pattern is one of mutual dependence for crucial resources (Rhodes, 1990). The structure of major production industries has often been a consequence of government funding, and governments have often granted effective representational monopoly to the industry's peak organisation, to the exclusion of other interests. Civil servants and ministers find it convenient to be able to negotiate with a single group about subsidies or regulation in these complex areas. But these corporatist features go along with the dependence of the state agency involved on the peak organisation.

This pattern also implies that while some environmental pressure groups were able to gain a degree of access to marginal decisions by limiting their demands, many others had no such insider status, even if they aspired to it. Similarly environmental regulatory agencies within government itself had to operate within the working assumptions of the policy community, relying on voluntary compliance and negotiations – a voluntarist approach which has been typical in Britain since the nineteenth century (Vogel, 1986).

In administrative terms, the dominance of separate policy communities has meant that responsibilities for environmental regulation have been scattered over many different central government departments, including the Department of Environment (DoE), the Ministry of Agriculture, Fisheries and Food (MAFF), the Department of Energy (DEn), the Department of Trade and Industry, the Department of Employment (DE), and the Department of Health and Social Services (DoH), plus the Scottish and Welsh Offices. Many quasi governmental agencies (QGAs) have key roles to play, as well as local authorities and quangos. These complex overlaps of responsibility have led in the past to major implementation problems.

Some specifically environmental quasi-governmental agencies have existed for a long time, such as the Nature Conservancy Council (NCC), the Countryside Commission

(CC), and the National Parks. But they have generally suffered from a chronic lack of resources to implement policy. The NCC has been particularly hard-pressed given its commitments under the Wildlife and Countryside Act of 1981. Moreover the proposal in the Green Bill to merge the operations of the NCC and CC in Scotland under the Scottish Office, with a similar merger in Wales under the Welsh Office, has received heavy criticism, although there is a certain logic to integrating concern for landscape and conservation when the two do not necessarily go hand-in-hand. Clearly, one motive for the proposed merger is the cutting of costs. Over and above that, critics have argued that the NCC is being punished for its open opposition to the Scottish Office, and also to Nicholas Ridley when he was minister at the DoE, over several key conservation issues: afforestation of the 'Flow Country' in Caithness; conflicts between peat digging and habitats of rare geese on Islay; conflicts between conservation and the extension of skiing facilities in the Cairngorms. Under the control of the Scottish Office, which has consistently favoured economic development over conservation, the merged Scottish NCC and CC might be gagged. The fear is that nationalism may prevent an effective response on issues affecting the whole of Britain, even if some coordination is achieved. The NCC and CC are also excluded from vital economic decisions about agriculture, while local authority planning legislation has never been applied to agricultural operations. And these agencies' own organisational ideologies focused upon the preservation of what is rare or outstanding in its class (for NCC, species of plants, insects or animals; and for CC, areas of natural beauty) rather than on protecting the 'everyday' countryside. All these features make effective environmental control measures difficult.

A wide variety of bodies, including the Labour Party, the parliamentary select committees on the environment, and the Natural Environment Research Council, have called for a US-style Environmental Protection Agency based within a new ministry, no longer encumbered by the local government and other non-environmental function of the DoE. As early as 1976, the Royal Commission on Environmental Pollution had called for greater institutional integration, on the grounds that the interconnectedness of environmental problems led to displacement effects, if aspects were treated in isolation. Such a major administrative change might greatly increase the degree of integration of environmental policy and give more weight to environmental considerations in Whitehall. However, there are countervailing forces at work too, including the growing realisation of the international nature of environmental problems and the lack of effective mechanisms for international coordination.

From 1987 onwards the government has taken some steps to rationalise the system and proposes to take this further in the 1990 Green Bill. Control of atmospheric emissions was previously spread across local authorities, the Health and Safety Executive (supervised by DE) and the Industrial and Air Pollution Inspectorate within the DoE, a body with a strong corporate identity and great autonomy. But in 1987 the new integrated HM's Inspectorate of Pollution located within the DoE was instituted, despite inter-departmental rivalries within Whitehall and lobbying by business pressure groups such as the National Farmers' Union (NFU) and Confederation of British Industry (CBI), which wished to maintain cosy 'insider' relations with existing regulatory agencies. Under the Green Bill, the Inspectorate will attempt to implement Integrated Pollutions Control, with major pollutors requiring an overall site licence based upon the working criterion of 'best practical environmental options'. This principle is a departure from 'best practical means' criteria previously applied to particular aspects of the problem in isolation (O'Riordan and Weale, 1989).

Despite the apparent victory won, many environmentalists have only given a qualified welcome to these changes. Firstly, the Inspectorate has been chronically underfunded and has had great difficulty in obtaining qualified staff; and this has undercut its capacity to implement legislation. Secondly, certain functions remain unintegrated: for instance, the Green Bill actually enhances local government powers in relation to atmospheric pollution. Critics argue that some well-established branches of the Inspectorate will still have a great deal of autonomy and are likely to maintain 'cosy' relationships with the regulated industry; moreover the 'best practical environmental option' criteria enshrines the British tradition of negotiation behind closed doors between pollutors and professionals. Measures in the 'Green Bill' to open pollution records, including those held by local authorities, the Pollution Inspectorate and the National Rivers Authority (NRA), to public scrutiny might seem to allow pressure groups to bring private prosecutions, thus opening up the regulatory process. Following pressure by industrialists only average emissions, rather than peak emissions, will be disclosed. This may disarm such attempted action (*New Scientist*, 16 December, 1989).

Since 1987, the system of separate policy communities has come under much more generalised stress, partly because of economic pressures, partly because of the government's changing policy technologies (for example giving up public ownership of industries and shifting to a regulatory stance), and partly because of growing domestic and international environmental concerns. We review recent changes in detail for four key areas – electricity, transport, agriculture and water – arguing at many points that despite appearances environmental policies have not changed all that much. The one large-scale change on nuclear power policy has been an unanticipated side-effect of electricity privatisation.

Energy and Electricity Privatisation

The key developments in the politics of energy and the environment since 1987 are associated with the government's plans to privatise the electricity industry. The conflicts between the government's economic policies and its avowed environmental goals and the distributional implications of the government's preferred solutions to the conflict, parallel those discussed below in relation to water privatisation. The electricity policy community in Britain has been underpinned by a commitment to nuclear power as a cheap and clean means of generating electricity, and by a 'supply side' orientation towards meeting electricity demand, which is seen as both environmentally growing and relatively immune to influence by the state (Coyne, 1978; Massey, 1988; Seward, 1990).

However, the nuclear power programme has been thrown into turmoil by the economic pressures of privatisation. In March 1987, after a protracted public inquiry, the government gave the go-ahead for the building of a PWR (pressurised water reactor) at Sizewell in Suffolk (O'Riordan *et al.*, 1988). The CEGB planned to build up to four more PWRs by the year 2000, the reactor at Hinkley Point in Somerset being next in line. In this it was hoped that economies of scale could be realised by building a sequence of similar reactors and Britain could enter the lucrative export market for PWRs and associated technologies. The logic of dividing the CEGB into two halves rested on the nuclear commitment. National Power, under the chairmanship of Lord Marshall, the former head of the UK Atomic Energy Authority, was to take over all nuclear power stations in England and Wales, its 70 per cent share of the generating market being justified in terms of the need to be able to absorb the financial risks of nuclear power. The twelve area electricity boards, to be privatised as distribution companies, were to take 20 per cent of their supplies from nuclear sources, a 4 percentage points increase over the current figure.

In the light of the comparatively poor economic record of nuclear power in Britain, as finally publicly disclosed by the CEGB at the Sizewell and Hinkley Point public inquiries, there was scepticism about the economic case for nuclear power – especially among institutional investors. One commonly accepted figure is that British nuclear electricity costs 40 per cent more than 'best practice' coal-produced power. The government's decision to legislate in favour of nuclear power was seen as a 'nuclear tax' on consumers and investors, despite the possibility of importing cheaper French nuclear generated power. In order to sugar the nuclear pill for investors, the government initially set aside £2.5 billion for waste disposal and decommissioning of existing plant, including the ageing first-generation Magnox reactors, the Advanced Gas Cooled Reactors and the Sizewell PWR; in last-minute changes to its programme it withdrew the Magnox reactors from the privatisation and promised to bear the full costs of waste disposal and decommissioning for existing plant. Despite this additional £4.5 billion package, investors remained

worried, especially in the light of major cost overruns at
Sizewell. Fearing the likely failure of the electricity privatisation programme the new Energy secretary, John Wakeham,
finally withdrew all nuclear power plants from the sell-off, in
November 1989. Plans to extend the nuclear programme were
scrapped, although the Sizewell PWR is to proceed.

This announcement threw the government's privatisation
plans into turmoil, setting back the schedule by at least six
months, and leading to the resignation of Lord Marshall. All
nuclear capacity is now to be vested in a new public corporation, Nuclear Electric. The rationale for dividing the CEGB's
assets between National Power and Power Generation has
been undercut, opening up the whole question of competition
in electricity generation. The government tries hard to paint
its nuclear commitment green, on the grounds that expanding
the nuclear programme would reduce emissions from coal
burning plants. It is more plausible that a combination of the
desire of the government to constrain the coal miners and the
institutional ideologies of the major actors in the policy
community were at work. Although such commitments have
shifted in a dramatic way, given overwhelming economic
pressures the traditional disinclination to take energy conservation seriously may still be in place.

Despite extensive criticism from the opposition, environmental pressure groups, and the energy conservation industry
(represented by the Association for the Conservation of Energy),
the government refused to write in specific targets on energy
conservation, renewables, and emission control into the Electricity Bill, merely inserting a weak clause that environmental
questions should be considered when planning new capacity.
The argument is that energy conservation – which has none of
the major environmental hazards associated with nuclear
power – is the least-cost and most technically feasible option
for reducing emissions. Conservation should be supplemented
by a much greater reliance upon renewable sources of energy,
such as wind, wave and tidal power, than that envisaged by
the CEGB. Also energy efficiency should be increased, the
development of combined heat and power plant encouraged
and greater emphasis placed upon technologies such as fluid-
ised bed coal burning, which promise to reduce emissions.

Consumers would need to be given financial help to conserve energy, as they have been by other privately owned electricity supply and distribution systems, notably in the US.

The government's argument has been that market forces will promote conservation: as real energy costs rise, conservation becomes economically rational, and it pays producers to invest in plant generating smaller emissions both to save on fuel bills and to avoid pollution taxes. Although the government tightened energy conservation requirements in building regulations in 1989, it has, at the same time, reduced its small energy conservation promotions budget by 15 per cent since 1987, and plans to halve it again by 1991. In the face of growing evidence that consumers are poorly informed about conservation, and lack the capital necessary to invest in making long-term savings, these cuts occasioned criticism by the all-party Select Committee on Energy and the National Audit Office.

To the extent to which the privatisation introduces market values, this may be inimical to energy conservation. Low-cost contracts offered to large industrial users by National Power and Power Generation may encourage a switch to electricity from more energy-efficient direct burning of fossil fuels. It may be difficult for the grid system (to be jointly owned by the distribution companies) to be run in either an energy-efficient or a cost-efficient manner when there are competing suppliers of power. Electricity prices to the consumer, already increased by 9 per cent in the year 1987–8 as privatisation loomed, may increase at well beyond the rate of inflation, hitting poorer consumers and reducing many families' ability to invest in conservation. Research and development, and projects regarded as high-risk by institutional investors (such as combined heat and power) are likely to go by the board. British Nuclear Fuels Ltd (BNFL) may be further encouraged to take on re-processing and storage of foreign nuclear waste.

Similarly, the old CEGB had plans to reduce emissions of oxides of nitrogen (NOx) from its coal-fired power plants by some 40 per cent over the next ten years by fitting low NOx burners. This commitment will, probably, be carried over by National Power and PowerGen. However, there are doubts about whether financial markets will fund the necessary investment. The costs of NOx 'scrubbing' have also meant that Britain has refused to join the 'club' of nations aiming to reduce sulphur dioxide emissions by 30 per cent by 1995, and to contemplate tougher EC standards, despite some planned investment in retro-fitting coal plant with scrubbers (McCormick, 1989: ch. 5). Recent delays and cost-overruns in fitting SO_2 scrubbers suggest that, in the absence of financial penalties, privatised producers will be loth to proceed with them, and that existing EC standards may not be met (Milne, 1989).

Christopher Patten, the new Secretary of State for the Environment, has expressed a strong interest in pollution taxes, including the fossil-fuel tax advocated by his new adviser, Professor David Pearce (Pearce *et al.*, 1989, pp. 162–7). If such a tax were introduced, electricity producers might reduce emissions. But this would depend on the existence of a strong regulatory regime able effectively to monitor pollution levels.

Transport

The Thatcher government's transport policy shows few signs of any 'green' awareness. On the contrary it has so far focused on exactly the sort of programme advocated by the roads lobby, the dominant ideological force within the transport policy community (Hamer, 1987). Although such a programme will generate opposition among key groups of Conservative voters, the active membership of such groups is electorally insignificant, while sympathisers can often be bought off by cosmetic measures. Because of downward pressure on public expenditure, road-building 'crowds out' investment in public transport. One affected group, the 'transport poor' in towns and the countryside, are unlikely to vote Tory, and their political influence has been minimal in the last decade. Although some commuters on grossly undercapitalised rail links in the South East may see a linkage between road-building and their worsening journeys to work, and worry about the environmental impact of the car, they tend to be relatively well-off and hence benefit from better roads for non-commuting, car-borne journeys.

Since 1987 car sales in Britain have grown very rapidly on the back of the expansion in consumer credit. From April 1988 to April 1989 alone, car sales grew by 15 per cent. At the same time, there has been a rapid growth in all forms of road traffic, including road freight. The deregulation of the buses, increased fares on public transport in general, and the continuing tax subsidies on company cars (albeit at a somewhat diminished level) have all contributed to this increase. In the face of intense pressure from the CBI, the AA, the RAC and the Road Haulage Association and faced with increased overcrowding of roads, especially those in the South East, the government announced in May 1989 an increase in public expenditure on road-building from £5 billion to £12 billion over the next ten years, along with measures to encourage private consortia to build new roads. In December 1989, a major new programme of road-building in London was considered. At the same time, the government again forced major price increases upon commuters by further reducing rail subsidies. It held back rail investment to improve overcrowding and poor reliability by imposing very stringent financial conditions on BR in the run-up to its possible privatisation.

The building of new roads is certain to generate the same sort of local opposition in the Tory heartlands as that caused by BR's plans to build a new high-speed rail link from Kings Cross to the Channel Tunnel. Initial plans for the link put forward in March 1989 led to intense local opposition in Tory-held constituencies, and backbench pressure on the government. In the end Thatcher 'persuaded' BR to make modified proposals to reduce the environmental impact of the link, at an additional cost of £500 million. So far the government has adamantly refused to fund these additional costs, leading BR to announce a twelve-month delay in bringing its private bill before Parliament. The hope is that BR can persuade corporate investors, made reluctant by cost overruns on the Channel Tunnel itself, to help fund the link. Many believe that, in the end, public money will be invested.

As the Channel Tunnel case suggests, the government is willing to modify its transport policies to reduce the more visible environmentally detrimental impacts of new projects.

However reassuring this is to voters, the consequences of the planned doubling of road traffic over the next twenty-five years will be serious, as pressure groups like Transport 2000 have suggested. Even though the British government reluctantly accepted EC regulations to fit catalytic converters to control emissions of nitrogen dioxide and unburnt hydrocarbons, and a great deal of publicity was got from associated measures to encourage the use of lead-free petrol, there remains the problem of emission of CO_2. The government's planned increases in road use would more than cancel out suggested savings in power station emissions of this greenhouse gas.

The Labour Party, too, is unwilling to grasp the electoral nettle of controlling private motoring, despite lip-service to an integrated transport policy. It, too, believes that major road-building is needed, despite growing evidence that this simply generates more traffic. Of course, expansion of public transport is also suggested; this, too, makes electoral sense given that Labour support is strong among public sector workers and the 'transport poor' dependent on public provision. While groups of voters who might swing to the left or to the right want increased access to high impact consumer goods such as the private car, the major parties cannot be expected to treat the causes of environmental harms associated with dominant transport policies.

Agriculture

The agricultural policy community, which has its foundations in the privileged access to decision-making given to the National Farmers' Union (NFU) in the 1947 Agriculture Act, has constituted one of the tightest corporatist relationships between the state and industry seen in Britain (Cox *et al.*, 1986; Smith, 1989). The farming lobby, now reinforced by food manufacturers and the pension funds, has fought alongside the MAFF in a largely successful attempt to maintain the boundaries of the agricultural policy community. As a result, despite increasing evidence of farm over-production in the UK, the government has been reluctant to transfer funds to conservation, preferring farm incomes to be maintained through alternative land uses and diversification of farming activities.

This insulation has been strengthened immensely by the key role of European Community decision-making in deciding agricultural policy (see Chapter 7). Although national governments have some discretion, there are major difficulties in reforming the EC's Common Agricultural Policy (CAP), and particularly the core orientation of policy towards boosting agricultural production. As far as Britain is concerned, the most notable area in which the CAP has been reformed in the 1980s is that of dairy production. The introductions of the co-responsibility levy and, later, milk quotas have, though, had mixed effects on the environment. Many smaller farmers have gone out of business and/or sold their quotas. Larger dairy herds are usually associated with more intensive practices. Although overall growth in expenditure under the CAP has been controlled since 1987, support levels still stimulate surpluses in some commodities, notably cereals. Cereal production in Britain has not been reduced, although there is less pressure to plough marginal land. Measures sponsored through, or tolerated under, the CAP which were apparently designed to support less intensive farming, such as the support available to upland farmers and in Environmentally Sensitive Areas, have been administered by MAFF in a conservative manner; while few farmers have taken up new subsidies to set aside land, despite the NFU's success in increasing the incentives to do so.

The subsidies available for agricultural intensification and conifer afforestation in the post-war period have led to a 'second agricultural revolution'. The predominant pre-war pattern of mixed farming was replaced by a more intense division of labour between arable and livestock farming, with greatly increased inputs of fuel, fertiliser and pesticides. By the 1960s growing production was patently leading to environmental problems, loss of amenity value, and breakdown of older rural communities. Although Britain's entry into the EC shifted the locus of some decision-making outside Whitehall, it made little difference in environmental terms: the CAP, too, was founded on the principle of increasing farmers'

incomes through intensification. Because quangos such as the
Nature Conservancy Council, the Countryside Commission
and the National Parks were largely excluded from key
decision-making over agriculture, they could only fight a
rearguard action.

Even well-established, relatively conservative pressure
groups were also marginalised (Lowe and Goyder, 1983,
ch. 4). One example of this was the Wildlife and Countryside
Act of 1981, which focused on rare species and on preserving
Sites of Special Scientific Interest, while enshrining the new
principle that farmers could be compensated for not damaging
such sites. The failure of the Wildlife and Countryside Act to
control damage of important sites has been one factor behind
the accelerating concern over the issue of countryside conservation and loss of faith in farmers as the guardians of the
countryside and its traditions (Lowe *et al.*, 1986, chs 6, 7). The
Conservative government with its crucial electoral constituency
in the shire counties, not least among the 'exurban' retired
and commuters who now dominate older rural communities
and small towns in the South East, is well aware of these
sentiments. At the same time, the inclination of the Prime
Minister and the Treasury has been to introduce market
forces and reduce subsidies. However, progress in these
directions has been slow, despite the electoral and financial
incentives.

Outside National Parks and Environmentally Sensitive
Areas the government has been reluctant to pay farmers to use
more sensitive management practices, although it has increased incentives to plant more broad-leafed trees (Blunden
and Curry, 1988, ch. 7). It has not supported research into
alternative farming practices and has, indeed, greatly reduced
expenditure on agricultural research and extension services
run by MAFF. In order to prop up farm incomes, which, the
NFU deemed, fell by an average of 25 per cent in 1988/9,
farmers have been encouraged to diversify into tourism,
processing their own products for sale on the farm, and niche
markets such as those for organic vegetable. Earlier initiatives
by Nicholas Ridley to free agricultural land for housing
development may be at an end, given Christopher Patten's
refusal in December 1989 to grant planning permission at

Foxley Wood on the Hampshire/Berkshire border, an important symbolic focus for groups like the Council for the Protection of Rural England who fear urban sprawl. Critics fear that if the government is not willing to support small, poorer farmers using relatively benign methods, falling incomes will lead them to further harm the countryside, especially that outside 'designated' areas.

At the start of the 1990s the agricultural policy community is undoubtedly under some strain. However, its power to protect established patterns is apparent in its ability to prevent extension of planning controls to agriculture (Shoard, 1987, chs 15, 16). Apart from measures to regulate the release of genetically engineered species, the only proposal in the Green Bill which will directly affect agriculture is the ban on stubble burning.

Water Pollution

The continued power of the agricultural and food industries is also evident in relation to the controversy over nitrate pollution, which has been central to the government's plans to privatise the water industry. Overall use of inorganic nitrate fertilisers has increased tenfold since 1945 and, particularly in cereal growing areas in the East of England, nitrates have seeped into acquifers and boreholes in increasing concentrations. Related problems include pollution of rivers by animal slurry from intensive livestock operations, phosphate runoff, and pesticide residues in drinking water, all of these being linked with agricultural intensification. Concern over agricultural pollution was joined to concern over sewage and industrial pollution of water courses in the run-up to the privatisation of the water industry.

Increasing levels of nitrates were first noticed in drinking water in the 1970s, particularly in the drought year of 1976. There is an established link with 'blue baby syndrome' – a failure of the oxygen metabolism of the newborn – and a possible link with stomach cancers, denied by the government and the industry. The issue of nitrates was, in effect, off the political agenda until 1987 and the run-up to privatisation. In

1980 a European Commission directive set a target date of 1985 for meeting agreed standards on nitrates. But the British government's response was for MAFF to negotiate a voluntary code of practice for farmers which did nothing to limit overall use of nitrates: however, if adhered to, it might limit runoff (Hill *et al.*, 1989).

Although several member states had already been taken to court over drinking-water standards, Nicholas Ridley at DoE after 1987 at first believed that no specific plans to meet EC targets would have to be written into the Water Bill, thus preserving the confidence of investors. However, after 1988 the European Commission took a very tough stance on this issue, demanding that specific investment plans for the water industry to meet current EC standards on nitrates, lead and other pollutants by 1993 should be made available before privatisation. Although some headway may be made by mixing water from different sources, and (with a timelag) by reducing use of fertilisers, investment in de-nitrification plants and sewage treatment will be required. Given the lack of capital investment consequent upon government policies towards nationalised industries in the 1980s, £2 billion may be needed in the early 1990s to meet existing EC limits and, perhaps, £20 billion may have to be invested over the next twenty years.

Given the profound unattractiveness of such investment to financial institutions and private investors, the Water Authorities lobbied hard for longer deadlines. However, pressure groups like Friends of the Earth and Greenpeace successfully used EC limits to paint the government as putting drinking-water standards at peril. It appeared that opposition in the Lords might see the Water Bill failing to pass through all its stages in the run-in to the 1989 summer recess. In the end the government wrote specific targets into the legislation and took residual powers to control nitrate use in designated sensitive areas near water supply sources. However, the government intends to rely, in the first instance, on voluntary compliance and subsidies for conversion of arable into grazing land, a clear violation of its own principle of 'the polluter pays'. The government avoided measures like a nitrate tax which would have a broad effect on the environment right across Britain and beyond the specific issue of drinking-water quality. The outcome clearly demonstrates the power of the agricultural lobby. The government will also allow the newly privatised water authorities to increase prices at 5 per cent over the rate of inflation for the next ten years. This may help account for the fact that opinion polls in 1989 suggested that 75 per cent of voters were opposed to the privatisation, although the electoral effects are likely to be more ambiguous than this might suggest. The government's claims that privatisation will liberate the water industry to invest in pollution control seems doubtful: higher charges might, instead, be turned into profits for investors in the privatised industry, with EC pressures being ignored.

The previous pattern of overlapping responsibilities, under-resourcing, and successor agencies is likely to carry over old modes of operation in relation to the new regime for regulating water quality. Under the Water Act 1989 the National Rivers Authority (NRA) is responsible for the quality of rivers, while the Pollution Inspectorate will monitor drinking-water quality. Previously the ten regional water authorities controlled the full water cycle, from extraction through purification, sewage treatment and disposal, as well as policing emissions into the river system. The Pollution Inspectorate has been highly critical of the water industry. But in the run up to water privatisation, the Inspectorate did not have the resources to monitor water authority applications for relaxed pollution controls on more than a thousand sewage works, and was dependent upon Water Authority expertise. The National Rivers Authority may have the institutional autonomy to act more toughly. However, its staff and modes of operation have been drawn directly from the old water authorities. Moreover, the NRA lacks adequate qualified staff to regularly monitor emissions.

European and International Dimensions

The new agenda for environmental politics – acid rain, global warming, depletion of the ozone layer, marine pollution – all involve transboundary problems of pollution control. The need for concerted international collective action raises the problem of freeriding: the national economic and political interest may suggest a strategy of imposing the costs of solution upon others by refusing extensively to control national emissions, thus 'hijacking' others into bearing the burden (Taylor and Ward, 1982). This is a strategy which Britain has pursued over dumping in the North Sea, sulphur dioxide pollution, and production of chloro-fluorocarbons. However, Britain has come under increasing international pressure. The EC is attempting to harmonise environmental policy, partly because industrialists in member states where polluters pay little get unfair trade advantages (European Documentation, 1987, p. 15). As the EC uses majority voting more often under the Single European Act, Britain will no longer be able to block environmental initiatives. The European Commission's resort to the European Court of Justice puts considerable pressure on deviant governments like Britain.

As we saw above, Britain has come into conflict with the EC over nitrate pollution and her failure to meet EC requirements for bathing-beaches. UK attitudes here mirror these in an area of marine pollution in which the EC has not been directly involved. In 1983, the British government, together with West Germany, Belgium, Denmark, France, the Netherlands, Norway and Sweden, signed the Breman Declaration committing signatories to reducing industrial pollution of the North Sea, together with pollution due to nitrate runoff from agriculture and the emission of sewage. In extended subsequent negotiations, although the British government made some concessions over the imposition of statutory limits on emissions of heavy metals, nitrates, phosphates, pesticides and other pollutants, they generally favoured negotiations with polluters, and would not countenance tighter controls in advance of specific scientific proof of harm. Although agreement was reached in 1987 to halve emission of some toxic and hazardous substances by 1994, in the run-up to the privatisation of the water industry, Britain refused to bow to pressure to stop sea-dumping of sewage sludge. Besides the issue of post-privatisation profitability, Britain's attitude betrays long-standing preferences for voluntary over statutory control and a history of conservatism over scientific proof. Both have also been factors in transboundary air pollution negotiations. As in the case of acid rain discussed above, Britain may also have been encouraged to free-ride by the fact that her pollution tends to circulate towards the Continent (Milne, 1987).

Some forms of environmental pollution, however, have global effects. Chloro-fluorocarbon gases (CFCs) are a classic case in point. Developed fifty years ago, CFCs have become a mainstay of modern life. They are used in aerosols, refrigeration, air conditioners, foam-filled furniture, fast-food packaging and as cleaning agents in the electronics industry. As long ago as the early 1970s, halogenated CFCs were implicated in the destruction of stratospheric ozone. Since then, scientists have demonstrated that the chlorine contained in the long-lived CFCs (which do not break down for a century or more) and the bromine contained in substances known as halons, destroy ozone. Figures concerning the rate of ozone depletion vary and scientists remain unclear about the specific processes through which CFCs deplete ozone. Yet a consensus has clearly emerged that CFCs destroy stratospheric ozone at a faster rate than it is regenerated, with implications for increases in rates of malignant skin cancer, agricultural yields and, crucially, the growth of oceanic phytoplankton – the basis of the oceanic food chain and a crucial 'pollution sink' for the 'greenhouse' gas CO_2 (Gribbin, 1988). Despite the British government's keenness to claim a leading role in the elimination of CFCs its position has been strongly influenced by that of ICI, Europe's largest producer of CFCs, with a market share estimated to be worth around £100,000 million annually (Johnston, 1987).

In 1980, the United Nations Environment Programme (UNEP) asked governments to·reduce production and consumption of CFCs, but it was not until 1985 that the Vienna Convention for the Protection of the Ozone Layer was adopted by 21 states and the EC. However, the Vienna Convention only dealt with international cooperation and research; it did not contain any specific controls. Within the EC, strict CFC controls were only supported by a handful of nations, including Denmark, West Germany and the Netherlands. Other countries, most notably Britain, France and

Italy, seemed more responsive to the wishes of the chemical manufacturers for a 'go-slow' approach, with Britain taking the lead in forming a blocking coalition.

Increasing pressure, particularly from the US, led the Vienna Convention countries and six other states to sign the Montreal Protocol in September 1987. The protocol treated the production and consumption of CFCs separately. Based on 1986 levels, the protocol called for a freeze in per-capita consumption by 1989, followed by a 20 per cent reduction by 1994 and a further 50 per cent reduction by 1999. Production, however, was to be allowed to increase by 10 per cent up to 1990 but was required to fall to 90 per cent of 1986 levels by 1994 and to 65 per cent by 1999. This difference between production and consumption was allowed since it was felt that it was only fair to allow developing countries, who had benefited little from CFCs, to increase their consumption up to a ceiling of 0.3kg per capita. However, almost immediately after the protocol had been signed, a major scientific expedition returned from the Antarctic with the message that ozone depletion was much worse than had been expected, and there is now evidence for severe ozone depletion in the Arctic. Given that the amount of chlorine in the atmosphere would treble by 2020 under the Montreal Protocol, there is a clear scientific consensus that controls are inadequate.

Partially as a result of shifts in the position of its own scientific advisers, Britain's attitude changed during the course of the 1987 negotiations to support for a 40–50 per cent CFC cutback. But its revised position still contained the proviso that timescales should be long enough for the development of alternatives to CFCs, an area in which ICI has basic research strengths, which would, however, take some time to exploit. Even in the light of the growing evidence of the scale of the problem, Britain has been reluctant to accept a total ban on CFCs, although pressure from other EC environment ministers in the lead-up to Thatcher's hastily arranged 'Saving the Ozone Layer' conference in March 1989 led to Nicholas Ridley accepting the need to push for a complete ban by the year 2000. Even then, in line with Ridley's free market philosophy, the Department of the Environment has refused to include legislative controls in the Green Bill, preferring instead a voluntary reduction in the use of CFCs, led by 'green consumers' refusing to buy products containing CFCs. If Britain's change in position is a function of changing information, electoral pressures, and a genuine, if limited, change of heart by Thatcher herself, all along the slow pace of change in perceptions of market possibilities by such major industrial interests as ICI has acted as a constraint.

Where global environmental issues are concerned, redistribution between rich metropolitan countries in the North and poor, peripheral countries in the South is a necessary condition for change (World Commission Environment and Development, 1987). The issue of securing the commitment of such countries as China and India to reducing CFC emissions has become a serious one, given their growing industrial capacity and their perception that rich countries have already benefited from CFC production. At the first official meeting of the signatories of the Montreal Protocol in Helsinki in May 1989, it was agreed that financial aid was required to encourage developing nations to take up the ozone-friendly, but costly, technologies. However, the notion of an 'international funding mechanism' was blocked by a number of industrialised countries, principally the US and Britain, which favoured bilateral aid and 'soft' World Bank loans. Given Britain's poor record on aid, and the strong possibility that bilateral aid would be tied to buying British technology, this position is unhelpful. On the issue of CFCs, as on the issue of global warming, powerful industrial nations wish to achieve solutions which protect their own positions while leaving developing countries to bear costs, associated with much lower per-capita emissions of pollutants. Alone among the parties, the Greens are willing to take the issue of international redistribution seriously.

Conclusions

The proposals in the Green Bill 1990 to move away from statutory limits upon emissions and towards pollution taxes may well increase the degree of inequality in society, for such taxes will often be passed onto consumers of products for which expenditures constitute a higher proportion of the incomes of poorer people (Burrows, 1979, pp. 144–9). These regressive effects are certainly likely to occur in the case of water and electricity, where it is the government's firm intention to allow the costs of pollution control to be passed onto consumers. Whether by accident or design, the government's preferred strategy may have electoral advantages: relatively speaking, poorer, Labour voters will bear a higher proportion of the costs of clean-up than those members of the middle classes who have the highest demand for environmental measures, and who are likely for other reasons to vote Tory. Given the crucial importance of attracting middle-class voters back into the Labour camp, this strategy might also tempt Labour; especially as poorer groups are, in any case, unlikely to vote Conservative.

Many capitalist states are currently doing much more than Britain is to overcome environmental problems, either against the opposition of individual industries, or in step with a redefinition or renegotiation of what the industry's economic interests are. This suggests that there is room for more reform in Britain: when other electricity supply industries find it profitable to promote conservation, it seems plausible that the CEGB's successors may come to do so too; when US car manufacturers are willing to accept measures in California to introduce radically cleaner cars running on electricity or natural gas, there seems little to suggest that, in the long term, British car manufacturers would find such a car incompatible with their profitability; when Mayor Chirac is taking measures to keep cars out of Paris, it is plausible that a British government might one day take on the road lobby and do the same in London. These arguments suggest that if there is an 'imprisoned zone' of politics beyond which a capitalist state will not go to search for solutions to environmental problems, the boundaries of the zone are elastic (Lindblom, 1977; Vogel, 1987). However, we would do well to recall the case of the Dutch government brought to the point of defeat by radical policies of cutting car use and pollution, which provoked a major negative reaction in business confidence and threats of disinvestment. As our discussion of CFCs suggests, change in policy moves in step with the market perceptions of major corporations like ICI. In the short to medium term the fundamental contradiction between the desire to consume more, on the one hand, and to clean up the environment on the other, which even 'environmentally sensitive' consumers and voters exhibit, means that Green products will only have a small market niche. Thus there will be crucial economic and electoral barriers to fundamental change and to the growth of green politics, over the next few years at least.

11

Foreign and Defence Policy

STEVE SMITH

The late 1980s was a period of unprecedented change in the post-war world. British foreign and defence policy is now having to be made and implemented in a rapidly changing world. A decade that started out with the Soviet invasion of Afghanistan, the election of Ronald Reagan to the White House, and the development of a second cold war, ended with earnest discussion in Washington of Francis Fukuyama's 'The End of History' (1989), an article arguing that the cold war was over, and that the West had 'won'. There was no longer any alternative to Western values; the 'end' of the great ideological conflicts which had shaped history were nigh. Yet only the previous year the most popular book in Washington had been Paul Kennedy's *The Rise and Fall of the Great Powers* (1988), interpreted as prophesying not the end of history on US terms but rather the decline of US power.

The key external change for British foreign and defence policy has been Mikhail Gorbachev's radical programmes of *glasnost* (openness) and *perestroika* (economic restructuring), which promise to change the nature of the Soviet economic and political systems. For *perestroika* to succeed the Soviet economic system will have to move towards the Western market model, an imperative which has forced Gorbachev to push for mutual US–Soviet arms reduction, most notably in the 1987 INF Treaty which scrapped an entire class of intermediate nuclear systems. In the early 1990s major arms control agreements are likely in the areas of strategic nuclear arms (the START talks), conventional arms in Europe (the CFE talks), and chemical weapons. Meanwhile the other superpower is undergoing a massive budget problem, which requires the Bush administration to reduce expenditure by something in the order of $100 billion by 1993 in order to comply with budget reduction legislation. The Reagan administration managed to double the federal budget deficit (from $78 to $155 billion) and triple the national debt (from $989 billion to $2,600 billion) in its eight years in office, leaving the new Bush administration to find out how to balance the books. This makes arms control a very attractive option for the US.

Within Europe these superpower changes towards detente have had two effects. First, and most spectacularly, the Gorbachev era has suddenly transformed Eastern Europe. The path towards liberalisation and pluralism trodden slowly in Poland and Hungary in the late 1980s was much more swiftly followed in East Germany, Czechoslovakia and even Bulgaria during 1989. The collapse of the Ceausescu regime in the Romanian revolution in December 1989 marked the demise of the only East European government to set its face against all reform. The implications of these epoch-making changes have only just begun to be considered, but they leave many longstanding assumptions of British foreign and defence policies looking anachronistic in a new age.

The second effect of the new detente is on West European security structures. For forty years the NATO alliance was a given in East–West relations. Yet the effect of the US budget crisis, the improvement in US–Soviet relations, and liberalisation in Eastern Europe is that a withdrawal of some US forces from Europe now seems inevitable. This will involve conventional forces but, more importantly, will also involve short-range nuclear systems as the two superpowers extend the logic of the INF Treaty to include *all* land-based nuclear missiles in Europe. These forces provide a central link between the defence of Europe and US strategic nuclear forces, a link whose fragility has continually worried European leaders, and which Thatcher is determined to maintain.

East Germany and West Germany are central to developments in the two halves of Europe, and, given the changing nature of the superpower relationship, especially the decline of the Soviet 'threat', the result is a Europe in flux. And, if the security dimension of Europe is in flux so too are the economic and institutional dimensions (see Chapter 7). Not only is there the assortment of arrangements involved in the creation of a single market (the 1992 measures) but there is also the prospect of the non-EC West European countries, especially Austria and Sweden, and some East European countries, applying to join.

While all countries have to frame their policies in this changing environment only Britain has both a major involvement in the European Community as well as participating in NATO's defence decision-making as a nuclear power. Britain will have to face all these problems in a way that is unlike any other state, and it is this combination of issues that will form the policy agenda for the 1990s.

The Traditional Model

The traditional view sees the content of foreign and defence policy as involving the diplomatic relations between Britain and other states, with the core agenda being one of military and political security. The 'central core' or the 'central column' of the decision-makers are the Prime Minister, Cabinet and the two great ministries, the Foreign and Commonwealth Office (the FCO) and the Ministry of Defence (MOD) (Vital, 1968). In addition a 'surrounding mantle' consists of other branches of government with an interest in foreign and defence policy but no authority to match the core bodies. Students of British politics have tended to stick to this traditional account because politicians talk about foreign and defence policy as if the world had not changed. The key term in the debate remains 'sovereignty', with all the emphasis on choice and capability that this implies. What is more, some features of policy have remained constant, while others have changed in the face of increasing interdependence with other states.

Constant Features

Clarke (1988) argues that there are four unchanging aspects of the domestic environment which continue to make the traditional view of foreign policy plausible. First, the Prime Minister and the executive continue to dominate the foreign policy process, with domestic political influences being of little importance. The cabinet system also remains important, not in terms of its formal meetings, which occur only once or twice a week, but in terms of its informal activities, such as the secret subcommittees and its *ad hoc* procedures for consultation and coordination. The personality of the Prime Minister is particularly important for foreign policy. Not only will it matter greatly how much the Prime Minister wants to be involved in foreign policy, but also crucial will be the relationships between the Prime Minister, the Foreign Secretary and the Secretary of State for Defence. In the 1980s a common view has been that Thatcher has been able completely to control some foreign policy issues against the views of the FCO and the Foreign Secretary.

Second, in foreign and defence issues the legislature plays a subordinate role. Although formally Parliament can be involved in foreign policy in a variety of ways, this rarely happens. When it does, Ministers hold all the trump cards, notably in being able to define the national interest. More critically, the Select Committee system, which was expected to give Parliament a renewed role, has not done so, mainly because the committees have very small staffs and have to stick to a brief given them by government. For example, because of its terms of reference the Committee that looked into the government proposal to buy the Trident missile in 1981 could only discuss *which* type of system was best, not whether any such system was needed. Similarly, government can time the announcements of decisions to undermine the work of committees; again on Trident, the government managed to announce its decision on purchasing Trident a few days before the committee published its report. Select Committees are

limited by the fact that they can only look at the implementation of policy, not the policy itself, and by their lack of power
either to cross-examine civil servants or to get governments to
listen to their conclusions. Finally, they are constituted on
party lines reflecting the government's majority. As for Parliament itself, debates on foreign policy issues are rare, are often
conducted at very general levels and tend to follow strictly
predictable party lines. Question-time is not a good way of
scrutinising foreign policy decisions, and the net effect is that
the legislature cannot effectively serve as anything more than
a general constraint on foreign policies of governments.

Third, the style or ethos of British foreign policy has been
stable. There have been few changes in the way the elite is
recruited, or in the perception of the perennial concerns for
British foreign policy, or in the received traditions of carrying
out foreign policy. For example, it is assumed that Britain is a
nuclear power, that it is in a fixed alliance structure (NATO),
and that the Soviet Union is the enemy. More generally, a
long tradition of British foreign policy stresses negotiation,
compromise, moving at the pace of the slowest, thinking of
other commitments, and not rocking the boat – a tradition
often inimical to Thatcher's approach.

> Mrs Thatcher was visibly irritated by the pragmatism of
> British foreign policy and the emphasis on continuity. She
> disliked the FCO tendency, particularly on EEC matters, to
> split the difference, to support the initiatives of others rather
> than to take them and to regard foreign policy as a matter
> best left to a particular Whitehall elite. Even a government
> as vigorous as that of Mrs Thatcher was not able to inject
> the 'ism' of its leader – Thatcherism – very effectively into
> the foreign policy process. (Clarke, 1988, pp. 76–7)

Fourth, the public salience of foreign and defence affairs has
broadly continued (except for a fairly brief politicisation of
nuclear defence issues between 1981 and 1988). Other foreign
and defence policies do not matter greatly in domestic politics.
Elite opinion is interested to an extent, but mass opinion is
rarely concerned with external issues and then tends to see
things in a decidedly nationalistic way. Public opinion may be
becoming more interested in EC issues, for the simple reason

that these have more impact in Britain than they used to, yet most voters are concerned only with things that directly affect them, which rules out the vast majority of foreign policy questions. Even in EC matters, such as membership of the European Monetary System (EMS), most people simply want the government to look after 'Britain's interests,' taking the government's word on what these interests are.

A fifth unchanging feature, not mentioned by Clarke (1988) but closely related to his list, is that Britain has continued to devote more resources to national defence than have its European allies. Britain's defence spending averages just over 5 per cent of GNP, compared to averages of around 2.5 to 4 per cent for Belgium, Denmark, France, Germany, Italy, the Netherlands and Norway. Some of this has gone to support the outposts of Empire that remain, but most of it has gone to support Britain's role within NATO, both at the nuclear and the conventional level. The most obvious indicator of this continuing commitment to being a leading military power is the independent nuclear deterrent, which has survived a strong domestic challenge from Labour between 1981 and 1988, when the party withdrew its pledge to scrap the UK's weapons.

A closely connected issue is the 'special relationship' between Britain and the United States in the area of military and intelligence cooperation. This unique linkage can be exaggerated, but was most evident in the Falklands War, when the US gave Britain invaluable intelligence data and military assistance, and in the development of the British nuclear deterrent, which, with the exception of the warheads, relies wholly on missile systems bought off-the-shelf from the US. At the military level, then, British governments have made concerted efforts to stay as one of the leading powers. Britain is still one of only five declared nuclear powers, and plans to upgrade its deterrent at an estimated cost of some £10 billion in the next decade with the purchase of the Trident system from the US.

Changing Features

Two major and long-term trends arising from internal causes have continued to affect British foreign and defence policy in the 1980s. First, the decline of British power perhaps slowed but has not been halted in the last decade. In 1945 Britain was a world power, at least in name, yet by 1990 it has become very much a regional, middle-level power. Successive British governments slowly adjusted to this 'descent from power' (Northedge, 1970, 1974; Calleo, 1968; Calvocoressi, 1978). Key arenas in this transition were the 'loss' of the Common- wealth and the military withdrawal from East of Suez (see Darby, 1973, 1977).

British governments and public opinion have still fully to square their perceptions of Britain's role with the rhetoric of Britain's history and consequent influence in the world. Critical to explaining this decline of power is the decline of the British economy (Gamble, 1990; Chalmers, 1985) as well as the rise of other powers to dominate the international political system (see Chapter 16). Because this change was a relative rather than an absolute decline it was much less easy to adjust to. The historical experience of being a great power has left British politicians and civil servants with a set of mental baggage that even in the early 1990s reflects Britain's previous position. Two potent examples of this carry-over from Britain's past role are the continuing debates over Britain's commitment to the European Community and over the independent nuclear deterrent. It is particularly interesting to note the linkage between the UK's decline and its military role. Britain has undergone a substantial relative loss of power which has affected its commitments overseas and has led to a withdrawal from its previous role, yet it has remained a leading military power by consistently devoting a much larger share of GDP to defence than other middle or regional powers. The continued military role both masks the relative decline and continues to give the impression of great power status.

Second, there has been a gradual but crucial move towards Europe. Britain's reorientation towards Europe in the 1960s and 1970s (see Camps, 1965, 1967; Hill, 1979; Kitzinger, 1973) was a lengthy process of adjustment, one that was not complete by the time Britain formally joined the European Community in 1973. Indeed, it was only after a tortuous renegotiation of the terms of entry and a referendum in 1975 that Britain could be said to be firmly part of Europe. Even then, the experience of the 1980s was that this is a very specific commitment to a certain type of 'Europe', one that is state-based and decidedly inter-governmental rather than supra-national (see Chapter 7).

Nevertheless, the main focus of British foreign policy is now Europe. And being involved so deeply in Europe, especially with the completion of the internal market in 1992, has altered the content, process and definition of foreign policy. Put simply, the foreign policy agenda is now distinctly different from what it was two decades ago; the mechanisms for making and implementing foreign policy are different; and the actors involved in making foreign policy are more numerous than implied by the formal traditional model discussed previously.

External Influences on British Policy

The external setting affects British foreign and defence policy by placing constraints on British governments' freedom of manoeuvre. In the last twenty years or so the *nature* of these external constraints has changed, because of three main, and closely related, trends: modernisation, multilateralism, and interdependence.

Modernisation

Modernisation refers to the increasing and continuing indus-trialisation of societies, the changes brought about by the industrial and scientific revolutions, which have three main effects on foreign policy (Morse, 1970, 1976). First, the dis-tinction between foreign and domestic politics has broken down. Second, the distinction between 'high' and 'low' politics that used to apply (with governments seeing the 'high' politics of security as the core of foreign policy) has been reversed, so that 'trade policy is foreign policy' (Cooper, 1972–3, pp. 18–36). Third, governments are less able than before to control events in their internal and external environments.

In the British context, modernisation has resulted in major changes in the policy agendas. The headlines are full of foreign policy issues, which are really economic ones. The

Prime Minister and her Chancellor of the Exchequer defend British foreign policy interests, *by defending the value of the pound.* The balance of payments crisis of 1989 is just one example of the way in which modernisation has altered the policy agenda. The huge monthly deficits weakened sterling, so the British government struggled to control the pound's slide on the foreign exchanges by increasing interest rates, but thereby imposed severe domestic hardship and risked economic recession. Such problems have long bedevilled British politicians, but the last twenty or so years have seen them assume more importance than ever, especially as governments of modernised countries are increasingly dependent for their popularity on continuing prosperity and rising living standards. Economic issues have gradually, but irreversibly, crept up the foreign policy agenda.

Multilateralism

Multilateralism refers to the massive increase in the number of international organisations in which Britain has to operate. As this chapter was being completed, the British Prime Minister was busy at the Commonwealth Heads of Government conference trying to persuade the other leaders to give South Africa time to change. Britain's South Africa policy *has* to be carried out in part in the Commonwealth forum, Similarly, British defence policy has to be worked out within the NATO context; for example, the Falklands War required the British government to undertake a very involved set of negotiations with its NATO partners in order to move the equipment and personnel to fight the war. Similarly what happened in the United Nations (UN) during the Falklands War was of vital importance to Britain's world standing and to the process of persuading the Argentine government to agree to a settlement. If the UN had not been taken seriously, an adverse resolution carried there could have had crucial consequences for the British government's attempts to gain active and passive support for its actions. Finally, as the EC becomes the dominant arena of British foreign policy, it follows that much of that policy has to be negotiated in an EC institutional setting. It is simply not possible for Britain to act either unilaterally or even bilaterally over EC issues (see Chapter 7). Britain can no longer concentrate on bilateral state-to-state foreign policy, nor can the British government pursue its *domestic* politics without taking into account the plethora of international bodies to which the UK belongs and which are concerned with common welfare questions. In addition the British government also has to deal with a growing number of transnational bodies, such as multinational corporations. The result of both these trends is that it has become impossible to think of Britain as in any sense a closed and distinct entity.

Interdependence

Interdependence is the major cause of the post-war transformation of foreign policy. The term had its origins in economics and refers to the increasing linkages between national economies (for the best overview, see Keohane and Nye, 1977; Cooper, 1968). Along with the other OECD countries, Britain is now in a predicament resulting from the:

> rapid and continuing changes in technology, communications and industrial and financial integration which have eroded national boundaries and the powers of governments but left the structure – and the rhetoric – of national politics in place. (Wallace, 1986, p. 367)

Wallace believes that successive governments have not thought through the implications of interdependence, primarily because doing so would require exposing the underlying issues and dilemmas in British foreign policy. British governments respond that interdependence is nothing new, that it has always been with us. But in previous eras Britain was either the hegemonic economic power or could retain a position of privilege because of Atlantic or Commonwealth links. Wallace notes that the eventual move to join the EC led to arguments about a once-and-for-all transfer of sovereignty, and this superficial view remains the level of the public debate. Yet interdependence is much more complex than this debate implies. It may not remove formal sovereignty, but it clearly affects effective sovereignty and national autonomy. The debate about the effects of the single European market and the harmonisation of social policy is likely to be conducted at the level of sovereignty, but this is merely the tip of the iceberg. Interdependence is far more pervasive in its effects on British foreign policy than the sovereignty argument implies.

If the formal EC setting is therefore only one arena for the effects of interdependence, what are the others? Wallace (1986) identifies the following key dimensions of international integration that together constitute the basis of increased interdependence. First is the integration of international production, whereby national companies have increasingly been replaced by multinational corporations. Good examples of this trend are the automobile, electronics, computer and textile industries. A quarter of UK trade now consists of trade flows between affiliates of the same parent company (Wallace, 1986, p. 376). 'There are fewer and fewer industrial sectors in which the British market is in the appropriate frame of reference; the European or the global market now includes the British, and British companies as well as British policy have to adjust their horizons' (1986, p. 376).

A second economic area is the integration of international business, where British companies have been earning more and more of their revenue overseas. In 1983 the seventy largest UK-based multinationals accounted for £70 billion of production in Britain and £100 billion abroad (Wallace, 1986, p. 377). Similarly, British firms have become prime targets for foreign investment and acquisition, especially as the integrated European market draws closer.

Third, international financial integration has increased, creating a global financial market. The development of round-the-clock trading has meant that British financial institutions have to become more and more oriented to the international rather than the national economy. This has speeded up since the 'big bang' in 1986, with the result that the international financial market is even more tightly integrated than before.

A fourth area concerns the integration of international communications, with the explosion in data transfer technology and the development of satellite and cable television making it possible for governments to control the transfer of information across national frontiers. Moreover, global communications clearly undermine national cultures.

A fifth area of change, a result of the last two factors, and is increased international market instability. International financial and monetary markets are now more unstable than ever, and, crucially, defy *national* attempts to control them.

Two areas of change concern defence specifically. One involves military procurement, where cost escalation, economies of scale and increasingly specialised markets have created a market in which there are now very few national procurement programmes; even nationally designed and built weapons include large numbers of foreign-made components. The other is the integration of military intelligence, command and control, which is particularly marked in the British case given the need for target information and satellite intelligence in order to be able to operate its 'independent' nuclear deterrent.

All these changes have cumulated in a major increase in intergovernmental collaboration. The decline of US economic hegemony has left the 'Big Seven' western economic powers (USA, Japan, West Germany, France, the UK, Italy and Canada) in a situation of having to try collective international economic management. From 1982 to 1985 Margaret Thatcher attended some eight to ten 'heads of government' meetings a year; in contrast, from 1970 to 1974 her Conservative predecessor, Edward Heath, attended only one or two a year (Wallace, 1986, p. 378). A similar picture applies to senior civil servants. All these extra meetings require preparatory meetings, and lead to lengthy ongoing follow-ups. As a result, complex bargaining and information-sharing groups develop, which make the national setting rarely a natural one for decision-making or alliance formation.

Wallace paints a picture of Britain caught up in a complex network of interdependence, one that he believes will become even more complex, with interdependence increasing. There is a mis-match between the fact of international economic, financial and industrial integration and the formal political structure of democratic accountability. Britain is unavoidably caught up in a set of interactions which fundamentally transform the context, agenda and processes of foreign policy.

The Contemporary Foreign Policy-Making Process

Summarising the transformations in the foreign policy environment of the 1990s, the domestic/foreign divide has largely lost its meaning. It is no longer easy to distinguish between foreign policy and domestic policy, as the boundaries between them have become increasingly blurred. This is especially clear in the EC. Similarly the distinction between politics and economics has largely broken down. Economic issues are now central to policy-makers and occupy much of their time. As a result, they are more likely than before to involve sections of the domestic public, with the result that foreign policy activity becomes increasingly opened up to domestic pressures, and the distinctive character of foreign policy fades away.

Foreign policy is also now more politicised than before, as a consequence of the content of foreign policy changing so markedly. The fact that foreign policy now involves areas of life that are enormously salient to people means that publics are, to an unprecedented extent, likely to make demands of their politicians concerning action in the foreign policy arena. And more actors are now involved in the foreign policy process. Not only are more governmental actors involved than hitherto, but also more pressure groups and transnational bodies. The EC provides the best example, with any EC discussion on a specific area of economic policy involving a host of national, transnational, subnational and international groupings.

The complexity of the contemporary foreign policy environment means that it is difficult for governments to coordinate policy. There are conflicting desires for specialisation in the many areas of foreign policy and, at the same time, for centralisation and control over the process. This trend has particularly important ramifications for the role of the Foreign and Commonwealth Office in particular, posing the question whether it should serve as *the* foreign policy ministry, or whether it should, instead, have a much narrower role in running the diplomatic service, leaving the primary concern for foreign policy with the Cabinet Office. It is also becoming increasingly difficult to ensure the implementation of foreign policy decisions. Decision-makers in London may find it harder to follow up effectively on decisions. Critically, much 'British' foreign policy is now implemented in Brussels, or relies for its success on joint action by actors in Bonn, Paris or Rome.

Overall, governments may be losing *effective* control of their foreign policy. The combination of a broadened agenda, a much more diffuse policy-making process, and a fundamentally more problematic implementation process threatens the ability of governments to control their foreign policies. The situation of structural complex interdependence makes it difficult for 'conviction' politicians like Thatcher to get their way. The Prime Minister's office fought a long battle with the FCO throughout the 1980s because she saw it as too accommodating and too 'pragmatic'. Yet she found it very difficult to change that view.

Finally, there remains a stark contrast between the terms in which the public debate about foreign policy is carried out and the day-to-day reality of foreign policy behaviour. The central term in the public debate is 'sovereignty', which tends to be defined very formally. This is shown most vividly in the contrast between the rhetoric of Thatcher's 1988 Bruges speech about the future of the EC and the UK's actual involvement in the Community. Formal sovereignty may exist, whereas effective sovereignty may not.

The Contemporary Defence Policy-Making Environment

Defence policy-making in the 1980s was rather different in several ways. The issues involved rarely penetrate into domestic debate, and relatively few politicians are interested in detailed defence matters. Parliament is less involved in defence issues, and the executive controls the agenda. The number of participants is, therefore, much more limited than in the foreign policy environment. Secrecy is also much greater. Governments can effectively hide behind the cloak of 'national security interests' to restrict the flow of information.

Implementation and control are easier in defence than in foreign policy. Implementation is more state-to-state than in most foreign policy issues, and control is more centralised. The MoD retains more of this control than does the FCO over foreign policy issues. Although defence became much more politicised in the 1980s than before, this politicisation is very patchy. There continues to be widespread support for the British nuclear deterrent and nationalism remains a very powerful force. On most defence issues governments have a free hand and do not have to worry about domestic reactions or interest. There remain very few Commons votes on defence issues even if a 'credible' defence policy is a prerequisite for electoral success. As a result, it is still feasible to analyse defence policy within the traditional model of British politics. The area is one in which it is easy to talk of Britain having 'interests', and this focuses attention on those in government rather than on the inter-party debate.

However, the change in the situation in Eastern Europe 1989–90 altered the context of British defence policy more than any other event since 1945. It will be very difficult indeed for governments of whatever political persuasion to continue to devote such a high percentage of GNP to defence when the public sees the collapse of the Eastern European bloc and a less aggressive Soviet Union. Not only this but the unfolding events in Eastern Europe will result in both superpowers reducing their commitments to Europe, especially given their own internal financial problems. There are many possibilities, but the most likely outcome will be a large reduction in conventional and nuclear forces in Europe, with Conventional Forces Europe (CFE) and Short-range Nuclear Forces (SNF) agreements being reached in 1990–2. These will reduce the number of Soviet and US forces in Europe, and lead to a reduction of British forces in West Germany (the British Army of the Rhine). In addition the future relationship between East and West Germany poses considerable problems for British decision-makers, to say nothing of the problems it poses for Soviet and French politicians. A reunited Germany could be so powerful economically that it would dominate both economic and security debates within Europe. Any moves towards reunification would first require the conclusion of a peace treaty between the German state and the allied powers – France, the UK, the USA and the Soviet

Union. A further agreement would also be needed over the status of Berlin. It is unlikely that these will be easy to negotiate.

Any moves towards reunification could also lead to such tensions within both NATO and the EC that each would find it difficult to agree on what to do. The Soviets are likely to propose the abolition, or at least the restructuring, of the two defence alliances, NATO and the Warsaw Pact Treaty Organization. Yet Thatcher and many other Western leaders see the continuation of NATO as essential to manage change in Europe. For the Soviets a united Germany is currently out of the question, as are any changes in existing boundaries. This does not mean that the Soviets oppose change in Eastern Europe – far from it – only that there are clear limits to that change. Nevertheless, it will be very difficult for Western politicians to say anything that implies less than total support for the peoples of Eastern Europe in their demands for 'freedom' and democracy. The difficulty will come when these demands lead to a restructuring of the existing Warsaw Treaty Organization, and a restructuring of Soviet defence forces. How will NATO react to a reduction of US conventional and nuclear forces, especially if the Soviet threat seems to be declining? The critical difficulty is that West Germany is the main actor in any discussions about NATO's defence posture, since this is where the two alliances meet head on, and is the main Western participant in any discussion about the future of Eastern Europe, by virtue of the German question. What would the West German government do if faced with a choice between reunification and NATO?

For British governments this situation poses fundamental questions of a kind that have not been faced in the last forty years. Should the British encourage the growth of a German super-state, one that might soon become the leading European military power in much the same way that West Germany dominates European economic matters? Yet can the British government publicly deny the German people their right to call for unity? The likely outcome is a public debate which accepts and welcomes the movement of Eastern Europe towards the West, yet a private policy-process trying to ensure that this move does not lead to an overpowerful Germany.

Paradoxically the changed superpower relationship and the transformed situation in Europe, may give the independent nuclear deterrent more of a role than ever before, since its existence could be seen as a factor promoting stability in a rapidly changing world. At least there will be the claim that with so much changing this is not a good time to get rid of the British deterrent; yet, at the same time, the superpowers are planning to reduce their nuclear forces considerably, so why should not the British bomb be reduced too? This implies a major public debate on the future of the British nuclear deterrent.

In terms of conventional forces, the transformation of the defence environment will almost certainly occasion a review of the UK's defence commitments, resulting in a large reduction in British defence expenditure, and in a shift in resources between the services, taking resources away from the Army and transferring them to the Royal Air Force and mainly the Royal Navy. British defence priorities will shift away from the stationing of large numbers of troops in West Germany and towards a more narrowly defined protective role for naval and air forces.

Current Problems

There remain a number of potential trouble spots and problems for British policy, mainly associated with the hangovers from Empire. The long-running dispute with Spain about Gibraltar remains unresolved, although as EC integration develops it seems unlikely to flare up in future, and Gibraltar's military garrison will shortly be withdrawn. By contrast, the Falklands garrison remains fully functional and the dispute with Argentina continues. However, a change of president in Argentina in 1989 did not produce any marked alteration of relations for the worse, as the FCO at one stage feared that it might.

British policy on South Africa has remained controversial within the Commonwealth, where the UK remains isolated in opposing any strengthening of sanctions against the apartheid regime. Thatcher has consistently pinned her hopes on a gradual liberalisation of South Africa's racist laws by the Nationalist Government arguing that sanctions can only penalise blacks by damaging South Africa's economy. With a shift towards democratic practices occurring widely in Eastern Europe and even the Soviet Union, the South African regime's denial of the suffrage to black voters remains an increasingly conspicuous exception to the trend – from which any non-Thatcherite British government would quickly withdraw its support.

At present the most visible potential crisis for the UK policy-makers centres still on Hong Kong. Most of the colony's territory is held on a lease from China which expires in 1997, and the British government in 1984 negotiated with the People's Republic of China (PRC) a treaty to govern the handover period. Under the terms of the agreement, only limited democratisation of Hong Kong's colonial government system would occur in the 1990s, thus facilitating its assimilation into China's quite different political and administrative system. At the same time the PRC guaranteed to respect the different economic and legal systems of Hong Kong, which indeed is in China's interest if the city's economy is to be maintained as an asset to the mainland.

In the spring of 1989, coinciding with a visit by Gorbachev to Beijing, China's political stability was rocked by large-scale and continuing demonstrations for democracy, focusing on Tiananmen Square in the capital. This unprecedented dissent stimulated greater optimism in Hong Kong about the prospects for political liberalisation in the mainland, quickly dashed when Chinese troops brutally crushed the Tiananmen Square protest in June 1989. The subsequent execution of protest leaders and a purge of sympathisers from the Communist party leadership all contributed to a marked hardening of the Chinese government line and created increased anxiety in Hong Kong about the 1997 handover.

Britain has resisted pressure from the colony for increased democratisation but at the end of 1989 the government announced plans to provide rights of entry to the UK for a small number of Hong Kong government officials and their dependants. The aim here is to keep the colony running efficiently up to 1997 by preventing any 'brain drain' of key personnel to other countries, since officials granted UK rights of abode will know that they can safely leave after the transition date. This attempted settlement seems to have alienated all parties. Millions of Chinese UK passport holders in Hong Kong will be denied rights of abode. China has denounced the policy as violating the 1984 agreement on transfer and the policy is controversial within the UK as well. Tory right-wingers criticise the policy as renewing the threat of large-scale immigration into the UK, while the Liberal Democrats favour granting rights of abode to all UK passport holders in Hong Kong.

Overlaying all these tensions, the UK government became embroiled in an international row at the end of 1989 about the position of some 57,000 refugees from Vietnam who had reached Hong Kong by boat and been interned in camps there. A British government proposal to compulsorily repatriate most of these people to Vietnam attracted widespread criticism, including that of the USA. At the time of writing both the Vietnam refugees issue and the broader questions about the transfer of Hong Kong remain unresolved. Only a dramatic liberalisation of the Communist regimes in China and Vietnam would seem able to resolve these issues without causing further major problems for UK policy – and developments of this kind seem very unlikely.

Conclusions

A fundamental transformation in the British foreign policy environment has taken place over the last twenty years, with a similar transformation now under way in the British defence policy environment. The changes of the late 1980s are certain to be the most important shifts to have occurred in the British defence environment since the war, shaking the fixed assumptions and concepts of the defence debate. In the near future the foreign policy and foreign economic policy environment will undergo even more change, since 1992 will create an EC setting in which it is almost impossible to talk of a distinctive *national* economic policy.

Yet, in both foreign and defence policy the public debate

will be phrased in terms of sovereignty, independence and national interests. This language will cloud the underlying structural changes in global politics. The foreign and defence policy environments have to coexist with strictly national structures of political organisation, accountability, and rhetoric. The reality of British foreign and defence policy in the 1990s is that it has to be made within an increasingly interdependent world. British policy-makers face a policy environment in the 1990s that is fundamentally different from any that they have faced since 1945, perhaps marking the beginning of a new and more unstable phase of history.

Note

I would like to thank the following for their helpful comments on previous drafts of this chapter: Richard Crockatt, John Street and, especially, Marysia Zalewski.

PART THREE

Current Issues

12

Northern Ireland and the Anglo-Irish Agreement

BRENDAN O'LEARY

Northern Ireland's politics are antagonistic. The Anglo-Irish Agreement (AIA), signed at Hillsborough in November 1985 by the Prime Ministers of the UK and the Republic of Ireland, Margaret Thatcher and Dr Garret FitzGerald, was designed to replace antagonism with accommodation, to promote peace and reconciliation between the two traditions in Northern Ireland and within both parts of Ireland, and to consolidate better relations between Britain and Ireland (Kenny, 1986).

The AIA also had five more immediate goals (O'Leary, B., 1987a). First, Irish and British policy-makers were persuaded that 'something had to be done' to stop the rise in support for Sinn Féin, the revolutionary nationalist party which supports the IRA. In four elections from 1982 to 1985 Sinn Féin captured between 35 and 43 per cent of the nationalist vote, threatening to eclipse support for the moderate nationalists of the SDLP. John Hume, the SDLP's leader lobbied hard for a political initiative in the British Isles, Europe and the USA. Halting Sinn Féin required measures to remove the causes of the alienation of the nationalist community in Northern Ireland. Second, both governments were concerned about security, and wished to reduce the violence associated with the conflict. Although the annual death toll had fallen from its

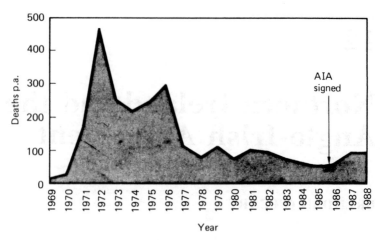

FIGURE 12.1   *Political   deaths   in   Northern   Ireland: annual   death   toll,
1969–88*

Source: Drawn from RUC data.

peak in the early 1970s it remained unacceptably high (see
Figure 12.1), as did all other indicators of violence (injuries,
shootings, explosions, and acts of intimidation). Third, both
governments wished to break the stalemate which had prevented an internal political settlement in Northern Ireland.
Unionists were not prepared to share devolved governmental
power with nationalists, and those nationalists who would
share power would only do so if an 'Irish dimension' accompanied it, i.e. some institutional recognition of their national
identity. Fourth, the Irish coalition government of Fine Gael
and Labour was anxious to promote the position of the
nationalist community in the North, if only to protect the Irish
party system from the impact of Sinn Féin. Although not
averse to gaining a first foothold in the long march to Irish
unification, its priority was peace before Irish unity (Mair,
1987). Finally, the British government was anxious that the
Irish government share responsibility for the management of
Northern Ireland, if not power, to help reduce the international embarrassment caused by its most troublesome
territory.

The Content of the Agreement and Its Rival Interpretations

The AIA is an accord between the British and Irish states which contains an agreed definition of how the status of Northern Ireland might be changed (Article 1). The electorate of Northern Ireland are free to choose, by majority vote, to remain part of the UK or to become part of the Republic of Ireland if they so wish. It established an Inter-Governmental Conference (IGC) where both governments discuss public policy matters affecting the government of Northern Ireland and make 'determined efforts ... to resolve any differences' (Article 2). It also commits both governments to promote a devolved government based on the 'co-operation of constitutional representatives ... of both traditions' that would 'secure widespread acceptance throughout the community' (Article 4). Until this devolved government is achieved the Irish government represents the interests of the nationalist minority in the Inter-Governmental Conference (Article 5).

The AIA contained thirteen articles in total – as the superstitious observed. Their content and the accompanying communiqué suggested a renewed British commitment to reform Northern Ireland, especially the administration of justice; and to guarantee equality by working 'for the accommodation of the rights and identities of the two traditions which exist in Northern Ireland', by protecting 'human rights' and preventing 'discrimination' (Articles 4(a) and 5). The governments pledged themselves to political, legal and security cooperation over Northern Ireland (Articles 5–8) and also to cross-border cooperation on security, economic, social and cultural matters (Articles 9 and 10).

Reactions to the AIA varied widely (O'Leary, B., 1987a, pp. 5–8). It was backed solidly by British and Irish public opinion. It was overwhelmingly supported in the House of Commons but only passed the Irish parliament, Dáil Éireann, against the opposition of the largest party in the Irish Republic, Fianna Fáil. Within Northern Ireland it was vehemently opposed by the two main unionist parties, the Ulster Unionist Party (UUP) and the Democratic Unionist Party (DUP), and by Sinn Féin. It was enthusiastically supported by the SDLP and, after misgivings, by the non-sectarian Alliance party.

Interpretations of the AIA also ranged dramatically. Minimalist supporters of the Agreement backed it for pragmatic reasons. It would establish inter-state institutions for managing civil unrest, provide mechanisms for dampening violence, and by quarantining the conflict help prevent destabilising spillovers into the core Irish and British political systems. For them, the AIA was fundamentally about containment: stopping Sinn Féin and the IRA. Maximalist proponents of the Agreement, by contrast, understood it as a principled framework for a long-run political solution. They differed considerably over what that long-run solution should be, especially over whether it would lead to Northern Ireland's integration into Britain or into the Irish Republic, but agreed in endowing the AIA with heroic rather than pragmatic significance. It was variously interpreted as a prelude to the creation of an all-Ireland federal state (Palley, 1986); to the exercise of joint authority by the British and Irish governments over Northern Ireland (Kenny, 1986); and, most commonly, to the establishment of a power-sharing devolved government within the province under modified British sovereignty (O'Leary, B., 1987a, 1989).

The opponents of the Agreement were also differentiated, and found in all parts of the British Isles. Sceptics alleged that the AIA was little more than an exercise in symbolic politics, a venture which pretended to address the sources of the conflict. It would be a continuous media event which would restate existing problems in the guise of solving them. Zealous critics by contrast contended that the AIA was a major constitutional turning-point. Ulster unionists lamented that the AIA marked the end, or the beginning of the end, of the union of Great Britain and Northern Ireland (Haslett, 1987; Smith, P., 1986). One iconoclastic former Irish government minister shared these perceptions: 'The AIA constitutes a deal between Irish Catholics and the British at the expense of Irish Protestants in their "Ulster" bastion ... accompanied by a great deal of verbiage about "reconciling the two traditions" in Northern Ireland, ... [and] cant ... of the hollowest description' (O'Brien, 1988, pp. xxxiii, xxxvi). However, this viewpoint is difficult to reconcile with the fact that the AIA has been equally bitterly opposed by many Irish Catholics and nationalists. Irish republicans assert that the AIA effectively surrenders official Irish efforts to 're-integrate the national territory' as pledged in the Irish Constitution of 1937. The AIA betrayed the spirit if not the letter of the Constitution of Ireland in return for implausible reassurances from 'perfidious Albion' that the Northern minority would be treated better in future (Coughlan, 1986). The AIA was the continuation of British direct rule in the province by other means: a shameful 'contract with the enemy' (Boland, 1988). It was 'in the final analysis ... about stabilising British interests ... [by] insulating the British from international criticism of their involvement in Irish affairs' (Adams, 1986, p. 105). The best way to evaluate these varying reactions is to examine the Agreement's impact upon Anglo-Irish relations, the political process in Northern Ireland, social reform and the administration of justice; and violence and security issues.

Anglo-Irish Relations

The most obvious development has been the institutionalisation of British and Irish cooperation, culminating in the Review of the Agreement published in May 1989. The signs of institutionalised 'intergovernmentalism' (Cox, 1987) include the regular sessions of the Intergovernmental Conference, the working of the joint administrative secretariat at Maryfield, and the attempts to harmonise their statements and policies by both governments after they have engaged in serious negotiations.

However, there have been many visible tensions in British–Irish governmental relations since November 1985. First, general elections and prospective changes of government in both countries threatened difficulties. The Irish general elections of 1987 and 1989, expected to produce majority Fianna Fáil governments, posed the most serious danger. Fianna Fáil had initially opposed the AIA, and raised doubts about its constitutionality. The danger proved hollow because Fianna Fáil failed to win an overall majority on both occasions

(O'Leary, B., 1987b; O'Leary, B., and Peterson, 1990), and because its leader, Charles Haughey, decided he would work the Agreement before the first election. He appointed the emollient Brian Lenihan as Foreign Minister and co-chairman of the IGC; and moved to repair his strained relations with Mrs Thatcher and the SDLP. However, in 1987 controversy was created when the Secretary of State for Northern Ireland, Tom King, used the occasion of the Irish election to encourage Unionists to negotiate a devolved government – arguing that the election had led to 'a pause' in the operation of the AIA. This ploy was not an attempt to renege on the Agreement – although it was insensitive to the interests of the outgoing Irish government. However, both Irish general elections gave a decisive boost to the AIA: Sinn Féin decided to contest elections to Dáil Éireann but polled a derisory 1.9 per cent of the first preference vote in 1987, followed by a mere 1.2 per cent in 1989. One objective of the Agreement – halting the growth of Sinn Féin throughout Ireland – had been realised.

The British general election of June 1987 was much less of a threat to the AIA. All three major party groupings expressed bi-partisan support for it in their election manifestos. The unionists hoped that a 'hung parliament' would enable them to negotiate the suspension of the AIA, but the Conservatives' majority shattered this wishful thinking. The British general election did affect the AIA because it prompted personnel changes, on top of those created by the new Irish government. With the departure of Nicholas Scott, after six years in the Northern Ireland Office (NIO), and simultaneous changes among leading civil servants, some of the major figures involved in the negotiation of the AIA had moved on. These changes contributed to the significant deterioration in the coordination of British–Irish relations in late 1987 and 1988 when several well-publicised episodes caused temporary crises, if not fiascoes.

The second danger to stable British–Irish relations was posed by disagreements between the two governments over the meaning of the Agreement, especially Article 1. British declarations that it marked the end of Irish governments' aspirations to achieve a united Ireland (as suggested by King in December 1985) produced hostile reactions from Irish political parties, and the SDLP – and 'We told you so' responses from Sinn Féin. Article 1 could be construed as confirming British sovereignty over Northern Ireland; but also as confirming the Irish Republic's constitutional claim to Northern Ireland. The AIA states how the 'status' of Northern Ireland can be changed – through the consent of the majority – but not what *is* its actual constitutional status. The rival understandings of the constitutional meaning of the AIA, which flow from deliberate ambiguities in the text, create multiple tensions. British efforts to reassure Unionists about their status as Britons conflict with Irish governments' defence of the AIA against ultra-nationalist critics. Both governments are in the curious position of wanting to say that only the other state has made major concessions on sovereignty in the AIA. The ambiguity of Article 1 was deliberately designed to make the AIA proof against a constitutional challenge in the Republic's Supreme Court (and did ensure its survival against its first challenge by the McGimpsey brothers in 1988) but it has served to inflame Unionist anxieties.

The third source of British–Irish conflict has been over the objectives and priorities of the IGC. Press releases, communiqués and interviews permit informed judgements as to the respective governments' objectives and priorities. Initially the British wanted improved security, especially in cross-border relations and extradition, as their primary goal. They also sought to reassure Unionists that the AIA is not against their interests, and promoted the idea of a devolved government. Finally, they moved, very slowly, to reform Northern Ireland in ways which would meet some nationalist criticism. Increased IRA activity in 1987 and 1988 strengthened the British emphasis upon security, crisis-management and the defeat of Sinn Féin and the IRA and reduced their commitment to reform.

Irish objectives and priorities differed. According to Peter Barry, the Irish foreign minister, the Fine Gael–Labour government in 1985 primarily sought to reform Northern Ireland by advancing minority interests and aspirations, in the administration of justice. They also wished to see a devolved government established. Finally, they sought cooperation on security. The Fianna Fáil government of February 1987–June 1989 was sceptical of, if not opposed to, devolution, and suggested that it should be accompanied by a broader North–South settlement as well as a British–Irish settlement embracing the 'totality of relationships' between the two islands. Their foreign minister Lenihan claimed to have three equally important goals: the promotion of the welfare of the minority, easing the fears of the majority, and reforming Northern Ireland (*Irish Times*, 11 May 1987). The Fianna Fáil–Progressive Democrats coalition government, formed after the June 1989 election, by contrast, restored devolution as an objective of the Irish government. These conflicting, and changing, objectives and priorities have generated intermittent strain and slowed the reforming momentum initiated by the AIA.

The fourth reason why British–Irish relations have occasionally deteriorated involves specific legal and security affrays which received global publicity. In late 1987 the Irish government amended the Extradition Act passed in 1986, to ensure that *prima facie* evidence that an offence had been committed would be required before suspects would be handed to the British. This amendment was passed after the refusal of the British government to change the court system in Northern Ireland – Dr FitzGerald claimed that these two issues had been linked in the negotiation of the AIA – and because of public anxieties about the treatment of Irish suspects in British courts. Irish underconfidence in British justice was reinforced in January 1988 when the Court of Appeal rejected the appeal of those convicted of the Birmingham pub bombings in 1974, despite suspicions about both the forensic evidence and the nature of the confessions which formed the basis of the convictions. The Irish government did not blame the British government because English judges found the idea that the West Midlands police could behave illegally 'too appalling to contemplate'. However, it could, and did, complain vociferously when the British Attorney General decided, in the same week, that it would not be in the national interest to prosecute RUC officers, despite evidence of a conspiracy to pervert the course of justice produced by inquiries into allegations that the police had engaged in 'shoot-to-kill'

policies in the early 1980s (Stalker, 1988). Nationalists
throughout Ireland reacted furiously: in their view the Attorney
General had decided to cover up an issue discussed in the
Inter-Governmental Conference.

Soon afterwards an unarmed Catholic civilian was shot
dead on the border by a British soldier in suspicious circumstances. The fires of this event were fanned when the only
British soldier to have been sentenced for a manslaughter
charge since 1969 was released by the Home Secretary in
February 1987. Having served a three-year sentence, he was
back with his former regiment. Events then flowed thick and
fast: the Home Secretary, Douglas Hurd, announced that the
Prevention of Terrorism Act was to be made permanent,
despite the fact that it contained 'internal exile' clauses
offensive to Irish sensibilities and civil libertarians. The
British Attorney General, badly briefed about the nature of
the amendment to the Irish Extradition Act, accused the Irish
government of breaching extradition agreements. The killing
of three unarmed IRA terrorists by the SAS in Gibraltar on
6 March 1988, in circumstances where they might have been
arrested, increased tension still further. The funerals of the
IRA personnel were subsequently attacked by a loyalist
paramilitary, resulting in three murders on 16 March, and on
19 March two British soldiers who drove into the resulting
funeral cortège in Andersonstown were lynched by members
of the procession.

The culmination of these events forced both governments to
get a better grip on their relations, and to agree on the need for
closer and better crisis-management and crisis-avoidance.
However, in December 1988 another major public row occurred when the Irish Attorney General refused to extradite
Father Patrick Ryan, despite *prima facie* evidence sufficient
to warrant a prosecution on terrorist charges, because the
public comments of the British Prime Minister and other
Conservative MPs had prejudiced his prospects of a fair trial.
Instead he invited his British opposite number to use the
Criminal Law (Jurisdiction) Act, which enables the prosecu-
tion of suspects in one jurisdiction for offences committed in
another. However, the British attempt to use this Act in the
Ryan case failed in 1989 because of lack of evidence – and

amidst rumours that witnesses were not prepared to travel to Ireland.

These events, intentionally or otherwise, appeared to show to the Irish that security, counter-insurgency and national sovereignty prerogatives matter more to British governments than good relations with the minority in Northern Ireland and the Irish government, or the preservation of the rule of law by the security forces. Cases in Britain such as the Guildford Four, the Maguires, the Birmingham Six and the Winchester Three – all convicted by English courts of IRA-related offences in controversial circumstances – became *causes célèbres* in Ireland. On the other hand the same episodes appeared to show to some British politicians that the Irish were insufficiently resolute in 'the fight against terrorism' and 'irrationally prejudiced' about British courts. Though none of these episodes revealed a British or Irish desire to renege on the AIA, in the British case they suggested a lack of coordination between the government ministries dealing with Northern Ireland. (The NIO does not handle all matters which affect British–Irish relations). Dr FitzGerald put matters more harshly in June 1989: 'The failure of the Irish to understand how stupidly the British can act is one of the major sources of misunderstanding between our countries ... Their system is uncoordinated. Because there's a Northern Ireland Secretary people think there's a Northern Ireland policy – but there isn't' (McKittrick, 1989). However that may be, both governments, in the jointly published Review of the AIA, showed themselves sensitive to the charge that the Inter-Governmental Conference lacked strategic coordination and had degenerated into a forum for mere 'crisis management'. They resolved to order their affairs better in future and avoid the temptations of 'megaphone diplomacy'.

The Political Process in Northern Ireland

Political developments since Hillsborough have been dominated by the apparently implacable hostility of most unionists to the AIA. 'Ulster [meaning Protestant Ulster] says No' has been the slogan of their resistance. Unionists rejected Article 1 of the Agreement because it suggested a lack of commitment in Westminster to retain the province in the UK. They condemned all the other articles because they give a 'foreign power' a say in the affairs of the UK. They refused to negotiate a power-sharing devolved government on the grounds that it would be discussed 'under duress', that it was not British to have permanent coalition governments, and because the Inter-Governmental Conference would be left intact even if a devolved government were agreed.

When the British government rejected a call for a local referendum on the Agreement unionist MPs cooperated in resigning their Westminster seats and forcing a 'mini-referendum' of fifteen by-elections in January 1986. The by-elections backfired when they failed to win their target of half a million votes and lost Newry and Armagh to the SDLP's deputy leader Seamus Mallon, but they did show the depth and breadth of Unionist opposition to the AIA. The by-elections were followed by boycotts of Westminster and the Northern Ireland Office; use of the facilities of the Northern Ireland Assembly – which nationalists had boycotted since its formation in 1982 – for political protests (O'Leary, C. *et al.*, 1988); the sundering of the last links between the Conservative party and the UUP; mass demonstrations; a one-day general strike; and a civil disobedience campaign involving non-payment of rates and taxes as well as the refusal of unionist councillors to set rates in local government districts. In the spring of 1986 loyalist paramilitaries attacked RUC officers' homes in retaliation for their 'collaboration' with the AIA; intimidated large numbers of Catholics into leaving their homes in areas of 'mixed residence'; and recommenced their practice of murdering Catholic civilians, dormant since 1977. The British government stood firm in the face of these protests, and faced down unionist opposition. It closed the Northern Ireland Assembly in June 1986, and enforced the law against illegal actions by Unionist politicians and paramilitaries. In consequence the strength of unionist constitutional, quasi-constitutional and paramilitary action against the AIA was dissipated by late 1986 and early 1987.

After their failure to persuade the British government to abandon the AIA, divisions and shifts of opinion erupted among Unionists. A minority broke away from the UUP to campaign for complete integration into Britain, arguing that British political parties should organise in Northern Ireland (Roberts, 1987). Most of these former Unionists sought to organise Conservative party branches in the province but their overtures were initially rejected by British Conservatives – although in 1989 it was agreed that some Conservative party branches could be formed. The think-tank of the loyalist paramilitary organisation, the UDA, published *Common Sense* in January 1987, in which they called for the establishment of a power-sharing devolved government ('co-determination'), subject to the abandonment of the AIA. In June 1987, after long consultations, the secondary leadership of the UUP and DUP produced the *Task Force Report*, which also suggested that a power-sharing devolved government was no longer 'unthinkable'. In response Ian Paisley and James Molyneaux entered into 'talks about talks' with the NIO which lasted until May 1988. However, they insisted that the AIA had to be suspended before broader talks with the SDLP or the Irish government could begin. This demand was unacceptable to both governments and the SDLP.

The posture of the unionist leaders effectively shelved the interest in the power-sharing option expressed in the *Task Force Report*, and their tactics thereafter seemed to be based upon waiting for the AIA to collapse as a result of discord between the British and Irish governments. On occasions they even hinted at their willingness to embrace direct negotiations with Dublin for a new agreement covering the 'totality of relationships' within the British Isles – but such suggestions were widely decoded as a stratagem to destroy the AIA. However, although agreed on hostility to the AIA, unionist political parties remained in a state of ferment. The UUP was divided between a majority of integrationists and a vocal minority prepared to accept a power-sharing devolved government; and the DUP was divided over whether to embrace more extreme action against the AIA, and over whether to maintain its united front with the UUP.

Among the nationalist minority the initial widespread backing for the AIA, which fed into increased support for the SDLP, waned as the Inter-Governmental Conference failed to deliver rapid, dramatic and effective reforms of Northern Ireland. Indeed by April 1988 in one opinion poll only 16 per cent of Catholics believed the AIA had benefited the nationalist community (Wilson, R., 1988). The British government's early caution and immobility on reforms owed something to its desire to reassure unionists but the predictable consequence was to reduce nationalist support. Sinn Féin sought to capitalise upon this vicious circle (Sinn Féin, 1989), but owing to the nature of IRA activity in the period after Hillsborough, and the resurgence of the SDLP, it has been unsuccessful. However, nationalist support for the Agreement has mostly depended upon the negative fact that it is opposed by unionists.

The most significant development within the nationalist bloc since the AIA was the holding of talks between the SDLP and Sinn Féin in the first eight months of 1988. John Hume's SDLP tried to persuade Sinn Féin of the futility of the IRA's campaign, which they believe is not only morally wrong but also the major obstacle to Irish unity. Sinn Féin used the talks to try to legitimise itself as a political party within the nationalist community. When the talks broke up both sides published their position papers and Hume later went on a renewed campaigning offensive against both Sinn Féin and the IRA, accusing them of being fascists who, far from 'defending' the Catholic minority, had killed more Catholics than any other organisation since 1969. The talks did succeed, if nothing else, in further isolating Sinn Féin from the broader nationalist community in Ireland but were predictably condemned by the unionists as unprincipled.

Since Hillsborough the SDLP has rejected all unionist calls for negotiations on a political settlement which have demanded either the abandonment or the suspension of the AIA. Nonetheless informal discussions and talks between representatives of the constitutional parties have continued since 1986, and occasionally have come close to producing a formula for 'talks about talks' – as appeared to be the case after cross-party discussions at Duisberg in West Germany in February 1989. However, despite other subterranean signs of political dialogue since then the internal politics of Northern Ireland remain in stalemate. Unionists are not prepared to negotiate under the AIA, the SDLP are not prepared to negotiate without it staying in place. Political leaders in both communities remain aware that compromise may be interpreted as surrender by their party colleagues and rivals in other parties, and at the time of writing, there are few signs which suggest good prospects for an agreed devolved government.

The AIA was intended to shake up trends in party support: to stem and reverse the growth of Sinn Féin; to stabilise support for the SDLP; and to encourage productive attitudes towards devolution among unionists – by strengthening power-sharing devolutionists within the UUP at the expense of both extremists within the DUP and integrationists within the UUP (O'Leary, B., 1987a, pp. 11–12). So what impact has the Agreement had in these respects? Within the unionist bloc the DUP has lost ground since Hillsborough. Table 12.1 demonstrates that in all three elections held after the signing

TABLE 12.1   *Party performance before and after the Anglo-Irish Agreement: per cent of the vote of Unionist and Nationalist blocs*

Unionists

	DUP		
	Before	*After*	*Net change*
Westminster	1983: 20	1987: 12	−8.3
Local Government	1985: 24	1989: 18	−6.5
European	1984: 34	1989: 30	−3.7
	UUP		
	Before	*After*	*Net change*
Westminster	1983: 34	1987: 38	+3.8
Local Government	1985: 30	1989: 31	+1.9
European	1984: 22	1989: 22	0

Nationalists

	SDLP		
	Before	*After*	*Net change*
Westminster	1983: 18	1987: 21	+3.2
Local Government	1985: 18	1989: 21	+3.3
European	1984: 22	1989: 26	+3.4
	Sinn Féin		
	Before	*After*	*Net change*
Westminster	1983: 13	1987: 11	−2.0
Local Government	1985: 12	1989: 11	−0.5
European	1984: 13	1989: 9	−4.1

Notes:
All figures in per cent. The figures are rounded except for the 'Net Change' figures which are to one decimal place. The figures for Local Government and European elections are percentages of all first preference votes; for Westminster of the total vote.

of the AIA, including the European election of 1989, Paisley's party failed to match the share of the vote it obtained in the corresponding elections held before the Agreement. However, the DUP and UUP have cooperated both politically and electorally since Hillsborough, so these figures, alone, are misleading. Moreover, power-sharing devolutionists have made little headway within the UUP. But the overall showing of the unionist bloc in the three elections held after the Agreement is also significant. Its total share of the Northern Ireland vote (55 per cent in the Westminster election of June 1987, 49 per cent of the first preference vote in the Local Government Districts elections of May 1989 and 51 per cent of the first preference vote in the European elections of June 1989) fell below its level in each of the last comparable elections, and the two 1989 elections produced the lowest and second lowest shares for the unionist bloc since the 'troubles' began (O'Leary, B., 1990). Some unionists undoubtedly abstained, disillusioned with constitutional politics or with their 'natural parties' campaigning against the AIA. However, although the AIA has produced some movement in the direction of squeezing loyalist extremists, it has not, as yet, produced a decisive accommodating response on the question of power-sharing from within the UUP or the DUP. Indeed, judging by opinion polls, Protestants increasingly favoured full integration of Northern Ireland into Britain (47 per cent) rather than devolved government with power-sharing (17 per cent) as their first preference solution (Wilson, R., 1988). On the other hand, after the 1989 local government elections many councillors from the UUP engaged in cross-party cooperation with the SDLP and the Alliance party in the allocation of committee duties and elected posts, suggesting some willingness to engage in local power-sharing.

The impact of the AIA on nationalist voting and party political behaviour has more clearly achieved the British and Irish governments' objectives. First, it has halted the growth of the Sinn Féin vote, and shows some signs of reversing it. Table 12.1 shows that Sinn Féin's share of the vote fell in each of the elections, Westminster, Local Government Districts and European, held after Hillsborough, by comparison with the corresponding three elections before the AIA was signed.

Second, the SDLP's position within the nationalist bloc has been decisively restored, as the sharp fall in Sinn Féin's share of the combined SDLP and Sinn Féin shows. Indeed the SDLP's performance in the 1989 European poll was its highest ever share of a Northern Ireland election. Extremist nationalism has thus been somewhat squeezed, although substantive reform of Northern Ireland will be required to reduce it further.

Social Justice and Legal Justice

The British government insist that major reforms have been facilitated by the AIA (Northern Ireland Office, 1989). They point to: the repeal of the Flags and Emblems Act of 1954, which outlawed the display of Irish nationalist insignia; the Public Order (NI) Order of 1987 which strengthened the law on incitement to hatred and gave powers to the police to control marches likely to cause provocation; the establishment of an Independent Commission for Police Complaints; measures to promote police–community relations and monitor allegations of misconduct by the security forces; the modification of the Emergency Provisions Act, 1987, in a more liberal direction; the publication of a new code of conduct for RUC officers in 1988; legislation which now enables citizens of the Republic resident in Northern Ireland to vote in local government elections (Elected Authorities (NI) Act, 1989); the Fair Employment Act, 1989, which allegedly strengthens the law against religious discrimination and promotes equality of opportunity in employment; and finally, measures to facilitate the use of the Irish language. They also point to the 'Making Belfast Work' project established in July 1988, and the extra expenditure directed to Northern Ireland under the 'International Fund for Ireland', set up to accompany the AIA, which has received contributions from the USA, Canada, New Zealand and the EC.

Why then has the commitment of the British government to social reform in Northern Ireland been questioned by nationalists? According to Irish officials many of the reforms have the character of being 'too little, too late'; what the government has 'given with one hand it has taken back with the other' by accompanying reforms with regressive repressive measures; and the 'British present a mythical picture of making concessions and reforms, while the reality is of little substantive change' (Source: non-attributable interviews). Their two areas of prime concern, shared by nationalists in Northern Ireland, are fair employment and the administration of justice.

Fair Employment

The communal inequalities in Northern Ireland are rooted in past and present direct and indirect discrimination (Standing Advisory Commission on Human Rights (SACHR), 1987; Smith, D., 1987; Eversley, 1989), and are illustrated in Figure 12.2, which shows that Catholic males are two-and-half times as likely to be unemployed as Protestant males, despite British 'reforms' since 1972. Injustice in the labour market can no longer be held to be the responsibility of the former Stormont parliament since it has persisted under direct rule. The Fair Employment Act of 1989, which sets out to remedy the weaknesses in the previous 1976 Act, has been criticised on

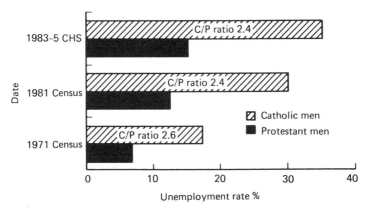

FIGURE 12.2 *Unemployment rates for Protestant and Catholic males*

Note: CHS = Continuous Household Survey Data.

Source: D. Smith (1987, table 2.1).

several grounds. The White Paper and first draft of the Bill which preceded it were flawed (McCrudden, 1988); and despite some key concessions made by the British government in the bill's passage through Westminster critics believe the final legislation lacks the 'teeth' required to address the entrenched direct and indirect discrimination in Northern Ireland's notorious labour markets with effective programmes of 'affirmative action'. Fair employment is vital in ending the alienation of the minority, and reducing support for Sinn Féin in the most deprived Catholic districts of Northern Ireland.

There is considerable suspicion that the British government was primarily motivated by the need to respond to the 'MacBride principles' campaign in the United States, which has sought to oblige US companies in Northern Ireland to practise fair employment in recruitment and promotion or be obliged to disinvest (Osborne and Cormack, 1989). The success of the supporters of the MacBride principles in passing relevant legislation in American states and in the US Congress has prompted the British government to engage in 'symbolic politics', to appear to be doing something about inequality. Kevin McNamara, the Labour party spokesperson on Northern Ireland, points out that Whitehall has spent more in lobbying in the USA to try to defeat the innocuous MacBride principles than in its efforts to stop the publication of *Spycatcher* (Doherty, 1988). The Conservative government may also have worried that radical legislation facilitating extensive 'affirmative action' on religious discrimination in Northern Ireland might produce awkward demands for similar legislation to rectify sexual and racial discrimination in England, Scotland and Wales.

Legal Justice

Nationalist discontent with British reforming efforts has been more marked in the administration of justice. 'In national conflicts, law, order and justice are not just some of the issues that happen to arise from other causes. National conflicts, once they are fully developed, revolve around these matters' (Wright, 1989, p. 153). Before the negotiation of the Agreement some of these matters were discussed, and although agreements in principle were reached they were excluded from the Hillsborough communiqué (Moloney, 1986). They included agreement to remove powers of arrest from the Ulster Defence Regiment, the locally recruited section of the British Army which is over 90 per cent Protestant; to guarantee a numbering system for UDR soldiers; to make RUC constables pledge to defend the 'two traditions'; and to increase the representation of Catholic judges on the Belfast high court. The Hillsborough accord and communiqué publicly included commitments to ensure 'police accompaniment' of the British Army and the UDR; to consider the reform of the controversial Diplock courts (which have a single judge and no jury), either by creating 'mixed' (i.e. British and Irish judges on the bench) or three judge courts; and to contemplate the establishment of a Bill of Rights.

On all these matters the Irish government and nationalists complain that the British government has either failed to deliver change or has done so half-heartedly. The courts have not been reformed, partly because of the resistance of Lord Hailsham, when he was Lord Chancellor, and Lord Lowry, the Lord Chief Justice of Northern Ireland. There has been no move on a Bill of Rights, partly because it would be incompatible with most of the British government's 'counter-insurgency' legislation, namely the Emergency Provisions Act and the Prevention of Terrorism Act. The British have also failed to deliver properly on 'police accompaniment'. The UDR, some of whose soldiers have continued to be involved in sectarian murders of Catholics and in overlapping membership of loyalist paramilitary organisations, has remained a fundamental concern. In August and September 1989 evidence that the files of IRA suspects had been given to loyalist paramilitaries who had used them to carry out murders again raised questions about the partiality of both the UDR and the RUC.

At a meeting of the Inter-Governmental Conference in 1989 in Dublin, Peter Brooke, the new Northern Ireland Secretary, met the new Irish foreign minister, Gerry Collins. This longest-ever session of the IGC broke up without any resolution of these issues. The Irish government pressed for a renewed British commitment to reform the security forces, especially their recruitment policies, and to ensure police accompaniment. In the subsequent press conference Collins pointed to the extensive 'gap' between both governments which needed to be closed, and warned ominously: 'If we don't do that then the Anglo-Irish Agreement will be held up to question as to whether or not there is any reason for having it at all.' After four years the AIA shows few signs of achieving minority confidence in the administration of justice and the security forces.

Violence and Security

The IRA and Sinn Féin, of course, have been desperate to ensure that the AIA will not produce minority confidence in British government. After November 1985 they deliberately set out to raise the tempo of their 'long war' to break Britain's will, to prevent an internal political settlement within Northern Ireland, and to encourage the British government into embarrassing repressive actions. In the summer of 1986 the IRA widened its definition of 'legitimate targets' to include civilians engaged in economic relations with the security forces, provoking a predictable response from the Ulster Freedom Fighters, the pseudonym for the militarily active section of the still legal Ulster Defence Association (UDA), that it too would widen its definition of 'legitimate targets'. The two sets of paramilitaries had a shared interest in ensuring that the level of violence would rise after the AIA, so they could both say it was not working. The monthly death toll not surprisingly rose in the years after the AIA by comparison with the preceding three, although preliminary data for 1989 suggest that it has since fallen. The more dramatic indicator of rising violence after the Agreement was in the levels of serious injuries caused by political violence. However, the death-rate still remained well below the levels of 1971–6 (see Figure 12.1) and it was inflated by internal feuds within paramilitary organisations. The IRA continually executed alleged informers; the Marxist paramilitaries of the Irish National Liberation Army (INLA) (who had killed Conservative spokesman Airey Neave in 1979) collapsed in an internal bloodbath; and the UDA remained so prone to faction-fighting that some of its members colluded in helping the IRA kill their deputy leader John McMichael (co-author of *Common Sense*) in December 1987. The IRA was fortified by renewed military supplies from Libya, following Thatcher's support for the American raid on Tripoli in April 1986. This helped it increase its campaigns in 1987–8. It also extended its campaign to England, and to attacks on British security force personnel on the European continent, the latter being more successful than the former. However, the IRA suffered several notable reversals. They lost eight men in an attack on Loughall RUC police station in May 1987. Their personnel regularly made 'mistakes' which brought them almost universal condemnation. The most notorious was the murder of 11 Protestant civilians and the injury of 63 others after a bomb at a Remembrance Day ceremony in Enniskillen in November 1987. In consequence Sinn Féin was unable to reap any benefits from the nationalist discontent over the pace of reform in Northern Ireland.

There is a long tradition of British policy-making in Ireland of ineffectively combining reform and repression (Townshend, 1983). The tradition seems to have survived the Hillsborough treaty. New repressive measures, introduced in the wake of Thatcher's anger when the IRA killed eight off-duty soldiers in August 1988, include the following: the Home Secretary's broadcasting ban on Sinn Féin, a legal political party (albeit in imitation of a similar ban by the Irish government); the requirement in the Elected Athorities Act, 1989, that all councillors in Northern Ireland take an oath repudiating the use of violence; and the removal of the right of the accused to have no inferences drawn from their silence by judges directing juries. The latter action was announced during the trial of three Irish people (the Winchester Three) exercising their common law 'right to silence'. They were accused and subsequently found guilty of plotting to murder Tom King. Making the Prevention of Terrorism Act permanent, despite it being in conflict with the judgements of the European Court of Human Rights, has also not helped win minority confidence in the forces of order.

The AIA has led to improvements in cross-border security operations, the sharing of intelligence between the two governments, the Irish government's signature of the European Convention on the Suppression of Terrorism, and, eventually, to improved extradition arrangements, but there is no overall success story to report in these domains. British security-policymaking since Hillsborough still seems to merit the satirical description in Adrian Mitchell's poem, 'A Tourist Guide to England': 'No. Please understand./We understand the Irish./Because we've been sending soldiers to Ireland/For hundreds and hundreds of years.' British ministers continue to equivocate between saying on the one hand that terrorism can be defeated and on the other that the IRA cannot be defeated militarily – as Peter Brooke suggested in the winter of 1989. Until security and reform policies march hand-in-hand the AIA cannot deliver the framework for a long-term settlement.

Conclusion

In late 1989 there was evidence of disillusionment with the Agreement among its supporters both outside and inside Northern Ireland. The AIA, while entrenched, appeared to have become little beyond 'machinery for muddling through' (Thompson, 1989). Unionists still remained adamant in their opposition. However, there still are tempered hopes about restoring the reforming momentum of the Agreement (Boyle and Hadden, 1989), which the British Labour party promises to renew if it wins the next general election (McNamara *et al.*, 1988). It is perhaps better to think of the Agreement as 'still muddling, but not yet through', a long-run venture best illuminated by a Chinese proverb often cited by Peter Barry: 'The journey of a thousand miles starts with a single step.'

Note

The author acknowledges the benefit of a Nuffield Foundation travel grant which enabled him to conduct interviews in Britain and Ireland in 1989.

13

The Political Economy of Regulation

CENTO VELJANOVSKI

Supply-side reforms have been the hallmark of the Thatcher government's first decade in office. Privatisation, liberalisation, deregulation, and attempts at fiscal and monetary restraint are all attempts to fundamentally alter the role of the state in the British economy. They are based on a political philosophy which contends that the state should provide a framework which enables economic and political freedoms and private initiative to flourish. Nonetheless the Thatcher decade has been one of contradiction and paradox. Despite a government committed to the withering-away of the state, it remains large. Taking any measure, numerical or otherwise, the state has not diminished appreciably during the 1980s.

Yet there can be no doubt that there have been significant and radical changes. Most of the nationalised industries have been privatised, other markets liberalised (the financial and labour sectors, the professions and buses) and there have been reforms of the education and health systems. Accompanying these policies has been the growth of regulation. Many of the nationalised industries have been privatised as large entities with considerable market power. These will continue to require pervasive regulation to reduce their ability to exploit their customers and suppliers. Those sectors of the economy which have been opened to competition, such as financial services and broadcasting, now confront complex legal controls. There has also been considerable institutional innovation. The privatised utilities – British Telecom, British Gas, BAA, the Water Authorities and soon the various companies which will constitute the electricity supply industry – are all subject to price controls, service obligations and a myriad of regulatory constraints administered by a new breed of regulatory watchdogs. In other areas market-based regulation, or 'economic instruments', are proposed, such as pollution taxes, pricing of the radio spectrum, the auction of broadcast franchises and the greater use of litigation to enforce competition law.

What is Regulation?

Regulation is a synonym for law backed by the police power of the state or the exclusionary powers of some association of individuals, the latter often referred to as 'self-regulation'. The state has a monopoly of the legitimate power to tax, proscribe, coerce and punish.

Regulation has grown significantly in the last decade both in terms of the number of laws (Table 13.1) and the proliferation of regulatory watchdogs (Table 13.2). Much of this growth is a statistical artifact. It often makes explicit the type of controls and constraints which nationalised industries exercised as self-regulators or where imposed on them by central government and the Treasury. In other sectors regulation has

TABLE 13.1   *Growth of legislation, 1982–9*

Year	Acts (pages)	Statutory Instruments (numbers)
1982	2072	1900
1983	1420	1966
1984	2876	2065
1985	3233	2082
1986	2844	2356
1987	1956	2279
1988	2210	2311
1989	2490	2400 (estimate)

TABLE 13.2   *The major regulatory agencies*

	Budget £m	Staff	Date formed	Self-financing
Established agencies:				
Office of Fair Trading	10.2	307	1973	No
Monopolies and Mergers Commission	4.4	108	1941	No
Independent Broadcasting Authority*	69.5	1,310	1954	Yes
Civil Aviation Authority	30.0	6,436	1971	Yes
New agencies 1984 onwards:				
Office of Telecommunications	4.5	120	1984	Yes
Office of Gas Supply	1.4	28	1986	Yes
Cable Authority	0.4	5	1984	Yes
National River Authority	30.0	6,500	1989	Yes
Office of Water Services	–	–	1989	Yes
Office of Electricity Regulation	–	–	1990	Yes
Independent Television Commission	–	–	1990	Yes
Radio Authority	–	–	1990	Yes
Broadcasting Standards Council	0.5	14	1987	No
Securities & Investment Board	1.30	180	1985	Yes
Self Regulatory Organisations**	14.8#	300	1986	Yes
	(# approximate)			

Notes:
  * The IBA is both a regulator and the provider of the transmission network. The figures therefore must be discounted to arrive at the true cost of regulation.
  ** There are five SROs – The Stock Exchange Association (TSA), Financial Intermediaries, Managers and Brokers Regulatory Association (FIMBRA); Investment Management Regulatory Organisation (ISRO); Association of Futures Brokers and Dealers (AFBD); Life Assurance & Unit Trust Regulatory Organisation (LAUTRO).
  Source: Annual Reports.

without question increased substantially. This is particularly so in the financial services sector. The Financial Services Act 1986 ushered in a new era of investor protection and spawned changes in the business practices of all financial and investment institutions.

Competing Models of Regulation

There are two competing models of government intervention – the public interest and the economic models.

  The public interest model, or its counterpart developed by economists – the market failures framework – asserts that regulation is designed for and has the effect of remedying the deficiencies and inefficiencies of the market (Kay and Vickers, 1989). For reasons of monopoly, externality and imperfect information, markets fail to achieve efficient outcomes. Moreover, the outcomes of even competitive markets are often seen as unjust because they give rise to significant disparities in wealth. Markets are based on winners and losers, and a competitive market-place only affords equality of opportunity not outcome. According to the public interest model, government can and does act to remedy inefficiency and smooth out inequalities in wealth. It also has a role in macroeconomic stabilisation – controlling the money supply and demand management through fiscal policy.

The public interest model fails to explain regulation in practice. Market failure and the public interest are elastic and vague concepts sufficient to justify nearly any intervention. Moreover, the success of governments in East and West in out-performing the market, or providing their citizens with better and more goods and services, greater and more evenly distributed wealth than the market economy, is patchy at best, not true in general.

Some economists have proposed a model of government regulation which accords more with experience. This is frequently referred to as the capture model, since it often concludes that regulation operates for the benefit of those regulated rather than those protected by the law. However, the model is more general than this, claiming only that politics like goods and services responds more often to the forces of demand and supply than to idealism. This economic model of regulation is most associated with the work of Stigler and the Chicago School of economics (Stigler, 1988). The supply of regulation is seen as the outcome of forces operating in the political arena. Legislators and regulators are the monopoly suppliers of laws; industry and pressure groups demand legislation to increase their wealth and privileges. The currency of this 'market' in regulation is votes and influence. Regulation is used to win in the political arena what groups fail to in the market. Thus, if the costs of forming a cartel are high, government will be enlisted to achieve by fiat an environment in which a cartel can operate effectively.

This view of regulation underpins many of the Thatcher government's reforms. Its diagnosis of the failures of the Heath, and previous Conservative and Labour governments, was that they over-regulated the economy, creating legally protected pockets of monopoly and inefficiency. The corporatism, which was a feature of the mixed economy and consensus politics of the 1960s and 1970s, made government the instrument of industry and trade unions. As a government White Paper (DTI, 1988, para. 1.3) states:

> Corporatism limited competition and the birth of new firms whilst, at the same time, encouraging protectionism and restrictions designed to help existing firms.

Supply-side economics views government not as a benign force but pernicious and destructive. The market, by which is meant free autonomous individuals trading and working in markets under the rule of law, maximises the wealth of a nation and the welfare of its members. Government has limited though important functions. It must establish and enforce a system of private and public property rights which will encourage private initiative and enterprise. It also should have responsibilities for defence, law and order, maintaining the value of the currency and alleviating pockets of real deprivation. Some regard even this list as excessive. For example, increasingly it has been argued that politicians cannot be trusted with control of the money supply because they are congenitally prone to debasing the currency by inflationary policies.

Reality is, of course, more complex than the competing visions of political parties. Nonetheless, the basic tenets of Thatcherism are now accepted by Left and Right, and provide a new consensus which accords the market a significantly greater role.

Nationalisation – Designed to Fail

The failure of the state is seen in the unworkable character of British post-war nationalisation. The Labour government of

Clement Attlee (1947–51) created nationalised industries with vague objectives and few controls. They were required to break-even taking one year with another, and to operate in the public interest. The Attlee nationalisations were in retrospect a massive error, the consequences of which unfolded in the subsequent three decades. They were, in short, designed to fail.

Their failure arose from three basic factors – monopoly, weak financial and managerial discipline, and political interference.

Nationalisation confused public ownership with monopoly. Many key industries – the so-called commanding heights of the economy – were rationalised into large industrial monoliths sometimes bringing hundreds of separate firms under one management, e.g. the gas industry. These nationalised monoliths grew cumbersome, festered with inefficiency, and increasingly insensitive to their workers and customers. They exhibited all the problems of monopoly.

The control problem manifested itself in the failure of the Attlee government and those which followed to devise appropriate managerial and financial disciplines for the nationalised industries. Recommendations and proposals for investment and pricing rules were generally ignored and the regulatory structure deeply flawed. The much quoted study by the National Economic Development Office (NEDO, 1976) pulled few punches in its assessment of the failure of the regulatory structure within which the nationalised industries operated. It painted a vivid picture of *ad hocery*, confusion and blatant political manipulation. The regulatory framework was described as 'unsatisfactory and in need of radical change'. Among the catalogue of deficiencies was the lack of trust and mutual understanding between government and management, confusion about their roles, and the absence of an effective system for measuring performance and managerial competence.

The politicians also found interference unavoidable and irresistible. They intervened in the day-to-day affairs of the nationalised industries because nearly every significant investment, employment and production decision became a political matter, often decided on political not commercial grounds. At other times the politicians shamelessly used the nationalised industries to control inflation and wages, and promote regional and employment policies unrelated to providing efficient service to customers.

The Evolution of Regulatory Policy

The growth of regulation did not start with a theory. It evolved to deal with the more intractable problems posed by privatisation and liberalisation and was often seen as quite distinct from these policies (Graham and Prosser, 1987; Veljanovski, 1988).

The growth of regulation comes from three sources – privatisation, liberalisation and the European Community.

Privatisation

Privatisation of the nationalised industries is the most significant of the Thatcher government's supply-side policies (Veljanovski, 1988, 1989). Prior to 1984 the industries which were privatised did not raise particular concerns requiring new regulation. This altered with the privatisation of British Telecom (Table 13.3). BT had and still has a dominant position in the provision of basic telecommunications in the UK, and a monopoly of the local domestic telephone system. It therefore has the ability to wield substantial market power to raise prices and lower the quality of service to the customer. The government decided that a new system of regulation was required in addition to competition law. The broad terms of the economic regulation of BT were sketched out by Professor Stephen Littlechild (Littlechild, 1983), now a regulator in his own right as Director General of the Office of Electricity Regulation, who proposed that in those areas where BT had a monopoly, the average price of a bundle of these services should increase by no more than the retail price index minus 3 per cent (revised to 4.5 per cent in 1989), the so-called 'RPI minus x' formula. In effect, the real price of these services would fall. This control was seen as a stop-gap until competition arrived from other telecommunications providers such as

TABLE 13.3   *UK privatisations, 1977–89*

Company	Date of sale*
Public offerings 1977–89:	
Amersham International	February 1982
Associated British Ports	February 1983
	April 1984
BAA	July 1987
British Aerospace	February 1981
	May 1985
British Airways	February 1987
British Gas	December 1986
British Petroleum	June 1977
	November 1979
	September 1983
	October 1987
British Telecom	November 1984
Britoil	November 1982
	August 1985
Cable & Wireless	October 1981
	December 1983
	December 1985
Enterprise Oil	June 1984
Jaguar	July 1984
Rolls Royce	May 1987
Water Authorities	December 1989
Private sales 1979–87:	
British Shipbuilders	May 1985–March 1986
British Technology Group (NEB)	December 1979–August 1984
National Bus Company	August 1986–March 1988
National Freight Company	February 1982
Rover Group	January–June 1987
British Rail	March 1983–July 1984
British Airways	March 1983–September 1986
British Gas Wych Farm	May 1984
Royal Ordnance	October 1986–April 1987

Note: * Dates of flotation of tranches.

Source: Veljanovski (ed.), *Privatisation and Competition: A Market Prospectus*, London: Institute of Economic Affairs, 1989, tables 1 and 2, pp. 192–3.

Mercury Communications and the new generation of broadband cable systems (Beesley and Laidlaw, 1989).

In subsequent privatisation – British Gas, BAA, water and electricity – the government followed a pattern – develop a system of economic regulation administered by a new watchdog. However, the guiding principles of the Littlechild Report, that regulation should be simple, transparent and rely on competition wherever possible, have been severely compromised. Often competition has been deliberately restricted, most notably in the cases of British Gas and the electricity supply industries. This has required more elaborate and complex regulations to substitute for competition, and placed a heavy burden on the regulator. Second, the nature of price control has also altered. It is now a permanent feature of regulation, not the stop-gap initially envisaged. It has become more elaborate and complex. In all privatisation where it is used, apart from BT, certain costs are passed through to the customer on the grounds that they are unavoidable. In the water and electricity industries the concept of yardstick competition has been used which seeks to set x (the so-called efficiency factor) by reference to some industry average level of efficiency improvement. The scope and detail of the formula has increased, covering more prices in more elaborate arithmetical formulations. The principle of simplicity has disappeared. Third, there has been a tendency to transform the RPI-minus-x formula into rate of return regulation. Littlechild saw price and rate of return regulation as alternatives. Rate of return gives an industry a 'reasonable' rate of return on 'allowable costs'. It was disparaged as 'US-style regulation' which was inflationary and encouraged cost-padding. However, a regulated industry's profitability has become one of the touchstones in the revision of the RPI-minus-x formula every five years (Oftel, 1988).

Liberalisation

Liberalisation has been another source of increased regulation, most evident in the financial services sector. In 1985 the Gower Report (Gower Report, 1985) made recommendations for a new system of investor protection to accompany the restructuring of the City known popularly as Big Bang of October 1986. This was touted as self-regulation backed by statute. A private company limited by guarantee, the Securities and Investment Board (SIB), was designated to administer investor protection laws, draft a rulebook and ensure that the self-regulatory organisation, or SROs, provided investors with rules which afforded them equivalent protection. A series of insider trading and illegal share dealing 'scandals' pressed the SIB to draft a very detailed set of rules. After the stock market crash of 1987, financial institutions began to realise that the FSA and the proposed rules drafted by the SIB would impose considerable costs and retard innovation in the financial sector. Sir Kenneth Berrill had been hand-picked to develop light regulation. Yet, instead of employing an economically based and flexible approach, he created a legalistic, complex and detailed set of rules, some of which were publicly criticised by the Office of Fair Trading as excessively costly and not in the interests of the consumer (Seldon, 1988). Under mounting pressure he was not re-appointed. Within a matter of months the SIB rulebook had been redrafted and key provisions of the Act repealed.

European Community

The European Community has become another major source of new regulation as part of its Single Internal Market programme. The purpose of SIM is to create a market allowing the free movement of goods, services, capital and people. In order to achieve this the European Commission set out a detailed legislative programme of 300 Acts to remove non-tariff barriers to trade by 31 December 1992. EC regulation has given rise to several particular concerns. One is the confusion between removing a barrier to trade and harmonisation which fails to take into account the different circumstances of each member state. This uniformity can act as a barrier by imposing differential costs on industry and regions. Second, many directives are interventionist, imposing higher standards than necessary to ensure the free efficient movement of goods and services. Third, the political and social dimensions of the SIM programme have caused considerable opposition from the British government because they are seen as inefficient and unnecessary regulation of industry – such as minimum wage legislation under the EC Commission's proposal for a 'Social Charter', and eroding national sovereignty (Dahrendorf *et al.*, 1989). Finally, the quest for monetary union through membership of the European Monetary Union (EMU), Exchange Rate Mechanism, and proposals for a single European central bank and common currency, all foreshadow increased centralised regulation.

The Proliferation of Watchdogs

The growth of regulation has been accompanied by the proliferation of regulatory watchdogs modelled on the Office of Fair Trading.

Six new regulatory authorities have so far been established – the Office of Telecommunications (Oftel) and the Cable Authority in 1984, the Office of Gas Supply (Ofgas) in 1986, the Office of Water, and the National Rivers Authority in 1989. When the electricity supply industry is privatised the Office of Electricity Regulation will assume its full responsibilities.

In other sectors new watchdogs have been established. In the financial sector the SIB and five SROs have been created to administer the Financial Services Act. The broadcasting sector will see the abolition of the Independent Broadcasting Authority and the Cable Authority to be replaced with three new watchdogs – the Independent Television Commission (ITC), the Radio Authority and the Broadcasting Standards Council (BSC).

Many of the existing watchdogs, such as the Office of Fair Trading (OFT), the Monopolies and Mergers Commission (MMC), and the Civil Aviation Authority (CAA) have had their powers extended. Prior to privatisation the MMC could only examine the efficiency and costs of the nationalised industries. Now, the Secretary of State can make a 'privatised undertaking' reference to the MMC to examine the competition aspects of those utilities which are now in the private sector. It would not have been conceivable under nationalisation for British Gas to be called to book as it was recently for overcharging its industrial customers (Monopolies and Mergers Commission, 1989).

These watchdogs have a range of responsibilities. They have the power to monitor performance, prices and the quality of service, and to ensure that the consumer is afforded protection. They typically combine a number of functions: they administer economic regulation under the RPI-x price rule where relevant, ensure that the privatised (or liberalised) firms comply with the terms of their licenses, have a general brief to 'promote' or 'enable' competition in the industry, and to detect anti-competitive practices, act as a conduit for consumer complaints and in some cases, most notably the broadcasting and City regulators, are responsible for licensing new firms.

The rise of the regulatory watchdog has established a new layer of largely unaccountable public administration in the UK. Baldwin and McCrudden (1987) describe them as 'constitutional anomalies' because they combine functions normally kept separate in the British system of public administration. The watchdogs also have wide powers and considerable discretion. Thus a small number of powerful regulators are able to make decisions about basic pricing and investment decisions which will affect the whole British economy. The system of control over the agencies is weak. The prospect of judicial review by the courts will generally prevent the agency from acting beyond the scope of its powers (*ultra vires*) and breaching natural justice. Although the scope of judicial review has been increased by the courts in recent years, its impact on good decision-making by regulatory agencies can be expected to be minimal, since the English courts are reluctant to examine the merits of the decision and the watchdogs can often judgement-proof their decisions by not giving reasons.

The Techniques of Intervention

A number of innovative techniques have been employed by the Thatcher government. These include the use of incentive regulation (RPI-minus-x price caps), new consumer rights (e.g. compensation for delays in the repair of a telephone) and pro-competitive common carrier laws. In other industries licensing and competitive franchising and so-called 'economic instruments' (OECD, 1989) of regulation such as pollution taxes, marketable pollution rights, pricing auctions, and the greater use of private litigation as a way of enforcing the law have been used. Other innovations have been competitive tendering, contracting out and executive agencies.

The move to regulation has had some clear benefits. For the privatised industries the move from nationalisation to regulation separates management from the task of regulating its own affairs in the public interest, and opens to public scrutiny the actions of the privatised industries and the regulator. Regulation is more 'transparent' than control through nationalisation. In addition, consumers have been given more rights and compensation payments for delay and interruption of services. Most of these privatised utilities are subject to investigation by the MMC if they engage in anti-competitive practices designed to harm customers, suppliers and competitors. The public interest, in short, is no longer defined by their management.

Yet there are defects with the way the new economic regulation has evolved. It has grown in a piecemeal and idiosyncratic fashion, often the outcome of the short-term constraints imposed by the need for the successful sale of a nationalised industry. The regulatory frameworks have become increasingly complex, often substituting for competition. There has been a failure to subject the new regulatory schemes and specific regulatory proposals to genuine cost–benefit appraisals. The use of cost–benefit techniques under clearly understood procedures and guidelines, independently audited, is essential if over-regulation is to be avoided.

In other areas of regulation there is a belated realisation that legalistic controls should be replaced with 'economic instruments' such as taxes, marketable permits and auctions, which are more effective and cheaper methods of regulation. These approaches, which have recently been proposed for the regulation of broadcasting and the environment, rely on market-like mechanisms to ensure compliance at the least cost (Pearce *et al.*, 1989; OECD, 1989).

Prospects for the Future

The withdrawal of the state from the ownership of industry and the liberalisation of markets has led to increasing intervention by regulation, much of which is ill-thought-out and likely to generate continuing inefficiencies and rigidities in the economy. Moreover, the locus of power to determine prices and investment decisions has shifted from politicians and trade unions to management and regulators; both these coalitions can harm industrial performance. Regulation has its own internal momentum. This is because regulation initially focuses on easily regulated variables and squeezes monopoly problems into less obvious areas requiring further regulation. Oftel has on a number of occasions threatened to regulate prices of BT services outside the RPI-minus-x formula, and reached informal agreement for price caps on others. Regulation has been extended to the quality of service in response to public disquiet. Whether true or not there was a perception that price controls lead to poor service and hence the need for the regulator to control service. The ideal of 'simple' limited regulation is a mirage. As long as monopoly exists and government is involved, regulation will grow and become increasingly complex. It starts with regulating the most obvious monopoly abuses, squeezing the problems into progressively harder to regulate areas. Soon the regulator discovers that he is shadowing management, second-guessing them and virtually running the company. The worst conceivable outcome is that we move slowly into a regulatory crisis (in much the same way as the US did in the 1970s). The policy prescription is as simple as it is obvious and is consistent with the basic tenets underlying the government's new industrial policy – rely on individual enterprise and competition. Only when these two have been maximised should we rely on regulation. When regulation is used it should be the least restrictive way to mimic the results which would have been achieved by the competitive market-place.

14

The Politics of the 1988 Education Reform Act

GEOFF WHITTY

The political origins of the Education Reform Act can be located in the crisis of the social democratic settlement of the post-war years (Centre for Contemporary Cultural Studies (CCCS), 1981; Whitty and Menter, 1988). This led to a breakdown and reassessment of the traditional compromises between old humanists, industrial trainers and public educators which had shaped the development of state education (Williams, 1965), and to the dissolution of the partnership between central and local government and the teaching profession which is often seen as the basis of the post-war settlement (Kogan, 1975). In that settlement, central government had provided broad policies, which were then administered and interpreted by county or district councils acting as local education authorities, which in turn entrusted curriculum decision-making largely to professionals on the ground. The settlement worked best in the period when the contradictions between the various functions ascribed to education, and the different aspirations of the parties involved, could be broadly reconciled in an expanding system.

However, a growing economic crisis generated calls for a reduction of the growth in state spending and the specification of clearer priorities for the education service. At the same time, deficiencies in the education service were themselves looked to as a possible cause of economic decline. A critique of the consequences of the post-war settlement was begun by a series of Black Papers on education published during the late 1960s and 1970s (Cox and Dyson, 1971), but it received official recognition in a speech by Labour prime minister James Callaghan at Ruskin College Oxford in October 1976, which launched a 'Great Debate' on education. This reflected an acceptance by the Labour leadership that the sort of progressive education that had developed in a period of relative professional autonomy in the 1950s and 1960s was out of step both with the needs of British industry and the wishes of parents. Among the solutions canvassed were the development of a core curriculum for all schools and new mechanisms of accountability.

The case was strengthened by widespread media coverage of events at William Tyndale Junior School in Islington, North London, where the head and a group of teachers were eventually dismissed after an official enquiry into allegations that they had abused their autonomy and manipulated the curriculum for politically motivated purposes. Dale (1989) argues that this affair facilitated attempts by the state to restructure and redirect the education service. It led, in particular, to the 'scapegoating' and closer monitoring of teachers and to an articulation of parent power with a conservative educational programme.

Labour's Great Debate was essentially an opinion-forming exercise, guided by a stream of documents from Her Majesty's Inspectorate of Schools and from the Department of Education and Science, and did not itself result in any major legislation. However, it served to legitimate a number of themes which were taken up with greater vigour by the first two Thatcher administrations. The 1980 Education Act, introduced by Mark Carlisle, Thatcher's first Secretary of State for Education and Science, sought to make schools more accountable by extending parental choice and began to erode the power of local education authorities. Despite his failure to endorse a more radical approach to these issues in the form of education vouchers, both these processes were accelerated under Sir Keith Joseph and reflected in the two Education Acts of 1986. A Technical and Vocational Education Initiative, sponsored by the Manpower Services Commission, sought to modernise the school curriculum and make it more relevant to the needs of industry. As demographic changes removed the threat of mass youth unemployment and replaced it with the spectre of massive skills shortages, the role of further and higher education in the economy also came under increasing scrutiny. Meanwhile, a start was made on rationalising vocational qualifications and certificating competences achieved in non-traditional educational settings.

The relationship of these various initiatives to each other and to existing provision remained unclear and it was only with the Great Education Reform Bill introduced by Joseph's successor, Kenneth Baker, in 1987 that the government has been seen to be altering radically the settlement enshrined in the 1944 Education Act. Johnson (1989) argues that only in this fifth phase of Thatcherite education policy – which he terms Bakerism – has there also been a concerted attempt to harmonise the various Tory tendencies which had influenced earlier initiatives. He believes that, as a result, the main configurations of formal schooling will be unrecognisable in many respects by the mid-1990s.

The Great Education Reform Bill

Even so, there is little evidence that the Bill itself was conceived as a grand design for education, since it effectively brought together in one piece of legislation a number of specific measures that had been mooted by the right over the years as ways of curbing the worst excesses of the existing system. The Bill was summed up by the Secretary of State in the House of Commons as embodying 'standards, freedom and choice' (1 December 1987). At its centre was a National Curriculum of core and foundation subjects (English, mathematics, science, technology, history, geography, art, music, P.E. and a modern foreign language) and an associated system of attainment testing for all children in state schools at ages 7, 11, 14 and 16. It also sought to make state schools more responsive to market forces by permitting open enrolment to schools in accordance with parental preference rather than letting local education authorities impose artificial limits on particular schools to maintain the viability of others. All larger schools and colleges were to be freed from the detailed bureaucratic control of LEAs by a system of devolved budgets and local management (LMS), while some parents were to be given the opportunity to vote to take their schools right out of LEA control as free-standing Grant Maintained Schools. City Technology Colleges, another new sort of school outside of LEA control announced at the 1986 Conservative Party conference, were also to be given a statutory basis by this Bill. In addition, it embodied some earlier White Paper proposals for the reform of university and public sector Higher Education. These involved the replacement of the University Grants Committee with a Universities Funding Council and the establishment of a new Polytechnics and Colleges Funding Council, which removed most of the major public sector institutions from LEA control. As originally published, the Bill also gave individual inner London boroughs the opportunity to opt out of the Inner London Education Authority.

Many of these items can be seen to respond directly to criticisms, on the one hand, of teacher autonomy and, on the other hand, LEA (especially left-wing LEA) bureaucracy and interference. Some sought to increase the accountability of educational institutions to central government, while others were intended to expose them more directly to the rigours of market forces. Some appeared to reflect centralising tendencies, while others seemed to imply decentralisation. Some signalled modernising tendencies, others a return to traditional values. This has produced an Act which appears to lack internal coherence, but some of the different elements can be interpreted as a response to different strands within the thinking of the New Right. Thus the imposition of a National Curriculum can be seen as a response to a neo-conservative emphasis on culture, tradition and nationality, while the clauses on open enrolment, local financial management and opting-out can be seen to reflect neo-liberal thinking.

Nevertheless, both can also be seen as part of a broader attempt to atomise educational decision-making within a clear legislative framework, using central government powers to remove or dissipate the influence of intervening powers such as LEAs, trade unions and entrenched professional interest groups. The strength of the state is then being used to remove anything that interferes with the operation of market forces or with the development of an appropriate sense of self and nation on the part of free citizens and consumers. On this interpretation, not only do the powers of local education authorities and the teachers' trade unions over the structures of education need to be reduced, it also becomes imperative to police the curriculum to ensure that the pervasive collectivist and universalistic welfare ideology of the post-war era is restrained so that support for the market, enterprise and self-help can be encouraged. The paradoxical suggestion by junior minister Bob Dunn, in an address to the Institute of Economic Affairs, that 'a study of the life and teachings of Adam Smith should be compulsory in all schools' (quoted in *Education*, 8 July 1988) was perhaps only an extreme version of that way of thinking.

The two central strands of New Right thinking come together particularly clearly in the writings of an influential pressure group on education, the so-called Hillgate Group (1987). This predominantly neo-conservative group seems to accept that market forces should ultimately be seen as the most effective way of determining a school's curriculum, but argues that central government intervention is necessary as an interim strategy to undermine the power of vested interests that threaten educational standards and traditional values. The government's own long-term preference for market forces is perhaps reflected in the fact that it has felt it appropriate not to impose its National Curriculum and the associated attainment targets and testing arrangements on independent schools (including those in receipt of public funds through the Assisted Places Scheme) and only in broad terms on the new City Technology Colleges. The inclusion of Grant Maintained Schools in the arrangements presumably implies that they will take some time to throw off their local education authority origins and develop the responsive new working practices that the government would like to see emerge. Seen in this light, there is arguably more consistency in the Bill than at first appeared. The apparent inconsistencies can be seen to reflect what Johnson (1989) terms a 'dirty' neo-liberal approach, in which policies at odds with the 'pure' form of that ideology are given support in the short term. Advocates of this approach, who seem to have considerable influence with the Thatcher administration, recognise a need for prior reconstruction before a free market in education can successfully operate.

Opposition to the Bill

Nevertheless, the underlying tensions within the New Right were reflected in the public debates around the Bill. Neo-liberal suspicions of a 'nationalised curriculum' were embodied in Lord Joseph's unsuccessful attempts to make the National Curriculum advisory rather than mandatory. Furthermore, the final format of the National Curriculum was itself a compromise between those seeking to modernise schools for industry through a massive injection of technology and neo-conservatives nostalgic for a return to the traditional grammar-school curriculum. The debate over religious education and collective worship, neither of which figured prominently in the original version of the Bill, brought other important tensions to light. However, with the possible exception of the Lords' vote against the arrangements for ballots on Grant Maintained status, most of the successful amendments (other than those proposed by the government) reflected the continuing, though muted, power of the traditional establishment. The most successful campaigns in the House of Lords were mounted by the Church of England, partly in moderating the more extreme demands of the New Right, by the universities in seeking to preserve some minimal assurances of academic freedom (an issue on which the polytechnics remained ominously silent), and by paternalistic peers who sought to protect the interests of children with special educational needs.

Despite considerable political and professional opposition to many elements of the Bill outside parliament, consultation periods on most of the major provisions were kept to a minimum and little notice apparently taken of their outcomes (Haviland, 1988). Mainstream opposition challenges and those inspired by the trade-union and LEA lobbies made virtually no impact. Not one of the many amendments proposed by the Association of County Councils was successful. Indeed, most of the main changes to the Bill as it passed through parliament reflected growing confidence by the government itself that its approach was essentially correct or needed strengthening. The number of new powers assigned to the Secretary of State is reported to have increased from 200 to 400 during the passage of the Bill (*Guardian*, 18 July 1988). Other changes, such as the outright abolition of the ILEA, proposed by an alliance between Norman Tebbit and Michael Heseltine, merely confirmed that any initial caution on the government's part was unnecessary. Even the Lords' amendments mentioned above were eventually incorporated into the Act in a form that limited their impact.

Effects of the Education Reform Act

A Bill that started as an amalgam of disparate measures has thus ended up as a more coherent codification of the right's approach to educational policy in the late twentieth century. The effects of the Act's implementation, however, have yet to be felt. Nevertheless, as we have already noted, some commentators have predicted that the new Act will reverse many of the changes that have taken place in education since the war. In many ways, this was intended and supporters of the Act see it as likely to raise standards through the rigours of the market. But critics argue that this is merely rhetorical cover for using education to legitimate existing inequalities. Although, at this stage, it is only possible to estimate what the likely effects of this Act will be, many observers fear that popular schools will either become larger or more selective in their intakes, leaving the others (and the children in them) to their fate. In general terms, the loss of pupils to the 'popular' schools will clearly have a damaging effect on other schools, both in terms of resources (especially in the context of local financial management) and in terms of morale. It is likely to encourage the reintroduction of covert selective admission to those 'popular' schools, which would further erode the comprehensive ideal and the principle of education for all.

The open market orientation of the proposals could also exacerbate divisions which already exist in society, by favouring those with the cultural resources to make informed choices, and create a stratum of 'sink' schools where pupils will have less than equal opportunity unless LEAs are able to intervene to ensure that they have adequate resources. Commentators from urban areas have expressed additional fears that such a policy will lead to racially segregated schools. The government has made much of the fact that Grant Maintained Schools will not normally be permitted to change their character or admissions policies within five years of opting out, but the governors may then apply to change by publishing statutory proposals for public comment. This too has been seen by critics as a backdoor means of reintroducing academic selection, albeit after a delay, though even that may not be necessary if there are changes in local circumstance. Some have suggested that the identification of individual schools' costs through devolved budgets is a halfway house to the identification of per capita costs which can then be used as a basis for the introduction of vouchers (Demaine, 1988; Maclure, 1988).

There are those who argue that, taken together, the provisions of the Act will establish a clear hierarchy of schools, perhaps running from independent schools through City Technology Colleges and Grant Maintained Schools, leaving under-resourced LEA or 'Council' schools as agencies of social control in the inner cities (Bash and Coulby, 1989). Certainly, some of the draft formulae for devolving budgets to schools have confirmed the worst fears of their critics, in so far as they appear to take resources away from hard-pressed inner city schools and redistribute them to those suburban schools which are already benefiting from increased parental fund-raising. However, the early indications are that the effects of the Act will be rather more uneven than the neater speculative scenarios suggest. Margaret Thatcher's view that most schools would eventually want to opt out of LEA control does not appear to be supported by the initial applications and some of these have come from schools whose proven worth is far from demonstrable. Meanwhile, some independent schools, as well as LEA maintained schools, are concerned about competition from 'free' Grant Maintained Schools and City Technology Colleges.

But it is in the implementation of the proposals on curriculum and assessment that some of the most contradictory developments seem to be taking place. Despite some evidence of a political veto over appointments to the new statutory bodies in this area, the reports produced by government-appointed working parties have largely embodied the collective wisdom and continuing influence of that 'liberal educational establishment' that is blamed by the New Right for a decline in standards. Most ironically of all, Black Paper editor Brian Cox has threatened to resign as chair of the English working party if its relatively liberal proposals are overturned by the government and its National Curriculum Council.

Meanwhile, the Confederation of British Industry has argued that the changes the government has made to other working party proposals run contrary to industry's needs by giving 'too much importance to narrow academic knowledge and too little to the fostering of transferable skills' (Jackson, 1989). The nineteenth-century conflicts between old humanists, industrial trainers and public educators (Williams, 1965) have thus by no means been resolved by the Education Reform Act. Many commentators have pointed to an apparent down-grading of the 'modernising' Technical and Vocational Education Initiative in the National Curriculum and the resemblance between the latter and the traditional curriculum that has so often been blamed for the decline of England's industrial spirit (Wiener, 1981; Barnett, 1986).

On the other hand, many critics of the government's higher education reforms believe that they will undermine traditional academic standards and values. This is partly because of the anticipated influence of industrialists on the new funding councils, but also because a new system of competitive bidding for funds is expected to force down unit costs and lead to production-line approaches to education and training. Yet, despite its declared commitment to increasing access to higher education, the government's recently announced decision to introduce student loans is regarded by many commentators as likely to reduce the already low level of working-class participation in English higher education. Indeed, one vice-chancellor has claimed that it will produce a 'hereditary graduate class', an outcome decidedly at variance with the declared aspirations of the 'Thatcher revolution'.

Some of the complications surrounding the implementation of the Education Reform Act arise from the different interests of those involved in implementing policy. For example, the Act has provided a political context in which officials at the Department of Education and Science have been able to assume a curriculum role in schools that had partially been usurped by the Department of Employment when the Manpower Services Commission/Training Agency sponsored the Technical and Vocational Education Initiative. Furthermore, TVEI is itself an example of a central government initiative that, within limits, has been significantly shaped by teachers in schools and sometimes used for progressive purposes (Dale, 1989), even if their claims to have 'hi-jacked' its agenda can be exaggerated (Jones, 1989). The different histories of the various parts of the education system also remain significant, and the differing dispositions of political forces in and around schools and higher education suggest that one should not necessarily expect identical outcomes in the different sectors.

Other policy issues also impact upon the implementation of the Act. The issue of teacher supply seriously calls into question the extent to which its school reforms can be implemented in a manner consistent with its declared aims. The lack of suitably qualified teachers in mathematics, science, technology and modern languages, and some absolute teacher shortages in areas like inner London, make highly problematic the equitable delivery of the National Curriculum and the achievement of the standards it was intended to ensure. It is also sometimes suggested that there is a tension between the enhanced standards of professionalism the government has been calling for and the close monitoring of teachers associated with current policies. While it remains to be seen whether the programmes of study and testing arrangements associated with the National Curriculum effectively serve to de-skill teachers at classroom level, there are certainly elements of current policies that have undermined the strength of teaching as an organised profession and this may have longer-term implications (for good or ill) for the quality of the teaching force.

There are clear indications that this attack on organised teachers has been a deliberate policy and one consistent with others pursued by the Thatcher government. On the one hand, the abandonment of collective pay bargaining in 1987 and the subsequent imposition of pay deals recommended by an interim pay body have involved the use of the powers of central government to undermine vested interests. On the other hand, the Reform Act itself has introduced devolution and deregulation as tools for disciplining the workforce. Local management of schools is likely to limit the power of trade unions at national and LEA levels, while at least one of the new City Technology Colleges is planning not to recognise trade unions in pay bargaining and opting instead for a non-strike agreement with its staff association. A provision which permits the Secretary of State to licence people with only two years of higher education, and no pre-service training, re-verses the trend of the past twenty years towards teaching becoming an all-graduate profession and is seen by many within the teaching profession as gainsaying the government's declared commitment to improving teaching quality.

A New Politics of Education?

The Education Reform Act was a coming together of a variety of measures which partly responded to immediate demands for action on specific issues and partly represented the cul-mination of broader pressures towards new modes of account-ability in education. While some measures derived from a recognition of serious deficiencies within the education sys-tem, the apportionment of blame and the particular solutions proposed were clearly influenced by various fractions of the New Right. To what extent, then, has the passage of the Act signalled a significant change in the politics of education in England?

There is no doubt that organised teachers are no longer a significant partner in the initiation and implementation of educational policy and that LEAs have been consigned to a distinctly subordinate role in its implementation. Within central government, politicians have reclaimed for themselves some of the influence over education policy that had been increasingly passing into the hands of state bureaucrats (Salter and Tapper, 1981). Raab (1989) has asked whether the end of the old partnership signals the abandonment of an earlier thrust towards a corporatist mode of educational politics or even of the special interest group mode of pluralism that characterised the post-war settlement. The new arrangements seem to put LEAs and teachers into an 'agency' relationship with central government rather than a partnership, while some of the reforms point towards a form of dispersed pluralism in educational policy-making, the ideal version of which is the atomised market. But Raab also points out that the government can still be seen as engaging in special interest group politics, by identifying more amenable new partners, in the form of parents and industry. These 'operate from a weaker, more fragmented, and less continuously active power base' than do central government's traditional partners in education policy-making, the LEAs and teacher trade unions, and arguably they are more open to manipulation by central government. Certainly, in ignoring parental votes against the abolition of the ILEA and the establishment of at least two City Technology Colleges, the government has demonstrated that 'parent power' is a tool to be employed when it helps to legitimate desired policies but ignored when it contradicts them.

As Raab (1989) puts it, 'the negotiative, bargaining style that seemed the hallmark of British twentieth-century democracy has gone out of fashion as the middle levels of influence are excluded or circumvented. The locus of decision-making shifts to an unreconciled and an inchoate mixture of central government and a newly-enfranchised, dispersed, pluralist array of decision-makers.' Yet, while downgrading the significance of some traditional contexts of educational decision-making, the Act has also produced an increase in the number of potentially significant arenas for educational politics and some of these may be highly susceptible to the influence of other vested interests, including ironically the liberal educational establishment. Indeed, recent research has indicated that, on the newly powerful governing bodies of schools, professionals and parents tend to act together (Golby and Brigley, 1989).

Nevertheless, at the level of policy formation and initiation in education, the role of central government has clearly been strengthened by recent legislation, even if, at the level of implementation, the outcomes of the new arrangements remain less clear. It may well be that a more open pluralist model of decision-making will apply at that level, but it cannot be seen independently of the strengthened role of central government in determining who are legitimate parties in that decision-making process and the context in which it is carried out. To this extent, the new arrangements can be seen as a reworking of the dual polity approach to contemporary politics rather than as a straightforward abandonment of any semblance of corporatist planning in favour of market forces.

There is anyway little doubt that the ideology both of the revised structure of the education system and the likely content of the national curriculum will undermine the notion that collective struggle, as opposed to individual decision-making, is a legitimate way of fighting for social justice in any arena. As such, the Act is likely to sustain structural inequalities rather than challenge them while at the same time fostering the idea that its championing of standards, freedom and choice in itself provides equal opportunities for all those individuals who wish to benefit from them. Yet the notion that a market approach can be justified in education remains highly contested. Ranson has argued that, if 'professional accountability' was dominant in the period from 1944 until the mid-1970s, and 'market accountability' is now the favoured approach to controlling the education system, what is needed in future is 'public accountability' in which individuals exercise choice as citizens, concerned with the well-being of others and the health of society, rather than merely as self-interested consumers (Ranson, 1988). The realisation of that vision must await another Act.

15

Industrial Relations

COLIN CROUCH

If British industrial relations policies in the 1970s moved in a Scandinavian direction – a deep involvement of organised labour and employers in economic management, a tripartite active labour market policy – during the 1980s they became like those of early Fifth Republic France. Reflecting a general political division in which political groups and individuals were either part of a *majorité* (insiders, trusted, able to participate in public life) or relegated to a *minorité* (excluded, unconsulted, marginalised), organised labour was pushed to or beyond the boundaries of political respectability. And for much of the time trade unions responded to this by retreating into an outsider's protest role.

This basic pattern was set early on in the Thatcher government's period. Did the final three years of the 1980s contribute anything new? In my view, very little; if anything the pattern was reinforced, in one area of policy – training – quite dramatically so. Whether one surveys industrial relations *per se* on the ground, changes in legislation, developments at the tripartite level, that basic thesis holds. The only differences are to be found in the conduct and strategy of the unions and their associated Labour Party. We shall deal with these themes in turn.

Industrial Relations on the Ground

With the exception of the 1984–5 miners' strike and some other major conflicts, levels of industrial conflict have been

318

TABLE 15.1   *Industrial conflict in the UK, 1950–88*

Years	Average annual figures for five-year periods		
	No. of strikes	Workers involved (000)	Working days lost (000)
1950–54	1701	583	1903
1955–59	2530	738	4602
1960–64	2512	1493	3180
1965–69	2380	1208	3929
1970–74	2885	1564	14077
1975–79	2335	1658	11663
1980–84	1363	1298	10486
1985–88*	944	797	3893

* Average of four years only.

Source: *Department of Employment Gazette (rounded figures).*

relatively low (see Table 15.1). Numbers of strikes, already in decline in the latter 1970s, are now at their lowest post-war levels. Worker involvements and aggregate days lost did not decline markedly until mid-decade, but then did so steeply. There were signs of a change in 1989, with important disputes in several public services and major private firms, but it is too early to consider whether this constitutes a real change of trend.

The later years of the 1980s also saw no real let-up, despite economic recovery, in the numerical decline of both trade-union membership and the manual working class in which unionism has been rooted. As Table 15.2 shows, union membership has returned to levels typical of the late 1960s.

TABLE 15.2   *Trade-union members, UK, 1975–87*

Years	Union members (000)	Density (%)*
1975	12,026	53
1980	12,947	56
1985	10,821	52
1986	10,539	50
1987	10,475	49

* Union members as a percentage of employees in employment (i.e. excluding unemployed).

Source: *Department of Employment Gazette (percentages rounded).*

How viable are current levels of union membership, given that the workforce is increasingly to be found in non-manual, private-sector, female or low-skilled occupations, while unions have their main strength among male, relatively skilled manual workers and among workers of all kinds in the public sector? It is clearly these developments that lie behind the union decline, but in order to assess their likely long-term impact we need to bear in mind several points. First, the public-sector decline is a very recent phenomenon, largely associated with privatisation. For much of the 1980s public employment actually increased; membership of the main public-service unions has been the most stable; and the main privatised monopolies and oligopolies have not seen an important decline in union membership. Since it is in these public and semi-public services that unions are most able to break through the gender and white-collar barriers, the continued strength of this kind of membership remains a major source of union stability.

Second, the decline in male manual employment had set in well before the 1980s and was a factor during the time of the rise in union membership during the 1970s. Further, unions initially reached a 40 per cent representation level in the early post-war economy that was much more 'male manual manufacturing' than the present one, so in some senses their current membership presence represents a remarkable achievement. Proportions of female and white-collar members have indeed risen steadily over the years, even if they remain small; the fastest growing union during the 1980s has been the Banking, Insurance and Finance Union. Unions' biggest difficulties in recruitment are among people in irregular, low-skilled employment, or pseudo-self-employment, where conditions are simply too precarious for workers to risk joining unions. But the capacity of employers in such firms to behave the way they do is itself part of a political context that can change rather than an ineluctable economic destiny.

There is widespread agreement among observers that where unions had already established collective bargaining arrangements with employers, these were unlikely to be destroyed by management. A Confederation of British Industry report in 1989 (Ingram and Cahill, 1989) found that the proportion of private manufacturing firms who bargained with unions had remained virtually static between 1979 and 1986 (falling from 72 per cent to 70 per cent), such decline as there was being concentrated in firms with less than 100 workers and therefore affecting only a small minority of employees. Of the 249 plants they surveyed that had bargained with unions in 1979, only ten had ceased to do so by 1986, while nine of the 132 not recognising unions in 1979 had started to do so by 1986.

However, managers, especially perhaps those in the public sector, have been quick to take advantage of labour's weakened economic and political position to increase their control over work practices, work speeds, etc. – that is, to strengthen their position within collective bargaining (Edwards and Heery, 1989; Richardson and Wood, 1989). Employers have also sought to bring collective bargaining more under their control by negotiating with unions at company level; the multi-employer agreements between a group of unions and a branch-level employers association that had been such a feature of industrial relations from the 1930s to the 1960s have become a rarity. Ingram and Cahill (1989) found that 87 per cent of employees had their basic pay fixed through bargaining at company level alone in 1986 (compared with 53 per cent in 1979). Only 4 per cent were subject to multi-employer bargaining only (12 per cent in 1979) and 9 per cent to both (35 per cent in 1979). Since 1986 the change has continued in the same direction. During 1988 alone multi-employer bargaining came to an end in banking, retail multiples, newspapers, water and independent television (Kelly and Richardson, 1989). One important cause of the change is the sheer growth of giant, foreign-owned corporations that have little need of membership of a British association; another is the explicit policy of the government to try to end national bargaining in local government and other public services; but another was the shift to localised bargaining initiated by the shop steward movement in the 1960s.

These changes do seem to have been reflected in increased productivity in industry as managements have taken more unilateral control over the conduct of work in their plants (Metcalf, 1989; Richardson and Wood, 1989). But there has possibly also been a concomitant worsening of industrial safety (Grunberg, 1986).

Government Intervention

From its early days the Conservative government developed a clear pattern in its interventions in industrial relations. First, it abandoned all attempts of its predecessors at either incomes policy or mediation in disputes. Second, it would substitute for incomes policy (i) tight central guidelines on pay rises in the public sector and (ii) a general policy stance (initially primarily through monetary policy, later mainly through interest rates) that would inhibit demand and therefore inflation. Third, it would pursue a gradual, step-by-step programme of legislation that would (a) reduce the scope of regulations designed to protect labour and (b) increase the scope of regulations controlling trade-union behaviour.

The government in no way deviated from this pattern in the final years of the decade. Cash limits governed most pay rises in the public sector; apart from some expansionary budgets, interest rate policy has been used as the sole counter-inflationary weapon in the private sector; and the legislative programme has been continued. The main items of deregulation since 1987 have concerned the lifting of protection from women workers – a convergence of free market and feminist concerns. And in 1989 it ended the Dock Labour Scheme, which for many years had protected dock workers from irregular employment by limiting access to dock work to workers registered with a scheme run jointly by port employers and unions.

More generally applicable was the Employment Act 1988. This continued the pattern of earlier legislation (1980, 1982, 1984) of extending the scope of the civil law over certain elements of union conduct – primarily over picketing, strike calls, the closed shop, political activities and the election of officers. There was however a major difference. Earlier legislation had placed legal remedies in the hands of employers: a firm could sue a union that subjected its premises to heavy or secondary picketing, or that organised an official strike without having held a prior ballot. The 1988 Act gives such rights to *workers*. A worker may now sue a union: (a) for attempting to punish him/her for failing to support a strike, even if the strike has been approved by a majority in a properly conducted ballot; or (b) for putting pressure on an employer to make union membership a condition of employment.

Workers also acquired the right to be able to demand a ballot in the event of their union calling a strike without having held one. The same Act also extended the provision of the 1984 Act requiring union executives to be elected by ballots; these ballots must now be conducted by post, with workers voting at home, and may not be conducted, even if secret, at the work place.

The Act is therefore an extension of union democracy, though it is democracy of a guided kind, giving workers the right to do things that the government would like them to do. There is no right to demand a strike ballot from a union that is *refusing* to call a strike; no protection against disciplinary action from an employer by workers participating in strikes preceded by properly conducted ballots. In a code of practice issued in 1989 the government proposed to tighten restrictions further by recommending that strikes should not take place unless there is a 70 per cent majority in favour; and even then unions should not call the strike if there is a chance of further negotiations. On the other hand, a union should not organise a strike ballot unless it is firmly committed to taking strike action; in other words, ballots should not be used as a bargaining tactic to strengthen the union's hand in negotiations. Such codes of practice do not have legal force but, like the Highway Code, they can be cited in Court as evidence of whether or not a party has followed good practice.

As in the earlier part of the decade, unions did little to contest implementation of the new legislation and tried to obey it. The few unions that did contest it – or whose members engaged in spontaneous disputes from which the unions did not adequately dissociate themselves – found themselves in the courts and received heavy fines.

In 1989 the Department of Employment issued a Green Paper, *Removing Barriers to Employment*, which promised even more legislation to reduce union power. It proposed, *inter alia*, a final end to the closed shop and rights for self-employed members of unions to demand ballots to try to prevent strikes by employed members that might adversely affect their businesses.

Tripartism

The years 1987–9 saw the removal of an extraordinary anomaly in the government's approach to tripartite relations in general and trade-union participation in public life in particular. The Manpower Services Commission had been set up by an earlier Conservative government in 1973 to run training policy and employment services. Despite being tripartite with a strong union involvement and despite being an instrument for public intervention in the economy, the Commission thrived for most of the Thatcher years.

However, during the election campaign of 1987 the Conservative manifesto promised to reduce the role of trade unions in the management of the MSC. Events then moved fast. The Commission lost responsibility for employment matters and was left with organising training outside the context of overall employment trends; it was renamed the Training Commission. Then, early in 1988 it was given the task of overseeing a new scheme for making receipt of unemployment pay by young people conditional on their acceptance of direction to a training course. For many trade unions this was the last straw, and despite the pleading of Neil Kinnock, the Labour Party leader, that the unions should remain engaged in this surviving national policy-making institution, the 1988 Trades Union Congress voted not to cooperate with the new policy, though they wished to remain part of the Commission.

Within days the Secretary of State for Employment had abolished the Training Commission and replaced it with the Training Agency, which is a direct arm of government and contains no employer or union representatives. During 1989 the local infrastructure of union–employer cooperation in running training schemes that the MSC had established was also abolished and replaced by new training and enterprise councils (TECs). These comprise local businessmen, serving as individuals, not representatives of trade associations. They are permitted to appoint a very limited number of individuals from trade unions and educational institutions if they wish. Care has been taken to ensure that the boundaries of TECs do not coincide with those of local education authorities so that they are independent of existing structures of training and education. And thus the anomaly of the MSC came to an end.

The Unions and Politics

In the wake of three consecutive general election defeats for the Labour Party, continuing high unemployment, an increasingly constricting web of legislation, exclusion from all but the most humdrum role in public life and the disaster of the 1984–5 mining strike, most trade unions seem to have decided to mend their fences and wait for better times in the future. The former has involved them in considerable constructive activity, while the latter is not as Micawberish as it sounds. Before considering these aspects it is however necessary to consider one major internal setback that the TUC has suffered – though even there the response suggests a strategy of cautious and sober optimism.

Some employers, especially Japanese multinationals setting up British plants, have offered to various individual unions sole representation rights in exchange for acceptance of the firm's approach to dispute settlement procedures. In a period where representation rights in new plants have been difficult to achieve, the offer has been very difficult to refuse, even though it implies a handicapped approach to disputes and a competitive struggle with other unions to get the sole representation prize. While the former is the grander cause, it is the latter that threatens unions as organisations and places strain on the TUC's ability (once impressive) to avoid recognition quarrels among its members.

The TUC attempted a working solution to the dilemma by drawing a distinction between existing and new ('green field') sites. Where a new factory or service location is being established, Congress has not objected to unions trying to secure recognition deals, even if this has sometimes involved the indignity of unions lining up to be judged the most pliable by the employer. It has drawn the line at agreements at existing sites, where a number of unions already have long-established recognition and where a single-union deal means the expulsion of several of them. It is a useful but not a watertight distinction: what happens if a firm is building a new plant instead of expanding an existing one? Or actually transferring operations to a new site?

Several unions have been involved in tricky deals of this kind, but two in particular were making a specialism of them: the Amalgamated Engineering Union (AEU), the second largest in the TUC; and the Electrical, Electronic Telecommunications and Plumbing Union (EETPU), the fifth largest. Several unions were seeking some punishment for this behaviour, but the EETPU caused particular offence. It signed a single representation agreement with Rupert Murdoch's News International newspaper firms after he had summarily transferred operations from Fleet Street to Wapping in East London, ended recognition of the printing unions and dismissed all their members. After trying and failing to secure guarantees of good behaviour from the EETPU, the TUC had no option but to expel it.

This is potentially a very damaging situation for the TUC. Following the miners' strike there has been a rival mining union outside the TUC, the Union of Democratic Mineworkers (UDM). Will it and the EETPU try to form a rival confederation with the small number of white-collar and breakaway unions also outside the TUC? And would the government begin to appoint members from this grouping, rather than from the TUC, to the few remaining public bodies that have union members? Would employers, including the government in the public service, try to give representation privileges to these unions? Will a vindictive struggle between the EETPU and the TUC's unions now develop?

While major conflict could erupt at any time, and the EETPU and the UDM are certainly in contact, there have so far been no dramatic developments. The EETPU has signified its desire to stay attached to the mainstream of the labour movement by retaining its affiliation to the Labour Party. The TUC has tried not to exacerbate the situation; it has rejected as 'premature' a request for affiliation from the small organisation of former EETPU members who opposed the union's conduct in getting itself expelled from Congress. An important factor in the situation is that the EETPU is engaged in long-running discussions of a merger with the AEU. Should these eventually succeed the resulting union would be the largest in the country, and its relationship to the TUC would need to be clearly established.

Meanwhile, most unions have been getting on with their day-to-day business. For many, especially those representing relatively skilled workers in south-eastern England, this is now much the same as in the past: securing wage increases somewhat higher than would be justified by changes in productivity because labour markets are tight. They have also, however, turned their attention to the difficult tasks of demonstrating their relevance to female workers (primarily a matter of proving that they are interested in problems of part-time workers), to the nominally self-employed and to workers in the service sectors and white-collar employment. No union is likely to try a straight political confrontation with the government either over industrial relations legislation or in the style attempted by the National Union of Mineworkers (NUM), though public-service unions may well become involved in strikes with the government as employer.

While there has been much public debate over a 'new model' of unionism being prefigured by the EETPU, the AEU and others, much of this is over-dramatised. The idea that British unions are particularly militant and avoid cooperative relations with employers has never been more than a part truth, and before the late 1960s was a highly inaccurate view. Some new developments in management thinking may lead to the construction of novel institutions for organising cooperation, but this hardly amounts to a drastic change. Employers' current enthusiasm for company- rather than industry-level bargaining may prove temporary, but is in any case highly consistent with the long-term preference of both employers and unions in Britain for rather decentralised structures.

Meanwhile, the unions' general strategy of waiting for

matters to improve is based on two realistic possibilities, the first concerning the Labour Party and the second the European Community.

With the support of most, though by no means all, affiliated unions the Labour leadership has set about returning to the centre-left of the political spectrum (see Chapter 4), where it had made its home since the 1920s apart from little leftward excursions such as that on which it embarked in the early 1980s. An aspect of this today – though it was not so in the past – is acceptance of elements of the Conservative industrial relations legislation, at least those parts concerning the use of ballots in union elections and strike votes. Most unions are not inclined to oppose this; partly because they are already learning how to communicate with their members and win ballots. To date, every union that has held a ballot on the future of its political fund (required under the 1984 Act) has been successful in retaining its fund, and in 1988 eight unions that previously lacked such funds acquired them through ballots. Also in that year there were 280 ballots held over industrial action, and unions secured approval for their proposed action in 90 per cent of cases (Kelly and Richardson, 1989, p. 142). In addition, having tasted a decade in the wilderness the unions want the return to an involvement in public life that would come with the return of a Labour government.

Somewhat less candidly discussed in Labour and union circles is whether a Labour government would again call on unions to pursue policies of wage moderation and modernisation of work practices. It almost certainly would do so, as a Labour government would take office in a situation of extreme economic difficulty and would be reluctant to use high unemployment as its principal weapon to solve the problem of labour cooperation. In some respects the unions would now be better equipped to pursue such a policy than in the past: they have tasted what an alternative to incomes policy is like, and they have to operate within a difficult legal framework which it is unlikely a Labour government would dismantle except on strict conditions.

On the other hand, the strategy of the Conservatives and many employers during the 1980s has made effective tripartite cooperation much less practical. Multi-employer bargaining has been fragmented and neither unions nor employers associations have anything like the meagre authority they used to possess. And there is still little willingness to admit that wage restraint would be a requirement of any strategy aimed at avoiding mass unemployment.

The other and most surprising source of optimism in the TUC is the European Community – to which British unions were for so long opposed. Events have moved rapidly. First, under the influence of the same neo-liberalism that informs British Conservative policy, the EC embarked on a policy of deregulating markets to create a single market among the member nations of the Community. This would be achieved by each government being willing to accept the minimum standards of all other member countries. The predictable consequences would be a movement of capital to countries where legal systems and general conditions were most favourable to capital, and a shift to general acceptance of whatever standards (including working and environmental conditions) were lowest. On these terms the Thatcher government was the most enthusiastic in the Community for moving towards the single market. Trade unions and the political left were inclined to see this as a 'businessman's Europe' that held little for them.

But matters have not rested there. Some European politicians, most notably Jacques Delors, the French socialist who is currently chairman of the European Commission, were concerned at the prospects of alienating labour from the new integrated Europe. Trade unions in countries with high labour standards – especially the Germans with their treasured co-determination system – were also alarmed at the prospect of employment fleeing to those locations in Europe where the worst labour standards would be accepted. From this emerged the doctrine: yes, every country must accept the standards of all the others – but first every country's standards must meet certain minimum conditions. The single market strategy was to acquire its so-called 'social dimension'. Suddenly the stage was set for a new level of social politics. Trade unions and socialist parties are now busy trying to devise a new Europe-wide labour and social policy.

British unions have clearly seen a ray of hope here, symbolised by the extraordinary welcome they gave to M. Delors when he addressed the 1988 Congress. Perhaps this partly reflects the new relevance that French patterns of industrial relations now have in Britain. But more important was the fact that the unions see scope for a new political arena in which they can participate, having been excluded so long from public life at home. They see the Thatcher government forced on to the defensive within Europe on social and labour policy.

It is far too early to judge the outcome of what will be a complex and protracted process. Will minimum standards merely mean minimal standards? Business interests remain far more powerful at Brussels than labour ones; policy-making will still be conducted primarily through national governments, the balance of which within Europe is slightly to the centre-right. There should be no easy assumption that the social dimension will result in imaginative new policies and a general raising of labour standards. Indeed, some wry observers have suggested that it is evidence of how low British labour has sunk that it can feel it may have something to gain from a policy that will be mainly concerned with raising standards in Greece and Portugal.

'Delors is our shepherd', said Norman Willis, general secretary of the TUC. British unions feel they have caught a scent of green pastures, though for the present they still languish in the shadow of the valley of death.

PART FOUR

Conclusion

16

The Thatcher Decade in Perspective

ANDREW GAMBLE

The Conservative government elected in 1979 and re-elected in 1983 and 1987 has attracted extremes of adulation and hostility. Many of its policies have been radical and controversial. There has been much debate on how far the government has achieved its aims and on the wider impact of its policies. The developments that have taken place during the Thatcher decade raise fundamental questions for understanding British politics. Can the changes be best explained by the personality of the Prime Minister and the ascendancy of a new public philosophy? Or are they a reflection of new times and new circumstances? Can political will and ideological conviction make a difference and alter the direction of long-term trends? Or is the role of politicians confined to finding the words for what is happening anyway?

Thatcherism

Much of the controversy has come to centre on the concept of Thatcherism, introduced originally by Stuart Hall (Hall, 1988). The term is used in three main ways:

(1) the political style and personal qualities of Margaret Thatcher as Conservative leader;

(2) the ideological doctrines of the New Right;
(3) the policies of the Thatcher government.

Those who have written on Thatcherism divide into radicals and sceptics. Radicals argue that the advent of the Thatcher government in 1979 marks a major discontinuity in recent British political history, and the reversal or substantial alteration of several of the long-term trends of British political and economic development. Sceptics dispute the coherence and the consistency of Thatcherism and doubt that many if any of the changes of the 1980s were the result of government actions and decisions.

Interpretations of Thatcherism

For radicals 1979 represents a watershed, comparable in importance to 1945 or 1906. Three different kinds of watershed are recognised – an electoral watershed, an ideological watershed, and a policy watershed. The thesis of an electoral watershed treats 1979 as a realigning election which saw a large swing of support to the Conservatives, particularly among skilled workers. The election result followed by the victories in 1983 and 1987 signalled the end of the post-war two-party system based on a stable pattern of class voting. The increase in electoral volatility and support for third parties since the 1950s indicated that the solidarity of class loyalties was weakening (see Chapter 3). The class alignment of voters was no longer as central as it had once been to British politics. A long period of Conservative dominance was in prospect. The thesis of an ideological watershed asserts that Thatcherism has broken the hold of collectivism on intellectual opinion and the policy-making elites (see Chapter 2). Keynesianism and universalist welfare have been discredited, and a new public philosophy has been established which stresses the superiority of market allocation to any form of political or bureaucratic allocation and advocates the application of free market principles in deciding the content and the priorities of public policy (see Chapters 8 and 9). The thesis of a policy watershed argues that Conservatives have not merely transformed the policy agenda by winning electoral and ideological ascendancy, but have carried through a revolution in policy in several areas by successfully implementing key parts of their programme. After ten years they had reversed economic decline, restored state authority, and reasserted British sovereignty.

In these ways Thatcherism is said to have introduced discontinuity into the development of British politics. It marked a sharp break with central aspects of the post-war era – the two-party system, the collectivist ethos of the governing elites, and the policy consensus on Keynesian economic management and public welfare provision. Sceptics reply that it is highly misleading to ascribe all change in the 1980s to the effect of Thatcherism. They point out that Thatcherism lacks internal coherence and consistency. There is no agreement on what the term means or to which policies and events it refers.

The idea of an electoral watershed overstates the swing of support to the Conservatives in 1979 which was substantial but not exceptional. Their share of the vote increased by 8 percentage points but they failed to increase their share of the vote in either 1983 or 1987, despite winning many more seats. The split in the opposition is more important in explaining Conservative success than positive conversion to the Conservatives. At 43 per cent of the vote the Conservative position is strong but not unassailable. Many specialists on voting behaviour also argue that the decline of class voting has been exaggerated (see Chapter 3).

The idea of an ideological watershed ignores the continuing hold of Keynesian and collectivist ideas among intellectuals and opinion-formers, as well as many Conservatives. Some of the new doctrines, such as monetarism, have been quickly discredited in their turn. Opinion surveys show that popular support for the new thinking remains low, and attachment to the values of the old consensus remarkably high (Crewe, 1988).

The idea of a policy watershed ignores the substantial continuities which link the policies of the Thatcher government – for example on economic management, on local authority cuts, on military procurement, and on the European Community – with those of its Labour predecessor, suggesting that the real break in policy comes in 1975/6 rather than in 1979. Examination of particular policies shows that the government did not work from detailed plans prepared in opposition. Policies were amended and revised according to circumstances and the pressures of office. New Right ideas were one input but only one. The outcomes in all policy fields have been mixed and talk of a policy revolution is premature (Marsh and Rhodes, 1989).

It is hardly surprising, given the strength of the sceptics' case, that many social scientists dislike using the term 'Thatcherism' at all. It is often hard to find firm evidence of connections between the political style, the ideology, and the policies. If Thatcherism means a coherent set of policies consistently applied then there is no Thatcherism.

Thatcherism as a Political Project

Thatcherism however can also be analysed not as a specific programme of policies but as a political project of the Conservative leadership, which emerged in the 1970s in response to the Conservative election defeats in 1974 and the political and economic crises of the 1970s (Bulpitt, 1985; Jessop *et al.*, 1988). It came to have three overriding objectives – the restoration of the political fortunes of the Conservative Party, the revival of market liberalism as the dominant public philosophy, and the creation of the conditions for a free economy by limiting the scope of the state while restoring its authority. Whether or not it was successful in any of these aims and helped transform British politics remains open. What makes Thatcherism distinctive as a political project is the scope of its ambitions, and the tenacity with which its leaders pursued them. Thatcherites were convinced that a dramatic break with many existing institutions and policies was necessary if the errors of the past were to be corrected and if Britain was to escape from its long, debilitating decline.

If Thatcherism had been only electoral rhetoric, it would have meant no more than Churchill's call in 1950 to set the people free, a tactic designed principally to unify the Conservative Party and win back electoral power from Labour. But the electoral objectives of Thatcherism were combined with a more precise ideological purpose, and a determination to translate the ideas of the New Right into policies in government. The Conservatives under Margaret Thatcher sought to restore their lost hegemony not simply electorally, but in ideological and policy terms also. The Thatcherites believed that in order to restore the ascendancy of their party they needed to carry through a substantial reordering of the state and its institutions. Such opinions made the Thatcher government appear radical and at times unConservative and controversial, not least within the Conservative Party, a party not ordinarily given to ideological enthusiasms.

A political project of this kind is not guaranteed success. Holding to a consistent policy line is difficult enough in opposition; in government it rarely occurs. Events and circumstances soon deflect even the most radical and determined government from its path. Premeditated doctrines are only one influence on policy and rarely the most important one. The attempt to achieve the objectives of a political project as ambitious as that of Thatcherism was certain to encounter obstacles and resistance.

By its own criteria for success the achievements of the Thatcher revolution can seem meagre. Yet what the government never quite lost throughout its period in office was a strategic sense of the direction in which it wished to move. Ministers have experimented with many different policies, and some of the most successful policies, such as privatisation, were stumbled on by accident. Pragmatism, administrative necessity, and electoral calculation have shaped the development of policy. New Right ideas have had a role, but never a dominant one. But they have enabled the government to renew its radical momentum after periods such as 1985–6 when it seemed to succumb to the inertia of administration.

The concept of Thatcherism draws attention to the way in which electoral calculation, ideological argument, and policy change were harnessed together by the Conservatives in the 1970s and 1980s in a political project which sought to overturn the established political wisdom and recreate the traditional Conservative dominance of British politics.

Theories of British Politics

The debates on the meaning of Thatcherism and on the scope of the changes introduced by the Thatcher government are part of wider debates about British political development. Three problems in particular have shaped these debates and provided distinct ways of understanding British politics: political legitimacy, the growth of government, and decline.

The first problem gave rise to the Westminster model which focuses attention on Parliament, the constitution, and party politics, and analyses the conditions and obstacles for representative and responsible government. It attaches great weight to political thought and action in shaping events and determining outcomes. Other perspectives have challenged the emphasis given to Parliament in the Westminster model. The two discussed in this chapter give priority to the institutions of the extended state and the relationships between the state and the economy. They direct attention to long-term trends, such as the growth of government, or the relative decline of the British economy on which government policies have little impact. The emphasis is placed on long-term developments in British politics, rather than on what politicians can change by their actions.

Studies inspired by the Westminster model have been concerned with the beliefs and ideologies of the political parties, the personalities and conflicts of the political leaders, and the events and circumstances of each changing period. Studies of the extended state and of state-economy relations focus instead on public policy and political economy, and analyse the constraints within which policies are framed and implemented. Thatcherism, understood as a project to restore the authority of Parliament and the political fortunes of the Conservative Party, fits snugly within the assumptions of the Westminster model. But to achieve these aims the Thatcherites declared that the state had to be rolled back and Britain's relative economic decline halted. The restoration of political legitimacy was linked to the reversal of the two trends that had dominated British politics for so long. Thatcherism needs therefore to be evaluated not simply as party politics, but also as public policy and political economy. These are three distinct ways of understanding British politics and the Thatcher decade.

Parliament and the Constitution

The traditional study of British politics meant the history of British political institutions and the ideas and principles embodied in them. The close link between theory and practice, and between ideas and institutions, were understood historically, as the outcome of a long process of historical development. The British historical experience was regarded as unique, and was used to explain the special character of British institutions and the distinctiveness of British political thought.

The key political institution was Parliament because for so long Parliament had been the source of both power and legitimacy in the British state. The success of this state was demonstrated by the unbroken continuity of British institutions since the seventeenth century, in sharp contrast to the experience of most states. External invasions and internal coups and revolutions had often forced on them abrupt changes in constitutional arrangements. Alone among the great powers Britain survived for three hundred years without a major break in the development of its institutions.

Representative and Responsible Government

This performance inspired both admiration and complacency. British institutions came to be seen as providing a unique blend of representative and responsible government. The British system was sufficiently flexible and pragmatic to permit the accommodation of new interests and demands, by periodically changing the basis on which the Parliament was elected. The principle was eventually accepted, although only after some fierce conflicts, that no group, class, or gender should be excluded from representation in Parliament.

The British system promoted responsible government by ensuring that British governments were strong and independent. Although accountable to Parliament, they were not subordinate to it. A British government, backed by a majority in Parliament, enjoyed the full authority and legitimacy of that body, and could act decisively to carry through its policies. Once it lost that support it had to resign. This balance between the executive and representative functions of government was considered by many observers to have reached a state close to perfection in England. Ever since Montesquieu praised English institutions in the eighteenth century for ensuring a balanced but not deadlocked constitution, English institutions have not been short of either foreign or domestic admirers.

What made this balance possible in England in the view of many observers was the character of British political culture, the broad consensus on the framework within which conflicts of interests and values could take place and disagreements could be resolved. In his classic study *Modern British Politics* Samuel Beer wrote:

> Happy the country in which consensus and conflict are ordered in a dialectic that makes of the political arena at once a market of interests and a forum for debate of fundamental moral concerns. (Beer, 1965, p. 390)

The Westminster Model

The traditional study of British politics was a study of the development of this unique political tradition. There was a great deal of attention paid to the key institutions – the Crown, the Cabinet, the Prime Minister, Parliament, and the political parties; to the conventions of the constitution; and to the doctrines of parliamentary sovereignty and accountability. Such studies gave rise to what John Mackintosh called 'the Westminster Model' (Mackintosh, 1982).

At the heart of this model was Parliament. The voters elected the Parliament, and from the Parliament were chosen the ministers of the Crown, who were accountable to Parliament for their actions. Ministers formulated policies in consultation with their civil servants, but these policies had to be approved by Parliament, which was the ultimate source of authority. Civil servants' task was to inform and to advise ministers, but ministers had to take responsibility for the decisions of their departments and were answerable to Parliament for them. The bureaucracy was subordinate to the executive and the executive was accountable to Parliament which was elected by all the citizens. Control of the executive depended on retaining the support of Parliament, which was elected by the people. Parties competed for the right to form a government and oversee and direct the formulation and implementation of policy within the rules, procedures, and conventions of the parliamentary system.

The Westminster model puts forward an ideal of a sovereign body elected by the votes of all the citizens, empowered to create and dismiss governments, to pass and to amend laws, to make ministers accountable and to protect the rights of citizens. Behind it is the idea of a cohesive and homogeneous British nation which despite internal conflicts and disputes has achieved sufficient consensus on procedures to give the decisions of the Parliament unquestioned legitimacy. This model still provides an important way of understanding British politics. It directs attention to some central questions about British political institutions, such as the role of Parliament and the organisation of the political parties. But it has met increasing criticism because it is not an accurate description of how government actually works in Britain or anywhere else, and it ignores other institutions and relationships that have often been more important than Parliament in determining how British politics have developed.

Decline of Representative Government

During this century Parliament has been widely perceived as an institution in decline, no longer effective either in representing the electorate or acting as a check on the executive. Many critics allege that British institutions no longer guarantee representative government.

(1) *The electoral system.* The simple plurality rule ensures that there are major discrepancies between the votes cast for parties nationally and the number of seats they win.

(2) *The territorial system.* The unitary character of the British state, and the dominance of England within it, restricts

the autonomy of regions, nations, and districts within the state.

(3) *National sovereignty.* The concept of the sovereign nation-state is a key aspect of the Westminster model. Parliament has to be sovereign not just in the formal sense that it can take binding decisions, but also in the sense that whatever it decrees is implemented. The erosion of the independence of nation-states in economic, military, and cultural affairs threatens this conception by reducing the number of decisions genuinely taken at national level (see Chapters 7 and 11). As interdependence has grown and sovereignty has been pooled, so the ability of the Westminster Parliament to represent its electorate has weakened.

(4) *Corporatism.* Many important interests, particularly producer interests have sought representation not primarily through Parliament but through other channels, often established by government itself. Parliament loses its role as the arena where conflicts between interests are sorted out.

(5) *Media.* Modern media have become the most important means of communication between politicians and the electorate, as well as the most important arena for ideological argument and the construction and dissemination of dominant ideas.

Decline of Responsible Government

Critics also allege that British institutions no longer guarantee responsible government.

(1) *Party discipline.* Mass parties subordinate MPs to their party leaders, and ensure that the executive generally dominates the legislature.

(2) *The political business cycle.* Governments learn to use discretionary fiscal and monetary policies to manipulate the economy so as to improve their chances of re-election. Competition for votes leads parties to promise more than they can deliver. Electors develop excessive expectations about what governments can achieve. In seeking to maintain full employment and rising living standards governments adopt lax monetary policies which create inflation. The inflation rate rises from one cycle to the next. The balance between the four

elements of the political economy of capitalist liberal democracies – full employment, stable prices, free collective bargaining, and democracy – becomes unsustainable, threatening the survival of democratic institutions, either through mass unemployment or uncontrollable inflation (Jay, 1976; Brittan, 1977).

(3) *Overloaded government.* The expansion in the range of government activities means that governments have too many tasks and too few resources to carry them out. Their expenditure commitments run ahead of their ability to raise taxes, and create a fiscal crisis, which is often resolved by forms of borrowing that are inflationary. The difficulty of coordinating the sprawling bureaucracies of the modern state makes government generally incompetent and ineffective at carrying out the popular will. Modern governments are therefore weak governments, because they lack the authority or the resources to implement the programmes on which they are elected (Birch, 1984).

(4) *Adversary politics.* The parties which alternate in government are representative of activist opinion within their parties rather than majority opinion within the electorate. Each party uses its majority in Parliament to push through the radical programme it adopts in opposition, and to reverse many of the measures its predecessor enacted. By the time the pressures of office and falling popularity have forced a return to pragmatic, centrist policies it is too late for the governing party to win back support, and it loses power to the opposition, which under pressure from its activists has endorsed a new radical programme. Major discontinuities in policy result every time the government changes hands (Finer, 1975).

(5) *Elective dictatorship.* The doctrine of parliamentary sovereignty and the *de facto* control of Parliament by the party with a majority of the seats in the House of Commons allows the executive to ignore all opposition to its policies if it so chooses. The opposition in the Commons is almost always outvoted, and opposition from the Crown, the House of Lords, or the courts can be overridden provided the executive is sufficiently determined. The position of the executive is reinforced by its powers of patronage, by news management, and by secrecy. Governments can act dictatorially and have

no need to tolerate opposition, or to respect civil liberties and the rights of minorities (Hailsham, 1978; Johnson, 1977).

Rebuilding Legitimacy

The Thatcher government believed strongly in parliamentary sovereignty, the unitary state, and the Westminster model as the proper basis of political authority. Unlike previous Conservative governments it made constant reference to the 'mandate' it had received from the electorate for its policies. But it did not seriously attempt to redress the balance of power between legislature and executive, or set new constitutional limits to government. In the 1970s Conservatives had urged that the authority and importance of Parliament be restored. Many wished to weaken and if possible remove the corporatist institutions which had supplanted the role of Parliament and provided a rival source of political legitimacy.

In practice, however, the Thatcher government did very little to reverse the decline of Parliament. It strengthened the representative character of Parliament in one area by sweeping away the institutions of corporatist bargaining. The trade unions were systematically excluded from national decision-making (see Chapter 15). The government however strongly opposed other reforms, including electoral reform, a bill of rights, a more representative second Chamber, and regional devolution.

Britain's electoral system was increasingly out-of-step with electoral systems in most other democracies in the 1980s. In the 1989 elections for the European Parliament the Green party in Britain polled a higher percentage of the vote than the Greens in any other EC country, yet unlike them won no seats. Britain is also an anomaly in European terms because it is both a multinational state and a highly centralised unitary state. The Thatcher government continued to give full support to both, refusing to devolve powers to the regions and nations within the British state. It found no means to remedy either the breakdown of Westminster's authority in Ulster, although it did sign the Anglo-Irish Agreement (see Chapter 12), or the decline of Unionism as a political force in Scotland.

It fought hard to retain national sovereignty, especially in relation to the EC (see Chapter 7). But even while the government proclaimed the importance of allowing the Westminster Parliament to take the final decisions, it was a signatory to the Single European Act which allowed numerous decisions affecting Britain to be decided by its European partners. Britain continued to differ from other European states in the priority it gave to its Atlanticist rather than to its European links. But despite its public rhetoric the Thatcher government appeared both unable and unwilling to halt further erosions of British sovereignty by the increasing pace of European integration (George, 1990). One of the government's proudest boasts was that it had made Britain respected once more throughout the world. But Britain's powerlessness to deal with the problems of Hong Kong gave a more accurate picture of British power than the special circumstances of the Falkland's War (see Chapter 11).

The government also did little to change the balance between Parliament and the media. The most important change, the televising of Parliament, was agreed against the opposition of Margaret Thatcher herself. The Conservatives continued the trend towards ever more sophisticated news management and the projection of their ideas and their image through the modern media, bypassing Parliament and its antiquated procedures.

The failure to make Parliament more representative and more central to political debate made the executive more like an elective dictatorship than ever. The large Conservative majorities in Parliament emphasised the executive's domination of the legislature. The government's attempts to remove powers from local authorities and other intermediate institutions between the central state and the citizen, as well as the uninhibited use it made of its powers of patronage and news management, confirmed its image as a government determined to overcome all internal opposition. The government did reform the Select Committees, but they still had relatively few powers compared to committees in other legislatures. Their ability to compel ministers and civil servants to attend and supply information was limited. Few concessions were made to the calls for more open government.

The absence of a codified constitution entrenching rights

and the separation of powers sharply distinguishes Britain from other European states. The British continue to insist on unfettered parliamentary sovereignty and resist the formal checks and balances provided by a written constitution. Despite its enthusiasm for setting limits to the state the Thatcher government proposed no reforms and made full use of the powers that were available to it through the doctrine of parliamentary sovereignty (Graham and Prosser, 1988; Gamble and Wells, 1988). Conservative electoral success in the 1980s did calm many of the fears that had been expressed in the 1970s about the health of British democracy. Many former critics of elective dictatorship and adversary politics found them less disturbing once a Conservative government was in power again. Conservative election victories in the 1980s interrupted the cycle of adversary politics that had run between 1959 and 1979. The alternation of the parties in government ceased, allowing an extended experiment with new policies.

The Conservatives found the political business cycle easier to manage than many predicted. Full employment was abandoned but even three million unemployed and much greater poverty were found not to threaten political stability or the Conservatives' electoral prospects, so long as the living standards of the prosperous two-thirds of the population continued to improve at the same time. During the 1980s the government became adept at aligning the economic cycle with the political cycle and maximising its chances of re-election. The government was committed to prevent the overloading of government that had been diagnosed in the 1970s by rolling back the state. It sought to reverse what has been one of the most persistent trends in British political development over the last one hundred years – the expansion of the size and the scope of government. It wanted to make government strong again and this could only be done by limiting its powers and responsibilities.

Public Policy

A return to limited government might halt the decline of Parliament. Parliament having willed the expansion of the state must now will its contraction to save itself. But can it be done? From a different perspective than that of the Westminster model it is the growth of government that is the central process in British politics and the problem that has to be explained. The emphasis is placed on public policy and the policy-making process rather than on Parliament and the political parties.

The expansion of government can be measured in a number of ways: government spending and taxation expressed as a proportion of gross domestic product (GDP); the size of the publicly owned sector of the economy; public employees as a percentage of all employees; and estimates of the range of government responsibilities and powers. All these indicators show a substantial enlargement of the role of government in the twentieth century. The trend has not been constant. Major upward leaps in expenditure levels occurred during the two world wars, but afterwards the level of public expenditure and taxation did not return to the level that had previously existed (Peacock and Wiseman, 1967).

The steady enlargement of public spending and taxation and the increase in public responsibilities gathered an irresistible momentum. The expansion of government was supported on grounds of interest, of expediency, and of ideology. From below, new lobbies and organised interests began to push for higher spending that would benefit their members. From above, the need to accommodate the demands of the working class and provide the infrastructure for a modern industrial society was acknowledged. Collectivist doctrines, justifying new responsibilities for the state, and favouring government intervention over *laissez-faire* began to gain ground in all parties.

The expansion of government and the public sector offers a very different perspective on British politics from the Westminster model. The complexity and size of modern government makes parliamentary scrutiny and control in the traditional sense impossible. The executive that presides over and manages the complex and far-flung public sector becomes the key institution for understanding British politics. Just as Bagehot in the nineteenth century argued that real power in the British system had passed from Parliament to the Cabinet, so many contemporary historians and political scientists have argued that in the twentieth century it passed to the informal policy networks established between the permanent state bureaucracy and the major organised interests such as the employers, the trade unions and professional groups (Middlemass, 1979).

The Policy-Making Process

The persistent trend during the twentieth century towards the growth of government shifts attention from the formal representastive institutions to the informal processes of the policy-making process that are involved in the management of the public sector. An important and influential literature has emerged which analyses the policy-making process and the politics of public services (see Chapters 5 and 9). Parliament and the political parties have a role in this but it is no longer the central one.

Research into the policy networks and policy communities which crisscross the public and private sectors reveals government as a complex structure (see Chapters 5 and 6), which far from responding to the directives of an executive that is answerable to Parliament, is composed of numerous bureaus, each with their own relative autonomy from the centre. The flow of commands and information does not proceed smoothly through an orderly hierarchy. Central agencies have to negotiate implementation of their policies with the agencies of subcentral government, which includes many different boards and enterprises, as well as local and regional authorities.

Why Government Grows

In this perspective politics is a highly constrained activity, concerned with processes of bargaining, consultation, and decision-making within the bureaucracies of the public sector. But there is disagreement over why this public sector has grown so much. Three particular arguments have been developed.

The first stresses the functional requirements of a modern industrial society. The needs and welfare of modern urban communities make necessary a large public sector. Demographic patterns by fixing the numbers and proportions in different social groups according to age and social needs also dictate the necessary policy response – for example the number of teachers or old people's homes required. Such models sometimes exhibit a sociological determinism in which politics becomes merely the translation into workable programmes of needs defined by long-established social trends. Party politics becomes a distraction from the business of administration. Public administration itself is viewed as a disinterested, benign activity. The public interest is secured primarily through the neutrality and professionalism of the civil service rather than through the detailed scrutiny of legislation by a representative Parliament.

The second explanation is found in the economic models of politics developed by the public choice school which have strongly influenced the New Right. They take a much less favourable view of public sector activity and policy-making. The growth of government is ascribed to defects in the political market and defects in the organisation of government. As a result there can be no painless translation of social needs into government programmes through a system of rational planning as envisaged in the public administration approach. Defects in the political market explain negative features of the Westminster model such as the political business cycle and overloaded government. In their compulsive search for votes, governments are constantly tempted to take on new powers and responsibilities, to launch new programmes, and to impose new taxes to boost their revenue. Pressures from mass electorates for more services and subsidies are reinforced by pressures from the permanent bureaucracies established to administer them. Those providing the services have an interest in increasing the size and budgets of their bureaus. Since government departments are often monopoly suppliers of the services they provide and since government can use its coercive powers to expand its revenue base, the public choice theory predicts that there will be a constant tendency for governments to expand (Tullock, 1976).

A third explanation of the growth of government analyses

the constant interplay between the functions that public sector activity serves and the way in which those functions are interpreted and defined in the course of political debate and competition. There is a substantial degree of freedom in determining policy agendas, and in formulating and implementing policies. The policy process is conceived as an arena in which there is a continual contest both over how problems are defined and priorities identified, and over how agreed policies are implemented. This approach still recognises severe constraints on policy-making imposed by the difficulty of stating policy objectives clearly, mobilising the resources and winning the acquiescence of groups needed to implement them. But it conceives policy outcomes as rather more open than either public choice or sociologically derived theories of the policy process are inclined to do (Jordan and Richardson, 1987).

Rolling Back the State

All three explanations indicate the powerful forces working through the political process that have led to the expansion of government programmes and responsibilities. The Thatcherite project planned to reverse the trend to big government and rebuild parliamentary authority by dismantling corporatist institutions and cutting spending programmes.

The government was more successful in limiting the scope than in reducing the size of government. Through its privatisation programme (see Chapter 13) it effected a major change in the boundaries between the public and private sectors, and it phased out a number of major spending programmes, including regional aid. It was also successful in reducing the number of civil servants, and abolishing many government agencies.

The size of government, however, measured by taxation and by spending altered little through the 1980s. It rose at first as a percentage of GDP before falling back as the economy grew rapidly in 1986–8. But by the end of 1989 it was only slightly below the level that the Conservatives had inherited ten years previously. For all the confrontations between central and local government over spending (see

Chapter 6) the overall level of public spending stayed close to the long-term trend. There were few signs that the Thatcher government had succeeded in breaking from the pattern of big government which it inherited. The major spending programmes – health, education, social security (see Chapters 9 and 14) – remained intact.

What the Thatcher government did introduce were major institutional reorganisations, some of which, like the provisions for hospitals and schools to opt for self-management, were often suspected by its critics of preparing the ground for future privatisation. In the meantime, however, the government continued to spend and tax as much as its recent predecessors. In comparative terms the size of the state in Britain remained broadly similar to that of other states in the OECD. Britain did not have either the largest or the smallest public sector in terms of spending and taxation. Where Britain did stand out was in moving so rapidly from having one of the largest nationalised sectors to one of the smallest during the 1980s (see Chapter 13) and in having a higher than average expenditure on defence as a percentage of GDP (see Chapter 11).

The organisation of the public sector in Britain was marked by direct state provision of public services. In a comparative context the extent of this was unusually high, and rather puzzling since the conditions that had established it elsewhere, such as a politically dominant Labour movement, were generally lacking. The acquiescence of the Conservatives in the past to such a statist organisation of the public sector is what requires explanation. The changes introduced by the Thatcher government which have brought greater variety and decentralisation into the provision of services in the public sector are moving Britain more towards a European norm than away from it (Dunleavy, 1989a).

Political Economy

A second alternative to the Westminster model's preoccupation with parliamentary institutions treats the historical problem of British decline as the key to understanding British politics. The decline as a great power and the decline of the British economy are closely linked. The economic decline has not been absolute but relative. It has always coexisted with steady if unspectacular growth (around 2 per cent per annum). But this growth has been accompanied by a tendency for Britain to perform less well than other leading economies.

The decline has not been uniform. In the last hundred years there have been periods of recovery and stability, as well as periods of economic difficulty and crisis. The overall trend however has been unmistakable. Britain's economic import-ance has been reduced, and although still one of the leading economies in the world economy, Britain no longer occupies the pivotal role which it once enjoyed.

Anxieties about decline have been a persistent feature of British politics in the last hundred years. There have been major debates about how it should be remedied, and many new policy initiatives, programmes, and institutions. Focus-ing on decline as the central problem of modern British history has helped make political economy a key approach in contemporary analysis of British politics. It has produced some major theories of the historical relationship of state and economy in Britain which provide criteria for judging the success or failure of the Thatcher government's bid to end decline. Four examples of such theories include:

(1) the relationship between democracy and institutional sclerosis (Olson, 1982);
(2) the absence of a British developmental state (Marquand, 1988);
(3) the overextension of British power (Kennedy, P., 1988);
(4) the peculiarities of British capitalism (Anderson, 1987; Nairn, 1981).

Institutional Sclerosis

Olson's work uses economic models to explain political de-velopments. His building blocks are individuals who are conceived as rational and egoistic, and utility maximisers. In the economic sphere the actions of individuals are coordinated through markets and the system of prices. In the political sphere the market is imperfect, and there is no similar way of assessing rationality. Much political action is also collective rather than individual, conducted through parties or pressure groups.

In his recent work Olson seeks to explain why some nations rise and others decline. Drawing on his theory of the logic of collective action (Olson, 1965) he argues that individuals join an organisation if they are offered selective incentives to do so. Organisations in the political sphere provide such incentives by seeking to obtain the largest possible share of benefits from public agencies for their members, while loading the costs of their actions onto non-members.

Interest groups of the kind Olson describes flourish in the legal and political conditions of democratic, pluralist societies. The longer such conditions have been established the denser the network of organised interests, and hence the more formidable the obstacles to policies that promote rapid economic growth. Major internal or external shocks such as wars, invasions, and revolutions can create the conditions for economic success by overcoming the institutional sclerosis that a long period of stable democratic rule creates. Applied to Britain, Olson's analysis finds support from studies that show how powerful interests have often resisted major changes intended to improve economic performance. The reversal of British decline is seen as requiring either that interests be persuaded to subordinate themselves to a higher public good, or that the power of existing interests be confronted and destroyed. Neither is easy to achieve.

The Developmental State

David Marquand's analysis also addresses the problem of how organised interests can be reconciled with decision-making in the public interest. But he traces the problem not to deficiencies in the political market and the logic of collective action, but to the absence in Britain of the conditions for a developmental state. Such a state is active and interventionist in support of the long-term development of the private sector. Its interventions are aimed at creating a framework of rules, institutions, and services which ensures that the decisions individuals and companies take maximise economic and social benefit. Its task is to think strategically for the whole society. The failure to create such a developmental state in Britain contrasts unfavourably with Japan, but also with France, Germany, and Sweden. In these countries different institutional means ensured that the state took responsibility for providing the long-term framework for development. In Britain the organisation of government and the liberal ethos which it fostered created major obstacles and has repeatedly frustrated attempts at modernisation.

Imperial Overextension

Paul Kennedy explains the decline as a consequence of Britain having once been a world power. Those powers that became first great powers and then world powers as a result of their economic and industrial success eventually confronted a similar dilemma: how to provide sufficient resources for military defence, domestic consumption, and investment against the challenge of rivals who were not similarly burdened. From this perspective British decline reflects the inability of the British state to protect the claims of investment against those of security and consumption. Its pursuit of a global role long after the conditions for such a role had disappeared imposed heavy costs on the British economy. A strong pound, and high levels of overseas military spending, defence-related research programmes, and foreign investment reflected policy priorities which put domestic restructuring of the economy around export industries rather lower than the preservation of Britain's place in the world.

The Unfinished Revolution

Perry Anderson and Tom Nairn emphasise the peculiarities of British capitalist development in a European context, and how these legacies from the past continue to block attempts to modernise the British economy and British society. The civil war of the seventeenth century was a struggle not between aristocracy and bourgeoisie but between two components of the landowning class. It was the least pure capitalist revolution

of any major European country. It removed important juridi-
cial and constitutional obstacles to capitalist development but
it left the social structure intact. When an independent
industrial capitalist class did emerge in the nineteenth century
it did not overturn the landowners' state but instead merged
its interests with theirs. The interpenetration of landed,
commercial, and industrial capital was consolidated within
the framework of the old constitutional state and with the help
of new institutions such as the public schools. Two lasting
legacies were a state whose institutions and ethos were pre-
democratic, and a balance of power in which manufacturing
interests were generally subordinate to those of finance and
commerce.

This old constitutional state successfully presided over
overseas territorial and commercial expansion as well as
domestic industrialisation, but it was often resistant to the
kinds of changes that economic and social modernisation in
the twentieth century required. The successful incorporation
of the Labour movement into this state in return for collectivist welfare programmes and redistributive fiscal policies
reinforced a consensus against modernisation.

Decline or Recovery?

Nowhere did the Thatcher government make greater claims
for its success in transforming British politics than in the
performance of the economy. The issue for both supporters
and critics of the government's policy is whether the buoyant
state of the British economy between 1986 and 1988 reflected
adroit management of the economic cycle or a more permanent economic recovery.

The main evidence for lasting change is the substantial
improvement in manufacturing productivity which for a time
outpaced all other economies and contributed to a much
higher rate of output. Some economists believe that the tough
monetary regime of the early years of the Thatcher government restored financial discipline through unemployment and
bankruptcy which forced companies and workers to become
more efficient. The stranglehold of subsidies, inefficient
management and powerful trade unions was broken. The

conditions for a new enterprise economy were created (Maynard, 1988).

There are also, however, signs that the economic recovery of the 1980s was not strong enough to change the long-term trend of British economic performance (see Chapter 8). If the whole cycle 1979–88 is compared with previous cycles the growth performance in the 1980s is not remarkable. The spurt in the late 1980s only compensated for the very steep falls in output in the early 1980s. Some of the obstacles to free markets were tackled by the Thatcher government, but most of the institutional weaknesses remained and some were intensified. Levels of investment, training, and research and development all marked Britain out as an economy still performing much less well than the world leaders. The losses of manufacturing capacity in the slump of the early 1980s were particularly serious and were responsible for the emergence of a widening trade gap in the late 1980s. Policy options to prevent the trade deficit causing a collapse of sterling and a resurgence of inflation threatened to return the United Kingdom to a regime of slow growth and familiar problems.

Britain continued to stand out in the 1980s as an economy without any form of institutional integration between government, banks, and industry which underpinned successful industrial strategies in other countries. The historic division between industry and finance in Britain which lay behind this institutional failure had long given the British economy a special position within the world economy (Ingham, 1984). This position was not changed but further reinforced by the Thatcher government. One consequence was that national prosperity became increasingly uneven, with growth and employment concentrated in the regions of the south and east (Smith, 1989).

The End of Class Politics

Watersheds often hide deeper continuities. The 1980s are better understood as an important period of transition rather than as a revolutionary transformation of British politics and society. What did not change is often as revealing as what did.

The Thatcher project has been a strange and often novel mixture of radical and very conservative elements. It succeeded in its most immediate purpose – to restore the political fortunes of the Conservative Party after the débâcle of 1974. But its wider aims of rolling back the state and reversing decline achieved only limited success.

One major change which is claimed for the Thatcher years is the waning of a politics centred on class. This claim has been made about political behaviour: individuals' class identity has become less important for the way in which they behave politically; and about ideology: class issues no longer dominate ideological and policy disputes. The first class claim is subject to fierce debate among voting specialists and is explored in detail in Chapter 3. The second is also controversial. Some Marxists have argued that the Thatcher government with its consistent bias in favour of employers and the rich, and its determination to break all resistance to its policies, represents a return to undisguised class government, not a retreat from it.

Others suggest that the nature of capitalism and the working class has changed radically, making a politics organised primarily around class increasingly irrelevant and futile. The challenge of the new times is to accept the new pluralism and diversity of modern industrial societies, and to organise a politics around demands for citizenship rights, choice, and the extension of democracy (Hall and Jacques, 1989).

What is certain is that Labour has begun to abandon the old Labourist version of class politics. This change may come to be seen as the Thatcher government's greatest achievement. By abandoning the defensiveness Conservatives used to show to the advance of collectivism the Thatcher government broke the consensus on the position of the trade unions and the balance of the mixed economy. It won major confrontations with sections of organised labour and with Labour-controlled councils (see Chapters 15 and 6). It frequently acted to curtail the powers of those institutions controlled by its opponents, reinforcing the dominance of the central state.

The sustained assault on the culture and the institutions of the Labour movement which the Thatcher government encouraged during the 1980s combined with the internal split within the Labour Party came close to producing a realignment of forces in British politics and a new party system. Labour's recovery after 1985 and the collapse of the centre after 1987 (see Chapter 4) prevented that. The Labour Party was substantially remodelled during the 1980s and has begun to look more like a European socialist party, with looser ties to the trade unions, and firmer commitment to market economics and the European Community.

The British Conservatives have changed much less. In the past there has always been a considerable contrast between the British Labour and Conservative parties and the parties of left and right in Europe. The gap between Labour and the European left is closing fast, but there is still a major difference between the Conservatives and the European right which is dominated by Christian Democratic parties. It was underlined in 1989 when the Thatcher government rejected the proposals for a Social Charter which every other Conservative government in the European Community accepted.

The triumphs of the Thatcher government have hastened the decline of the old Labour movement, but a durable Thatcherite consensus has not been consolidated, as the chapters of this book show. The emergence of new social movements, particularly the Green movement (see Chapter 10), and new issues can only with difficulty be forced within the straitjacket of the old class-based two-party system. A new political agenda centred on Europe, disarmament, the environment, the quality of public and private services, and citizenship rights has already become well established in many countries of the European Community. In the 1990s it is poised to dominate political developments in Britain.

Guide to Further Reading

Chapter 2 Ideology

By far the best account of both the fixed and the shifting political ideologies of Conservative and Labour is Greenleaf (1983, 1987). Barry (1987) and Green (1987) give accounts of the neo-liberal critique of the old consensus. King (1987) covers similar ground but from a much more critical standpoint. King also includes a discussion of socialist theories of citizenship. The Thatcher years are critically surveyed in a number of Andrew Gamble's publications (see especially Gamble, 1988). Marquand (1988) expertly diagnoses the failure of the consensus, and yearns, in a rather melancholy way, for its reconstruction on more rational grounds.

Contemporary revisionist socialists have yet to produce a volume to match C. A. R. Crosland's *The Future of Socialism* (Crosland, 1956). However, Hattersley (1987), Gould (1985), and Radice (1989) are useful books by practising politicians. Radice's book is good on the new 'constitutionalism' that has featured strongly in socialist thinking in recent years. A much neglected book is Luard (1979). Hoover and Plant (1989) is both critical of conservative public policy and original in its rethinking of socialist welfare theory. For a critique of contemporary welfare theory, see Barry (1990).

Theoretical treatments of market socialism include Miller (1989) and Estrin and Le Grand (1989). Works on the more traditional socialism are thinner on the ground but Benn (1982) covers the main ground.

Chapter 3 Voting and the Electorate

In-depth analysis of the British electorate has a very short history. The first nationwide study of the British electorate, *Political Change in Britain* (Butler and Stokes, 1969, 1974), was published less than three decades ago and most current work addresses themes raised in that volume. It is still well worth reading, even though it does not go beyond the 1970 election. Electoral behaviour in the 1970s is covered in Miller (1981), and Sarlvik and Crewe (1983). On the

1983 general election, see Heath *et al.* (1985) and Dunleavy and Husbands (1985). On the 1987 election, see Miller *et al.* (1990), and Crewe (1987). An excellent, short summary of Crewe's views on dealignment appears as Crewe (1984).

To get the 'feel' of recent general elections as well as a wealth of information and analysis, see Butler and Kavanagh (1980, 1984, 1988) or Crewe and Harrop (1986 and 1989). For a longer perspective see Butler (1989). Craig (1989) contains only tables and facts, but is invaluable for testing theories and putting current events in a proper historical context.

On electoral behaviour at local elections, see Miller (1988); on electoral behaviour at byelections, see Norris (1990); on electoral behaviour at Euro-elections, see Butler and Jowett (1985).

Chapter 4   Parties, Pressure Groups, and Parliament

There is an extensive literature on the nature of Thatcherism and its impact on British politics. Of particular interest are Gamble (1988) and Hall (1988). Also useful is Riddell (1989). Much less has been written about the Conservative party than about Thatcherism during these years though readers who wish to trace changes in party organisation will find much useful information in Butler and Kavanagh (1988). The Labour party is better served with a useful collection of essays by Whiteley (1983) and Kavanagh (1982). On Liberal party politics Bogdanor's excellent collection (Bogdanor, 1983) remains valuable and for recent material see Wilson (1987). On Scottish politics Kellas (1989) and the annual Yearbook of Scottish Government should be consulted. On pressure groups a useful general collection is Marsh (1983) and there are some excellent case-studies such as Whiteley (1983). For Parliament and pressure groups see Rush (1990). On Parliament the most comprehensive guide is Griffith, Ryle, and Wheeler-Booth (1989). A shorter general overview can be found in Silk and Walters (1987). A useful collection of essays is Judge (1983); Norton (1985) provides an overview of recent developments. Drewry (1989) is essential on the new Select Committees. On the Lords see Shell (1988).

Chapter 5   Government at the Centre

The British central state has been documented by a number of systematic studies, notably Rose (1987) on Whitehall ministries, and Dunleavy (1989c, 1989d) on a much wider range of agencies. A more difficult treatment is given in Dunsire and Hood (1989).

Core executive (PM, Cabinet and central institutions) have been very scantily studied during the 1970s and 1980s. However, *Public Administration* (Spring 1990) is an important source for academic studies adopting new directions, while Hennessy (1986) provides a reasonable condensation of the older journalistic-cum-institutionalist approach. A recent, eye-opening case study is Linklater and Leigh (1986) – worth reading more than a chestful of ministerial memoirs.

On the civil service, a key and very readable modern source is the Efficiency Unit's (1988) report – with its schizophrenic message at once proclaiming the progress made in 1980s efforts to improve management in government, while at the same time condemning them as ineffective and urging a radical change of direction. The House of Commons, Treasury and Civil Service Committee report (1988) is also interesting. The deep background to the current reorganisation is lengthily if chattily explored in Hennessy (1989).

The intelligence services continue to be documented only in bizarrely inflated journalistic studies, but Andrew (1985) at least provides a historical grip.

Chapter 6   Government Beyond Whitehall

For a straightforward introduction to local government, see the book by Byrne (1986). Look out for the most recent edition. A more advanced account is provided in Stoker (1988). The book by Gyford, Leach and Game (1989) draws on their research for the Widdicombe Committee and provides an excellent insight into the growing influence of party politics in local government. For a comprehensive account of the world of sub-central government, see Rhodes (1988).

To get a flavour of the conflict and turmoil of the 1980s, see the books by Newton and Karran (1985), Jones and Stewart (1985), and Parkinson (1987). Lansley, Goss and Wolmar (1989) describe the rise and fall of the urban left.

For those interested in theoretical issues, see Stoker (1988) chapter 10. See also Bulpitt (1983) and Dunleavy (1986). For a colourful New Right account, see Pirie (1988). The concepts of Fordism and post-Fordism are discussed in the chapter by Stoker in Stewart and Stoker (1989). King's chapter in the same book reviews normative perspectives on local government.

Up-to-date accounts of changes in local government and an

assessment of their implications are provided in Stewart and Stoker (1989) and Klein (1989). The following journals should also be consulted: *Policy and Politics, Local Government Studies, Local Government Policy-Making, Public Administration*, as well as the weekly magazine *Local Government Chronicle*.

Chapter 7   Britain and Europe

The literature on Britain and the EC is patchy and much is written in other European languages. For an up-to-date account of the workings of the EC, see Nugent (1989). This should be supplemented by a glance at the EC Treaties, since the language and content of the basic texts need to be understood. Pryce (1987) provides a commentary on the changes embodied in the Single European Act and their potential implications for political integration.

For the policy process, see Wallace, Wallace and Webb (1983), though it needs to be supplemented on more recent developments by more specialised literature. The reports of the House of Lords Select Committee on the European Communities provide valuable commentaries on particular policy issues.

The most comprehensive survey of Britain and the EC is by De la Serre (1987). See also Butler (1986) and Tugendhat (1986), both practitioner accounts, and O'Nuallain (1985), which contains a chapter by Edwards on British management of EC policy.

Other useful sources include the publications of the Royal Institute of International Affairs and the University Association for Contemporary European Studies and among the journals *Government and Opposition, Integration* (Bonn), the *Journal of Common Market Studies* and the *Revue du Marché Commun*.

Chapter 8   Economic Policy

The best book on Britain's economic decline, presenting a powerful critique of post-war policies, is Pollard (1982). For readable discussions of the monetarist experiment by the Thatcher Government two books are particularly useful: Keegan (1984) and Smith (1987). For readers with a taste for the more technical debates in economic policy-making two collections of papers are particularly good, Dornbusch and Layard (1987) and Britton (1989). For a comparative perspective on the economic crises of the 1970s, and the divergent policy responses of governments to the economic problems of advanced industrial countries see Keman, Paloheimo, and Whiteley (1987).

Chapter 9   Social Policy

A useful review of post-war social policy, focusing on the Thatcher years, is provided by Deakin (1987), who both sets social policy in the context of economic policy and covers the 1985–6 social security reviews in detail. Digby (1989) offers a masterpiece of compression from both the historical and comparative perspective. On health services Allsop (1984) and Ham (1985) provide sound introductions, the former usefully including a selection of primary documents. The second edition of Klein's (1989) work on the politics of the NHS is not to be missed, conveying better than any alternative the flavour of health politics in the UK. Goodin and Le Grand (1987) summarise the evidence on the middle-class welfare state, and Ringen (1987), though an advanced book, offers comparative evidence of its general effects. Klein and O'Higgins (1985) contains a series of papers offering a valuable antidote to the 'crisis of the welfare state literature' usefully represented in Mishra (1984).

Chapter 10   Environmental Politics and Policy

The following reviews of environmental politics in the early 1980s are useful: Goldsmith and Hilyard (1986), and Blowers (1987). For an alternative review of the period covered here, see Secrett and Porritt (1989). For information on Green politics, see Rudig and Lowe (1986) and Eckersley (1989). For the policy style of environmental regulation in Britain, see Vogel (1986). For the ideas of the green movement, see Porritt (1985).

Chapter 11   Foreign and Defence Policy

There are few up-to-date histories of British foreign policy. The best introductions remain Northedge (1974), Frankel (1975) and Jones (1974). A good discussion of the future of British foreign policy is Tugendhat and Wallace (1988). The foreign policy process is best dealt with in Wallace (1976); Hennessy (1986) offers a powerful analysis of the developments in Cabinet government. On British defence policy, see Baylis (1983, 1989) for general discussions. On the Falklands War, see Freedman (1988). For a good, if dated, account of British nuclear weapons policy, see Freedman (1980). The special relationship is discussed in Louis and Bull (1986), and from the nuclear side in Simpson (1986). A good analysis of the economic aspects of defence policy is Chalmers (1985). Two recent collections of essays on the topic of foreign and defence policies are Smith, Smith and White (1988) and Clarke and Freedman (1990). For an introduction to the nature of interdependence, see Keohane and Nye (1977); modernisation is extensively discussed in Morse (1976). The impact of interdependence on British foreign policy is very well dealt with in Wallace (1986). The best discussions of contemporary British foreign policy are found in the quarterly journal *International Affairs*.

Chapter 12   Northern Ireland and the Anglo-Irish Agreement

There is an enormous literature on Northern Ireland and the selection below is merely the tip of an iceberg of over 7,000 publications since 1969. There are several good introductions to the conflict: Arthur (1984), and Boyle and Hadden (1985). Key historical treatments are in Buckland (1981), Farrell (1980), Kennedy (1988), Miller (1978), and Stewart (1986). There are several surveys of the social science literature: Lijphart (1975) and Whyte (1978, 1988, 1990). The unionist perspective is represented by Wilson, T. (1989) and the republican perspective by Farrell (1980). Stimulating interpretations of the conflict can be found in Bruce (1986), Guelke (1988), MacDonald (1986), and O'Malley (1983). An excellent discussion of inequality and discrimination can be found in Standing Advisory Commission on Human Rights (1987). British policy before Hillsborough is the subject of Bew and Patterson (1985). Further and more detailed discussants of the Anglo-Irish Agreement include McGarry (1988) and O'Leary, B. (1987a, 1989). Discussion of 'solutions' can be found in Boyle and Hadden (1985), McGarry and O'Leary (1990), Rea (1982), Rose (1975), Teague (1987) and Watt (1981). There is an excellent political directory in Flackes and Elliott (1989).

Chapter 13   The Political Economy of Regulation

The development of the privatisation programme under the Thatcher government is explored in detail by Veljanovski (1988). For the political and legal issues involved in regulation of industry, see

Barnes and Winward (1989), Kay and Vickers (1989), and Vel-janovski (1990). The degree of regulation of industry that is desirable for the European Community as it moves towards 1992, is debated in Dahrendorf *et al.* (1989).

Chapter 14   The Politics of the 1988 Education Reform Act

McNay and Ozga (1985) provide a useful basic collection of theoretical and empirical papers on education policy-making. There is no detailed study for England which compares with recent study of policy-making in Scotland (McPherson and Raab, 1988). Much of the important work by Kogan (e.g. Kogan, 1975) is now dated, but Ball's study (Ball, 1990) will be a significant new addition to the literature. Other books and readers contain accounts and analyses of particular policies of the 1970s and 1980s (e.g. Edwards *et al.*, 1989, Hargreaves and Reynolds, 1989), while that by Ranson and Tomlin-son (1986) provides some useful material on changes in central/local government relations in education.

Centre for Contemporary Cultural Studies (1981) is one of a number of books that explore the rise and fall of the post-war social democratic consensus in education. That by Dale (1989) on the role of the state in education in the post-war years includes a useful discussion of education policy under Thatcher, as will a new book from the Department of Cultural Studies, Birmingham University (1990). Knight (1990) discusses the development of Conservative education policy from 1950 to 1986, while Jones (1989) analyses the components of the Conservative 'revolution in education'.

A growing literature on the Education Reform Act itself includes two books produced while the Bill was passing through Parliament. That by Haviland (1988) brings together the written responses to the Bill, while Simon (1988) offers a critical commentary. Among later books, Maclure (1988) provides the best summary of the content of the Act, while Flude and Hammer (1989) and Bash and Coulby (1989) contain analyses of various elements of it. The contribution of the New Right can be approached both via their own commentaries upon the Bill (e.g. Hillgate Group, 1987) and by secondary analyses (Jones, 1989; Flude and Hammer, 1989).

Chapter 15   Industrial Relations

It is too early for any major assessments of the later 1980s, but readers can keep up to date through articles in *The British Journal of*

Industrial Relations and *The Industrial Relations Journal*. An overall
summary of the decade can be found in Crouch (1990). Important
works on the earlier 1980s include Batstone and Gourlay (1986) and
Millward and Stevens (1986). A major survey of the changing legal
system is Wedderburn (1986).

Chapter 16   The Thatcher Decade in Perspective

There is a large and growing literature on Thatcherism and the
Thatcher government. For general surveys see Kavanagh (1987)
and Riddell (1989). Theories of Thatcherism are analysed in
Gamble (1988) and Jessop *et al.* (1988). Hall (1988) contains the
original essays that launched the concept. King (1985) and Young
(1989) are the best guides to Margaret Thatcher's political style.
Skidelsky (1988) is a collection of essays on different aspects of
Thatcherism, while Hoover and Plant (1989) examine its ideological
character. International perspectives are contained in Krieger
(1986) and Overbeek (1990). Strong positive assessments of the
Thatcher record can be found in Holmes (1989) and Maynard
(1988). The best critique of the concept of Thatcherism is Rhodes
and Marsh (1989).

Different approaches to the study of British politics are analysed
by Dearlove and Saunders (1984) and Dunleavy (1986b; and forthcoming). See also Burch and Moran (1987). For the Westminster
model, see Mackintosh (1982), Birch (1964); and for more recent
work, Norton (1984). For public policy perspectives, see Dunleavy
and O'Leary (1987), Jordan and Richardson (1987), and Rose
(1985). For the literature on decline, see Gamble (1990) and Sked
(1987). The future of class politics in Britain is analysed by
Miliband (1983), Hobsbawm (1989), and Hall and Jacques (1989).

Bibliography

Adams, G. (1986) *The Politics of Irish Freedom*, Dingle, Brandon Books.

Adler, M. (1988) 'Lending a Deaf Ear: The Government's Response to Consultation on the Reform of Social Security', in Davidson, R. and White, P. (eds), *Information and Government*, Edinburgh, Edinburgh University Press.

Alderman, G. (1989) 'Anglo-Jewry and the 1987 General Election', paper presented to the Political Studies Association Conference, Warwick.

Allsop, J. (1984) *Health Policy and the National Health Service*, London, Longman.

Anderson, P. (1987) 'The Figures of Descent', *New Left Review*, no. 161, pp. 20–77.

Andrew, C. (1985) *Secret Service: The Making of the British Intelligence Community*, London, Heinemann.

Anwar, M. (1986) *Race and Politics: Ethnic Minorities and the British Political System*, London, Tavistock.

Arthur, P. (1984) *The Government and Politics of Northern Ireland*, London, Longman.

Ascher, K. (1987) *The Politics of Privatisation: Contracting Out in the NHS and Local Authorities*, London, Macmillan.

Atkinson, A. B. (1988) *Income Maintenance for the Unemployed in Britain and the Response to High Unemployment*, London, Suntory Toyota International Centre for Economics and Related Disciplines, Discussion Paper WSP/37.

Bain, A. D. (1982) *The Control of the Money Supply*, Harmondsworth, Penguin.

Baldwin, R. and McCrudden, C. (1987) *Regulation and Public Law*, London, Weidenfeld & Nicolson.

Ball, S. (1990) *Politics and Policy-Making in Education*, London, Routledge.

Balogh, T. (1982) *The Irrelevance of Contemporary Economics*, London, Weidenfeld & Nicolson.

Barnes, F. and Winward, J. (1989) *In the Absence of Competition – A Consumer View of Public Utilities Regulation*, London, National Consumer Council.

367

Barnett, C. (1986) *The Audit of War*, London, Macmillan.
Barry, N. P. (1987) *The New Right*, London, Croom Helm.
Barry, N. P. (1990) *Welfare*, Milton Keynes, Open University Press.
Bash, L. and Coulby, D. (eds) (1989) *The Education Reform Act: Competition and Control*, London, Cassell.
Batstone, E. and Gourlay, S. (1986) *Unions, Unemployment, and Innovation*, Oxford, Blackwell.
Baylis, J. (ed.) (1983) *Alternative Approaches to British Defence Policy*, London, Macmillan.
Baylis, J. (1989) *British Defence Policy: Striking the Right Balance*, London, Macmillan.
Beer, S. (1965) *Modern British Politics*, London, Faber.
Beesley, M. and Laidlaw, B. (1989) *The Future of Telecommunications*, London, Institute of Economic Affairs.
Benn, T. (1980a) *The Case for Party Democracy*, London, Institute for Workers Control.
Benn, T. (1980b) *Arguments for Socialism*, Harmondsworth, Penguin.
Benn, T. (1982) *Parliament, People, and Power: Agenda for a Free Society*, London, Verso.
Berrington, H. (ed.) (1984) *Change in British Politics*, London, Cass.
Beveridge, W. (1942) *Social Insurance and Allied Services*, London, HMSO, Cmd 6404.
Bew, P. and Patterson, H. (1985) *The British State and the Ulster Crisis*, London, Verso.
Birch, A. (1964) *Representative and Responsible Government*, London, Unwin.
Birch, A. (1984) 'Overload, Ungovernability, and Delegitimation: The Theories and the British case', *British Journal of Political Science*, vol. 14, no. 2, pp. 135–60.
Blowers, B. (1987) 'Transition or Transformation: Environmental Policy under Thatcher', *Public Administration* vol. 65, pp. 227–295.
Blunden, J. and Curry, N. (1988) *A Future for Our Countryside*, Oxford, Blackwell.
Bogdanor, V. (ed.) (1983) *Liberal Party Politics*, Oxford, Oxford University Press.
Bogdanor, V. (1988) 'Against the Overmighty State: A Future for Local Government in Britain', London, Federal Trust for Education and Research.
Bogdanor, V. and Butler, D. (eds) (1983) *Democracy and Elections*, Cambridge, Cambridge University Press.
Boland, K. (1988) *Under Contract With the Enemy*, Cork, Mercier Press.

Boyle, K. and Hadden, T. (1985) *Ireland: A Positive Proposal*, Harmondsworth, Penguin.

Boyle, K. and Hadden, T. (1989) 'Breathing New Life into the Accord', *Fortnight*, no. 272, April, pp. 11–12.

Bradshaw, J. R. and Holmes, H. (1989) *Living on the Edge*, London, Tyneside CPAG.

Brindley, T., Rydin, Y. and Stoker, G. (1989) *Remaking Planning*, London, Unwin Hyman.

Brittan, S. (1973) *Capitalism and the Permissive Society*, London, Macmillan.

Brittan, S. (1975) 'The Economic Contradictions of Democracy', *British Journal of Political Science*, vol. 5, no. 2, pp. 129–60.

Brittan, S. (1977) *The Economic Consequences of Democracy*, London, Temple Smith.

Brittan, S. (1983) *The Role and Limits of Government*, London, Temple Smith.

Brittan, S. (1988) *A Restatement of Economic Liberalism*, London, Macmillan.

Britton, A. (1989) *Policymaking with Macroeconomic Models*, London, Gower.

Browning, P. (1983) *Economic Images*, London, Longman.

Bruce, S. (1986) *God Save Ulster: The Religion and Politics of Paisleyism*, Oxford, Oxford University Press.

Buchanan, J. (1975) *The Limits of Liberty*, Chicago, University of Chicago Press.

Buchanan, J. and Tullock, G. (1962) *The Calculus of Consent*, Michigan, Ann Arbor.

Buckland, P. (1981) *A History of Northern Ireland*, New York, Holmes & Meier.

Buiter, W. H. and Miller, M. (1981) 'The Thatcher Experiment: The First Two Years', *Brookings Papers on Economic Activity*, 2, pp. 315–79, Washington, The Brookings Institution.

Buiter, W. H. and Miller, M. (1983) 'Changing the Rules: Economic Consequences of the Thatcher Regime', *Brookings Papers on Economic Activity*, 2, pp. 305–65, Washington, The Brookings Institution.

Bulpitt, J. (1983) *Territory and Power in the United Kingdom*, Manchester, Manchester University Press.

Bulpitt, J. (1985) 'The Discipline of the New Democracy: Mrs. Thatcher's Domestic Statecraft', *Political Studies*, vol. 34, no. 1, pp. 19–39.

Bulpitt, J. (1990) 'Walking Back to Happiness? Conservative Party Governments and Elected Local Authorities in the 1980s', *Political Quarterly* (forthcoming).

Burch, M. and Moran, M. (eds) (1987) *British Politics: A Reader*, Manchester, Manchester University Press.

Burrows, P. (1979) *The Economic Theory of Pollution Control*, Oxford, Martin Robertson.

Butler, D. (1989) *British General Elections since 1945*, Oxford, Blackwell.

Butler, D. and Jowett, P. (1985) *Party Strategies in Britain: A study of the 1984 European Elections*, London, Macmillan.

Butler, D. and Kavanagh, D. (1980) *The British General Election of 1979*, London, Macmillan.

Butler, D. and Kavanagh, D. (1984) *The British General Election of 1983*, London, Macmillan.

Butler, D. and Kavanagh, D. (1988) *The British General Election of 1987*, London, Macmillan.

Butler, D. and Stokes, D. (1974) *Political Change in Britain*, London, Macmillan.

Butler, M. (1986) *Europe: More than a Continent*, London, Heinemann.

Byrne, T. (1986) *Local Government in Britain*, Harmondsworth, Penguin.

Calleo, D. (1968) *Britain's Future*, London, Hodder & Stoughton.

Calvocoressi, P. (1978) *The British Experience 1945–75*, London, Bodley Head.

Campbell, D. (1988) 'They've got it taped', *New Statesman and Society*, 12 August, pp. 10–12.

Camps, M. (1965) *What Kind of Europe?*, Oxford, Oxford University Press.

Camps, M. (1967) *European Unification in the Sixties*, Oxford, Oxford University Press.

Caves, R. E. and Krause, L. B. (1980) *Britain's Economic Performance*, Washington, The Brookings Institution.

Centre for Contemporary Cultural Studies (CCCS) (1981) *Unpopular Education: Schooling and Social Democracy in England since 1944*, London, Hutchinson.

Chalmers, M. (1985) *Paying for Defence: Military Spending and British Decline*, London, Pluto.

Charter 88 (1988) *Charter 88*, London, New Statesman and Society.

Clarke, H. C. and Whiteley, P. F. (1989) 'Perception of Macroeconomic Performance, Government Support, and Conservative Party Strategy 1983–87', *European Journal of Political Research* (forthcoming).

Clarke, M. (1988) 'The Policy-Making Process', in Smith, Smith and White (1988), pp. 71–95.

Clarke, M. and Freedman, L. (eds) (1990) *British Foreign Policy*, Cambridge, Cambridge University Press.

Congdon, T. (1989) 'Will the Lawson Boom Cause As Much Inflation As the Barber Boom?', *Economic Affairs*, vol. 9.

Cooper, R. (1968) *The Economics of Interdependence*, New York, McGraw-Hill.

Cooper, R. (1972–3) 'Trade Policy is Foreign Policy', *Foreign Policy*, no. 9, pp. 18–36.

Coughlan, A. (1986) *Fooled Again? The Anglo-Irish Agreement and After*, Cork, Mercier Press.

Cox, C. B. and Dyson, A. (eds) (1971) *The Black Papers on Education*, London, Davis-Poynter.

Cox, G., Lowe, P. and Winter, M. (1986) 'From State Regulation to Self Regulation: The Historical Development of Corporatism in British Agriculture', *Policy and Politics* no. 14, pp. 475–90.

Cox, W. H. (1987) 'Managing Northern Ireland Intergovernmentally: An Appraisal of the Anglo-Irish Agreement', *Parliamentary Affairs*, vol. 40, no. 1, pp. 80–97.

Coyne, P. (1978) 'Nuclear Power and the Growth of Corporatism' in Elliot, D. (ed.), *The Politics of Nuclear Power*, London, Pluto.

Craig, F. W. S. (1989) *British Electoral Facts 1832–1987*, Aldershot, Gower.

Crewe, I. (1984) 'The Electorate: Partisan Dealignment Ten Years On', in Berrington, H. (ed.), *Change in British Politics*, London, Cass.

Crewe, I. (1987) 'Why Mrs Thatcher was Returned with a Landslide', *Social Studies Review*, vol. 3, no. 1, pp. 2–9.

Crewe, I. (1988) 'Has the Electorate become Thatcherite?', in Skidelsky, R. (ed.), *Thatcherism*, pp. 25–50.

Crewe, I. and Harrop, M. (eds) (1986) *Political Communications: The General Election Campaign of 1983*, Cambridge, Cambridge University Press.

Crewe, I. and Harrop, M. (1989) (eds), *Political Communications: The General Election Campaign of 1987*, Cambridge, Cambridge University Press.

Crosland, C. A. R. (1956) *The Future of Socialism*, London, Cape.

Crouch, C. (1990) 'United Kingdom: The Rejection of Compromise', in Baglioni, G. and Crouch, C. (eds), *European Industrial Relations: The Challenge of Flexibility*, London, Sage.

Curtice, J. and Steed, M. (1988) 'Analysis', in Butler, D. and Kavanagh, D., *The British General Election of 1987*, London, Macmillan, pp. 316–62.

Dahl, R. A. (1985) *Controlling Nuclear Weapons: Democracy versus Guardianship*, Syracuse, Syracuse University Press.

Dahrendorf, R. *et al.* (1989) *Whose Europe? Competing Visions for 1992*, London, Institute of Economic Affairs.

Dale, R. (1989) *The State and Education Policy*, Milton Keynes, Open University Press.

Darby, P. (1973) *British Defence Policy East of Suez 1947–68*, Oxford, Oxford University Press.

Darby, P. (1977) 'East of Suez Reassessed', in Baylis, J. (ed.), *British Defence Policy in a Changing World*, London, Croom Helm, pp. 52–65.

De la Serre, F. (1987) *La Grande-Bretagne et la Communauté Européene*, Paris, Presses Universitaries de France.

Deakin, N. (1987) *The Politics of Welfare*, London, Methuen.

Dearlove, J. and Saunders, P. (1984) *Introduction to British Politics*, Cambridge, Polity.

Demaine, J. (1988) 'Teachers' Work, Curriculum and the New Right', *British Journal of Sociology of Education*, vol. 9, no. 3, pp. 247–64.

Department of Cultural Studies, University of Birmingham, *Under New Conditions: Educational Policies, Practices and Alternatives Since 1979*, London, Unwin Hyman.

Department of Employment (1989) *Removing Barriers to Employment*, London, HMSO.

Department of the Environment (1988) *Local Authorities' Companies: A Consultation Paper*.

DHSS (1985) *Reform of Social Security*, London, HMSO.

DTI (1988) *Enterprise*, London, Department of Trade and Industry.

Digby, A. (1989) *British Welfare Policy*, London, Faber.

Doherty, P. (1988) 'MacBride Effort: US Map Keeps on Getting Darker', *Fortnight*, no. 264, July–August, pp. 11–12.

Donoghue, B. (1987) *Prime Minister: The Conduct of Policy Under Harold Wilson and James Callaghan*, London, Cape.

Dornbusch, R. and Layard, R. (1987) *The Performance of the British Economy*, Oxford, Clarendon Press.

Drewry, G. (1989) *The New Select Committees*, Oxford, Oxford University Press.

Duncan, S. and Goodwin, M. (1988) *The Local State and Uneven Development: Behind the Local Government Crisis*, Cambridge, Polity.

Dunleavy, P. (1986a) 'Explaining the Privatisation Boom', *Public Administration*, vol. 64, no. 1, pp. 13–34.

Dunleavy, P. (1986b) 'Topics in British Politics' and 'Theories of the State in British Politics', in Drucker, H. *et al.* (eds), *Developments in British Politics 2*, London, Macmillan.

Dunleavy, P. (1989a) 'The United Kingdom: Paradoxes of an Ungrounded Statism', in Castles, F. (ed.), *The Comparative History of Public Policy*, Cambridge, Polity.

Dunleavy, P. (1989b) 'The End of Class Politics?', in Cochrane, A. and Anderson, J., *Politics in Transition: Restructuring Britain*, London, Sage/Open University.

Dunleavy, P. (1989c) 'The Architecture of the British Central State: Part I, Framework for Analysis', *Public Administration*, vol. 67, no. 3, pp. 249–75.

Dunleavy, P. (1989d) 'The Architecture of the British Central State: Part II, Empirical Findings', *Public Administration*, vol. 67, no. 4, pp. 391–418.

Dunleavy, P. (1990) 'Reinterpreting the Westland Affair: Theories of the State and Core Executive Decision-Making', *Public Administration*, vol. 68, no. 1, pp. 29–60.

Dunleavy, P. (forthcoming) *Analysing British Politics*, London, Macmillan.

Dunleavy, P. and Husbands, C. (1985) *British Democracy at the Crossroads: Voting and Party Competition in the 1980s*, London, Allen & Unwin.

Dunleavy, P., Jones, G. W. and O'Leary, B. (1990) 'Prime Ministers in the House of Commons, 1868–1988', *Public Administration*, vol. 68, no. 1, pp. 123–41.

Dunleavy, P. and O'Leary, B. (1987) *Theories of the State: The Politics of Liberal Democracy*, London, Macmillan.

Dunleavy, P. and Rhodes, R. (1986) 'Governments Beyond White-hall' in Drucker, H. *et al.* (eds), *Developments in British Politics 2*, London, Macmillan.

Dunleavy, P. and Rhodes, R. A. W. (1990) 'Core Executive Studies in Britain: A Review', *Public Administration*, vol. 68, no. 1, pp. 3–28.

Eckersley, R. (1989) 'Green Politics and the New Class', *Political Studies*, vol. 37, no. 2, pp. 205–23.

Edmunds, M. (1985) 'Central Organisations of Defence in Great Britain', in M. Edmunds (ed.), *Central Organisations of Defence*, London, Pinter/Westview Press, pp. 85–107.

Edwards, A., Fitz, J. and Whitty, G. (1989) *The State and Private Education: an Evaluation of the Assisted Places Scheme*, Lewes, Falmer Press.

Edwards, C. and Heery, E. (1989) 'Recession in the Public Sector: Industrial Relations in Freightliner 1981–5', *British Journal of Industrial Relations*, vol. 27, no. 1, pp. 57–72.

Efficiency Unit (1988) *Improving Management in Government: The Next Steps*, London, HMSO.

Estrin, S. and Le Grand, J. (eds) (1989) *Market Socialism*, Oxford, Clarendon Press.

European Documentation (1987) *The European Community and the Environment Office*, Luxembourg, Office of Official Publications of the European Community.

Eversley, D. (1989) *Religion and Employment in Northern Ireland*, London, Sage.

Fair, F. (1984) *Specification, Estimation, and Analysis of Macroeconomic Models*, Cambridge, Mass., Harvard University Press.

Farrell, M. (1980) *Northern Ireland: The Orange State*, London, Pluto.

Finer, S. E. (ed.) (1975) *Adversary Politics and Electoral Reform*, London, Wigram.

Finer, S. E. (1988) 'Thatcherism and British Political History', in Minogue, K. and Biddiss, M. (eds), *Thatcherism: Personality and Politics*, London, Macmillan.

Fisher, S. (1987) 'Monetary Policy', in Dornbusch, R. and Layard, R. (eds), *The Performance of the British Economy*, Oxford, Clarendon Press.

Flackes, W. D. and Elliott, S. (1989) *Northern Ireland: A Political Directory, 1968–1988*, Belfast, Blackstaff Press.

Flude, M. and Hammer, M. (eds) (1989) *The Education Reform Act, 1988: Its Origins and Implications*, Lewes, Falmer Press.

Flynn, A., Gray, A., and Jenkins, W. (1989) 'Taking the Next Steps: The Changing Management of Government', Paper to the 1989 Political Studies Association Conference, University of Warwick.

Flynn, N. (1989) 'The New Right and Social Policy', *Policy and Politics*, vol. 17, no. 2, pp. 97–109.

Forbes, I. (ed.) (1979) *Market Socialism: Whose Choice?*, London, Fabian Society.

Frankel, J. (1975) *British Foreign Policy 1945–73*, Oxford, Oxford University Press.

Freedman, L. (1980) *Britain and Nuclear Weapons*, London, Macmillan.

Freedman, L. (1988) *Britain and the Falklands War*, Oxford, Blackwell.

Friedman, M. (1962) *Capitalism and Freedom*, Chicago, University of Chicago Press.

Friedman, M. (1968) 'The Role of Monetary Policy', *American Economic Review*, vol. 63, pp. 1–17.

Friedman, M. and Friedman, R. (1979) *Free to Choose*, Harmondsworth, Penguin.

Fry, G. (1988) 'Inside Whitehall', in Drucker, H. *et al.* (eds), *Developments in British Politics 2*, London, Macmillan.

Fukuyama, F. (1989) 'The End of History?', *The National Interest*, Summer.

Galbraith, J. K. (1965) *The Affluent Society*, Harmondsworth, Penguin.

Gallup Political Index (1986), 307 (March), London, Gallup Polls.

Gamble, A. (1988) *The Free Economy and the Strong State: The Politics of Thatcherism*, London, Macmillan.

Gamble, A. (1990) *Britain in Decline*, London, Macmillan.

Gamble, A. and Wells, C. (eds) (1988) *Thatcher's Law*, Cardiff, University of Wales Press.

George, S. A. (1990) *An Awkward Partner: Britain in the European Community*, Oxford, Oxford University Press.

Gilmour, I. (1983) *Britain Can Work*, Oxford, Martin Robertson.

Golby, M. and Brigley, S. (1989) *Parents as School Governors*, Tiverton, Fair Way Publications.

Goldsmith, E. and Hilyard, N. (eds) (1986) *Green Britain or Industrial Wasteland*, Cambridge, Polity.

Goodhart, C. A. (1984) *Monetary Theory and Practice*, London, Macmillan.

Goodin, R. and Le Grand, J. (eds) (1987) *Not Only the Poor*, London, Allen & Unwin.

Gould, B. (1985) *Socialism and Equality*, London, Macmillan.

Gower Report (1985) *Review of Investor Protection*, Cmnd 9125, London, HMSO.

Graham, C. and Prosser, T. (1987) 'Privatising Nationalised Industries: Constitutional Issues and New Legal Techniques', *Modern Law Review*, vol. 50, pp. 16–51.

Graham, C. and Prosser, T. (eds) (1988) *Waiving the Rules*, Milton Keynes, Open University Press.

Grant, W. (1989) 'The Erosion of Intermediary Institutions', *Political Quarterly*, vol. 60, no. 1.

Grantham, C. (1989) 'Parliament and Political Consultants', *Parliamentary Affairs*, vol. 42, no. 4.

Green, D. (1987) *The New Right*, Brighton, Wheatsheaf.

Greenleaf, W. H. (1983) *The British Political Tradition*, Volume I, *The Rise of Collectivism*; Volume II, *The Ideological Heritage*, London, Methuen.

Greenleaf, W. H. (1987) *The British Political Tradition*, Volume III, *A Much Governed Nation*, London, Methuen.

Gribbin, J. (1988) *The Hole in the Sky: Man's Threat to the Ozone Layer*, London, Friends of the Earth.

Griffith, A. G., Ryle, M. and Wheeler-Booth, M. (1989) *Parliament: Functions, Practice, and Procedures*, London, Sweet & Maxwell.

Grunberg, L. (1986) 'Workplace Relations in the Economic Crisis:

A Comparison of a British and French Automobile Plant', *Sociology*, vol. 20, no. 4, pp. 503–29.

Guelke, A. (1988) *Northern Ireland: The International Perspective*, Dublin, Gill & Macmillan.

Gyford, J., Leach, S. and Game, C. (1989) *The Changing Politics of Local Government*, London, Unwin Hyman.

Hailsham, Lord (1978) *The Dilemma of Democracy*, London, Collins.

Hall, S. (1988) *The Hard Road to Renewal*, London, Verso.

Hall, S. and Jacques, M. (eds) (1989) *New Times*, London, Lawrence & Wishart.

Ham, C. (1985) *Health Policy in Britain*, London, Macmillan.

Hambleton, R. (1989) 'Urban Government Under Thatcher and Reagan', *Urban Affairs Quarterly*, vol. 24, no. 3, pp. 359–88.

Hamer, M. (1987) *Wheels within Wheels*, London, Routledge & Kegan Paul.

Hanrieder, W. and Auton, G. (1980) *The Foreign Policies of West Germany, France, and Britain*, Englewood Cliffs, NJ, Prentice-Hall.

Hargreaves, A. and Reynolds, D. (eds) (1989) *Education Policies: Controversies and Critiques*, Lewes, Falmer Press.

Haslett, E. (1987) *The Anglo-Irish Agreement: Northern Ireland Perspectives*, Belfast, Unionist Joint Working Party.

Hattersley, R. (1987) *Choose Freedom*, Harmondsworth, Penguin.

Haviland, J. (1988) *Take Care, Mr. Baker!*, London, Fourth Estate.

Hayek, F. A. (1960) *The Constitution of Liberty*, London, Routledge & Kegan Paul.

Hayek, F. A. (1975) *Full Employment at any Price?* London, Institute of Economic Affairs.

Health Services Journal (1987) 'The Public Voices its Opinions on the NHS' (2 April) pp. 382–3.

Heath, A., Jowell, R. and Curtice, J. (1985) *How Britain Votes*, Oxford, Pergamon.

Heath, A., MacDonald, S. (1988) 'The Demise of Party Identification Theory?', *Electoral Studies*, vol. 7, no. 2, pp. 95–108.

Heath, A., Jowell, R., Curtice, J. and Evans, G. (1989) 'The Extension of Popular Capitalism', paper presented to the 1989 Political Studies Association Conference, University of Warwick.

Hendry, D. F. and Ericsson, N. R. (1983) 'Assertion Without Empirical Basis: An Econometric Appraisal of Friedman and Schwartz', *Bank of England Panel of Academic Consultants*, Panel paper 22, London, Bank of England.

Hennessy, P. (1985) 'Does the Elderly Cabinet Machine Need Oiling?' *The Listener*, 27 June, pp. 8–9.

Hennessy, P. (1986) *Cabinet*, Oxford, Blackwell.

Hennessy, P. (1989) *Whitehall*, Secker & Warburg.

Hill, C. (1979) 'Britain's Elusive Role in World Politics', *British Journal of International Studies*, vol. 5, no. 3, pp. 248–59.

Hill, C. (1988) 'The Historical Background: Past and Present in British Foreign Policy', in Smith, Smith and White (1988), pp. 25–49.

Hill, M., Aaronovitch, S. and Baldock, D. (1989) 'Non Decision-Making in Pollution Control in Britain: Nitrate Pollution, the EEC Drinking Water Directive and Agriculture', *Policy and Politics*, vol. 17, pp. 227–40.

Hillgate Group (1987) *The Reform of British Education*, London, Claridge Press.

Hirschman, A. (1985) *Shifting Involvements: Private Interests and Public Action*, Oxford, Blackwell.

HMSO (1980) *Financial Statement and Budget Report 1980–81*, H.C. 500, London.

HMSO (1982) *Financial Statement and Budget Report 1982–83*, H.C. 237, London.

HM Government (1987) *Housing: The Government's Proposals*, White Paper, Cm 214.

HM Government (1989a) *Caring for People: Community Care in the Next Decade and Beyond*, White Paper.

HM Government (1989b) *Working For Patients*.

Hobsbawm, E. (1989) *Politics for a Rational Left*, London, Verso.

Holmes, M. (1989) *Thatcherism: Scope and Limits 1983–7*, London, Macmillan.

Hood, C. (1987) 'British Administrative Trends and the Public Choice Revolution', in Lane, J. E. (ed.), *Bureaucracy and Public Choice*, London, Sage.

Hood, C. (1990) 'The End of the Public Bureaucracy State?', London, London School of Economics, Inaugural Lecture.

Hood, C. and Dunsire, A. (1989) *Cutback Management in Public Bureaucracies: Popular Theories and Observed Outcomes in Whitehall*, Cambridge, Cambridge University Press.

Hoover, K. and Plant, R. (1988) *Conservative Capitalism*, London, Routledge.

Hoskyns, J. (1983) 'Whitehall and Westminster: An Outsider's View', *Parliamentary Affairs*, vol. 36.

House of of Commons (1980) 'Memorandum by Milton Friedman to the House of Commons Select Committee on the Treasury and the Civil Service', *Monetary Policy*, HC 720.

Ingham, G. (1984) *Capitalism Divided*, London, Macmillan.

Ingram, P. and Cahill, J. (1989) *The Structure and Process of Pay Determination in the Private Sector 1979–86*, London, CBI.

Jackson, M. (1989) 'CBI Struggles to "Save" Curriculum from Baker', *The Times Educational Supplement*, 24 March.

Jackson, P. (1982) *The Political Economy of Bureaucracy*, London, Philip Allan.

Jacobs, M. (1989) 'The Green Dilemma', *New Socialist*, no. 62, August/September, pp. 11–14.

Jay, P. (1976) *Employment, Inflation, and Politics*, London, Institute of Economic Affairs.

Jessop, B., Bonnett, K., Bromley, S. and Ling, T. (1988) *Thatcherism: A Tale of Two Nations*, Cambridge, Polity.

Johnson, F. (1980) *Defence by Ministry*, London, Duckworth.

Johnson, N. (1977) *In Search of the Constitution*, Oxford, Pergamon.

Johnson, R. (1989) 'Thatcherism and English Education: Breaking the Mould, or Confirming the Pattern?', *History of Education*, vol. 18, no. 2, pp. 91–121.

Johnston, K. (1987) *Into the Void? A Report on CFCs and the Ozone Layer*, London, Corgi.

Jones, G. W. (1983) 'Prime Ministers' Departments Really Create Problems: A Rejoinder to Patrick Weller', *Public Administration*, vol. 61, pp. 79–84.

Jones, G. W. (1988) 'The Crisis in British Central–Local Relationships', *Governance*, vol. 1, no. 2, pp. 162–84.

Jones, G. W. (1989) 'A Revolution in Whitehall? Changes in British Central Government Since 1979', *West European Politics*, vol. 12, no. 3, pp. 238–61.

Jones, G. W. and Stewart, J. (1985) *The Case for Local Government*, London, Allen & Unwin.

Jones, K. (1989) *Right Turn: The Conservative Revolution in Education*, London, Hutchinson Radius.

Jordan, A. G. and Richardson, J. J. (1987) *British Politics and the Policy Process*, London, Allen & Unwin.

Joseph, K. (1976) *Stranded on the Middle Ground*, London, Centre for Policy Studies.

Joseph, K. and Sumption, J. (1979) *Equality*, London, Murray.

Jowell, R. and Witherspoon, S. (1985) *British Social Attitudes: the 1985 Report*, Aldershot, Gower.

Judge, D. (1983) (ed.) *The Politics of Parliamentary Reform*, London, Heinemann.

Kaldor, N. (1982) *The Scourge of Monetarism*, Oxford, Oxford University Press.

Kavanagh, D. (1987) *Thatcherism and British Politics*, Oxford, Clarendon Press.

Kavanagh, D. (1982) (ed.) *The Politics of the Labour Party*, London, Allen & Unwin.

Kay, J. and Vickers, J. (1989) 'Regulatory Reform in Britain', *Economic Policy*, vol. 7, pp. 286–351.

Keegan, W. (1984) *Mrs. Thatcher's Economic Experiment*, Harmondsworth, Penguin.

Keliher, L. (1990) 'Core Executive Decision-Making on High Technology Issues: the case of the Alvey Report', *Public Administration*, vol. 68, no. 1, pp. 61–82.

Kellas, J. (1989a) 'Prospects for a New Scottish Political System', *Parliamentary Affairs*, vol. 42, no. 4, pp. 519–32.

Kellas, J. (1989b) *The Scottish Political System*, Cambridge, Cambridge University Press.

Kellner, P. (1989) 'Decoding the Green Message', *Independent*, 7 July, p. 6.

Kellner, P. and Crowther Hunt, Lord (1980) *The Civil Servants: An Inquiry Into Britain's Ruling Class*, London, MacDonald & Janes.

Kelly, J. and Richardson, R. (1989) 'Annual Review, 1988', *British Journal of Industrial Relations*, vol. 27, no. 1, pp. 133–54.

Keman, H., Paloheimo, H. and Whiteley, P. (1987) *Coping with the Economic Crisis*, London, Sage.

Kennedy, D. (1988) *The Widening Gulf: Northern Attitudes to the Independent Irish State, 1919–49*, Belfast, Blackstaff Press.

Kennedy, P. (1988) *The Rise and Fall of the Great Powers*, London, Unwin Hyman.

Kenny, A. (1986) *The Road to Hillsborough*, Oxford, Pergamon.

Keohane, R. and Nye, J. (1977) *Power and Interdependence*, Boston, Mass., Little Brown.

King, A. (1985) 'Margaret Thatcher: The Style of a Prime Minister', in King, A. (ed.), *The British Prime Minister*, London, Macmillan.

King, D. (1987) *The New Right*, London, Macmillan.

King's Fund Institute (1989) *Efficiency in the NHS*, London.

Kitzinger, U. (1973) *Diplomacy and Persuasion: How Britain Joined the Common Market*, London, Thames & Hudson.

Klein, R. (1989) *The Politics of the NHS*, London, Longman.

Klein, R. and O'Higgins, M. (1985) *The Future of Welfare*, Oxford, Blackwell.

Knight, C. (1990) *The Making of Tory Education Policy in Post-War Britain, 1950–86*, Lewes, Falmer Press.

Kogan, M. (1975) *Educational Policy-Making – A Study of Interest Groups and Parliament*, London, Allen & Unwin.

Krieger, J. (1986) *Reagan, Thatcher, and the Politics of Decline*, Cambridge, Polity.

Labour Party (1989) *Policy Review*, London, Labour Party.

Laidler, D. (1981) 'Monetarism: An Interpretation and An Assessment', *Economic Journal*, vol. 91, pp. 1–28.

Lansley, S., Goss, S. and Wolmar, C. (1989) *Councils in Conflict*, London, Macmillan.

Lavoie, D. (1985) *Rivalry and Central Planning*, Cambridge, Cambridge University Press.

Lee, M. (1990) 'The Ethos of the Cabinet Office: A Comment on the Testimony of Officials', *Public Administration,* vol. 68, no. 2, forthcoming.

Le Grand, J. (1982) *The Strategy of Equality*, London, Allen & Unwin.

Lewis, J. and Townsend, A. (1989) *The North-South Divide: Regional Change in Britain in the 1980s*, London, Chapman.

Lijphart, A. (1975) 'The Northern Ireland Problem: Cases, Theories, and Solutions', *British Journal of Political Science*, vol. 5, no. 1, pp. 83–106.

Lijphart, A. and Grofman, B. (eds) (1984) *Choosing an Electoral System*, New York, Praeger.

Lindblom, C. (1977) *Politics and Markets*, New York, Basic Books.

Linklater, M. and Leigh, D. (1986) *Not With Honour: the Inside Story of the Westland Scandal*, London, The Observer.

Littlechild, S. C. (1983) *Regulation of British Telecommunications' Profitability*, London, HMSO.

Loughlin, M. (1986) *Local Government in the Modern State*, London, Sweet & Maxwell.

Louis, W. R. and Bull, H. (eds) (1986) *The Special Relationship: Anglo-American Relations Since 1945*, Oxford, Clarendon Press.

Lowe, P. and Goydor, J. (1983) *Environmental Groups in Politics*, London, Allen & Unwin.

Lowe, P., Cox, G., O'Riordan, P. and Winter, M. (1986) *Countryside Conflicts: The Politics of Farming and Conservation*, Aldershot, Gower/Temple Smith.

Luard, E. (1979) *Socialism Without the State*, London, Macmillan.

McCormick, J. (1989) *Acid Earth: The Global Threat of Acid Pollution*, London, Earthscan, ch. 5.

McCrudden, C. (1988) 'The Northern Ireland Fair Employment White Paper: A Critical Assessment', *Industrial Law Journal*, vol. 17, no. 3, pp. 162–81.

MacDonald, M. (1986) *Children of Wrath: Political Violence in Northern Ireland*, Cambridge, Polity.

McGarry, J. (1988) 'The Anglo-Irish Agreement and the Prospects for Power Sharing in Northern Ireland', *Political Quarterly*, vol. 59, no. 2, pp. 236–50.

McGarry, J. & O'Leary, B. (eds) (1990) *The Future of Northern Ireland*, Oxford, Clarendon.

Mackintosh, J. (1982) *The Government and Politics of Britain*, London, Hutchinson.

McKittrick, D. (1989) 'Fitzpatrick Attacks "Inept" Britain', *Independent*, 7 June.

Maclure, S. (1988) *Education Re-formed: A Guide to the Education Reform Act 1988*, London, Hodder & Stoughton.

McNamara, K. *et al.* (1988) 'Towards a United Ireland', Labour Front Bench Statement, House of Commons.

McNay, I. and Ozga, J. (eds) (1985) *Policy-Making in Education: The Breakdown of Consensus*, Oxford, Pergamon.

McPherson, A. and Raab, C. D. (1988) *Governing Education: A Sociology of Policy Since 1945*, Edinburgh: Edinburgh University Press, 1988.

Mair, P. (1987) 'Breaking the Nationalist Mould: The Irish Republic and the Anglo-Irish Agreement', in Teague, P. (ed.) *Beyond the Rhetoric: Politics, the Economy and Social Policy in Northern Ireland*, London, Lawrence & Wishart, pp. 81–110.

Mair, P. (1989) 'The Problem of Party System Change', *Journal of Theoretical Politics*, vol. 1, no. 3.

Marquand, D. (1988) *The Unprincipled Society*, London, Cape.

Marsh, D. (1983) (ed.) *Pressure Politics*, London, Junction Books.

Marsh, D. and Rhodes, R. (1989) 'Implementing "Thatcherism": A Policy Perspective', paper presented to the 1989 Public Administration Conference, University of York.

Marshall, T. H. (1950) *Citizenship and Social Class and Other Essays*, Cambridge, Cambridge University Press.

Martin, R. (1989) 'The Political Economy of Britain's North–South Divide', in J. Lewis and A. Townsend (eds), *The North–South Divide*, London, Chapman, pp. 20–60.

Massey, A. (1988) *Technocrats and Nuclear Politics*, Aldershot, Avebury, 1988.

Mather, G. (1989) 'Thatcherism and Local Government: An Evaluation' in Stewart, J. and Stoker, G. (eds), *The Future of Local Government*, London, Macmillan.

Maynard, G. (1988) *The Economy Under Mrs. Thatcher*, Oxford, Blackwell.

Metcalf, D. (1989) 'Water Notes Dry Up: The Impact of the Donovan Report Proposals and Thatcherism at Work on Labour Productivity in British Manufacturing Industry', *British Journal of Industrial Relations*, vol. 27, no. 1, pp. 1–31.

Middlemas, K. (1979) *Politics in Industrial Society*, London, Deutsch.

Miliband, R. (1984) *Capitalist Democracy in Britain*, Oxford, Oxford University Press.

Miller, D. (1978) *Queen's Rebels: An Anatomy of Loyalist Rebellion*, Dublin, Gill & Macmillan.

Miller, D. (1989) *Market, State, and Community: Theoretical Foundations of Market Socialism*, Oxford, Oxford University Press.

Miller, W. L. (1981) *The End of British Politics? Scots and English Political Behaviour in the 1970s*, Oxford, Oxford University Press.

Miller, W. L. (1988) *Irrelevant Elections? The Quality of Local Democracy in Britain*, Oxford, Oxford University Press.

Miller, W. L., Broughton, D., Sonntag, N. and McLean, D. (1989) 'Political Change in Britain During the 1987 Campaign', in Crewe, I. and Harrop, M. (eds), *Political Communications: The General Election Campaign of 1987*, Cambridge, Cambridge University Press.

Miller, W. L., Clarke, H., Harrop, M., Leduc, L. and Whiteley, P. (1990) *How Voters Change: The 1987 British Election Campaign in Perspective*, Oxford, Oxford University Press.

Milne, R. (1987) 'Pollution and Politics in the North Sea', *New Scientist*, 19 December, pp. 53–8.

Milne, R. (1989) 'British Power Stations Find it Hard to Come Clean', *New Scientist*, 23 March, p. 6.

Milward, N. and Stevens, M. (1986) *British Workplace Industrial Relations 1980–84*, London, Gower.

Minogue, K. (1978) 'On Hyperactivism in Modern British Politics', in Cowling, M., *Conservative Essays*, London, Cassell.

Mishra, R. (1984) *The Welfare State in Crisis*, Brighton, Wheatsheaf.

Moloney, E. (1986) 'A Good Deal for Unionists', *Fortnight*, no. 231, December–January, pp. 6–7.

Monopolies and Mergers Commission (1989) *British Gas*, London.

MORI (1989) *The Greening Consumer*, London, Mori.

Morse, E. (1970) 'The Transformation of Foreign Policies: Modernisation, Interdependence, and Externalisation', *World Politics*, vol. 22, no. 3, pp. 371–92.

Morse, E. (1976) *Modernisation and the Transformation of International Relations*, New York, The Free Press.

Mueller, D. C. (1979) *Public Choice*, Cambridge, Cambridge University Press.

Nairn, T. (1981) *The Breakup of Britain*, London, Verso.

NEDO (1976) *A Study of UK Nationalised Industries – Their Role in the Economy and Control in the Future*, London, National Development Office.

Newton, K. and Karran, T. (1985) *The Politics of Local Expenditure*, London, Macmillan.

Niskanen, W. (1971) *Bureaucracy and Representative Government*, New York, Aldine-Atherton.

Norris, P. (1990) *The Volatile Electorate: British Byelections since the War*, Oxford, Oxford University Press.

Northedge, F. (1970) 'Britain as a Second-Rate Power', *International Affairs*, vol. 46, no. 1, pp. 37–47.

Northedge, F. (1974) *Descent From Power: British Foreign Policy, 1945–73*, London, Allen & Unwin.

Northern Ireland Office (1989) *Developments since the Signing of the Anglo-Irish Agreement*, Belfast and London.

Norton, P. (1984) *The British Polity*, London, Longman.

Norton, P. (1985) *Parliament in the 1980s*, Oxford, Blackwell.

Norton-Taylor, R. (1988) 'Thatcher By-passes MI5 Old Guard for New Chief', *Guardian*, 13 January, p. 1.

Nugent, N. (1989) *The Government and Politics of the European Community*, London, Macmillan.

O'Brien, C. C. (1988) 'Introduction' to *Edmund Burke's Irish Affairs*, London, Century Hutchinson.

OECD (1989) *Economic Instruments for Environmental Protection*, Paris, Organisation for Economic and Cultural Development.

Oftel (1988) *The Regulation of British Telecom's Prices*, London, Office of Telecommunications.

O'Leary, B. (1987a) 'The Anglo-Irish Agreement: Statecraft or Folly', *West European Politics*, vol. 10, no. 1, pp. 5–32.

O'Leary, B. (1987b) 'Towards Europeanisation and Realignment? The Irish General Election, February 1987', *West European Politics*, vol. 10, no. 3, pp. 455–65.

O'Leary, B. (1989) 'The Limits to Coercive Consociationalism in Northern Ireland', *Political Studies*, vol. 37, no. 4, pp. 562–8.

O'Leary, B. (1990) 'Appendix 4. Party Support in Northern Ireland 1969–89', in McGarry, J. and O'Leary, B. (eds), *The Future of Northern Ireland*, Oxford, Oxford University Press.

O'Leary, B. and Peterson, J. (1990) 'Further Europeanisation: The Irish General Election, July 1989', *West European Politics*, vol. 13, no. 1.

O'Leary, C., Elliott, S. and Wilford, R. A. (1988) *The Northern Ireland Assembly, 1982–6: A Constitutional Experiment*, London, Hurst.

Olson, M. (1965) *The Logic of Collective Action*, Cambridge Mass., Harvard University Press.

Olson, M. (1982) *The Rise and Decline of Nations*, New Haven, Yale University Press.

O'Malley, P. (1983) *The Uncivil Wars: Ireland Today*, Belfast, Blackstaff Press.

O'Nuallain, C. (ed.) (1985) *The Presidency of the European Council of Ministers*, London, Croom Helm.

O'Riordan, T., Kemp, R. and Purdue, M. (1988) *Sizewell B*, London, Macmillan.

O'Riordan, T. and Weale, A. (1989) 'Administrative Reorganisation and Policy Change; The Case of Her Majesty's Inspectorate of Pollution', *Public Administration*, no. 67, pp. 277–95.

Osborne, R. D. and Cormack, R. J. (1989) 'Employment Equity in Northern Ireland and Canada', *Administration*, vol. 37, no. 2, pp. 133–51.

Overbeek, H. (1990) *Global Capitalism and Britain's Decline*, London, Unwin Hyman.

Palley, C. (1986) 'When an Iron Hand Can Beckon a Federal Union', *Guardian*, 20 January.

Parkin, S. (1989) *Green Parties: An International Guide*, London, Heretic.

Parkinson, M. (ed.) (1987) *Reshaping Local Government*, London, Policy Journals.

Peacock, A. (1961) *The Welfare Society*, London, Unservile State Paper, no. 2.

Peacock, A. and Wiseman, J. (1967) *The Growth of Public Expenditure in the United Kingdom*, London, Allen & Unwin.

Pearce, D., Markandya, A., and Barbier, E. B. (1989) *Blueprint for a Green Economy*, London, Earthscan.

Peele, G. (1989) 'Contemporary Conservatism and the Borders of the State', in Helm, D. (ed.) *The Economic Borders of the State*, Oxford, Oxford University Press.

Petchney, R. (1989) 'The Politics of Destabilisation', *Critical Social Policy*, Summer, pp. 82–97.

Peters, B. G. (1989) *Comparative Public Administration*, Tuscaloosa, Alabama, University of Alabama Press.

Piachaud, David (1979) *The Cost of a Child*, London, CPAG Cambridge.

Pinto-Duschinsky, M. (1989) 'Trends in British Party Funding 1983–87', *Parliamentary Affairs*, vol. 42, no. 2, pp. 197–212.

Pirie, M. (1988) *Micropolitics*, London, Wildwood House.

Pollard, S. (1982) *The Wasting of the British Economy*, London, Croom Helm.

Ponting, C. (1986) *Whitehall: Tragedy and Farce*, London, Hamilton.

Porritt, J. (1985) *Seeing Green: The Politics of Ecology Explained*, Oxford, Blackwell.

Powell, G. Bingham (1982) *Contemporary Democracies*, Cambridge, Mass., Harvard University Press.

Pressman, J. and Wildavsky, A. (1973) *Implementation*, Berkeley, University of California Press.

Pryce, R. (1987) *The Dynamics of European Union*, London, Croom Helm.

Raab, C. (1989) *Educational Policy: What Models for Research?*, paper presented at the Policy Studies Institute.

Radice, G. (1989) *Labour's Path to Power*, London, Macmillan.

Ranson, S. (1988) 'From 1944 to 1988: Education, Citizenship and Democracy', *Local Government Studies*, vol. 14, no. 1, pp. 1–19.

Ranson, S. and Tomlinson, J. (eds) (1986) *The Changing Government of Education*, London, Allen & Unwin.

Rea, D. (ed.) (1982) *Political Co-operation in Divided Societies*, Dublin, Gill & Macmillan.

Reform of Social Security (1985), London, HMSO, Cmnd 9517–19.

Rhodes, R. (1988) *Beyond Westminster and Whitehall*, London, Unwin Hyman.

Rhodes, R. (1990) 'Policy Networks: In Search of a Literature', in Marsh, D. and Rhodes, R. (eds), *Policy Networks in British Politics*, Oxford, Oxford University Press.

Richardson, R. and Wood, S. (1989) 'Productivity Changes in the Coal Industry and the New Industrial Relations', *British Journal of Industrial Relations*, vol. 27, no. 1, pp. 33–56.

Riddell, P. (1989) *The Thatcher Decade*, Oxford, Blackwell.

Ringen, S. (1987) *The Possibility of Politics*, Oxford, Oxford University Press.

Roberts, H. (1987) 'Sound Stupidity: The British Party System and the Northern Ireland Question', *Government and Opposition*, vol. 23, no. 3, pp. 315–35.

Rose, R. (1975) *Northern Ireland: A Time of Choice*, London, Macmillan.

Rose, R. (1980) 'British Government: The Job at the Top', in Rose, R. and Suleiman, E. N. (eds), *Presidents and Prime Ministers*, Washington, American Enterprise Institute, pp. 1–49.

Rose, R. (1985) *Do Parties Make a Difference?*, London, Macmillan.

Rose, R. (1987) *Ministers and Ministries: A Functional Approach*, Oxford, Oxford University Press.

Rose, R. and McAllister, I. (1986) *Voters Begin to Choose*, London, Sage.

Rüdig, W. and Lowe, P. (1986) 'The Withered "Greening" of British Politics: A Study of the Ecology Party', *Political Studies*, vol. 34, no. 2, pp. 262–84.

Rush, M. (ed.) (1990) *Parliament and Pressure Politics*, Oxford, Oxford University Press.

Salter, B. and Tapper, T. (1981) *Education, Politics, and the State*, London, Grant Macintyre.

Sarlvik, B. and Crewe, I. (1983) *Decade of Dealignment*, Cambridge, Cambridge University Press.

Saward, M. (1990) 'The Civil Nuclear Network in Britain', in Marsh, D. and Rhodes, R. (eds) *Policy Networks in British Politics*, Oxford, Oxford University Press.

Scruton, R. (1981) *The Meaning of Conservatism*, Harmondsworth, Penguin.

Secrett, C. and Porritt, J. (1989) *The Environment: The Government's Record*, London, Friends of the Earth.

Sedgemore, B. (1980) *The Secret Constitution*, London, Hodder & Stoughton.

Seldon, A. S. (1988) (ed.) *Financial Regulation – or Over-Regulation?*, London, Institute of Economic Affairs.

Seldon, A. (1990) 'The Cabinet Office and Coordination, 1979–87', *Public Administration*, vol. 68, no. 1, pp. 103–122.

Self, P. (1989) 'What's Wrong with Government? The Problem of Public Choice', Unpublished paper.

Shell, D. (1988) *The House of Lords*, London, Philip Allan.

Shoard, M. (1987) *This Land is Our Land: The Struggle For Britain's Countryside*, London, Collins, esp. ch. 15, but see also ch. 16.

Silk, P. and Walters, R. (1987) *How Parliament Works*, London, Longman.

Simon, B. (1988) *Bending the Rules: The Baker 'Reform' of Education*, London, Lawrence & Wishart.

Simpson, J. (1986) *The Independent Nuclear State: The United States, Britain and the Military Atom*, London, Macmillan.

Sinn Féin (1989) *Hillsborough. The Balance Sheet, 1985–88, A Failure*, Dublin, Sinn Féin Publicity Department.

Sked, A. (1987) *Britain's Decline*, Oxford, Blackwell.

Skidelsky, R. (ed.) (1988) *Thatcherism*, London, Chatto & Windus.

Smith, D. (1987) *Equality and Inequality in Northern Ireland*, London, Policy Studies Institute.

Smith, David (1987) *The Rise and Fall of Monetarism*, Harmondsworth, Penguin.

Smith, David (1989) *North and South*, Harmondsworth, Penguin.

Smith, M., Smith, S. and White, B. (eds) (1988) *British Foreign Policy: Tradition, Change, and Transformation*, London, Unwin Hyman.

Smith, M. J. (1989) 'The Annual Review: The Emergence of a Corporatist Institution', *Political Studies*, vol. 37, no. 1, pp. 81–96.

Smith, P. (1986) *Why Unionists say 'No'*, Belfast, Joint Unionist Working Party.

Social Services Committee (1987–8) *Resourcing the NHS: Short Term Issues*, London, HMSO, HC 264–I.

Socialist Conference (1989) *Socialist Policy Review*.

Stalker, J. (1988) *Stalker*, London, Harrap.

Standing Advisory Commission on Human Rights (SACHR) (1987) *Religious and Political Discrimination and Equality of Opportunity in Northern Ireland, Report on Fair Employment*, London, HMSO, Cm 237.

Stewart, A. T. Q. (1986) *The Narrow Ground: Patterns of Ulster History*, Belfast, Pretani Press.

Stewart, J. & Stoker, G. (1989) *The Future of Local Government*, London, Macmillan.

Stigler, G. S. (ed.) (1988) *Chicago Studies in Political Economy*, Chicago, University of Chicago Press.

Stoker, G. (1988) *The Politics of Local Government*, London, Macmillan.

Stoker, G. (1989a) 'Urban Development Corporations: A Review', *Regional Studies*, vol. 23, no. 2, pp. 159–73.

Stoker, G. (1989b) 'Creating a Local Government for a post-Fordist Society: The Thatcherite Project?' in Stewart, J. and Stoker, G. (eds) *The Future of Local Government*, London, Macmillan.

Stubbs, C. (1988) 'Property Rights and Relations: The Purchase of Council Housing', *Housing Studies*, vol. 3, no. 3, pp. 145–58.

Taagepera, R. and Shugart, M. S. (1989) *Seats and Votes: The Effects and Determinants of Electoral Systems*, London, Yale University Press.

Taylor, M. and Ward, H. (1982) 'Chickens, Whales, and Lumpy Public Goods: Alternative Models of Public Goods Provision', *Political Studies*, vol. 30, no. 3, pp. 350–70.

Teague, P. (ed.) (1987) *Beyond the Rhetoric: Politics, the Economy, and Social Policy in Northern Ireland*, London, Lawrence & Wishart.

Thompson, B. (1989) 'The Anglo-Irish Agreement, 1985, Machinery for Muddling Through', paper presented to the 1989 Political Studies Association Annual Conference, University of Warwick.

Thurow, L. (1983) *Dangerous Currents: The State of Economics*, Oxford, Oxford University Press.

Tooze, R. (1988) 'Security and Order – the Economic Dimension', in Smith, Smith and White (1988) pp. 124–45.

Townshend, C. (1983) *Political Violence in Ireland: Government and Resistance since 1948*, Oxford, Clarendon.

Townshend, C. (ed.) (1988) *Consensus in Ireland. Approaches and Recessions*, Oxford, Clarendon Press.

Travers, T. (1989) 'Community Charge and other Financial Changes', in Stewart, J. and Stoker, G. (eds), *The Future of Local Government*, London, Macmillan.

Treasury and Civil Service Committee (1988) *Eighth Report – Civil Service Management Reform: The Next Steps*, London, HMSO. House of Commons Papers 494–I and II.

Treaties establishing the European Communities (1987), London, HMSO.

Tugendhat, C. (1986) *Making Sense of Europe*, London, Viking.

Tugendhat, C. and Wallace, W. (1988) *Options for British Foreign Policy in the 1990s*, London, RIIA, Routledge.

Tullock, G. (1976) *The Vote Motive*, London, Institute of Economic Affairs.

Veljanovski, C. G. (1988) *Selling the State: Privatisation in Britain*, London, Weidenfeld & Nicolson.

Veljanovski, C. G. (ed.) (1989) *Privatisation and Competition – A Market Prospectus*, London, Institute of Economic Affairs.

Veljanovski, C. G. (1990) *Law and Economics*, London, Institute of Economic Affairs.

Vital, D. (1968) *The Making of British Foreign Policy*, London, Allen & Unwin.

Vogel, D. (1986) *National Styles of Regulation: Environmental Policing in Great Britain and the United States*, Ithaca, Cornell University Press.

Vogel, D. (1987) 'Political Science and the Study of Corporate Power: A Dissent from the New Conventional Wisdom', *British Journal of Political Science*, vol. 17, no. 4, pp. 385–408.

Wallace, H., Wallace, W. and Webb, C. (eds) (1983) *Policy-Making in the European Community*, Chichester, Wiley.

Wallace, W. (1976) *The Foreign Policy Process in Britain*, London, RIIA/Allen & Unwin.

Wallace, W. (1978) 'Old States and New Circumstances – The International Predicament of Britain, France, and Germany', in Wallace, W. and Paterson, W. (eds), *Foreign Policy-Making in Europe: A Comparative Approach*, Farnborough, Saxon House, pp. 31–55.

Wallace, W. (1986) 'What Price Independence? Sovereignty and Interdependence in British Politics', *International Affairs*, vol. 62, no. 3, pp. 367–89.

Wallace, W. and Wallace, H. (1990) 'Strong State or Weak State in Foreign Policy? The Contradictions of Conservative Liberalism', *Public Administration*, vol. 68, no. 1, pp. 83–102.

Wass, D. (1984) *Government and the Governed*, London, Routledge.

Watt, D. (1981) *The Constitution of Northern Ireland: Problems and Prospects*, London, Heinemann.

Weale, Albert (1986) 'Ideology and Welfare', *Quarterly Journal of Social Affairs*, vol. 2, no. 3, pp. 197–219.

Weale, A. (ed.) (1988) *Cost and Choice in Health Care*, London, King Edward's Hospital Fund.

Wedderburn, Lord (1986) *The Worker and the Law*, Harmondsworth, Penguin.

Weller, P. (1983) 'Do Prime Ministers' Departments Really Create Problems?', *Public Administration*, vol. 61, pp. 59–78.

Whiteley, P. (1983) *The Labour Party in Crisis*, London, Methuen.

Whiteley, P. and Winyard, S. (1987) *Pressure for the Poor: The Poverty Lobby and Policy-Making*, London, Methuen.

Whitty, G. and Menter, I. (1988) 'Lessons of Thatcherism: Education Policy in England and Wales, 1979–88', *Journal of Law and Society*, vol. 16, no. 1, pp. 42–64.

Whyte, J. (1978) 'Interpretations of the Northern Ireland Problem: An Appraisal', *Economic and Social Review*, vol. 9, no. 4, pp. 257–82.

Whyte, J. (1988) 'Interpretations of the Northern Ireland Problem', in Townshend, C. (ed.) *Consensus in Ireland: Approaches and Recessions*.

Whyte, J. (1990) *Interpreting Northern Ireland*, Oxford, Clarendon Press.

Widdicombe Report (1986) *The Conduct of Local Authority Business*, Cmnd 9797, HMSO.

Wiener, M. (1981) *English Culture and the Decline of the Industrial Spirit 1850–1980*, Cambridge, Cambridge University Press.

Wildavsky, A. (1980) *Speaking Truth to Power*, Boston, Little Brown.

Wiles, P. and North, G. (eds) (1984) *Economics in Disarray*, Oxford, Oxford University Press.

Williams, N.J., Sewell, J.B. and Twine, F.E. (1987) 'Council House Sales and the Electorate: Voting Behaviour and Ideological Implications', *Housing Studies*, vol. 2, no. 4, pp. 274–82.

Williams, R. (1965) *The Long Revolution*, Harmondsworth, Penguin.

Wilson, D. (1987) *Battle for Power*, London, Sphere.

Wilson, R. (1988) 'Poll Shock for Accord', *Fortnight*, no. 261, April, pp. 6–8.

Wilson, T. (1989) *Ulster, Conflict, and Consensus*, Oxford, Blackwell.

World Commission on Environment and Development (1987) *Our Common Future*, Oxford, Oxford University Press.

Wright, F. (1989) 'Northern Ireland and the British-Irish Relationship', *Studies*, no. 78, pp. 151–62.

Young, H. (1989) *One of Us*, London, Macmillan.

Index